Environmental Awareness Activities
for Librarians and Teachers

Environmental Awareness Activities for Librarians and Teachers

20 Interdisciplinary Units for Use in Grades 2–8

by MARTHA SEIF SIMPSON

McFarland & Company, Inc., Publishers
Jefferson, North Carolina, and London

British Library Cataloguing-in-Publication data are available

Library of Congress Cataloguing-in-Publication Data

Simpson, Martha Seif, 1954–
    Environmental awareness activities for librarians and teachers :
  20 interdisciplinary units for use in grades 2–8 / Martha Seif
  Simpson.
      p. cm.
    Includes index.
    ISBN 0-7864-0064-1 (sewn softcover : 50# alk. paper) ∞
    1. Environmental sciences—Study and teaching—Activity programs.
  2. Environmental education—Activity programs. I. Title.
  GE77.S56   1995
  372.3'57044—dc20   95-14827
                                                              CIP

Manufactured in the United States of America

McFarland & Company, Inc., Publishers
  Box 611, Jefferson, North Carolina 28640

For my husband, John, and our children,
Paul, Rose, Nicholas, and Shayna

CONTENTS

Acknowledgments   ix

How to Use This Book   1

ENVIRONMENTAL UNITS

I. Our Planet's Resources

    Our Earth   7

    The Atmosphere   19

    Water   30

    Energy   40

II. Our Planet's Natural Habitats

    Seas and Oceans   55

    Islands and Coral Reefs   65

    The Seashore   76

    Ponds and Wetlands   86

    Rivers and Lakes   97

    Rainforests   107

    Forests and Woodlands   117

    Mountains   128

    Grasslands   140

    Deserts   151

    Polar Regions   161

III. Preserving Our Planet

    Urban Environments   173

    Food and Farming   184

    Waste and Recycling   195

Endangered Species and Habitats   207
Environmental Awareness   219

Addresses of Organizations and Music Companies   233
Index   239

ACKNOWLEDGMENTS

In researching this book, I have made a special effort to include as many currently published titles as possible. By the time this book is in print, however, the status of some of these resources may have changed. I urge the reader to regularly check the catalogs of the publishers whose titles I have recommended for additional sources.

I would especially like to thank the following publishers who generously provided me with excellent, up-to-date resource materials. Their assistance is greatly appreciated.

> Carolrhoda Books
> Chelsea House Publishers
> Facts on File Publications
> Forest House Publishing Company, Inc.
> Franklin Watts
> Gallopade
> Gareth Stevens Publishing
> Lerner Publications
> Macmillan Publishing Company
> Marshall Cavendish
> Raintree Steck-Vaughn Publishers
> Thomson Learning

I would also like to thank my co-workers at Stratford Library Association, and especially Bob Roche, who worked miracles for me through Interlibrary Loan!

HOW TO USE
THIS BOOK

I wrote *Environmental Awareness Activities for Librarians and Teachers* with four main goals in mind:

1. **To increase students' awareness of nature and environmental issues.** The activities are designed to teach children to respect our Earth, its resources, habitats and wildlife — and to understand the threats to the environment. Once this appreciation is gained, it is my hope that students will choose to become involved in the conservation and protection of our planet.

2. **To provide an interdisciplinary curriculum for each environmental issue.** Each of the 20 units includes activities in 10 subject areas to enable students to gain a more comprehensive understanding of the environmental topic. Just as one element of the environment affects another, so too are the various subject areas interrelated.

3. **To encourage students to use a variety of current nonfiction sources to research these activities.** There are many excellent books and series on environmental topics on the market today, as well as an assortment of atlases and other general reference tools. Rather than sending students to a standard textbook to find all the answers, the activities are designed to develop the students' research skills by requiring them to consult a variety of nonfiction sources. In addition, my book will demonstrate to educators how current nonfiction can be used in the classroom as instructional material.

4. **To encourage students to work together in small groups.** Even when an activity is not specifically labeled as a cooperative project, students may benefit from experiencing it in a small group situation. Since in most cases, several books will need to be consulted in order to arrive at a complete answer, each student within the group can be assigned a book or books to read. They can then pool their answers. This cooperative learning approach will also enable students to sharpen their interpersonal and group communication skills.

Each environmental unit, as mentioned above, is broken down into ten subject or activity areas: library skills, arts and crafts, spelling/vocabulary, geography, math, music and theater arts, English composition, science, history/sociology, and topics for discussion. Within each subject, there are seven activities, labeled (a) through (g). They range in difficulty for students in grades two through eight. Thus, activity (a) is designed for students in grade two, (b) for grade three, and so on. Educators in the upper grades may wish to assign the given activity for that grade level, as well as one or more of the preceding activities. The activities are written to be read by the student. Sections marked "Notes" are directed toward the instructor.

In most cases, the activity is followed by a series of numbers which are keyed to the suggested resources listed in the unit. The suggested resources are nonfiction books in which all or part of the answer may be found. These books range in reading level difficulty. Resources listed for each activity include all relevant books, regardless of their reading level, to allow for students with varying reading abilities, and to give greater flexibility to educators who may wish to assign activities other than those recommended for their grade level.

Occasionally, no suggested resources are given. This is done in such cases as a local geography or music and theater arts activity where the answer would not appear in any of the books listed. Sometimes, the activity is so general that an answer can be found in most of the suggested resources, so none are singled out. For some activities, such as history/sociology questions that require the student to write a biography of a person, the suggested resources are meant to serve as starting points for the student's research. From there, the student will need to find a biography or other materials that are not listed in this book.

In addition to the suggested resources, a number of books for additional reading are recommended. "Younger" books are loosely defined as grades two through four, and "Older" as grades five through eight, although there is some overlap. Most of these titles are nonfiction, but there are a few fiction titles listed. It may often be useful to consult these titles, as well as sources listed in other units of this book, for further research. Given the budgetary constraints of most schools and libraries, educators may need to adapt some of the activities so that the answers can be found in the resources that are available to them.

At the time this book was written, the vast majority of recommended titles were listed in *Books in Print*. I have, however, occasionally included some out-of-print sources. I have also recommended several book series. Names of series are indicated in brackets [ ].

Although they are not listed outside of the library skills activities, students should also be encouraged to consult general library resources such as encyclopedias, atlases, and almanacs. In writing this book, I used *World Book Encyclopedia* for activities that ask the student to look up information in an encyclopedia, but others may be used as well.

I have quoted numerous statistics throughout the book, especially in the math activities. I have found that many sources offer conflicting statistics. In such cases, I tried to use the numbers that were most often cited. In the instances where I obtained the statistics from one or more books used in that particular unit, I have noted the source.

Whenever possible, I would suggest that educators take their classes on field trips. A walk in the woods to identify plants while studying forests and woodlands, for example, will bring the subject to life for the student. Additional science experiments can also be used in conjunction with each unit.

A list of organizations to which the students can write for more information appears at the end of each unit. The full addresses of these are given at the end of the book. There is also an index of all books, series, authors, and organizations cited in this book.

Environmental issues are a growing concern to both children and adults. At the same time, an interdisciplinary, whole-language approach to learning is becoming popular in many school systems. In this book I have attempted to combine these factors in order to create challenging and thought-provoking instructional units that will enable students to develop research, critical thinking, and communication skills, while learning what they can do to protect the Earth.

I
Our Planet's Resources

OUR EARTH

Our home planet, Earth, is billions of years old and always changing. Geological forces deep within the planet cause the movement of continents, the formation of mountains, and the birth of volcanic islands. Atmospheric forces spawn monsoons, droughts, and tornadoes. Clues to Earth's history are found in fossils and rocks. Earth provides us with air, minerals, water, food, and more. But the pressures humans place on Earth are often damaging. We must learn to appreciate and take care of our precious home.

LIBRARY SKILLS

a. Use *The Rand McNally Children's World Atlas* to answer the following questions: 1) Look up World — Terrain. What are the types of terrain that are shown on the map? What is the terrain where you live? 2) Look up World — Climate. What is the climate where you live? 3) Look up World — Life on the Land. What is the main type of economic activity where you live? 4) Look up World — Population. What is the population density where you live?

b. Use *World Book's Young Scientist Vol. 4 — Planet Earth* to do the following: 1) Look up All About Metals. Make a list of metals and how they can be used. Then look up Resources from Our Planet and find these metals on the chart shown. Note the year that Earth is expected to run out of each of these resources. When are Earth's fossil fuels expected to run out?

c. Find a map of a state of your choice in an encyclopedia or atlas. Use it to draw and label geographical features on your copy of the map. Include features such as rivers, lakes, mountain ranges and major peaks, national parks and forests, canyons and caves, waterfalls, etc.

d. Use *The World Almanac and Book of Facts* to answer the following questions about earthquakes and volcanoes: 1) List the dates and places of all earthquakes that measured 8.0 or more on the Richter Scale. 2) Where and when was the earthquake with the biggest death toll? 3) Which country has had the most number of major earthquakes? 4) Which country has had the greatest death toll from major earthquakes? 5) For the most recent year listed, where was the earthquake of the greatest magnitude? 6) How many active volcanoes are there, and what percent of them are located within the Ring of Fire? 7) Which volcano was responsible for the largest number of deaths? How? 8) Which country or island has the greatest number of active volcanoes? 9) Which volcano has been active for the longest time? 10) Name the tallest volcano that erupted during the most recent year listed.

e. Use a field guide, such as *Rocks and Minerals,* to make a list of properties of minerals. Then find 20 minerals or pictures of them. Mount each one and include a description of its properties.

f. Look up these Earth science terms in a dictionary. List the words alphabetically. Then divide each word into syllables and define it: geology, paleontology, speleology, evolution, oceanography, seismology, plate tectonics, geography, ecology, geochronology, paleoecology, biology, meteorology, mineralogy, geophysics, crystallography, topography, stratigraphy, petrology, hydrology, archaeology.

g. Use *Rocks and Minerals of the World* to color in areas on a map of the world where five minerals of your choice are located. Which countries are the main producers of these minerals?

ARTS AND CRAFTS

a. Earth is made up of many layers of rock. On a cross-sectional picture of Earth's layers, label and color the following: inner core (white), outer core (yellow), lower mantle (orange), upper mantle (red), crust (brown). Use these colors of modeling clay to make a three-dimensional model of the Earth. Start with a ball of white clay and add the other colors. Make sure the crust is very thin. When the ball is semi-hardened, have an adult slice it in half. Does your model look like your picture? (2, 6, 9, 10, 15, 16, 23, 26, 29)

b. Use plaster of Paris and modeling clay to make your own fossils and molds. (1, 6, 11, 18, 19)

c. Cut out pictures of natural rock formations, man-made stone carvings or buildings, or gems and crystals. Paste your pictures onto sheets of paper and label them. Bind your pictures into a book.

d. Color in a map of the world and draw lines to indicate the borders of Earth's seven large and five small geologic plates. Mount your map on paperboard and let it dry flat. Then cut along the plate lines to make a jigsaw puzzle of the Earth. (2, 3, 8, 9, 15, 16, 18, 24)

e. Earth contains many elements such as carbon, and compounds such as water, that make life on our planet possible. Each of these basic substances is recycled naturally. Create a picture or series of pictures that explains how one of these natural cycles works: water, nitrogen, phosphorus, sulfur, carbon, plant and soil, rock, or a food chain. (5, 9, 10, 17, 18, 25, 26)

f. Draw a cross-section of a cave system. Show how water on Earth's surface seeps underground and forms a series of cave chambers. Include formations such as stalactites. Label the features of your drawing. (4, 15, 23, 27)

g. Do one of these activities: 1) Draw a cross-section detailing the formation of a volcano. Label features such as descending plates and molten rock, and explain how these forces can cause a volcano to become active. 2) Build a clay model of a volcano and explain how it works. 3) Use a series of drawings or photographs of a volcano before, during, and after it erupts. Label what is happening in each picture. (3, 8, 14, 15, 16, 17, 18, 20, 23, 29)

SPELLING/VOCABULARY

a. Complete a crossword puzzle of terms that relate to soil: bedrock, clay, topsoil, bacteria, humus, fertile, erosion, earthworms, sand, loam, minerals, silt, gravel, pebbles, subsoil, acidity, peat, mud, decay, moss. (6, 9, 10, 11, 23, 25)

b. Complete a word search puzzle of rock names: flint, slate, basalt, sandstone, coal, limestone, pumice, clay, granite, chalk, gneiss, marble, obsidian, tuff, shale, amber, halite, schist, conglomerate, gabbro. (10, 15, 17, 23, 26)

c. Complete a word search puzzle of minerals and metals: borax, gypsum, quartz, sulfur, titanium, phosphate, uranium, asbestos, gold, talc, tungsten, lithium, copper, mica, platinum, bauxite, iron, mercury, feldspar, silver. (3, 11, 15, 23, 26)

d. Complete a crossword puzzle of mining terms: ore, smelt, refine, alloy, drill, leach, shaft, gemstone, deposit, metal, cleavage, mineral, dredging, excavate, strip mining, vein, quarry, deep mining, fossil fuels, crystal. (6, 9, 15, 17, 23, 26)

e. Define these terms that relate to the natural wearing away of Earth's features: water erosion, mudflow, lava, weathering, rockslide, sediment, avalanche, sinkhole, sheeting, canyon, desert erosion, glacier, cave, waterfall, wind erosion, scree, carbonic acid, ice erosion, chemical weathering, tropical erosion. (6, 8, 12, 13, 18, 20, 23)

f. Complete a fill-in-the-blanks exercise of terms that relate to Earth movements: transform (or strike-slip) fault, shock waves, continental plate, seismograph, fault scarp (or dip-slip fault), rifting, collision, spreading ridge, Richter Scale, ocean plate, volcano, earthquake, continental drift, fault line, aftershocks, subduction, epicenter, focus, Mercali Intensity Scale, deep-sea trench. (2, 3, 8, 10, 12, 15, 16, 18, 20, 22, 23, 24)

g. Complete a matching exercise of geological terms: crust, asthenosphere, lithosphere, magma, inner core, outer core, mantle, continental drift, fossil, crater, strata, magnetism, extrusive, mesosphere, tremor, Mohs Scale, moraine, intrusive, geyser, plate tectonics.   (2, 3, 6, 9, 12, 15, 16, 17, 18, 23, 29)

GEOGRAPHY

a. What is the Ring of Fire? On a map of the world, color in the Ring of Fire. (8, 16, 29)

b. On a map of the United States, color in the major earthquake zones (purple), moderate zones (blue), minor zones (green). Now look at a map that shows mountain ranges. How does it compare to your earthquake map? (12, 18, 24)

c. What is plate tectonics? On a map of the world, draw the seven large geologic plates with a solid line. Use dotted lines to show the five smaller plates. (2, 3, 8, 15, 16, 18, 24)

d. What are Pangaea, Gondwanaland and Laurasia? What relation do they have to Earth's continents? Draw a series of four or five pictures to show the progression of these land masses.   (2, 3, 9, 10, 16, 19, 20, 23)

e. On a cross-section of a shoreline and ocean floor, label these features: coastal mountain, continental slope, trench, magma, rift valley, continental shelf, abyss, volcanic island, spreading ridge, descending plate, subduction zone, convection currents.   (6, 10, 16, 23)

f. Make a list of areas that have had many disastrous earthquakes, volcanoes, tsunamis and hurricanes. Locate these places on a map of the world.   (3, 8, 12, 14, 18, 20, 22, 23)

g. On a map of the United States, draw the San Andreas Fault. What cities are located along the fault? List the places, dates, and magnitudes of some major earthquakes that have occurred along this fault.   (3, 8, 16, 20, 23, 24)

MATH

Note: Different sources use slightly varying figures.

a. Rocks and minerals are rated by how hard they are, according to the Mohs Scale of Hardness. A harder mineral will scratch a softer one. For example, copper can scratch gypsum but not calcite, so its hardness is 3. The Mohs Scale, from softest to hardest, is: 1-Talc; 2-Gypsum; 3-Calcite; 4-Fluorite; 5-Apatite; 6-Feldspar; 7-Quartz; 8-Topaz; 9-Corundum; 10-Diamond. Use the Mohs Scale to rate these minerals: 1) Cobalt can scratch apatite but not feldspar. 2) Malachite can scratch calcite but not fluorite. 3) Olivine can scratch feldspar but not quartz. 4) Garnet can scratch fluorite but not apatite. 5) Aquamarine can scratch quartz but not topaz. 6) Bauxite can scratch talc but not gypsum. 7) Emerald can scratch topaz but not corundum. 8) Limonite can be scratched by gypsum but not by talc.   (*Rocks and Minerals*)

b. Make a list of the seven continents and their areas in square miles. Arrange the list in descending order, from the largest continent to the small-est.   (16)

c. Eight minerals make up 98 percent of all the rocks on Earth. They are oxygen 46%, silicon 28%, aluminum 8%, iron 5%, sodium 3%, potassium 3%, calcium 3%, and magnesium 2%. The remaining 2 percent includes traces of other elements. Draw a pie chart to illustrate the mineral content of Earth's crust.

d. A carat is a measure used by jewelers in weighing precious stones. One carat is equal to .2 grams. Use a calculator to convert the following carat amounts of largest known gems to grams: black opal, 1,520 carats; emerald, 8,613 carats; sapphire, 2,302 carats; ruby, 8,500 carats; diamond, 3,106 carats; topaz, 22,892.5 carats. Larger stones are measured in pounds and ounces. Convert the following record-holding stones to ounces: amber, 33 pounds 10 ounces; gold, 472 lb. 8 oz. An unusually large boulder of jade weighed 291 tons. How many pounds is that? How many ounces?   (*The Guinness Book of World Records*)

e. Convert the following numbers to inches: 1) The longest stalactite in the world is a 195 ft. wall-supported column in the Cueva de Nerja in Spain. 2) The Flying Dragon Pillar in Nine Dragons Cave in China is the tallest stalagmite at 128 ft. 3) The deepest cave in the United States is Lechuguilla Cave in Carlsbad Caverns, New Mexico, at 1,565 ft. 4) The longest under-water cave ever explored is the Nohoch Na Chich cave system in Mexico. So far, 43,600 ft. of passages have been mapped. 5) The world's largest cave chamber is the Sarawak Chamber in Malaysia's Gunung Mulu National Park. It measures 2,300 ft. long, 980 ft. wide, and its lowest point is 230 ft. high.   (*The Guinness Book of World Records*)

f. Because of continental drift, the Atlantic Ocean is growing 3/4 inch wider every year. At that rate, how much wider will it be by the year 2100? How many feet is that? How many years would it take for the Atlantic to widen a mile?

g. Earth's outer layer, or crust, is about 20 miles thick. The mantle is about 1,800 miles thick. The outer core is about 1,400 miles and the inner core is about 800 miles. Convert these distance to kilometers. What is Earth's ap-proximate diameter in miles and kilometers?

MUSIC AND THEATER ARTS

a. Bells are often made of brass, ceramic, or other materials mined from the Earth. Listen to the ring of a variety of bells. Which ones have a higher pitch and which sound lower? Which ones are louder, which softer? Which echo the longest? With each student in the class holding one bell, try to ring out a tune.

b. There are many songs about the weather such as "Let It Snow" and "Singin' in the Rain." Sing along to some of these.

c. Brass, an alloy of copper and zinc, is used to make many musical instruments. Make a list of brass wind instruments and identify their pictures. Listen to live or recorded music of some brass instruments.

d. *Group project:* Act out some of the forces of Earth. For example, divide the class into two groups, each of which represents a continental plate. Pretend the plates are moving toward each other. When they collide, mountains are formed. How would you act this out? Other ideas to dramatize: how a hurricane forms, how Pangaea broke up into continents and islands, what happens to a fault line during an earthquake.

e. *Earth: A Day in the Life of a Planet* and *Earth, Sea & Sky* are collections of natural sounds by Nature Recordings. Listen to tracks on these or other environmental recordings and try to identify the sounds you hear.

f. Show how you would act in various situations during an earthquake, tornado, or other natural disaster. What would you do to protect yourself at home, outside, in a tall building, or at school? Act out different roles, such as a frightened child, a teacher, a police officer, a parent, etc.

g. *Group project:* In 1864, Jules Verne wrote a science fiction novel called *A Journey to the Center of the Earth.* Act out a scene from this book.

ENGLISH COMPOSITION

a. Write an adventure story about exploring a cave.   (4, 23, 27)

b. There are many language expressions, called similes, that use Earth terms in their descriptions: for example, black as coal, old as the hills, high as a mountain, slow as a glacier. Make up ten similes using names of rocks, minerals, or land formations. Use each of these similes in a sentence that describes something.

c. People often do not treat our Earth as well as they should. Write a poem or essay on the subject "Taking Care of Our Earth."   (2, 5, 7, 9, 10, 21, 25)

d. A variety of climates and weather conditions happen on Earth. Choose one type of weather in any part of the world. It can be stormy, such as a blizzard, or pleasant weather. Write a description of what you might observe outdoors during that weather. (8, 10, 20, 28)

e. Write an adventure story about how a person survives a natural disaster, such as an earthquake, volcano, landslide, tsunami, hurricane, or tornado. Describe what the person was doing when the disaster occurred, his/her reactions, and what happened afterward. (3, 8, 12, 14, 18, 20, 22, 23, 24, 28)

f. The ancient Greeks created many myths in an attempt to explain the natural processes of our planet. In fact, several of our words are derived from the names of Greek gods. For example, from Gaea, the Earth goddess, we get "geo" as in "geography." From Vulcan, the god of fire, we get "volcano." Read some Greek myths. Then create your own mythological character. Write a story about this character to explain an earthly phenomenon.

g. The actions of humans are causing serious damage to Earth's environment. Choose one environmental problem, such as global warming or desertification. Write an essay on the cause of the problem and how it affects the Earth. Give a possible solution to the problem. (2, 5, 7, 9, 10, 21)

SCIENCE

a. What are volcanoes? What causes them to be active? What is lava? Where does it come from? What are hot springs and geysers? With your teacher supervising, create an experimental volcano in class. (6, 8, 9, 10, 11, 14, 15, 16, 18, 20, 23, 29)

b. How is soil made? What makes soil fertile? What are some different types of soil? Why are earthworms good for soil? What other small animals live in soil? Look at various soil samples under a microscope. What do you see? (5, 6, 9, 10, 11, 15, 18, 21, 23, 25)

c. Why do earthquakes occur? Where are they most likely to happen? What is the Richter Scale and how is it used? What is a seismograph and how does it work? (2, 6, 8, 9, 10, 12, 15, 16, 20, 23)

d. What are stalactites and stalagmites? How are they made? Where can they be found? Make your own sample stalactite crystals using salt or baking soda dissolved in water. (4, 8, 10, 11, 15, 18, 23, 26, 27)

e. What are fossils? How were they made? What are fossil fuels? How were they made? How has the study of fossils proven the theory of continental drift? (1, 2, 9, 13, 15, 16, 17, 18, 19, 23, 26)

f. There are three main types of rock found on Earth's crust: igneous, sedimentary, and metamorphic. How are each of these formed? Divide a sheet of paper into three columns and label them igneous, sedimentary, and metamorphic. Then list the names of several rocks in the proper columns. (6, 9, 10, 15, 16, 17, 18, 19, 23, 26)

g. Use the theories of continental drift and plate tectonics to explain how block and fold mountains are formed. What causes undersea and dome mountains? Why are some mountains volcanic? Tell how some major mountain ranges, such as the Himalayas and Andes, were formed. (3, 6, 8, 16, 18, 20, 23)

HISTORY/SOCIOLOGY

a. What can we learn about the history of our planet by studying fossils? (1, 13, 15, 16, 17, 18, 19, 23, 26)

b. What was the Ice Age? How did it affect Earth's landscape? (6, 10, 13, 19, 23)

c. *Class project:* Make a timeline mural that details the various eras and periods of geological time. Include the names and approximate year spans of each era and period, information on how Earth and life forms developed, and pictures of animals that existed then. (2, 3, 6, 9, 15, 17, 18, 19, 23)

d. Earthquakes and volcanoes are violent examples of how Earth is constantly changing. Write a report about a major quake or volcanic eruption. When did it occur? How did it affect the surrounding area and nearby people? (3, 8, 12, 14, 18, 20, 22, 23, 24)

e. How have the growth of agriculture and ranching changed the Earth's soil structure and landscape? What are some local and worldwide consequences of these changes? (5, 6, 9, 21)

f. Until about the year 1500, most people believed the Earth was flat. What were some other mistaken beliefs people had about the Earth? What were some scientific theories and observations made by early scientists and philosophers? (2, 3, 18, 22, 23)

g. Various civilizations throughout history have created incredible structures out of rock. These include the Great Wall of China, Stonehenge, the Parthenon, the pyramids, and the stones of Easter Island. Choose one of these or another stone structure to research. Write a report including information about the size and content of the structure, the people who built it and the time in which they lived, and its purpose. If its purpose is not known, relate the mystery surrounding the structure's construction and purpose. (15, 18)

TOPICS FOR DISCUSSION

a. What are some causes of soil erosion and pollution? What are some of the dangers? What can be done to protect our soil? (5, 6, 7, 11, 25)

b. Natural forces on Earth can be very destructive. Name some of these, such as hurricanes and earthquakes. What are some safety measures people can take to protect themselves from nature's fury? (12, 14, 20, 22, 24)

c. What are some uses for various rocks and minerals? (10, 11, 15, 17, 22, 26)

d. What are some pressures humans have placed on Earth's landscape and resources? How have these pressures upset the balance of nature? (2, 5, 6, 7, 11, 21, 25)

e. Volcanoes and earthquakes are very destructive, but they are good for Earth's environment. What are some positive results of these so-called disasters? (3, 8, 12, 14, 18, 23, 29)

f. What are some natural factors, such as continental drift, that change the landscape of Earth's surface? What are some major changes that have occurred since the formation of our planet? How can you tell more changes are happening now? What are some landscape changes that have occurred because of the actions of humans? (2, 5, 8, 9, 15, 18, 20, 21, 23)

g. Humans have found many uses for Earth's fossil fuels, rocks and minerals. As the demand for these resources increases, we dig deeper into the Earth to extract them. How does mining affect Earth's appearance and environment? (2, 15, 21, 23)

SUGGESTED RESOURCES

(1) Aliki. *Fossils Tell of Long Ago* [Let's-Read-and-Find-Out]. Harper, 1990.
(2) Amato, Carol J. *The Earth* [Breakthroughs in Science]. Smithmark, 1992.
(3) Aylesworth, Thomas G. *Moving Continents: Our Changing Earth* [Earth Processes]. Enslow, 1990.
(4) Bender, Lionel. *Cave* [The Story of the Earth]. Watts, 1989.
(5) Bennett, Paul. *Earth: The Incredible Recycling Machine*. Thomson, 1993.
(6) Catherall, Ed. *Exploring Soil and Rocks* [Exploring Science]. Steck-Vaughn, 1990.
(7) The EarthWorks Group. *50 Simple Things Kids Can Do to Save the Earth*. Scholastic, 1990.
(8) Goodman, Billy. *Natural Wonders and Disasters* [Planet Earth]. Little, 1991.
(9) *How the Earth Works* [Science in Our World]. Grolier, 1992.
(10) Jennings, Terry. *The Earth* [Exploring Our World]. Cavendish, 1989.
(11) _____. *Rocks and Soil* [The Young Scientist Investigates]. Childrens, 1988.
(12) Knapp, Brian. *Earthquake* [World Disasters]. Steck-Vaughn, 1989. (Also other books in series.)

(13) Lauber, Patricia. *Dinosaurs Walked Here and Other Tales Fossils Tell*. Bradbury, 1987.
(14) _____. *Volcano: The Eruption and Healing of Mount St. Helens*. Bradbury, 1986.
(15) McConnell, Anita. *The World Beneath Us* [The World of Science]. Facts on File, 1985.
(16) Mariner, Tom. *Continents* [Earth in Action]. Cavendish, 1990.
(17) _____. *Rocks* [Earth in Action]. Cavendish, 1990.
(18) Markle, Sandra. *Digging Deeper: Investigations into Rocks, Shocks, Quakes, and Other Earthy Matters*. Lothrop, 1987.
(19) Niles, Gregory, and Eldredge, Douglas. *The Fossil Factory*. Addison-Wesley, 1989.
(20) *Our Violent Earth* [Books for World Explorers]. National Geographic, 1982.
(21) Peckham, Alexander. *Changing Landscapes* [Green Issues]. Gloucester, 1991.
(22) Poynter, Margaret. *Earthquakes: Looking for Answers* [Earth Processes]. Enslow, 1990.
(23) Silver, Donald M. *Earth: The Ever-Changing Planet* [Random House Library of Knowledge]. Random, 1989.
(24) Simon, Seymour. *Earthquakes*. Morrow, 1991.
(25) Stille, Darlene R. *Soil Erosion and Pollution* [New True Books]. Childrens, 1990.
(26) Symes, R. F. *Rocks & Minerals* [Eyewitness Books]. Knopf, 1988.
(27) Wood, Jenny. *Caves: An Underground Wonderland* [Wonderworks of Nature]. Stevens, 1991.
(28) _____. *Storm* [The Violent Earth]. Thomson, 1993. (Also other books in series.)
(29) _____. *Volcanoes: Fire from Below* [Wonderworks of Nature]. Stevens, 1991.

LIBRARY SKILLS RESOURCES

The Guinness Book of World Records. Facts on File, 1994.
Rand McNally Children's World Atlas. Rand McNally, 1989.
Rocks and Minerals of the World [Using and Understanding Maps]. Chelsea, 1993.
The World Almanac and Book of Facts. World Almanac, 1994.
World Book's Young Scientist, Vol. 4—Planet Earth. World Book, 1993.
Zim, Herbert S. and Shaffer, Paul R. *Rocks and Minerals* [Golden Guides]. Western, 1957.

ADDITIONAL READING—YOUNGER

Abels, Harriette. *Stonehenge* [The Mystery of . . .]. Crestwood, 1987.
Arnold, Caroline. *Land Masses* [Easy-Read Geographic Activities]. Watts, 1985.
_____. *Trapped in Tar: Fossils from the Ice Age*. Clarion, 1987.
Butler, Daphne. *First Look Under the Ground* [First Look]. Stevens, 1991.
Cole, Joanna. *The Magic School Bus Inside the Earth* [Magic School Bus]. Scholastic, 1987.
Dixon, Dougal. *Geology: Rocks, Minerals and Fossils* [Franklin Watts Science World]. Watts, 1982.
Greenburg, Judith E., and Carey, Helen H. *Caves* [Science Adventures]. Raintree, 1990.
Gunzi, Christiane. *Cave Life* [Look Closer]. Kindersley, 1993.

Jacobs, Una. *Earth Calendar*. Silver, 1986.

McNulty, Faith. *How to Dig a Hole to the Other Side of the World*. Harper, 1979.

Mitgutsch, Ali. *From Ore to Spoon* [Start to Finish]. Carolrhoda, 1981.

Norman, Lilith. *The Paddock: A Story in Praise of Earth*. Knopf, 1993.

Richardson, Joy. *Rocks and Soil* [Picture Science]. Watts, 1992.

Silver, Donald M. *One Small Square: Backyard* [Scientific American Books for Young Readers]. Freeman, 1993.

————. *One Small Square: Cave* [Scientific American Books for Young Readers]. Freeman, 1994.

Simon, Seymour. *Earth: Our Planet in Space*. Four Winds, 1984.

Sotnak, Lewann. *Carlsbad Caverns* [National Parks]. Crestwood, 1988.

Wheeler, Jill. *The Land We Live On* [We Can Save the Earth]. Abdo, 1990.

Whitlock, Ralph. *In the Soil* [Use Your Eyes]. Wayland, 1986.

Wood, Tim. *Natural Disasters* [The World's Disasters]. Thomson, 1993.

ADDITIONAL READING – OLDER

Barnes-Svarney, Patricia L. *Clocks on the Rocks: Learning About Earth's Past* [Earth Processes]. Enslow, 1990. (Also other books in series.)

Beiser, Arthur. *The Earth* [Life Nature Library]. Time, 1963.

Cox, Shirley. *Earth Science* [Science Fair]. Rourke, 1992.

Dailey, Robert. *Earth* [First Books – Planets]. Watts, 1994.

Dixon, Dougal. *The Changing Earth* [Young Geographer]. Thomson, 1993.

Kerrod, Robin. *Mineral Resources* [World's Resources]. Thomson, 1994.

Lambert, David, and the Diagram Group. *The Field Guide to Geology*. Facts on File, 1988.

Lauber, Patricia. *Seeing Earth from Space*. Orchard, 1990.

Laycock, George. *Caves*. Four Winds, 1976.

Lye, Keith. *The Earth* [Young Readers' Nature Library]. Millbrook, 1991.

McLaughlin, Molly. *Earthworms, Dirt, and Rotten Leaves: An Exploration in Ecology*. Macmillan, 1993.

Martin, Ana. *Prehistoric Stone Monuments* [World Heritage]. Childrens, 1993.

Milne, Lorus J. and Milne, Margery. *A Shovelful of Earth*. Holt, 1987.

Newton, David E. *Land Use A–Z* [Environment Reference]. Enslow, 1991.

Parker, Steve. *The Earth* [Science Project Book]. Cavendish, 1986.

Ross, Harriet, ed. *Greek Myths: Tales of the Gods, Heroes and Heroines*. Lion, 1993.

Rybolt, Thomas R., and Mebane, Robert C. *Environmental Experiments About Land* [Science Experiments for Young People]. Enslow, 1993.

Verne, Jules. *A Journey to the Center of the Earth*. Dodd, 1959.

The Visual Dictionary of the Earth [Eyewitness Visual Dictionaries]. Kindersley, 1993.

Whitfield, Philip. *Why Do Volcanoes Erupt?* Viking, 1990.

Wiggers, Raymond. *The Amateur Geologist: Explorations and Investigations* [Amateur Science]. Watts, 1993.

Williams, Brian, and Williams, Brenda. *The Random House Book of 1001 Questions and Answers About Planet Earth*. Random, 1993.

Winckler, Suzanne, and Rodgers, Mary M. *Soil* [Our Endangered Planet]. Lerner, 1994.

See also: books in ENVIRONMENTAL AWARENESS and MOUNTAINS units.

FOR MORE INFORMATION ABOUT OUR EARTH, WRITE TO:

American Cave Conservation Association
Earth Day U.S.A.
Earthwatch
Environmental Defense Fund
Friends of the Earth

International Erosion Control Association
The Kids' EarthWorks Group
National Speleological Society
Renew America
Soil and Water Conservation Society

THE ATMOSPHERE

Of all the planets in our solar system, Earth has the only atmosphere that can sustain life as we know it. The condition of our air affects our health, the land, water quality, and the weather. But the activities of humans are polluting this life-giving resource. The atmosphere knows no national boundaries. People all over the world must work together to clean up Earth's atmosphere and reduce the damage that has already been done.

LIBRARY SKILLS

a. Your teacher will show you ten books about the atmosphere, wind, air pollution, inventions that use air, or people that work with air. Which books are fiction? Which are non–fiction? Which are biographies? How can you tell? Where would you find these books in the library?

b. Use *Scholastic Environmental Atlas of the United States* to answer the following questions: 1) According to the chart on Air Quality in Major Cities, which cities have the worst air? The best? What is the air quality of cities listed from your state? 2) How did the rivers of Pittsburgh become polluted? How did the citizens clean up?

c. Look up Tornadoes in *Growing Up with Science* or another science encyclopedia. How does air cause tornadoes to form? Where is Tornado Alley? Why do more tornadoes occur there than any other place on Earth?

d. Use an online data base or *Reader's Guide to Periodical Literature* to look up some articles on smog, wind power, and atmospheric temperature. For each subject, list the names of two articles, the magazines, issue numbers, dates, and pages on which they appear. If you have the magazines in your school, find the actual articles.

e. Use *The World Almanac and Book of Facts* to make a graph of Total Releases of Toxic Chemicals into the Air by the Manufacturing Industry. Then list the ten manufacturing companies that released the largest amounts of toxic chemicals into the air.

f. In *The New State of the World Atlas*, look in the Environment section to find a pollution map. With this as your guide, color in the areas of air pollution on a map of the world. Then use the information on Acid Rain-Makers to draw up a chart on Amounts of Acid Rain Generated by Countries.

g. In an encyclopedia, look up information on the makeup of atmospheres of the planets in our solar system. How does Earth's atmosphere differ from the atmospheres of the other planets? Draw up a chart to compare temperature, quantity of certain gases, proximity to the sun, and other atmospheric factors.

ARTS AND CRAFTS

a. Fold sheets of paper in different ways to make paper airplanes. Which flies the fastest? The farthest? Why? Assemble a glider from pieces of cut balsa wood. How does it fly in comparison to the paper planes? (12, 14, 27)

b. You can't see air, but you can see that it moves. Make a mobile, kite, or weather vane. Why do they move the way they do? (3, 14, 20, 22, 27)

c. Make a papier-mâché piñata by blowing up a balloon. Paste strips of newspaper over the balloon, using a flour and water paste. When it dries, paint it. Cut a small hole in the piñata and fill it with goodies. What happened to the balloon? How did air help you make the piñata?

d. Make a collage or mural of various aircraft, things that use air, examples of wind power, or wind energy devices. (3, 6, 17, 22, 26)

e. Create a poster to make people aware of one danger of atmospheric pollution, such as the ozone hole, global warming, smog, or acid rain. (8, 9, 10, 18, 21, 23, 25)

f. Invent a machine that runs on wind energy. Draw a diagram or build a model of your invention. What does your creation do? Its purpose can be useful or silly. (3, 22, 26)

g. Design an air purification system or an anti–air pollution machine. Draw a diagram or build a model of your invention. Write an explanation of how it would work. (9, 10, 20, 23)

SPELLING/VOCABULARY

a. Complete a matching picture puzzle of things that use air: balloon, windmill, tire, sailboat, kite, lungs, weather vane, trumpet, glider, straws, parachute, vacuum cleaner, fire, bicycle pump, airplane, hair dryer. How does each one use air? (1, 3, 5, 14, 17, 22)

b. Complete a crossword puzzle of terms related to the properties of air:

air pressure, suction, air resistance, humidity, lift, compression, weather, gaseous, contraction, expansion, streamlining, kinetic energy, transparent, convection, density. (3, 14, 20, 22)

c. Complete a word search puzzle of the componants of Earth's atmosphere: hydrogen, helium, oxygen, nitrogen, neon, argon, krypton, xenon, methane, particles, aerosols, ozone, carbon dioxide, water vapor. (2, 8, 12, 16, 25)

d. Complete a crossword puzzle of air and weather-related terms: low pressure, high pressure, Beaufort wind scale, anemometer, barometer, jet stream, hurricane, condense, weather vane, currents, evaporate, tornado, front, climate, temperature, drought, El Niño, Fahrenheit, Celsius, precipitation. (13, 14, 20, 21, 27)

e. All animals need to breathe clean air in order to live. On a diagram of the human respiratory system, label the following: nasal cavity, mouth, bronchi, diaphragm, left lung, right lung, trachea, esophagus. Humans use air to speak. Label the following on a picture of the human larynx: trachea, epiglottis, vocal chords, cartilage. What are: alveoli, cilia, bronchiole, pharynx, tonsils, sinuses, mucous membranes, plural membranes? (15, 19)

f. Define some terms that relate to atmospheric pollution: smog, CFCs, acid rain, greenhouse effect, ozone hole, fossil fuels, fallout, DDT, particulate, radiation, fly ash, polystyrene, nitrous oxide, PH acidity, emissions, carbon monoxide. (4, 8, 9, 10, 11, 16, 20, 21, 23, 25)

g. Following are terms that relate to breathing problems or diseases caused by air pollution. Match each term to its meaning: hay fever, asthma, bronchitis, emphysema, sick building syndrome, hiccups, coughing, sneezing, pleurisy, pneumonia, tuberculosis, cataracts, the bends, hyperventilation, skin cancer, lung cancer. (4, 15, 19, 23)

GEOGRAPHY

a. Look around your community for places, such as busy intersections or factories, where a lot of pollution is added to the air. Locate these places on a local map. When you walk or drive by these places, can you tell if the air is polluted?

b. Find Antarctica on a globe or world map. On a picture of Antarctica, draw an outline of the ozone hole that exists in the atmosphere above it. How big is this hole in comparison to other countries on Earth? (4, 10)

c. Look at a United States map. Note the compass points north, south, east, and west. Then read a weather report to find out which way the wind is blowing. Point this out on your map. Keep a chart of wind direction for one week.

d. In *The World Almanac and Book of Facts,* look up Speed of Winds in the United States. Then look at a United States map. Mark in green the cities that have an average wind of 6.0–6.9 mph, in red cities with winds of 7.0–7.9 mph, blue 8.0–8.9 mph, orange 9.0–9.9 mph, purple 10.0–10.9 mph, brown 11.0–11.9 mph, and pink 12.0–12.9 mph. What is the windiest place in the country? Place a star there and record its average wind speed.

e. A one foot rise in sea level could cause the polar caps to melt, the sea level to rise, and the shorelines to recede 100 to 1,000 feet. Look at a map of the world that shows land elevations. How might the geography of the world change if global warming were to cause the seas to rise?   (4, 11, 16, 20, 21, 25)

f. What are trade winds? Why are they important to sailors? On a map of the world, draw and label northeast trade winds, southeast trade winds, summer monsoons, and westerlies.   (3, 4, 13, 22)

g. Parts of the world show the effects of air pollution caused by smog, acid rain, deforestation, wind erosion, the ozone hole, and other air pollution factors. Locate on a world map some areas that have been harmed. Note the type of air pollution responsible for the damage.   (9, 10, 16, 18, 25)

MATH

a. Air is made up of many invisible gases. Make a chart that shows the amounts of nitrogen, oxygen, and other gases that are contained in the air. What are some of these trace gases?   (4, 12, 14, 16, 24)

b. The Beaufort wind scale is used to describe the force of wind at different speeds. Look at a chart of the Beaufort wind scale to answer the following questions: 1) What type of wind blows at 3 mph? At 35 mph? 2) What happens at Beaufort #4? 3) How many mph is a strong gale? 4) Air blowing at 65 mph is what kind of wind? 5) Name the five types of breezes, their Beaufort numbers, and the mph range for each. 6) How hard does the wind have to blow in order to move a weather vane? In order to be a hurricane?   (27)

c. There is a hole in the ozone layer over Antarctica. It is as big as North America, and as deep as Mount Everest is tall. How many square miles is North America? How tall is Mount Everest? Use these figures to calculate the approximate size of the ozone hole.   (10)

d. The sun sends visible and invisible radiation to the Earth. 1) Of the radiation that reaches Earth, 15% is absorbed by the atmosphere, 6% is reflected by the atmosphere, 21% is reflected by clouds, 3% is absorbed by clouds, 5% is reflected by the ground, and 50% is absorbed by the ground. Draw a chart that illustrates this. 2) What types of radiation are there? Draw a chart of the electromagnetic spectrum.   (10, 11)

e. Look up a wind chill table. (One can be found in *The World Almanac and Book of Facts*.) How does wind speed affect weather temperature? Refer to this chart to answer the following questions: If it is 35°F with a wind chill factor (wcf) of 25 mph, what does the temperature feel like? If 50°F with a wcf of 40 mph; 10°F with a wcf of 5 mph; -20°F with a wcf of 30 mph; 0°F with a wcf of 20 mph; 30°F with a wcf of 45 mph; -10°F with a wcf of 10 mph; 15°F with a wcf of 40 mph?

f. Look up a table of apparent temperature or a heat index. (One can be found in *The World Almanac and Book of Facts*.) How does humidity combined with air temperature affect the body's ability to cool itself? Refer to the chart to answer the following questions: If the air temperature (air temp) is 85°F and the relative humidity (rh) is 30%, what is the apparent temperature? If air temp is 100°F and rh is 10%; air temp is 70°F and rh is 90%; air temp is 105°F and rh is 60%; air temp is 75°F and rh is 100%; air temp is 95°F and rh is 40%; air temp is 85°F and rh is 0%; air temp is 110°F and rh is 10%?

g. Answer these math problems concerning wind and weather: 1) A lightning bolt heats the surrounding air to a temperature of 30,200°C. Convert this number to degrees Fahrenheit. 2) The wind speed of a tornado may reach 250 miles per hour. Convert this figure to kilometers per hour. 3) Air in the jet stream travels from west to east, and can be as fast as 360 kilometers per hour. Convert this figure to miles per hour. 4) Light travels through the air a million times faster than sound, or about 5.5 seconds faster per mile. To judge how far away you are from a lightning storm, count the number of seconds between the time you see a lightning flash and the time you hear thunder. Divide by 5 to get the approximate number of miles. How far away is the storm if you count 90 seconds? 58? 32? 3?

MUSIC AND THEATER ARTS

a. Sing some songs about the air or things that fly, such as the pop song "Up, Up, and Away," or "Let's Go Fly a Kite" from the film *Mary Poppins*.

b. Count how many times you inhale and exhale in one minute. Then run or do exercises for five minutes. Count the number of times you inhale and exhale in one minute again. Is it more or less? Why? Pretend you are an athlete who just ran a marathon. How would you breathe?

c. Make believe it is a day with no wind. How would you walk? Then pretend it is a windy day. How would you walk? Next, show how you would walk in a gale wind.

d. Pretend you are an astronaut. Act out how the forces of gravity and air pressure would affect you during blast-off. When would you become weightless? Why? Act out how you would move around the space capsule while you were weightless. Pretend to land on the moon. Mime getting into a space suit and walking on the moon. How would the moon's air and gravity affect how you walk? What would you wear? Why?

e. Several musical instruments use wind power to make sounds. Most wind instruments require a person to blow through a mouthpiece. Can you think of other ways wind power can be used to make music? Make a list of wind-powered musical instruments. Divide your list into Reeds, Brass, and Other.

f. It is important to learn proper breathing techniques in order to project your voice on stage. Breathing exercises can also help relax the body to reduce stress. Practice some breathing exercises that are used in theater classes. (19)

g. There are many hobbies or sports that involve wind, such as flying a kite or sailing. Each person in the class can mime a wind hobby or sport. The rest of the class can try to guess the activity.

ENGLISH COMPOSITION

a. Read "Winnie the Pooh and the Blustery Day," by A. A. Milne. Then write your own story about a windy day.

b. Look around your neighborhood for examples of air pollution. Write a letter to your local newspaper or public official about what you see. Suggest a way to stop polluting the air. (9, 16, 23, 24, 27)

c. One source of air pollution is cigarette smoke. Write an explanation of how cigarette smoke affects the human body. (15, 19, 23)

d. Write a description of what happens when you breathe. What gas does your body use? How? Where does it go inside your body? What gas leaves when you exhale? (12, 15, 19, 23, 24)

e. Pretend you are a meteorologist. Write a weather report for a good or stormy day. Tell the current weather, and give a forecast for tomorrow's weather. Base your report on wind currents, high and low pressure areas, humidity, fronts, temperature, etc. Give an air quality report as part of your forecast. (13, 20, 27)

f. Pretend you are a delegate to the Global Summit to Preserve Earth's Atmosphere. Write an international law which you would propose to stop the harmful effects of air pollution and other atmosphere-destroying acts of humans. List your law's goals, and the rules all nations must agree to follow. (4, 9, 10, 11, 16, 21, 23)

g. Write a science fiction story that takes place in a time when Earth's atmosphere is severely polluted. How do people live when there is no clean air to breathe? How are plants and animals affected? What is the government's role?   (4, 9, 11, 16, 23, 25, 27)

SCIENCE

Note: Many science books contain experiments about air. These can be used along with this unit.

   a. List some properties of air. Conduct some experiments that demonstrate these properties.   (1, 8, 12, 13, 14)

   b. What does a barometer do? How does it work? Make a simple barometer in class.   (12, 13, 14, 27)

   c. What are the layers of the Earth's atmosphere? What are some characteristics of each layer? Prepare a chart that describes these facts.   (4, 8, 10, 14, 16, 20, 25)

   d. Carbon dioxide and oxygen are two gases that are in Earth's air. How is oxygen added to the air? What are some ways that humans add carbon dioxide to the air?   (4, 8, 12, 16, 24, 25)

   e. What is ozone? How does it differ from oxygen? Why are oxygen and ozone important? How can they be dangerous? What is the ozone layer? Why is it important? How is the ozone layer being damaged?   (2, 4, 8, 10, 16, 20, 25)

   f. Draw a chart that explains the carbon cycle or the water cycle. What would happen to Earth if either one of these systems were to become unbalanced?   (4, 8, 11, 20, 21)

   g. Explain the human respiratory system. What are the roles of: lungs, blood, mucous membranes, heart, diaphragm, larynx, pharynx, trachea. What is the purpose of coughs, sneezes, and runny noses?   (15, 19, 23)

HISTORY/SOCIOLOGY

   a. Read some true stories about the early days of aviation. Write a report about your favorite person, invention, or accomplishment.   (6, 26)

   b. Air pollution has been a problem throughout history. Look up information about one air pollution incident from recent or past history. How did the pollution affect people?   (4, 9, 23, 24)

   c. Many items we use, such as tires, are filled with air. Other inventions, such as airplanes, fly in the air. Choose one invention that uses air in some way and trace its history. Who created it, when, and how was it first used? How is it used now?   (6, 12, 26)

   d. Read a biography about an aviator or astronaut. Then list some facts about his/her life, such as when the person was born and what he/she accomplished in the air.   (6, 26)

e. How have people used wind power as a source of energy in the past? How is it used now?   (3, 22)

f. There have been a several tragedies throughout history that involved an aircraft, such as the crash of the *Hindenburg* or the *Challenger* explosion. Choose one such event to research. Tell when and where it happened. What is the theory of how and why it happened? What is being done to avoid a similar disaster?   (7)

g. Several scientists have developed theories or made discoveries about air and the atmosphere. Choose one scientist and state his/her discovery or theory. When and where did the scientist live? How did he/she attempt to prove the discovery or theory? What was the reaction to the news? Do we believe it today?   (2, 11, 12)

TOPICS FOR DISCUSSION

a. If you can't see air, how can you tell it is there?   (3, 5, 12, 13, 14, 17, 20, 22, 23)

b. Name some ways that we use air and wind for work, fun, and as an energy source.   (3, 5, 12, 17, 20, 22, 24)

c. What is air pollution? Name some causes of air pollution. What are some of its effects on plants, animals, people, water, buildings, and the environment?   (4, 8, 9, 16, 20, 23, 24, 27)

d. How can saving energy help prevent air pollution? List some energy-saving hints that would improve air quality.   (4, 9, 11, 16, 20, 21, 23, 24, 25)

e. What is sick building syndrome? What are some sources of indoor air pollution? What can we do to lower these levels?   (4, 10, 23, 24)

f. What causes acid rain? How does it affect the environment? Human health? What are some possible solutions to this problem?   (4, 8, 9, 16, 18, 20, 23, 25, 27)

g. What are some human activities that add greenhouse gases to our atmosphere? What might happen to Earth's land, water, and weather if this global warming trend continues? How might humans be affected?   (4, 8, 9, 11, 16, 20, 21, 25)

SUGGESTED RESOURCES

(1) Ardley, Neil. *The Science Book of Air.* Harcourt, 1991.

(2) Asimov, Isaac. *How Did We Find Out About the Atmosphere?* [How Did We Find Out About...?] Walker, 1985.

(3) Bailey, Donna. *Energy from Wind and Water* [Facts About]. Raintree, 1990.

(4) Baines, John. *Conserving the Atmosphere* [Conserving Our World]. Steck-Vaughn, 1989.

(5) Barkan, Joanne. *Air, Air All Around* [First Facts]. Silver, 1990.

(6) Boyne, Walter J. *The Smithsonian Book of Flight for Young People.* Atheneum, 1988.

(7) Coote, Roger. *Air Disasters* [The World's Disasters]. Thomson, 1993.

(8) Costa-Pau, Rosa. *Keeping the Air Clean* [The Junior Library of Ecology]. Chelsea, 1994.

(9) Hare, Tony. *Acid Rain* [Save Our Earth]. Gloucester, 1990.

(10) _____. *The Ozone Layer* [Save Our Earth]. Gloucester, 1990.

(11) Johnson, Rebecca L. *The Greenhouse Effect: Life on a Warmer Planet* [Discovery!]. Lerner, 1990.

(12) Johnston, Tom. *Air, Air, Everywhere* [Science in Action]. Stevens, 1988.

(13) Kahl, Jonathan D. *Weatherwise* [How's the Weather?]. Lerner, 1992.

(14) Kerrod, Robin. *Air in Action* [Secrets of Science]. Cavendish, 1990.

(15) Lambert, Mark. *The Lungs and Breathing* [How Our Bodies Work]. Silver, 1988.

(16) Leggett, Jeremy. *Air Scare* [Operation Earth]. Cavendish, 1991.

(17) Llewelyn, Claire. *First Look in the Air* [First Look]. Stevens, 1991.

(18) Lucas, Eileen. *Acid Rain* [Saving Planet Earth]. Childrens, 1991.

(19) Parker, Steve. *The Lungs and Breathing* [The Human Body]. Watts, 1989.

(20) Pollard, Michael. *Air, Water and Weather* [Discovering Science]. Facts on File, 1987.

(21) Pringle, Laurence. *Global Warming: Assessing the Greenhouse Threat.* Arcade, 1990.

(22) Rickard, Graham. *Wind Energy* [Alternative Energy]. Stevens, 1991.

(23) Snodgrass, Mary Ellen. *Environmental Awareness: Air Pollution.* Bancroft-Sage, 1991.

(24) Stille, Darlene R. *Air Pollution* [New True Books]. Childrens, 1990.

(25) Tesar, Jenny. *Global Warming* [Our Fragile Planet]. Facts on File, 1991.

(26) Wood, Tim. *Air Travel* [The World on the Move]. Thomson, 1993.

(27) Wyatt, Valerie. *Weatherwatch.* Addison-Wesley, 1990.

LIBRARY SKILLS RESOURCES

Growing Up With Science. Cavendish, 1988.

Kidron, Michael, and Segal, Ronald. *The New State of the World Atlas.* Simon & Schuster, 1991.

Mattson, Mark. *Scholastic Environmental Atlas of the United States.* Scholastic, 1993.

Reader's Guide to Periodical Literature. H.W. Wilson.

The World Almanac and Book of Facts. World Almanac, 1994.

ADDITIONAL READING – YOUNGER

Adler, David A. *You Breathe In, You Breathe Out: All About Your Lungs* [Discovering Science]. Watts, 1991.

Ames, Lee J. *Draw 50 Airplanes, Aircraft, and Spacecraft*. Doubleday, 1977.

Asimov, Isaac. *Why Is the Air Dirty?* [Ask Isaac Asimov]. Stevens, 1992. (Also other related books in series.)

Bennett, Paul. *Earth: The Incredible Recycling Machine*. Thomson, 1993.

Broekel, Ray. *Experiments with Air* [New True Books]. Childrens, 1988.

Churchill, E. Richard. *Fantastic Flying Paper Toys*. Sterling, 1990.

Devonshire, Hilary. *Air* [Science Through Art]. Watts, 1992.

_____. *Flight* [Science Through Art]. Watts, 1993.

Gibbons, Gail. *Catch the Wind!* Little, 1989.

Greene, Carol. *Astronauts* [New True Books]. Childrens, 1984.

Milne, A. A. *Winnie the Pooh and the Blustery Day*. Disneyland, 1989.

Planes [What's Inside?]. Kindersley, 1992.

Provensen, Alice, and Provensen, Martin. *The Glorious Flight: Across the Channel with Louis Bleriot*. Viking, 1978.

Steele, Philip. *Storms: Causes and Effects* [Weather Watch]. Watts, 1991. (Also other books in series)

Stille, Darlene R. *The Greenhouse Effect* [New True Books]. Childrens, 1990.

Taylor, Barbara. *Up, Up and Away! The Science of Flight* [Step into Science]. Random, 1992.

_____. *Weather and Climate: Geography Facts and Experiments* [Young Discoverers]. Kingfisher, 1993.

Taylor, Richard L. *The First Flight: The Story of the Wright Brothers* [First Books— Space Science and First Flights]. Watts, 1990. (Also other books in series.)

Wheeler, Jill. *The Air We Breathe* [We Can Save the Earth]. Abdo, 1990.

ADDITIONAL READING—OLDER

Blackman, Steve. *Planes and Flight* [Technology Craft Topics]. Watts, 1993.

Bramwell, Martyn. *Weather* [Earth Science Library]. Watts, 1994.

Clark, John. *The Atmosphere: Projects with Geography* [Hands On Science]. Gloucester, 1992.

Dolan, Edward F. *Our Poisoned Sky*. Dutton, 1991.

Gutnik, Martin J. *The Challenge of Clean Air* [Environmental Issues]. Enslow, 1990.

_____. *Experiments That Explore Acid Rain* [Investigate!]. Millbrook, 1992.

_____. *Experiments That Explore the Greenhouse Effect* [Investigate!]. Millbrook, 1991.

Hare, Tony. *Polluting the Air* [Save Our Earth]. Watts, 1992.

Heyman, LeRoy. *Aces, Heroes, and Daredevils of the Air*. Messner, 1981.

Lambert, Mark. *Aircraft Technology* [Technology in Action]. Bookwright, 1990.

Linsley, Leslie, and Aron, Jon. *Air Crafts*. Dutton, 1982.

Miller, Christina G., and Berry, Louise A. *Acid Rain: A Sourcebook for Young People*. Messner, 1986.

Parker, Steve. *Flight and Flying Machines* [See & Explore Library]. Kindersley, 1993.

Rosenblum, Richard. *Wings: The Early Years of Aviation*. Four Winds, 1980.

Royston, Angela. *Planes* [Eye-Openers]. Aladdin, 1992.

Rybolt, Thomas R., and Mebane, Robert C. *Environmental Experiments About Air* [Science Experiments for Young People]. Enslow, 1993.

Sandak, Cass. *A Reference Guide to Clean Air* [Science, Technology, and Society]. Enslow, 1990.

Walker, Jane. *The Atmosphere in Danger* [Man-Made Disasters]. Watts, 1993.
Yep, Laurence. *Dragonwings*. Harper, 1975.

See also: books in ENVIRONMENTAL AWARENESS and WATER units.

FOR MORE INFORMATION ABOUT THE ATMOSPHERE, WRITE TO:

The Acid Rain Foundation
Air and Waste Management Association
Alliance for Responsible CFC Policy
American Wind Energy Association
Environmental Action Coalition
Environmental Defense Fund
Friends of the Earth
Greenhouse Crisis Foundation
Natural Resources Defense Council
Sierra Club

WATER

All living things on Earth need water in order to survive. But, in spite of the fact that about two-thirds of the planet is covered with water, we are in the midst of a serious water crisis. Water mismanagement and pollution threaten our supplies of drinking water, and harm plant and animal life. We must change our water use habits to protect this most valuable resource.

LIBRARY SKILLS

a. Look in a dictionary. List all the terms you can find that begin with "water," such as waterfall.

b. Look in the card catalog or online catalog to find fiction books about bodies of water. What subject headings can you look under? List the titles and authors of five picture books or novels you find.

c. Look up Water in *The New Book of Knowledge*. Note some facts about these topics: sinkholes, erosion, and water purification.

d. Too much water in an area may result in flooding. Look up Floods, Tidal Waves in *The World Almanac and Book of Facts*. Which country has had the most flood-related deaths? In the past 20 years, which country has had the worst flooding problem? What part of the world seems to be especially prone to flooding?

e. Use an atlas or encyclopedia to find a precipitation map. On a map of the world, color tropical areas that receive a lot of rain in green, desert areas that receive little rain in red, and areas that are always covered with ice in blue.

f. Suppose you wanted to learn all about fishing. Where would you look in the library to find this information? Which references would you consult? Which subject headings? Which Dewey decimal numbers?

g. In the *New State of the World Atlas*, look up Urban Blight. On a map of the world, color in red the areas where less than half of the population has safe drinking water. Use diagonal lines to shade the areas where less than half the population has sanitation services.

ARTS AND CRAFTS

a. Paint a picture using watercolors.

b. Make a collage of pictures of water (rivers, waterfalls, rain, waves, etc.).

c. Draw a picture that illustrates the water cycle. Picture water going through at least five changes. Explain on your picture why the water cycle is important. (1, 2, 9, 12, 14, 15, 22, 23, 26)

d. Draw a poster encouraging people to stop polluting water, or to conserve water. (1, 8, 9, 12, 14, 19, 20, 22, 23, 24)

e. *Group project:* Create a bulletin board display about plant and animal life that is found in fresh or salt water.

f. *Group project:* Build a model of a water treatment plant or a water purification plant. Label what happens in each section. (1, 14, 19, 24)

g. There are many types of vessels in which people can travel on or through water, such as a canoe or submarine. Build a model of one seaworthy vehicle. (5, 6)

SPELLING/VOCABULARY

a. Complete a matching picture puzzle of animals that live in or near water: seal, duck, otter, shark, eel, frog, whale, fish, swan, turtle, alligator, crab, manatee, beaver, dragonfly, octopus, sea gull, dolphin, clam, pelican. (20, 26)

b. Complete a word search puzzle of water courses and bodies of water: ocean, brook, lake, river, waterfall, sea, glacier, gulf, stream, marsh, pond, swamp, iceberg, estuary, bay, brook, geyser, lagoon, cascade, tributary. (15, 18, 20, 25, 26)

c. Complete a fill-in-the-blanks exercise of things we do with water: irrigate, wash, drink, soak, heat, freeze, absorb, drip, dilute, swim, sail, spray, flush, cook, ice, boil, steam, dissolve, float, paint. (6, 15, 20, 24, 25)

d. Complete a crossword puzzle about the water cycle: cloud, evaporate, fog, runoff, rainfall, hydrologic, water vapor, precipitate, condense, humidity, groundwater, moisture, droplet, weather, stream, dew, frost, ice crystals, transpiration. (1, 5, 9, 14, 15, 18, 21, 23, 25, 26)

e. Explain the differences between fresh and salt water, soft and hard water, treated and untreated water, clean and polluted water. Which of these would be safe to drink? Explain the differences between a water treatment plant and a water purification plant, a lake and a reservoir, a waterspout and a whirlpool, groundwater and surface water. (9, 14, 15, 19, 21, 22, 24)

f. Define some terms associated with water pollution: runoff, eutrophication, thermal pollution, mercury, toxic waste, fly ash, leachate, strip mining, lead, THM, nitrates, phosphates, sewage, chemical fertilizers, acid rain, pesticides, infectious diseases, ocean litter. (8, 12, 14, 16, 19, 22, 23)

g. What is groundwater? Explain these related terms: aquifer, fossil water, cave, sinkhole, porous rock, permeable, zone of aeration, bedrock, artesian well, water table, stalactite, stalagmite, spring, limestone, geyser, zone of saturation, thermal spring. (9, 14, 16, 22, 23)

GEOGRAPHY

a. On a map of the United States, label the Great Lakes, the Mississippi River, and other important bodies of water.

b. On a map of the world, label the Earth's oceans. Also label some important seas and rivers.

c. How can water change the shape of beaches, mountains, valleys, and other landforms? Look up information about a specific place, such as Niagara Falls or the Grand Canyon, or a local beach, cave, river, etc. How has water affected the shape of the land? (18, 23, 26)

d. Many early explorers traveled across the oceans. On a map of the world, trace the routes of three explorers who set out from different countries. Note each explorer's name, the date of the exploration, and the starting and ending point of the journey. Use a different color for each explorer. (5)

e. Some parts of the world receive either too much rain and are prone to flooding, or too little rain and endure droughts. On a map of the world, color drought-prone areas in orange and flood-prone areas in purple. (10, 11, 14, 16)

f. Many dams have been built in the United States and around the world. Locate some of these on a map of the world. For what purpose were the dams built? Do dams help or hinder the environment? (10, 14, 17, 22)

g. On a map of the world, color in some areas that have been damaged by acid rain (red), oil spills (green), and toxic chemicals/wastewater (blue). (3, 8, 12, 13, 22)

MATH

a. Two-thirds of the Earth is covered with water. Of this amount, about 97% is in the oceans, 2% is in the glaciers, and 1% is fresh water. Draw a chart to illustrate these facts. (20)

b. A dripping faucet that leaks one drop of water per second will waste four gallons of water in a day. How many gallons will be wasted in a week? In a 30-day month? In a year?

c. Compile a list of ten interesting math facts about water. Suggestions: The amount of water a person should drink each day, the place on Earth that receives the most rain, the boiling and freezing points of water, how much of Niagara Falls is eroded each year, etc. (1, 4, 12, 15, 21, 23, 24, 26)

d. Pollution from factories that release smoke into the air is a major cause of acid rain. Weather systems, which travel from west to east across North America, spread the effects of acid rain. If smoke particles are blown 300 miles per day for three days, how far will the polluted air travel? 500 miles per day for two days? 425 miles per day for six days? 385 miles per day for a week? (13)

e. Look up a table of apparent temperature or a heat index. How does the amount of water vapor in the air affect the body's ability to cool itself? Refer to the table to answer the following questions: If the air temperature (air temp) is 100°F and the relative humidity (rh) is 0%, what is the apparent temperature? If the air temp is 75°F and rh is 70%; if air temp is 80°F and rh is 100%; if air temp is 110°F and rh is 50%; if air temp is 90°F and rh is 90%; if air temp is 70°F and rh is 10%; if air temp is 95°F and rh is 20%; if air temp is 75°F and rh is 50%. (23 or *World Almanac and Book of Facts*)

f. Taking a shower uses about 30 gallons of water, flushing the toilet uses 4 gallons of water, and running a faucet uses 2.5 gallons per minute. If, during the day, a person takes a shower, flushes the toilet 6 times, and runs water for a total of 47 minutes, how much water is used in one day? Most Americans use about 50-150 gallons of water per day. How does this compare to the person in this example? (14)

g. United States water use is about 47% for agriculture, 44% for industry, and 9% for household use. If Americans use a total of 450 billion gallons of water each day, how many gallons are used in each of these three categories? Make a chart to illustrate your answer. (14)

MUSIC AND THEATER ARTS

a. Pour different amounts of water into drinking glasses. Tap each glass with a spoon and listen to the sound it makes. See if you can play simple tunes with water-glass chimes.

b. There are lots of songs about rain and water. Sing and dance along to "Singin' in the Rain," "Raindrops Keep Fallin' on My Head," and other popular water songs.

c. Do a Show and Tell presentation of water litter. Choose one type of garbage, such as old cans, oil, or plastic six-pack rings, that people dump in rivers, lakes, or seas. Bring it or a picture of it to class and tell about the damage it does to the Earth's waters, vegetation, and wildlife.   (12, 19, 20, 23)

d. Act out something that happens in or with water, such as a fish swimming or a person washing. The rest of the class can try to guess the mimed activity.

e. Many musical compositions have been named for bodies of water. Listen to some music, such as "The Blue Danube" by Johann Strauss. How does the composer express his feelings for the body of water?

f. *Group project*: Many people don't conserve water because they don't believe there is a water shortage. Perform a skit to explain the water crisis, and to convince everybody to use less water.   (9, 12, 14, 16, 22)

g. Many types of weather, such as rain, snow, and hurricanes, involve water. Various forms of weather are often depicted in music, such as tinkling the high notes on a piano to indicate rain, or crashing symbols for thunder. What instruments would you use to portray snow, a calm sea, or a stormy sea? Listen to "The William Tell Overture" by Gioacchino Rossini. Do you hear a storm in the music? What do you imagine is happening?

ENGLISH COMPOSITION

a. Water has many uses. Write an essay about why you think water is a valuable resource. What is your favorite thing to do with water? Why? (1, 2, 6, 18, 25)

b. Write a story about the adventures of a drop of water. What different forms does it take? Where does it go?   (2, 4, 7, 15, 21, 24, 25)

c. Think up some picturesque adjectives for water, such as *crashing* waves or *babbling* brook. Describe: stream, pond, cloud, fog, ocean, brook, waves, waterfall, puddle, drop, river, sea, lake, snow, icicle, water, rain. Be creative!

d. Do one of these creative writing activities: 1) Pretend you are a desert plant or animal. Write a true story about how you are able to survive on a very small amount of water. 2) Pretend you are a river. Describe what happens as you flow from a mountain top toward the sea. 3) Pretend you are a green, leafy plant or tree. Tell how you gather and use water.   (2, 10, 21, 23, 26)

e. Look around your community for water pollution problems. Write a letter to the editor of your local newspaper, mayor or town council, congressman or senator. Express your concern about one of these problems.   (8, 9, 12, 14, 19)

f. Imagine what your life would be like during a severe drought or flood.

How would your family survive? Would your drinking water be rationed (drought) or contaminated (flood)? Would you be forced to leave your home? What would happen to plants and animals? Pretend you are living in a city or on a farm, in the United States or elsewhere. Write a one-week diary of how you survive the worst drought or flood in the area's history. (10, 11, 14, 16)

g. For two weeks, keep a journal of how you use water. Write down every time you turn on the water faucet, bathe or shower, flush the toilet, use water for cooking or watering plants, etc. Estimate how many seconds or minutes the water is left running. Try to limit your use of water after the first day. At the end of two weeks, write a report on your daily water use and how you can conserve water at home. (1, 9, 14, 22, 25)

SCIENCE

Note: There are many books of water experiments available. Students can conduct several simple water experiments in addition to doing the following activities.

a. What are the three forms water can take? Tell where water in each of these forms can be found. (1, 2, 4, 15, 18, 21, 25)

b. What is the chemical name for water? How is water made from two gases? What are some properties of water? Perform some simple experiments that illustrate these properties. (2, 4, 18, 21, 23, 24, 25)

c. How much of the human body is water? How do our bodies use water? What can happen to us if we do not consume enough water? (1, 2, 14, 19, 21, 22, 26)

d. How can water be used as an energy source? Name three methods of harnessing water power. State briefly how each one works. (1, 12, 18, 21, 25, 26)

e. What is acid rain? What causes it? Note some of the chemical pollutants involved. What are some of the effects of acid rain on the environment? (2, 8, 12, 13, 14, 17, 23)

f. What is desalination? What countries use this process? Why? How is it done? What is salination (or salinization)? How does it affect the water supply? (12, 14, 19, 22)

g. Explain these water effects on Earth's weather and atmosphere: 1) What causes us to see a rainbow? 2) What is humidity? How is it measured? 3) How are clouds formed? Hail? Frost? 4) What causes a hurricane? A tornado? (7, 15, 23)

HISTORY/SOCIOLOGY

a. Years ago, people could safely drink water directly from a stream or lake. Now, this is usually not safe. What has happened to make our untreated fresh water unsafe to drink? (1, 12, 19, 20, 25)

b. Many explorers traveled across the water. Look up information about one explorer or group of explorers. Note his/their names, country, where and when he/they sailed. What did he/they discover? (5, 6)

c. Droughts and floods have done much damage and affected millions of people throughout history. Find out some information about one flood or drought. Where and when did it occur? How did it affect the environment and the people who lived there? (10, 11, 12, 14)

d. Water sports have always been popular. Choose one water sport and trace its history. Name some famous athletes who participated in the sport. What records have been set?

e. The use of water to irrigate crops and as an energy source has been important throughout history. Choose one civilization from the past or present. Tell how they used water for either of these purposes. (9, 14, 16, 17, 19)

f. Look up information on one major incident of water pollution, such as the industrial pollution of the Cuyahoga River or the *Exxon Valdez* oil spill. Name the source of the pollution (accident, industrial, sewage, etc.). When did it occur? Is it still going on? How has the pollution affected the environment? What has been done to correct the problem? (3, 9, 12, 13, 14, 16, 22)

g. The United States federal government has passed several laws in order to control and clean up water pollution. In addition, many government and private organizations have been formed to regulate this problem. Choose one law or organization and write a report about it. Note when the law or organization came into being, the problem it addresses, and whether or not it has been successful. (13, 14, 16, 22, 23)

TOPICS FOR DISCUSSION

a. Why do water shortages occur? What are some ways that we can save water from being wasted? (1, 10, 12, 18, 19, 20, 24)

b. What are some sources of water pollution? What are some effects of pollution? (1, 2, 8, 12, 18, 19, 20, 24)

c. What are some measures we can take to make sure our water does not become polluted? (1, 8, 18, 19, 20)

d. Tell how water pollution can harm or kill humans via the food chain. (2, 12, 13, 14, 20, 22)

e. Why is the water resource in crisis? List some conditions of nature and problems caused by people that have contributed to the shortage of fresh water. (9, 10, 12, 13, 16, 19, 22)

f. Which of the following do you think is the worst water pollution problem: acid rain, groundwater contamination, oil spills, or dumping waste into rivers and seas? Defend your choice. (2, 8, 12, 13, 14, 19, 22)

g. How do farmers contribute to water pollution? To water waste? What are some agricultural methods that can conserve water and not contaminate groundwater? (2, 8, 9, 12, 14, 22)

SUGGESTED RESOURCES

(1) Baines, John. *Water* [Resources]. Thomson, 1993.
(2) Bennett, Paul. *Earth: The Incredible Recycling Machine.* Thomson, 1993.
(3) Blashfield, Jean F., and Black, Wallace B. *Oil Spills* [Saving Planet Earth]. Childrens, 1991.
(4) Broekel, Ray. *Experiments with Water* [New True Books]. Childrens, 1988.
(5) Coote, Roger. *The Sailor Through History* [Journey Through History]. Thomson, 1993.
(6) Davies, Eryl. *Water Travel* [The World on the Move]. Thomson, 1993.
(7) Flint, David. *Weather and Climate: Projects with Geography* [Hands On Science]. Gloucester, 1991.
(8) Hare, Tony. *Acid Rain* [Save Our Earth]. Gloucester, 1990.
(9) Hoff, Mary, and Rodgers, Mary M. *Groundwater* [Our Endangered Planet]. Lerner, 1991.
(10) Knapp, Brian. *Drought* [World Disasters!]. Steck-Vaughn, 1990.
(11) _____. *Flood* [World Disasters!]. Steck-Vaughn, 1990.
(12) Leggett, Dennis, and Leggett, Jeremy. *Troubled Waters* [Operation Earth]. Cavendish, 1991.
(13) Lucas, Eileen. *Acid Rain* [Saving Planet Earth]. Childrens, 1991.
(14) _____. *Water: A Resource in Crisis* [Saving Planet Earth]. Childrens, 1991.
(15) Pollard, Michael. *Air, Water and Weather* [Discovering Science]. Facts on File, 1987.
(16) Pringle, Laurence. *Water: The Next Great Resource Battle* [Science for Survival]. Macmillan, 1982.
(17) Rickard, Graham. *Water Energy* [Alternative Energy]. Stevens, 1991.
(18) Seixas, Judith S. *Water: What It Is, What It Does* [Greenwillow Read-Alone]. Greenwillow, 1987.
(19) Snodgrass, Mary Ellen. *Environmental Awareness: Water Pollution.* Bancroft-Sage, 1991.
(20) Stille, Darlene R. *Water Pollution* [New True Books]. Childrens, 1990.
(21) Taylor, Kim. *Water* [Flying Start Science]. Wiley, 1992.
(22) Tesar, Jenny. *Food and Water: Threats, Shortages and Solutions* [Our Fragile Planet]. Facts on File, 1992.
(23) Walker, Sally M. *Water Up, Water Down: The Hydrologic Cycle* [Earth Watch]. Carolrhoda, 1992.

(24) Walpole, Brenda. *Water*. Garrett, 1990.
(25) *Water* [Science in Our World]. Grolier, 1992.
(26) Wood, Jenny. *Waterfalls: Nature's Thundering Splendor* [Wonderworks of Nature]. Stevens, 1991.

LIBRARY SKILLS RESOURCES

Kidron, Michael, and Segal, Ronald. *The New State of the World Atlas*. Simon & Schuster, 1984.
The New Book of Knowledge. Grolier, 1994.
The World Almanac and Book of Facts. World Almanac, 1994.

ADDITIONAL READING – YOUNGER

Asimov, Isaac. *How Do Big Ships Float?* [Ask Isaac Asimov]. Stevens, 1993.
Bailey, Donna. *What We Can Do About Wasting Water* [What We Can Do About]. Watts, 1992.
Brandt, Keith. *What Makes It Rain? The Story of a Raindrop*. Troll, 1982.
Cobb, Vicki. *The Trip of a Drip* [How the World Works]. Little, 1986.
Cole, Joanna. *The Magic School Bus at the Water Works* [Magic School Bus]. Scholastic, 1986.
Devonshire, Hilary. *Water* [Science Through Art]. Watts, 1993.
Dorros, Arthur. *Follow the Water from Brook to Ocean* [Trophy Let's-Read-and-Find-Out Stage 2]. HarperCollins, 1993.
Fowler, Allan. *It Could Still Be Water* [Rookie Read-About Science]. Childrens, 1993.
Greene, Carol. *Caring for Our Water* [Caring for Our Earth]. Enslow, 1991.
McHugh, Christopher. *Water* [Discovering Art]. Thomson, 1993.
Peacock, Graham. *Water* [Science Activities]. Thomson, 1994.
Razon, Mark J. and Bix, Cynthia Overbeck. *Water, Water Everywhere*. Little, 1994.
Sanchez, Isidro. *Watercolor* [I Draw, I Paint]. Barron's, 1991.
Schmid, Eleonore. *The Water's Journey*. North-South, 1990.
Simon, Seymour. *Icebergs and Glaciers*. Morrow, 1987.
Swallow, Su. *Water* [Starting Points]. Watts, 1990.
Taylor, Barbara. *Sink or Swim: The Science of Water* [Step into Science]. Random, 1991.
Wheeler, Jill. *Every Drop Counts: A Book About Water* [Target Earth]. Abdo, 1993.
_____. *The Water We Drink* [We Can Save the Earth]. Abdo, 1990.

ADDITIONAL READING – OLDER

Babbitt, Natalie. *The Search for Delicious*. Farrar, 1969.
Barss, Karen J. *Clean Water* [Earth at Risk]. Chelsea, 1992.
Cossi, Olga. *Water Wars: The Fight to Control and Conserve Nature's Most Precious Resource* [Earth Care]. Macmillan, 1993.
Dahlstedt, Marden. *The Terrible Wave*. Houghton, 1989.
Ellis, Chris. *Water*. Parkwest, 1992.
[Exploration Through the Ages] series. Watts.

Gutnik, Martin J. *Experiments That Explore Oil Spills* [Investigate!]. Millbrook, 1991.

Kalman, Bobbie, and Schaub, Janine. *Wonderful Water* [Primary Ecology]. Crabtree, 1992.

Kaufman, Les et al. *Alligators to Zooplankton: A Dictionary of Water Babies* [New England Aquarium Books]. Watts, 1991.

Lambert, Mark. *Ship Technology* [Technology in Action]. Bookwright, 1990.

Leopold, Luna B. and Davis, Kenneth S. *Water* [Life Science Library]. Time, 1966.

Raynor, Ralph. *Undersea Technology* [Technology in Action]. Bookwright, 1990.

Richardson, Wendy, and Richardson, Jack. *Water: Through the Eyes of Artists* [Artists of the World]. Childrens, 1991.

Rybolt, Thomas R., and Mebane, Robert C. *Environmental Experiments About Water* [Science Experiments for Young People]. Enslow, 1993.

Seed, Deborah. *Water Science*. Addison-Wesley, 1992.

Stwertka, Eve. *Drip Drop: Water's Journey*. Simon & Schuster, 1990.

Taylor, Barbara. *Water and Life* [Science Starters]. Watts, 1991.

_____. *Water at Work* [Science Starters]. Watts, 1991.

Twist, Clint. *Rain to Dams: Projects with Water* [Hands On Science]. Gloucester, 1990.

West, Tracey. *Fire in the Valley* [Stories of the States]. Silver Moon, 1993.

See also: books in SEAS AND OCEANS, RIVERS AND LAKES, and PONDS AND WETLANDS units.

FOR MORE INFORMATION ABOUT WATER, WRITE TO:

The Acid Rain Foundation

American Water Resources Association

American Water Works Association

The Freshwater Foundation

Friends of the Earth

International Water Resources Association

The Izaak Walton League of America

Natural Resources Defense Council

The Oceanic Society

Soil and Water Conservation Society

ENERGY

There are many sources of energy. Some are hidden deep inside the Earth, and some are on its surface. Earth's major source of energy, the sun, is millions of miles away. Humans need energy for growth, work, travel, recreation, and comfort. As our energy needs increase, and the supply of finite fuels decrease, we must look to new ways to meet these demands. However, our biggest challenge may be to use Earth's energy resources in a way that will not harm our environment.

LIBRARY SKILLS

a. Your teacher will give you a list of nonfiction books about energy. Put them in order, according to their call numbers.

b. Use *Rocks and Minerals of the World* to do the following: On a map of the United States, mark with a colored dot the areas where oil (red), coal (black), natural gas (blue), and uranium (yellow) are found.

c. In *The New Book of Popular Science,* look up Energy. Answer the following questions: 1) How much has the United States' demand for energy risen since 1960? Why? 2) How has the increased need for energy affected the environment? 3) What are some modern uses for electricity?

d. Use *The Atlas of World Issues* to answer the following: 1) What countries are the biggest exporters of oil? Which are the biggest importers? 2) Which countries are the largest producers of energy? The largest consumers? 3) Make a chart of the number of nuclear reactors in each country.

e. Use *The World Almanac and Book of Facts* to find out: 1) The name of the current United States Secretary of Energy. 2) How many civilians are employed by the Department of Energy in the United States alone. 3) The date on which the cabinet-level Energy Department was created, and who was president at the time.

f. Look up the Industrial Revolution in an encyclopedia. When did it take place? How did it come about? What was it and where did it happen? How did it affect industry? How did it change people's way of life?

g. Refer to *The Information Please Environmental Almanac* to answer the following questions: 1) How has energy conservation benefited the energy industry? The consumer? The environment? 2) What is the IRP approach to utility regulation? How does your state rate on the Energy Report Card? 3) How does recycling save energy? How much energy can be saved by recycling a 12 ounce glass bottle? An aluminum can? A steel can?

ARTS AND CRAFTS

a. Create a collage of things that use electricity. (1, 12, 13, 15, 20)

b. Draw a poster that encourages people to conserve energy. (7, 8, 13, 17, 20)

c. Most cars today run on gasoline. Design a vehicle that runs on an alternative energy source. Your fuel can be realistic or whimsical. Draw a picture of your creation and tell how it would work. (7, 8, 13, 14, 15, 17)

d. Draw a flow chart that illustrates how energy can be converted from one form to another. For example: The sun's energy helps plants grow. Animals eat plants. People eat plants and animals. People use energy to do work. You can illustrate one way electricity is made, how solar energy works, etc. (9, 13, 17, 19, 21, 22, 25)

e. Draw a diagram or make a model of a generator. Show the type of fuel or power source it uses to make electricity. (3, 4, 7, 8, 14, 17, 22, 26, 27, 28, 29)

f. Create a diagram or model of an energy-efficient home. What types of energy does it use? What special energy-saving devices have you included? (8, 9, 14, 16, 17, 20, 24, 26)

g. Build a model of an alternative energy source in use or a power plant. Show how it harnesses and provides energy. (3, 7, 8, 9, 11, 14, 23, 24, 26, 27, 28, 29)

SPELLING/VOCABULARY

a. Match several types of energy to the pictures that illustrate them: wind (windmill), water (wave), magnetic (horseshoe magnet), chemical (battery), electricity (lightning), steam (whistling tea kettle), solar (sun), atomic (electron symbol), biomass (plant), geothermal (geyser), heat (flame), light (light bulb), sound (radio). (4, 5, 18, 22, 29)

b. Complete a crossword puzzle of terms associated with oil: drilling rig, pitch, refinery, gasoline, tanker, heating oil, kerosene, diesel, petroleum, fossil fuel, derrick, pipeline, crude oil, oil well, lubricant. (4, 7, 25, 29)

c. Complete a word search puzzle of terms that relate to electricity: hydroelectricity, cables, magnet, light bulb, ampere, battery, insulator, generator, conductor, turbine, volt, circuit, current, ohm, kilowatt, conduit, dynamo, meter, transformer, static electricity.   (3, 4, 5, 12, 20, 22, 28)

d. Complete a matching puzzle of terms associated with solar energy: absorptive, greenhouse, reflective, solar collector, passive solar, active solar, photovoltaic, array, silicon, heat, light, solar wind, panels, solar furnace, solar chimney, photons, radiation, solar pond, sunlight, solar cells.   (7, 14, 21, 26)

e. What is the difference between nuclear fission and nuclear fusion? Which process does the sun use? Which is used in producing nuclear energy? Complete a fill-in-the-blanks exercise of these related terms: nuclei, hydrogen, helium, atom, fallout, nuclear waste, steam, uranium, chain reaction, neutrons, radiation, meltdown, nuclear reactor, plutonium, fuel rods, boron, coolant, moderator, control rods.   (6, 7, 14, 29)

f. Match each of the following types of fuel to its energy source. Energy sources (may be used more than once): natural gas, coal, atomic, biomass, oil. Types of fuel: diesel, ethane, lignite, uranium, kerosene, dried animal dung, plutonium, coke, ethanol, anthracite, methanol, charcoal, propane, bitumen, wood, butane, gasoline, bituminous _____, methane.   (6, 7, 9, 10, 14, 23, 25, 29)

g. Choose one source of energy. It can be either a fossil fuel or an alternative energy. Create a dictionary of at least fifteen terms that relate to this energy source. Alphabetize your list of words and include definitions.   (3, 7, 8, 9, 10, 11, 14, 23, 24, 25, 26, 27, 28, 29)

GEOGRAPHY

a. On a map of the world, mark the countries that produce most of the world's petroleum (oil). On another map, mark the countries that use the most oil. How do the two maps compare?   (4, 7, 13, 25, 29)

b. What types of energy are available in your community? Where does your home's electricity come from? Are there any nuclear power plants, coal mines, oil wells, waste-to-energy plants, wind farms, etc. located in your state? Locate any energy-producing facilities on a map of your state.

c. Divide a sheet of paper into four columns and label them: coal, petroleum, natural gas, and uranium. List the countries that are the main producers of each type of fuel. Locate these countries on a map of the world. (4, 7, 8, 10, 14, 25, 29)

d. Some countries rely heavily on alternative/renewable sources of energy. On a map of the world, mark with colored dots the countries that widely use energy from the sun (red), wind (blue), water (green), biomass (yellow). Place a (purple) dot in countries that use geothermal energy.   (3, 7, 9, 11, 14, 24, 26, 27, 28)

e. On a map of the world, mark with a black dot some areas where major oil spills have occurred. About how much oil was spilled in each area?   (2, 14)

f. What is OPEC? Name the countries that belong to OPEC and locate them on a map of the world.   (7, 8, 14, 17)

g. The use of fossil fuels and atomic power have affected climate and atmospheric conditions in parts of the world. Make a list of some areas that have been affected by acid rain, ozone depletion, nuclear radiation, air pollution, and other energy-related climate or atmospheric problems.   (7, 8, 14, 17, 18, 22)

MATH

a. Take a poll in your class to find out what type of energy is used to heat your homes (oil, gas, electric). How many homes have solar panels? What type of energy is used in your school? Draw a chart to display the results of your poll.

b. In your home, you may find a watt-hour meter. It is used to find out how much electric power you have used every month. Look at a picture of some round dials such as those found on a watt-hour meter. Read the dials, from left to right, by noting which number the hand points to. If the hand is between two numbers, choose the lower number (but if the hand is between 0 and 9, choose the 9). Then answer the following questions: What is a watt? How many watts does it take to light a 40 watt bulb? A 75 watt bulb? A 100 watt bulb?

c. Find out the average prices for a gallon of regular and super gasolines in your area. If a car has an 18 gallon tank, how much would it cost for a fill-up of each type of gasoline? On a full tank, how many miles would that car go if it got 13 miles per gallon? 20 miles? 27 miles? 44 miles?

d. Power stations that convert fossil fuels into electricity waste about two-thirds of the energy they produce in the form of unused heat. And fossil fuels are rapidly being used up. Experts estimate there may be enough oil to last about another 33 years, gas for 60 years, and coal for perhaps 200 years. If scientists could find a way to utilize all (instead of one-third) of the energy from fossil-fueled power plants, how long will the Earth's supplies of oil, coal, and gas last?

e. Many engines are rated by their horsepower. Horsepower is the power needed to lift 550 pounds one foot in one second. At that rate, how many pounds can be lifted one foot in one second by a 2 horsepower engine?

5 HP? 12 HP? 27 HP? 40 HP? If an engine can lift 3,850 pounds one foot in one second, what is its horsepower? 11,550 pounds? 18,700 pounds? 24,750 pounds?

f. Nuclear fuels are very powerful. One pound of nuclear fuel will boil 120 million gallons of water, while one pound of coal will boil only 9.6 gallons of water. Make a chart to show how much water can be boiled by using 2, 3, 4, 5, 6, 7, 8, 9, and 10 pounds of each type of fuel. A second way to compare these two fuels is that one pound of uranium equals 1,500 tons of coal. Make another chart to show how much coal is needed to match the energy of 2, 3, 4, 5, 6, 7, 8, 9, and 10 pounds of uranium.

g. In the United States, we pay for electricity based on a unit called the kilowatt-hour. Home appliances vary in the amount of electricity they use. For example, a dishwasher uses one kilowatt (kw) of energy in 20 minutes, while a color television uses one kw of energy in 9 hours. Look at the following examples of the period of time that various devices can be used for in one kilowatt-hour. Dishwasher = 20 minutes, clothes dryer = 30 minutes, iron = 50 minutes, slow cooker = 8 hours, color TV = 9 hours, 100-watt bulb = 10 hours, refrigerator = 24 hours, freezer = 12. Answer the following questions. How many kilowatt-hours are used by: 1) A refrigerator in one week? 2) A dryer running for 6 hours plus an iron used for 100 minutes? 3) A 100-watt bulb on for 4 hours, plus 10 60-watt bulbs on for 1 hour? 4) A color TV on for 3 hours a day for 9 days? 5) A refrigerator and a slow cooker both in use for 192 hours?

MUSIC AND THEATER ARTS

a. What is potential energy? What is kinetic energy? Act out some examples of potential and kinetic energy. (5, 13, 19)

b. *Group project:* Pretend the students in the class are molecules. Act out these examples of heat energy: 1) Students walk slowly, in random directions, around half of the room. This is an example of cool temperature. Then, have students move quickly around the room, taking up a larger amount of space. This shows how molecules vibrate more rapidly and take up more space (expand) as heat rises, a property called convection. 2) Have children stand in a line. The person at one end takes one end of a rope. The rope is passed on to the students down the line, until the entire rope is stretched out from end to end. This is an example of conduction, the process of transferring heat from molecule to molecule. 3) Heat transmitted by radiation does not pass through molecules. Show this by having one student stand at one side of the room. A second student should stand at the opposite side, holding a bell. The first child can pretend to "zap" the other child with an infrared ray.

After a few seconds, the second child rings the bell to show the radiation has traveled across the room.   (13, 19)

   c. Pretend you are living in a time before homes had electricity. Act out how you would have prepared food, using an early energy source. Then pretend you are living in the future and show how you might prepare food.

   d. *Group project:* There are two types of nuclear reactions that produce energy: fission and fusion. Have half of the students act as protons, and half as neutrons. 1) To act out how nuclear fission works, all students except one acting as a neutron should stand together in a bunch (representing an atom of uranium). The lone neutron then runs into the atom, causing it to split into two equal groups (with a loud bang!). One neutron from each new atom comes loose during the split. Next, each new neutron runs into an atom, causing another split. This chain reaction continues until all atoms are split. 2) To show fusion, two students should form a group of one neutron and one proton. This is an atom of hydrogen. Three students should form an atom of helium, one neutron and two protons. The hydrogen atom runs into the helium atom. Both atoms become one group (with a loud bang!), and one proton separates.   (5, 6, 8, 13, 29)

   e. *Group project:* Energy conservation and recycling are two ways to save energy and help the environment. Act out a short play on one or both of these themes.   (7, 8, 14, 17).

   f. Sound is a form of energy that travels in waves. As the energy that flows through sound waves increases, the intensity of the sound increases. Intensity is measured in decibels. Look at an instrument that shows the decibel level of a stereo or other electronic musical device. Play different types of music and note the decibel levels for each one. Do some types of music generate a higher decibel level than others? What happens when you alter the volume, bass, treble, or other controls?

   g. *Group project:* Act out a short play about how people performed agricultural, construction, and manufacturing jobs before and after the invention of the steam engine. How did the Industrial Revolution affect people's lives? (7, 14, 15, 29)

ENGLISH COMPOSITION

   a. Write a true story telling how you use different types of energy in an average day. (1, 4, 13)

   b. Make believe you are water, wind, or the sun. Write a story about how you provide energy for people to use. (7, 21, 22, 26, 27, 28)

   c. Industrialized countries, such as the United States, use up more energy resources than countries that have little or no industry, such as India. Is this fair? Write an essay giving your opinion on this issue.   (7, 8, 17, 29)

d. Pretend you are a public relations representative for either the natural gas or petroleum industry. Design a catalog that shows all the wonderful products that can be made from gas or oil. Use drawings or pictures cut from advertisements in your catalog. Label each product.   (4, 8, 10, 25, 29)

e. Keep a journal for one week, noting each time you use electricity. Then tell what you might have done in each case if electricity had not been available. For example, if you used an electric stove to cook food, you might have cooked over a wood fire. Or, instead of watching television, you might have read a book.   (14)

f. Pretend you work for the United States Department of Energy. Draft a resolution for our government to become more energy-efficient. What energy conservation matters would be your top five priorities? State your recommendations for improving the country's energy production or utilization in these five areas.   (7, 8, 14, 17, 18)

g. Write a science fiction story about life in the year 2020. Tell what energy sources will be used to run machines and heat homes. Will there be more or fewer energy sources available than there are now? Will some present-day energy sources no longer exist? What new types of energy will be used? What will be some modes of transportation, and what will they use for fuel?   (7, 8, 14, 15, 16)

SCIENCE

Note: There are many books of science experiments that have to do with energy. The class can do some of these in conjunction with this unit.

a. What is the difference between energy and fuel? Name several types of energy and types of fuel. How can these fuels be converted into energy? (4, 10, 22, 25, 29)

b. What are some types of solar energy? Name some ways to collect and use solar energy.   (21, 26)

c. What are some sources of heat energy? How can heat energy be converted to other types of energy? Give some more examples of how one form of energy can be converted to another form.   (7, 9, 13, 19, 21, 22, 24, 29)

d. What is meant by the terms "non-renewable energy source" and "renewable energy source"? Divide a sheet of paper into two columns. List as many power sources or types of fuel as you can in each column.   (3, 7, 8, 9, 10, 11, 17, 24, 25, 26, 27, 28, 29)

e. Many types of energy can harm the environment in some way. Explain the types of environmental damage that can be caused by obtaining coal, wood, oil, gas, and steam from hot springs, and by building hydroelectric dams, wind farms, nuclear power plants, solar power stations, and garbage-fueled power plants. What damage can be done by utilizing these energy sources? (7, 9, 10, 14, 17, 18, 23, 24, 25, 26, 27, 28, 29)

f. There are many ways to obtain energy from water. Define and explain how the following water sources can provide energy: tidal power, hydroelectric power, power from waves. How can heat be obtained from the sea? (3, 8, 14, 17, 27, 29)

g. Refer to the source of energy you researched for the Spelling/Vocabulary exercise. Choose a specific form of that energy. For example, if your dictionary is about coal, you might choose coke. Explain, in scientific terms, one example of how that source generates electricity or heat, or powers a machine. You may use pictures to illustrate your explanation. (3, 7, 8, 9, 11, 14, 23, 24, 26, 27, 28, 29)

HISTORY/SOCIOLOGY

a. Before gas, oil, coal, and electricity were made available, people used other energy sources. Name some of them. For example, what type of energy was used to move a ship? A train? A mill that ground flour? How did people heat their homes before the use of gas, oil, coal, and electricity? (4, 5, 9, 21, 26, 27, 28, 29)

b. Give a brief history of the formation of Earth's fossil fuels. (4, 5, 10, 17, 25, 29)

c. Draw a timeline or make a chronological list of energy sources. What was the first form of energy used by humans? Include various types of fuel, from the past to the present. Note when they were first used. (2, 6, 7, 8, 11, 12, 14, 24, 26, 27, 28, 29)

d. Many scientists made discoveries and inventions that have led to our current widespread use of electricity. Write a report about one of these scientists. When and what was his/her great contribution in the field of electricity? What is the source of the word "electricity"? (2, 12, 15, 20)

e. Choose one type of alternative or renewable energy source. Trace its history. When and how was it first used? Which countries now use it as a major source of energy? What are the possibilities for its use as a major energy source in other parts of the world? (6, 8, 9, 11, 14, 23, 24, 26, 27, 28, 29)

f. Why did the United States suffer a shortage of oil in the 1970s? How did this energy crisis affect the country? What have Americans learned from this experience? (8, 14)

g. Several environmental disasters involving various sources of energy have occurred. Write a report on one incident, such as the *Exxon Valdez* oil spill. Tell when, where, and how it happened. What was the aftermath of this disaster? (2, 8, 14, 18, 23)

TOPICS FOR DISCUSSION

a. Discuss some safety precautions to take when using electricity, gas, and other types of energy or fuel at home and away from home. (12)

b. Do you think there will be more or less energy available in the future than there is now? Why? How will the availability of energy affect the way we live? Will people try to use more or less energy in the future? (5, 7, 8, 13, 14, 16, 29)

c. List some advantages and disadvantages of nuclear energy. Take a poll in your class to see how many students think the United States should continue to build and operate nuclear power plants and how many think we should stop using nuclear energy. (5, 6, 7, 8, 14, 17, 29)

d. Discuss the advantages and disadvantages of using coal, oil, and gas as energy sources. What effect does each one have on the environment? How versatile and efficient are these fossil fuels? (5, 7, 8, 10, 14, 17, 25)

e. There are several ways to generate electricity. Name some of them. Is electricity an efficient power source, or is it wasteful? Is it safe, reliable, and inexpensive? How do we rely on electricity? (3, 5, 7, 8, 11, 14, 17, 20, 26, 29)

f. Name some alternative and renewable sources of energy. Discuss the advantages and disadvantages of using each type. Consider their reliability, effects on the environment, availability, and efficiency. Why are some forms of energy better suited for use in certain parts of the world than in others? Which of these energy sources may be an option where you live? (3, 7, 8, 9, 11, 14, 17, 24, 26, 27, 28, 29)

g. Why do we need to use a variety of energy sources? How do cost and convenience affect the types of fuel used in a particular area? How do world politics affect our energy choices? (7, 8, 14, 17)

SUGGESTED RESOURCES

(1) Baker, Susan. *First Look at Using Energy* [First Look]. Stevens, 1991.
(2) Blashfield, Jean F., and Black, Wallace B. *Oil Spills* [Saving Planet Earth]. Childrens, 1991.
(3) Boltz, C. L. *How Energy Is Made*. Facts on File, 1985.
(4) Breiter, Herta. *Fuel and Energy* [Read About Science]. Raintree, 1988.

(5) Cobb, Vicki. *More Power to You!* [How the World Works]. Little, 1986.

(6) Fradin, Dennis. *Nuclear Energy* [New True Books]. Childrens, 1987.

(7) Gardiner, Brian. *Energy Demands* [Green Issues]. Gloucester, 1990.

(8) Gibson, Michael. *The Energy Crisis* [World Issues]. Rourke, 1987.

(9) Houghton, Graham. *Bioenergy* [Alternative Energy]. Stevens, 1991.

(10) Jackman, Wayne. *Gas* [Resources]. Thomson, 1993.

(11) Jacobs, Linda. *Letting Off Steam: The Story of Geothermal Energy* [Earth Watch]. Carolrhoda, 1989.

(12) Johnston, Tom. *Electricity Turns the World On!* [Science in Action]. Stevens, 1988.

(13) _____. *Energy: Making It Work* [Science in Action]. Stevens, 1988.

(14) Keeler, Barbara. *Energy Alternatives* [Overview Series: Our Endangered Planet]. Lucent, 1990.

(15) Lafferty, Peter, and Rowe, Julian. *The Inventor Through History* [Journey Through History]. Thomson, 1993.

(16) Lambert, Mark. *Homes in the Future* [Houses and Homes]. Lerner, 1989.

(17) Leggett, Jeremy. *Energy Gap* [Operation Earth]. Cavendish, 1991.

(18) Lucas, Eileen. *Acid Rain* [Saving Planet Earth]. Childrens, 1991.

(19) Olesky, Walter. *Experiments with Heat* [New True Books]. Childrens, 1986.

(20) Parker, Steve. *Eyewitness Science: Electricity*. Kindersley, 1992.

(21) Petersen, David. *Solar Energy at Work* [New True Books]. Childrens, 1985.

(22) Podendorf, Illa. *Energy* [New True Books]. Childrens, 1982.

(23) Pringle, Laurence. *Nuclear Energy: Troubled Past, Uncertain Future* [Science for Survival]. Macmillan, 1989.

(24) Rickard, Graham. *Geothermal Energy* [Alternative Energy]. Stevens, 1991.

(25) _____. *Oil* [Resources]. Thomson, 1993.

(26) _____. *Solar Energy* [Alternative Energy]. Stevens, 1991.

(27) _____. *Water Energy* [Alternative Energy]. Stevens, 1991.

(28) _____. *Wind Energy* [Alternative Energy]. Stevens, 1991.

(29) Seidenberg, Steven. *Fuel and Energy* [Information Library]. Stevens, 1992.

LIBRARY SKILLS RESOURCES

Middleton, Nick. *Atlas of World Issues* [World Contemporary Issues]. Facts on File, 1989.

The New Book of Popular Science. Grolier, 1994.

Rocks and Minerals of the World [Using and Understanding Maps]. Chelsea, 1993.

The World Almanac and Book of Facts. World Almanac, 1994.

World Resources Institute. *The Information Please Environmental Almanac*. Houghton, 1993.

ADDITIONAL READING – YOUNGER

Ardley, Neil. *Science Book of Energy*. Harcourt, 1992.

Bailey, Donna. *Energy from Oil and Gas* [Facts About]. Steck-Vaughn, 1990.

_____. *Energy from Wind and Water* [Facts About]. Steck-Vaughn, 1990.

_____. *What We Can Do About Conserving Energy* [What We Can Do About]. Watts, 1992.

Berger, Melvin. *Switch On, Switch Off.* Crowell, 1989.
Charman, Andrew. *Energy* [Science Through Art]. Watts, 1993.
Cobb, Vicki. *Why Doesn't the Sun Burn Out?* Dutton, 1990.
Harlow, Rose, and Morgan, Gareth. *Energy and Growth* [Fun with Science]. Warwick, 1991.
Hoban, Russell. *Arthur's New Power.* Crowell, 1978.
McKie, Robin. *Energy* [Science Frontiers]. Hampstead, 1989.
Mellett, Peter, and Rossiter, Jane. *Food Energy* [Science Through Cookery]. Watts, 1993.
Mitgutsch, Ali. *From Oil to Gasoline* [Start to Finish]. Carolrhoda, 1981.
Rickard, Graham. *The Chernobyl Catastrophe* [Great Disasters]. Bookwright, 1989.
Spence, Margaret. *Fossil Fuels* [World About Us]. Watts, 1993.
_____. *Solar Power* [World About Us]. Watts, 1993.
Twist, Clint. *Future Sources* [World About Us]. Watts, 1993.
_____. *Wind and Water Power* [World About Us]. Watts, 1993.
Ward, Alan. *Forces and Energy* [Project Science]. Watts, 1992.
Wheeler, Jill. *Earth Moves: Get There with Energy to Spare* [We Can Save the Earth]. Abdo, 1991.

ADDITIONAL READING – OLDER

Arnold, Guy. *Facts on Nuclear Energy* [Facts on]. Watts, 1990.
Asimov, Isaac. [How Did We Find Out About...] series. Walker.
Catherall, Ed. *Exploring Energy Sources* [Exploring Science]. Steck-Vaughn, 1991.
_____. *Exploring Uses of Energy* [Exploring Science]. Steck-Vaughn, 1990.
Godman, Arthur. *Energy Supply A–Z* [Environment Reference]. Enslow, 1991.
Gutnik, Martin J. *Electricity from Faraday to Solar Generators.* Watts, 1986.
_____. *Projects That Explore Energy* [Investigate!]. Millbrook, 1994.
Haines, Gail B. *The Challenge of Supplying Energy* [Environmental Issues]. Enslow, 1991.
Johnstone, Hugh. *Facts on Future Energy Possibilities* [Facts on]. Watts, 1990.
Kerrod, Robin. *Energy Resources* [World's Resources]. Thomson, 1994.
_____. *Future Energy and Resources* [Today's World]. Watts, 1990.
Lambert, Mark. *Energy Technology* [Technology in Action]. Bookwright, 1991.
Leone, Bruna, and Smith, Judy. *The Energy Crisis* [Opposing Viewpoints]. Greenhaven 1981.
Markle, Sandra. *Power Up: Experiments, Puzzles, and Games Exploring Electricity.* Atheneum, 1989.
Mason, John. *Power Station Sun: The Story of Energy* [Discovering Science]. Facts on File, 1987.
Moeri, Louise. *Downwind.* Dutton, 1984.
New Mexico People and Energy Collective. *Red Ribbons for Emma.* New Seed, 1981.
Pack, Janet. *Fueling the Future* [Saving Planet Earth]. Childrens, 1992.
Pifer, Joan. *Earthwise: Earth's Energy* [Earthwise]. W.P. Press, 1993.
Randle, Damian. *Natural Resources* [Young Geographer]. Thomson, 1993.
Twist, Clint. *Facts on Fossil Fuels* [Facts on]. Watts, 1990.

See also: books in WASTE AND RECYCLING and ENVIRONMENTAL AWARENESS units.

FOR MORE INFORMATION ABOUT ENERGY, WRITE TO:

Alliance to Save Energy
Alternative Energy Sources Organization
American Council for an Energy-Efficient Economy
American Petroleum Institute
American Solar Energy Society
American Wind Energy Association
Biomass Energy Research Association
Electric Power Research Institute
Gas Research Institute
Geothermal Education Office
Natural Resources Defense Council
Nuclear Energy Information Service
Renew America

II

Our Planet's Natural Habitats

SEAS AND OCEANS

Scientists believe that life on Earth began in the sea. From the early days of our planet's formation, a vast array of plant and animal life has thrived in these waters. But humans have polluted and abused the oceans. These actions threaten marine life and can alter Earth's atmosphere and weather. Protecting our oceans is important, not only to the creatures that dwell in the sea, but to all life on Earth.

LIBRARY SKILLS

a. Here is a list of ten things that are found in the sea. Put them in alphabetical order: fish, boats, tides, plants, coral, water, rocks, octopus, seaweed, dolphins.

b. Use the subject section of the card catalog or an online catalog to look up books about sea pollution. Note their Dewey decimal numbers and locate them on the shelves. What types of books are they near?

c. Find five books on whales in your library and compare them. Which books are the most recent? Which have the best pictures? Which have the most information? Which books are easy to read? Which books have information on the size and weight of various whales, migration patterns, how whales eat, how they breathe, whale hunting, saving the whales, whales and dolphins, whales and sharks, whales and humans? Which book do you like best? Why?

d. Look in an encyclopedia to compile a list of minerals and other resources that can be found in the sea. What resources are mined? What is the most plentiful resource?

e. Use *Reader's Guide to Periodical Literature* or an online data base to find magazine articles about sea pollution and endangered marine life. What subject headings did you use? List titles, magazine names and issues of two articles for each topic.

f. In *The New State of the World Atlas*, look in the Environment section to find a map of land and sea pollution. On a map of the world, color in areas of sea pollution (brown) and oil tanker spills (red).

g. Mount Everest is the tallest peak on Earth at 29,028 feet. Use *The*

World Almanac and Book of Facts to look up Principal Ocean Depths. List the names, locations, and depths in feet of all ocean trenches that are deeper than Mount Everest is tall.

ARTS AND CRAFTS

a. *Group project:* Make a bulletin board or mural of an ocean scene. Draw or cut out pictures of all types of sea plants and animals. Paste them onto a background of blue construction paper. You could include an island, a coral reef, a lighthouse, or other details in your picture.   (1, 17, 18, 21, 26, 27)

b. Look at some pictures of corals. Use colored modeling clay to make your own models of coral.   (1, 18, 21, 24, 26, 27)

c. Many forms of sea life are in danger of becoming extinct. Draw a poster to alert people to the problems facing dolphins, manatees, whales, coral reefs, or another sea species.   (2, 10, 11, 22, 26)

d. Draw a picture or make a collage that illustrates the food chain in the sea. Include different types of plants and animals.   (2, 3, 7, 10, 11, 12, 14, 21, 25)

e. *Group project:* Use clay or papier-mâché to make a relief model that illustrates continental drift. Show what happens on the ocean floor when geological plates drift apart or collide.   (13, 14, 18, 23, 25)

f. Make a model or diagram of a seagoing vessel from the past or present. Label its features.   (6, 8, 12, 25)

g. *Group project:* In the future, people may build homes or cities under the sea. Design an undersea city of the future. Use milk cartons, plastic bottles, and other materials to build a model of your creation. Label each feature to tell what it is. Consider: How will your city be powered? Where will the energy come from? Where will breathing air come from? What will be the food supply?   (12, 18, 25)

SPELLING/VOCABULARY

a. Complete a matching picture puzzle of sea mammals and birds: dugong, orca, seal, pelican, manatee, blue whale, dolphin, otter, sea gull, beluga, polar bear, narwhal, walrus, penguin, sea lion, puffin.   (2, 3, 5, 12, 17, 18, 21, 23, 24, 27)

b. On a picture of some waves, label the following parts: crest, trough, fetch, white cap, foam, swell, breaker, wavelength, ocean floor. On a picture of a coastline, label these features: beach, dunes, spit, sandflat, marsh.   (7, 19, 20, 25)

c. Complete a fill-in-the-blanks exercise of ocean motion: wave, current, wind, high tide, low tide, whirlpool, deep sea vent, water cycle, breaker, gyre, tsunami, Coriolis effect, El Niño, seiche, bore, upwelling, longshore drift.   (3, 7, 10, 14, 15, 18, 19, 23, 24, 25)

d. Complete a word search puzzle of fish and other cold-blooded creatures that are found in the deep sea: clam, starfish, manta ray, coral, mackerel, shrimp, mussel, shark, eel, octopus, lobster, squid, jellyfish, crab, krill, turtle, cod, herring, sardine, tuna. (2, 5, 7, 12, 14, 17, 18, 21, 24, 27)

e. On a picture of a fish, label these body parts: scales, gills, pectoral fin, air bladder, spine, dorsal fin, ventral fin, caudal fin, transverse line, lateral line. Name some types of: jawless fish, cartilaginous fish, bony fish, demersal fish. (7, 12, 17, 18, 21)

f. Complete a crossword puzzle of terms that relate to the ocean environment: photoplankton, zooplankton, seaweed, algae, salinity, nektonic, benthic, pelagic, hydrothermal vent, red tide, aquaculture, estuary, deep ocean, polar ocean, tropical ocean, intertidal zone, subtidal zone, eutrophic area, aerobic, anaerobic. (12, 15, 18, 23, 27)

g. Define these classes of sea animals and give three or more examples of each: zooplankton, worms, coelenterates, mollusks, crustaceans, echinoderms, jawless fish, cartilaginous fish, bony fish, reptiles, mammals, birds. (2, 12, 17, 18, 21)

GEOGRAPHY

Note: Some books divide Earth's global ocean into four parts: the Pacific, Atlantic, Indian, and Arctic oceans. Other books include a fifth division, the Antarctic or Southern Ocean. The Pacific and Atlantic Oceans may be further divided into North and South regions, for a total of seven seas. Teachers may adapt this information as they see fit.

a. Match the names of the continents and oceans to their correct places on a map of the world. (2, 5, 13, 14, 18)

b. On a map of the world, label the Earth's oceans. Also label some important seas, gulfs, and bays. (2, 3, 9, 10, 14, 25)

c. On a map of the world, draw the major surface currents of the oceans. Draw warm currents in red and cold currents in blue. How do ocean currents compare to wind currents? (2, 7, 12, 14, 18, 19, 23, 25)

d. On a map of the world, color in areas of the ocean that contain a lot of pollution. What are some of the pollutants? (4, 9, 11, 23)

e. On a map of the world, mark areas that have been hit hard by tsunamis, hurricanes, or cyclones. Where do many hurricanes and cyclones form? (20)

f. Draw a cross-sectional map of a view beneath the ocean surface. Include the continental shelf, continental slope, continental rise, abyssal zone, and the ocean floor. Add some of these other features: plain, atoll, plateau, island, volcano, trench, ridge, mountain, seamount, coral reef. Label each feature of your drawing.   (7, 12, 13, 14, 15, 18, 23, 24, 25)

g. What was Pangaea? What is continental drift? How does continental drift change the shape of the ocean floor and the surface lands? How are islands and mountains formed? What is the Ring of Fire? On a map of the world, label the geological plates and the Ring of Fire.   (13, 14, 23, 25)

MATH

a. Earth is commonly divided into seven continents and four oceans. List the continents in order of size, from the largest to the smallest. Make another list of the oceans. Does Earth contain more water or land? Make a chart to compare the amounts of land and water on Earth.   (3, 14, 19)

b. *Group project:* Make a chart of 30 marine animals, their sizes and weights. Arrange them from smallest to largest. What is the smallest animal you can find? What is the largest?   (10, 17, 18, 21, 23, 24, 27)

c. Answer these "fishy" math problems: 1) Add the number of arms of a sea star to the number of wings of a penguin. Multiply by the number of claws on a crab. 2) Multiply the number of legs on 2 lobsters by the number of arms on a squid. Divide by the number of arms on an octopus. 3) Add the number of gills on 6 fish to the number of tusks on 7 walruses. Multiply by the number of arms on an eel. Add the number of tails on 8 whales. Divide by the number of legs on an iguana.

d. The approximate surface areas of the ocean (in square miles) are as follows: Pacific, 64,186,300; Atlantic, 33,420,000; Indian, 28,350,500; Arctic, 5,105,700. The average depths of the oceans (in feet) are: Pacific, 12,900; Atlantic, 11,700; Indian, 12,600; Arctic, 3,400. Draw two bar graphs to illustrate these facts.   (*The World Almanac and Book of Facts*)

e. Look up these number facts about oceans: 1) The percent of Earth's surface that is covered by water. 2) The average salinity (saltiness) of sea water. 3) The depth of the deepest trench in the oceans. 4) The average depth of all the oceans. 5) The highest sea wave recorded. 6) The percent of Earth's water that is seawater. Write down six more interesting math facts about oceans.   (2, 10, 14, 18, 19, 23)

f. In the sea, water pressure increases about 14.7 pounds per square inch for every 30 feet of depth. How much would the water pressure be at a depth of 60 feet below the surface? At each of the following: 210; 870; 1,410; 2,280; 5,280; 13,500; 17,370; 19,530; 29,610?   (20)

g.   Scientists use echo sounding to measure the depths of the sea. Sound in the sea travels at about 4,800 feet per second. An echo sounder sends an ultrasonic signal to the ocean floor. When the signal echoes off the floor, the depth at that point can be measured according to the time required for the echo to bounce back, using the following formula:

$$\frac{\text{Time (in seconds)} \times 4800}{2} = \text{depth (in feet)}$$

(For example, at 3.2 seconds, the depth would be 7,680 feet.) Use this formula to figure out what the depth of the ocean floor would be given the following time amounts: 1.5, 2.2, 3.8, 4.9, 5.3, 6.0, 7.8, 8.1, 9.3, 10.5.

MUSIC AND THEATER ARTS

a.   Present a puppet show to act out the songs "Octopus's Garden" (by the Beatles) and "Under the Sea" (from Disney's *The Little Mermaid*).

b.   Pretend to be different sea animals. Act out how they move through the sea and how they catch their food.   (Nature Recordings)

c.   Listen to *The Sea, Ocean Moods* (Nature Recordings), *Ocean Dreams* (Soundings of the Planet), *Songs of the Humpback Whale* (Living Music Records), or another recording of ocean sounds. Discuss what you hear.

d.   *Group project:* Act out a famous sea battle, such as England's battle against the Spanish Armada, or a pirate adventure.   (6)

e.   *Small group project:* Act out an underwater diving expedition or a sea exploration from history. What are you exploring? How do you get there? What equipment do you need? What do you find?   (6, 10, 12, 18, 26, 27)

f.   Sing some old sea shanties such as "My Bonnie Lies Over the Ocean," "Sailing, Sailing," and "Blow the Man Down."

g.   *Group project:* Write and act out a skit about the legend of Atlantis, a story about the Greek sea god Poseidon, or another sea myth.

ENGLISH COMPOSITION

a.   Pretend you are a sea bird or a sea mammal. Write a story about your day.   (5, 12, 18, 21, 22)

b.   There are many legends about sea creatures, such as mermaids or sea monsters. Write a story or poem about one of them.   (3)

　　c. Make up a story to explain why sea water is salty.　(23)

　　d.　Choose one of these creative writing activities: 1) Pretend you are a diver exploring a coral reef. Describe what you see. 2) Pretend you are an archaeologist exploring the wreck of a ship under the sea. Describe your search methods and what you find. 3) Write a story about the mythical lost continent of Atlantis. Tell what you think life was like there and how it fell into the sea.　(10, 12, 17, 18, 25, 26, 27)

　　e. Write an essay about one way humans pollute the oceans. Describe the type of pollution and its effects. Tell what you think should be done about it.　(2, 7, 10, 11, 15, 23, 25)

　　f. Storms and other acts of nature at sea can be devastating. Pretend you are at sea and you observe a hurricane or an undersea volcano. Describe the effects of one of these events. What happens at sea? How does it affect a nearby island?　(19, 20, 23, 24, 25)

　　g. Overfishing, mining the sea's resources, pollution, and hunting are major problems threatening Earth's oceans. Pretend you are a delegate to a world summit concerned with one of these issues. Write a law that would try to improve conditions for the seas and their creatures.　(2, 10, 11, 12, 15, 18, 23, 24, 25)

SCIENCE

　　a. What are waves? How do they move? What is a tsunami? How powerful are waves? Make some waves at a water table. Locate a crest, trough, and breaker.　(2, 5, 7, 14, 18, 19, 20, 24, 25)

　　b. What causes tides? What is high tide and low tide? How are they different from spring and neap tides?　(2, 5, 14, 18, 19, 24, 25)

　　c. How do oceans affect the weather? How do they affect temperatures around the globe? Explain the water cycle as part of your answer.　(7, 9, 10, 14, 19, 23, 25)

　　d. What are ocean currents? Why are they important? How do they travel? What is the difference between warm and cold currents? Surface and deep sea currents?　(2, 7, 14, 18, 19, 23, 25)

　　e. Where and how are coral reefs formed? What are some types of coral? What animals live along a coral reef? What are the three types of coral reefs? How do they differ?　(1, 10, 15, 18, 21, 23, 24, 26, 27)

　　f. How do sea pollutants spread through the food chain? How else is sea pollution spread around the globe?　(2, 7, 9, 23, 25)

　　g. What happens to crude oil after it spills into the sea? Where does the oil go? How does the temperature of the water affect it? How does the oil affect plant and animal life? How can it be cleaned up?   (2, 4, 7, 9, 10, 23)

HISTORY/SOCIOLOGY

a. Look up pictures of boats from ancient times to the present. What materials were boats made of in the past? How were they powered? Compare them to modern boats.   (6, 8, 25)

b. Certain sea mammals have been hunted for many years. Now they are in danger of becoming extinct. Make a list of these endangered animals. Why have they been hunted? What is being done to solve this problem?   (2, 3, 9, 10, 21, 22)

c. Write a short biography of a famous sea explorer or group of explorers. Where and when did the person or group sail? Include a map of the journey. What was discovered?   (6)

d. Compare modern fishing methods to the ways people fished the oceans in the past. Also compare whaling in past and present times. How do modern techniques affect marine life and the environment?   (2, 7, 10, 11, 12, 18, 23, 24, 25)

e. Write a paper on one invention that helps sailors or oceanographers to explore the sea. This can be a navigational tool (such as sonar), a vessel (such as a submersible), or another device (such as the diving suit).   (6, 8, 12, 15, 18, 23, 24)

f. Write a report on a sea disaster of historical importance. It can be environmental (such as Iraq's release of oil into the Persian Gulf), a shipwreck (such as the sinking of the *Titanic*), or an act of nature (such as a tsunami). When, how, and why did it happen? What was the aftermath of the incident? (2, 4, 6, 10, 11, 16, 23, 24)

g. For centuries, people have made a living from the sea. Name some occupations that depend on oceans or ocean resources in some way.   (2, 6, 12, 15, 18, 23, 24, 25)

TOPICS FOR DISCUSSION

a. How do people use the oceans? Which of these are good uses? What are some bad uses?   (2, 3, 5, 7, 9, 10, 12, 14, 18, 25)

b. What minerals and other resources (excluding food) can be found in the sea?   (2, 7, 10, 12, 14, 18, 23, 24, 25)

c. What are some ways that humans pollute the sea? What are the effects of each type of pollution?   (2, 4, 7, 9, 10, 11, 14, 18, 22, 23, 25, 27)

d. What is the greenhouse effect? What causes it? What effect might this have on the world's oceans?   (10, 23, 24, 25)

e. How have human greed and modern technology endangered marine life?   (2, 7, 9, 10, 11, 14, 23, 25, 27)

f. Why are coral reefs in danger? How do people who enjoy coral reefs actually harm them?   (1, 4, 10, 11, 21, 23, 26, 27)

g. Name some ways, other than pollution, that people harm Earth's oceans. Which do you think does more damage—pollution or these other practices?   (2, 4, 9, 10, 21, 23, 25, 26, 27)

SUGGESTED RESOURCES

(1) Arnold, Caroline. *A Walk on the Great Barrier Reef* [Nature Watch]. Carolrhoda, 1988.
(2) Baines, John. *Protecting the Oceans* [Conserving Our World]. Steck-Vaughn, 1991.
(3) Baker, Lucy. *Life in the Oceans* [Life in]. Watts, 1990.
(4) Blashfield, Jean F., and Black, Wallace B. *Oil Spills* [Saving Planet Earth]. Childrens, 1991.
(5) Carter, Katherine Jones. *Oceans* [New True Books]. Childrens, 1982.
(6) Coote, Roger. *The Sailor Through History* [Journey Through History]. Thomson, 1993.
(7) Costa-Pau, Rosa. *Conservation of the Sea* [Junior Library of Ecology]. Chelsea, 1994.
(8) Davies, Eryl. *Water Travel* [The World on the Move]. Thomson, 1993.
(9) Hare, Tony. *Polluting the Sea* [Save Our Earth]. Gloucester, 1990.
(10) Hoff, Mary, and Rodgers, Mary M. *Oceans* [Our Endangered Planet]. Lerner, 1991.
(11) Leggett, Dennis, and Leggett, Jeremy. *Troubled Waters* [Operation Earth]. Cavendish, 1991.
(12) Mackie, Dan. *Undersea* [CHP Technology Series]. Penworthy, 1987.
(13) Mariner, Tom. *Continents* [Earth in Action]. Cavendish, 1990.
(14) _____. *Oceans* [Earth in Action]. Cavendish, 1990.
(15) Mattson, Robert A. *The Living Ocean* [The Living World]. Enslow, 1991.
(16) Nottridge, Rhoda. *Sea Disasters* [The World's Disasters]. Thomson, 1993.
(17) Parker, Steve. *Fish* [Eyewitness Books]. Knopf, 1990.
(18) Rice, Tony. *Ocean World* [Young Readers' Nature Library]. Millbrook, 1991.
(19) Simon, Seymour. *Oceans*. Morrow, 1990.
(20) Souza, D. M. *Powerful Waves* [Nature in Action]. Carolrhoda, 1992.
(21) Steele, Philip. *Sharks and Other Creatures of the Deep* [See and Explore Library]. Kindersley, 1991.
(22) Taylor, Dave. *Endangered Ocean Animals* [Endangered Animals]. Crabtree, 1993.
(23) Tesar, Jenny. *Threatened Oceans* [Our Fragile Planet]. Facts on File, 1991.
(24) Whitfield, Philip. *Oceans* [Strange and Amazing Worlds]. Viking, 1991.
(25) Williams, Lawrence. *Oceans* [Last Frontiers for Mankind]. Cavendish, 1991.

(26) Wood, Jenny. *Coral Reefs: Hidden Colonies of the Sea* [Wonderworks of Nature]. Stevens, 1991.

(27) Wu, Norbert. *Life in the Oceans* [Planet Earth]. Little, 1991.

LIBRARY SKILLS RESOURCES

Kidron, Michael, and Segal, Ronald. *The New State of the World Atlas*. Simon & Schuster, 1991.

Reader's Guide to Periodical Literature. H.W. Wilson.

The World Almanac and Book of Facts. World Almanac, 1994.

ADDITIONAL READING—YOUNGER

Base, Graeme. *The Sign of the Seahorse*. Abrams, 1992.

Biesty, Stephen. *Cross-Sections Man of War*. Kindersley, 1993.

Cole, Joanna. *The Magic School Bus on the Ocean Floor*. [Magic School Bus]. Scholastic, 1992.

Greenburg, Judith E., and Carey, Helen H. *Under the Sea* [Science Adventures]. Raintree, 1990.

Guiberson, Brenda Z. *Salmon Story*. Holt, 1993.

Heinrichs, Susan. *The Atlantic Ocean* [New True Books]. Childrens, 1986.

_____. *The Pacific Ocean* [New True Books]. Childrens, 1986.

Humphrey, Kathryn Long. *Shipwrecks: Terror and Treasure* [First Books—Examining the Past]. Watts, 1991.

Jaspersohn, William. *A Day in the Life of a Marine Biologist*. Little, 1982.

Jensen, Anthony, and Bolt, Stephen. *Undersea Mission* [Young Explorers]. Stevens, 1989.

McWilliams, Karen. *Pirates* [First Books—Examining the Past]. Watts, 1989.

Mitgutsch, Ali. *From Sea to Salt* [Start to Finish]. Carolrhoda, 1985.

Palmer, Joy. *Oceans* [First Starts]. Raintree, 1993.

Petersen, David. *Submarines* [New True Books]. Childrens, 1984.

Rand, Gloria. *Prince William*. Holt, 1992.

Ryder, Joanne. *Sea Elf* [Just for a Day Books]. Morrow, 1993.

Sabin, Louis. *Wonders of the Sea*. Troll, 1982.

[The Sea] series. Bookwright, 1991.

Steele, Philip. *About Life in the Sea* [Do You Know...?] Warwick, 1986.

Stille, Darlene R. *Oil Spills* [New True Books]. Childrens, 1991.

Taylor, Barbara. *Rivers and Oceans: Geography Facts and Experiments* [Young Discoverers]. Kingfisher, 1993.

ADDITIONAL READING—OLDER

Bramwell, Martyn. *Oceans* [Earth Science Library]. Watts, 1994.

Duane, Diane. *Deep Wizardry*. Delacorte, 1985.

Engel, Leonard. *The Sea* [Life Nature Library]. Time, 1963.

Fine, John Christopher. *Oceans in Peril*. Macmillan, 1987.

Ganeri, Anita. *The Oceans Atlas: A Pictorial Atlas of the World's Oceans.* Kindersley, 1994.

Hargreaves, Pat, editor. [Seas and Oceans] series. Silver, 1980.

Koch, Frances K. *Mariculture: Farming the Fruits of the Sea* [New England Aquarium Books]. Watts, 1992. (Also other books in series.)

Lambert, David, and McConnell, Anita. *Seas and Oceans* [The World of Science]. Facts on File, 1985.

Lampton, Christopher. *Tidal Wave* [Disaster!]. Millbrook, 1992.

McCall, Edith. *Pirates and Privateers* [Frontiers of America]. Childrens, 1980.

Martin, James. *Tentacles: The Amazing World of Octopus, Squid, and Their Relatives.* Crown, 1993.

Meyerson, A. Lee. *Seawater: A Delicate Balance* [Earth Processes]. Enslow, 1988.

[The Ocean World of Jacques Cousteau] series. Danbury.

Osborne, Mary Pope, adapter. *Mermaid Tales from Around the World.* Scholastic, 1993.

Phillips, Anne W. *The Ocean* [Earth Alert]. Crestwood, 1990.

Robinson, W. Wright. *Incredible Facts About the Ocean: Volumes 1, 2, 3, 4* [Ocean World Library]. Dillon.

Simon, Seymour. *How to Be an Ocean Scientist in Your Own Home.* Lippincott, 1988.

Smith, Roland. *Sea Otter Rescue: The Aftermath of an Oil Spill.* Dutton, 1990.

Waters, John F. *Deep Sea Vents: Living Worlds Without Sun.* Cobblehill, 1994.

Wu, Norbert. *Beneath the Waves: Exploring the Hidden World of the Kelp Forest.* Chronicle, 1992.

See also: books in WATER, ISLANDS AND CORAL REEFS, and THE SEASHORE units.

TO LEARN MORE ABOUT SEAS AND OCEANS, WRITE TO:

Center for Marine Conservation
Council on Ocean Law
The Cousteau Society
Friends of the Earth
Greenpeace U.S.A.

National Coalition for Marine Conservation
The Oceanic Society
Pacific Whale Foundation
World Aquaculture Society
Worldwatch Institute

ISLANDS AND
CORAL REEFS

Islands and coral reefs are homes to the most unusual and fragile creatures on Earth. Completely surrounded by water, these isolated patches are home to wildlife that has evolved differently from life on the mainland. So, too, have the original human populations of islands developed their own customs and lifestyles which may seem strange to people from the continents. These exotic lands are subject to harsh forces of nature and endangered by the "civilized" world. We must strive to preserve their unique beauty.

LIBRARY SKILLS

a. Place the following island countries in alphabetical order: Japan, Sri Lanka, United Kingdom, New Zealand, Cuba, Iceland, Philippines, Hong Kong, Madagascar, Fiji, Trinidad, Vanuatu.

b. Look through *Children's Atlas of People & Places* and find ten island countries. For each country, note its capital city and population.

c. Look up Important Islands and Their Areas in *The World Almanac and Book of Facts*. Match the following islands to the countries that own them: Falkland Islands, Corsica, Tierra del Fuego, Greenland, Baffin, Curacao, Zanzibar, Galápagos, Easter, Bermuda, Tahiti, Guam, Crete, Bali, Iwo Jima, Sardina, Mindanao, Madeira, Tasmania, Vancouver. Now find these countries on a world map. Which islands are owned by countries that are not near them?

d. Use an encyclopedia or atlas to locate these islands that are part of the United States: Hawaii, Long Island, Apostle Islands, Assateague, Nantucket, Key West, Mount Desert Island, Sanibel Island, Nag's Head, Martha's Vineyard, Aleutian Islands, Cape Hatteras, Kodiak Island, Channel Islands, Block Island, Hilton Head, Galveston Island, Merritt Island, St. George Island, Matagorda Island. To which states do each of these belong? The United States also owns several island territories and possessions in other parts of the world. Locate the following: American Samoa, Guam, Wake Island, Midway Island, Puerto Rico, Howland Island, Virgin Islands, Northern Mariana Islands.

e. Use *Rocks and Minerals of the World* to color in a map of volcanic islands in the Pacific Ocean. You will need to look at several pages to find all the islands. Include the names of any volcanoes that are given. Then, in red, mark the area known as the Ring of Fire. What islands are part of the Ring?

f. Use *Lands and Peoples* to locate these answers: 1) List ten islands that are considered to be part of the North American continent. 2) List ten European islands. 3) Approximately how many islands are there in East Asia? Name five island countries from this area. 4) Approximately how many islands are included in the region called Oceania? What is the total land area of these islands?

g. Use the *Endangered Wildlife of the World* series or a similar source to complete this activity. Divide a sheet of paper into four columns. Label them: Caribbean Islands, Islands of the Mediterranean, Islands of Southeast Asia, and Islands of the Pacific. In each column, list the names of endangered animals that live on these islands or in the surrounding waters.

ARTS AND CRAFTS

a. Many coral reef and island habitats have suffered abuse by humans. Draw a poster to encourage people to save a particular reef or island, or an animal that lives on a reef or island.   (5, 10, 12, 13, 15, 16, 19)

b. Draw the flag of an island country.   (*Children's Atlas of People & Places*)

c. People of the Caribbean Islands celebrate a carnival in the spring. Part of the celebration involves dressing up in colorful costumes and masks. Make a carnival mask and costume to wear in a carnival parade.   (18)

d. Choose one island. Make a model or craft of something that represents the island. For example: a model of a giant tortoise for the Galápagos Islands, the tower of London for England, a lei or grass skirt for Hawaii, etc.

e. There are many types of coral, and they all form different shapes. Use clay to make a model of staghorn coral, brain coral, gorgonian coral, or another type. Label your model with an explanation of the coral's life and special features.   (5, 6, 13, 14, 16, 19)

f. Make a diorama of a barrier reef, fringing reef, or coral atoll.   (2, 5, 6, 14, 19)

g. Choose one island country or archipelago. It may or may not be inhabited by humans. Make a collage of scenes from these islands. You may include pictures of plants and animals, landscapes, and a map of the area. If inhabited, you may include the flag of the island, pictures of traditional foods and costumes, etc. The collage can be two- or three-dimensional.

SPELLING/VOCABULARY

a. Complete a crossword puzzle of island features: beach, cliff, cave, arch, stack, atoll, lagoon, barrier reef, fringing reef, coral, water, erosion, ocean, shore, sand, plants, lava, wildlife. (2, 12, 14, 19)

b. Complete a word search puzzle of extinct or endangered island wildlife: dodo, kiwi, dugong, honeycreeper, sea lion, lemur, orangutan, albatross, moa, takahe, cormorant, tortoise, puffin, auk, fur seal, spoonbill, nene, key deer. (9, 10, 15, 21, 27)

c. Complete a word search puzzle of coral reef creatures: angelfish, anemone, crown-of-thorns, clown fish, sponge, sea star, sea horse, clam, shrimp, crab, snail, sea urchin, turtle, dugong, tube worm, barracuda, jellyfish, grouper, eel, damselfish. (5, 6, 13, 16, 19)

d. Complete a fill-in-the-blanks exercise of terms that relate to the formation of volcanic islands: seamount, ocean ridge, smoker, lava, limestone, crust, vent, fissure, tephra, pumice, sulfur, crater, eruption, caldera, ocean trench, guyot, cinder cone, hotspot, magma, fumarole. (2, 8, 10, 11)

e. The Galápagos Islands are home to many unusual plants and animals. Identify each of the following with a sentence that describes its unique features: land iguana, frigate bird, giant tortoise, lava lizard, blue-footed booby, waved albatross, sea lion, masked booby, swallow-tailed gull, marine iguana, cormorant, penguin, woodpecker finch, Sally Lightfoot crab, prickly pear cactus, sunflower, mangrove tree, Scalesia tree, palo santo tree, lava cactus. (3, 9, 10, 15)

f. Look up information on one island nation. Create a glossary of native terms spoken by the islanders. Include at least fifteen terms. Arrange them in alphabetical order and give their meanings. (4, 8, 18, 23, 25, 26, 27, 28, 29)

g. Complete a matching exercise of coral terms: Coelenterata, tentacles, polyp, corallite, calcium carbonate, skeletons, planulae, budding, zooplankton, nematocysts, coralline algae, zooxanthellae, spicule, hydrocorals, branching corals, soft corals, octocorals, boulder corals, stony corals, coral colony. (5, 6, 13, 16, 19)

GEOGRAPHY

a. What is the Great Barrier Reef? Where is it located? List several interesting facts about the Great Barrier Reef and its wildlife. (5, 16, 19)

b. What is an archipelago? Write the names of five or more archipelagos. (10, 21, 27, 28)

c. Choose one island anywhere in the world. Make a list of some plants and animals that are unique to that part of the world.   (10, 21, 27, 28)

d. Look up information on one archipelago country. About how many islands comprise it? How many are inhabited? List some of the major islands. Note their climates, major land features such as volcanoes, and forms of plant life. In what part of the world is the country located?   (21, 23, 25, 26, 27, 28, 29)

e. Divide a sheet of paper into four columns. Label them: Caribbean Islands, South Pacific Islands, Mediterranean Islands, and Southeast Asia. In each column, list some major crops grown on these island groups.   (4, 18, 21, 23, 25, 26, 27, 28, 29)

f. Create a statistical fact sheet for one island country. Include numbers on its area in square miles and length of coastline, latitude and longitude, average temperature range, amount of rainfall, highest altitude, population, monetary unit, and other numerical data.   (21, 23, 25, 26, 27, 28, 29)

g. Many islands form along the Mid-Ocean Ridge. What is it and how long is it? On a map of the ocean floor, locate the Mid-Ocean Ridge. Name some of the islands along the Ridge.   (1, 8, 11)

MATH

a. The Galápagos Islands are 600 miles west of South America, on the equator. Some very unusual plants and animals live there. Change the following measurements from feet to inches: 1) Frigate birds have long black wings that stretch 8 feet from tip to tip. 2) Sunflowers can grow as high as 60 feet tall. 3) Prickly pear cacti can grow to 30 feet tall. 4) The only penguins not at the South Pole live in the waters near the Galápagos Islands. They are only about 1 foot high. 5) The Galápagos marine iguana is the only iguana in the world that eats seaweed. It will dive down 20 feet or more into the ocean to find food.

b. In 1963, a volcanic island named Surtsey was born near Iceland. On November 17, a cinder cone broke through the surface of the Atlantic Ocean. Two days later, the new island was 33 feet above sea level. In three days, it was 130 feet, in five days it was 200 feet, and on the sixth day it stood at 230 feet high. Make a graph of Surtsey's growth during its first six days as an island. In June of 1967, the highest point on the island was 567 feet. How much had it grown since November 23, 1963?   (8, 9, 14)

c. Following is a list of the world's ten largest islands and their areas in square miles. Round off these numbers to the nearest 1,000. Then place the islands in descending order: Sumatra 182,860; New Guinea 311,737; Great

Britain 84,550; Ellsmere 75,767; Baffin 195,927; Greenland 840,004; Borneo 288,151; Victoria 83,896; Madagascar 226,658; Honshu 87,805.

d. The crown-of-thorns is a 16-armed starfish that feeds on the polyps of stony corals. During its life, it can eat about two square miles of coral. At that rate: 1) How many square miles of coral can 25 crowns-of-thorns devour? 40 crowns-of-thorns? 100? 2) How many of these starfish would it take to destroy a coral reef that covered an area of 60 square miles? 94 square miles? 130 square miles? (19)

e. Use a calculator to complete the following coral reef math problems: 1) There are over 2,500 species of coral. About 650 are stony corals whose limestone skeletons provide the basic structure of a coral reef. The rest are soft corals. What percent of all corals are stony corals? 2) The Great Barrier Reef is about 1,260 miles long. How many feet is that? 3) Staghorn coral is a major reef-building stony coral. Its colonies may form up to 75 percent of a reef. At that rate, how many miles of staghorn coral would be found in a reef that was 300 miles long? 1,000 miles? 1,260 miles? 4) Most coral reefs do not grow deeper than 150 feet below sea level. However, the Great Barrier Reef reaches almost 500 feet beneath the water's surface. How much deeper than usual is this?

f. Many island animals are endangered. Compute these math examples about endangered animals: 1) Once there were an estimated 250,000 giant tortoises living on the Galápagos Islands. Human visitors and settlers killed many of them. Now there are about 15,000 left. What percent of the giant tortoises were killed? 2) A few centuries ago, there were over 300 species of birds living in New Zealand; now 25 percent are extinct. How many bird species are left? 3) When Europeans landed on the Hawaiian Islands in the 18th century, there were about 25,000 nenes (Hawaiian geese). In 1949, after colonists and their animals hunted the nenes, there were only 30 birds left. What percent of the nene population was destroyed? Conservationists bred the birds and by 1980 their numbers were up to 750. What percent increase is this over 1949 figures? What percent of the 18th century population is the 1980 figure? 5) The key deer of the Florida Keys numbered about 40 million in the beginning of the 19th century. Today, there are about 8 million of them. What percent of the key deer population has been lost?

g. Refer to the math exercise in this unit, item **c**, for a list of the ten largest islands. Rank these in descending order by area. Then look up the population of each island. Rank them again in descending order by population. (21, 23, 25, 26, 27, 29)

MUSIC AND THEATER ARTS

a. Listen to *Asia — Misty Isle* (Nature Recordings), a collection of nature sounds from the island of Sri Lanka. What can you tell about this island from what you hear?

b. Some special occasions, such as Christmas, birthdays and weddings, are celebrated all over the world. Choose one island country and show how the people celebrate one of these events.   (4, 18, 21, 27, 28)

c. Listen to music from various island nations. (Some can be found in the Explorer series, produced by Elektra Nonesuch.) How do different cultures use music to celebrate special events?

d. Calypso and Reggae music are popular in the Caribbean islands. Listen to some Calypso and Reggae music (see Smithsonian/Folkways and Rykodisc Catalogs). How are the two forms of music similar? How are they different? How have these styles influenced modern American music?   (18)

e. Many island countries have folktales or legends that the inhabitants tell. Choose one island and read some of their folklore. Perform a puppet show about one of these stories.

f. Some Broadway plays are set on islands, such as the musicals *South Pacific* and *Once on This Island*. Listen to music from these plays. Then act out scenes from these or other plays set on islands.

g. *Small group project:* Each group should choose one island country. Pick a cultural activity or event from that country and act out a representation of it. Some examples: Japanese Kabuki theater, Martinique's Vaval carnival, or a Javanese puppet show.   (4, 18, 21, 23, 25, 26, 27, 28)

ENGLISH COMPOSITION

a. Pretend you are the first person to discover an island. Write a story about what you might find there. What animals and plants do you see? What is the weather like? How large is the island? What are your plans for the island?

b. Pretend you are a diver observing a coral reef. Write a story or poem about what you see. You may include descriptions of coral and some of the reef-dwellers there.   (5, 6, 13, 14, 19)

c. Pretend you are witnessing the birth of a new volcanic island. Write an eyewitness account of what you see.   (2, 8, 12, 14)

d. Write a nonfiction story about an animal that lives on or near a reef or island. Give some facts about where and how it lives.   (1, 3, 5, 6, 7, 10, 13, 14, 15, 16)

e. *Group project:* Many different foods are prepared on various islands around the world. Choose an island and write down a recipe of a traditional food from there. Include any additional information about the food, such as if it is eaten during a certain festival. Combine these recipes into an island cook book. For fun, cook a recipe and bring it in for the class to share at an international island food festival.   (18, 22)

f. The United States has many small islands, such as the Florida Keys, the Aleutian Islands, Assateague, and Nantucket. Create a nature guide for one American island or island chain. Describe the climate and physical features of the island(s). Tell about the plant and animal life there. (9, 20, 24)

g. In Norse Mythology, the Mid-Atlantic Ridge was represented as the Midgard Serpent. Read some Norse or Scandinavian legends of the Midgard Serpent. Write a plot summary of one story.   (1, 8)

SCIENCE

a. What are stony corals, soft corals, and gorgonian corals? Which type has skeletons which make up the basic structure of coral reefs? How do corals eat? What do they eat? In what type of water do corals live?   (5, 6, 16, 19)

b. What is a coral atoll? What was Charles Darwin's theory of how atolls develop?   (6, 12, 14, 19)

c. How do corals build reefs and islands? How can mangrove trees increase the size of an island?   (2, 5, 6, 9, 12, 14, 16)

d. Islands, by their nature, are isolated places. So how do plants and animals get to them?   (3, 8, 9, 10, 12, 14, 17)

e. Island plants and animals have evolved differently from mainland life forms. Choose one island plant and one island animal. Compare them to a similar mainland plant and animal. How do they differ in size, habits, physical appearance, what they eat, etc.?   (3, 9, 10, 12, 14, 15)

f. Three types of islands are oceanic (or volcanic) islands, continental (or coastal) islands, and tectonically formed islands. Explain briefly how each type is formed. Name at least one island that is an example of each of these three types.   (7, 9, 12, 17)

g. Refer to the lists of endangered island animals you created for the library skills exercise, item **g**. Choose one animal from each column. Write a fact sheet about these four animals. Include their descriptions, how they live, why they are endangered, and any efforts that are being made to save them from extinction.

HISTORY/SOCIOLOGY

Note: Earth has many island countries. Each has its own unique history and culture. In a social studies unit, the teacher may want to do an overview of life on several islands, have the class concentrate on a specific island or group of islands, or assign each student a different island to study. Adapt these activities to fit the scope of your lesson plans.

a. Choose one island. Who were the first people to inhabit it? Do they still live there? If other people moved to the island, where did they come from? (4, 18, 21, 27, 28)

b. Choose one island country. What is family life like there? What are the roles of the father, mother, children and extended family members? (4, 18, 21, 27, 28)

c. Choose one island country. What is the principal religion(s) there? What are some cultural traditions? List the names and times of year of some major holidays and festivals celebrated there. (4, 18, 21, 27, 28)

d. Although few people live on the Galápagos Islands, people from many nations have visited there throughout history. These include pirates, whalers, shipwrecked sailors, and scientists. Look up information about one or a group of these visitors. When did they visit? How did they use the island and its resources? Was the island disturbed or left alone? (9, 10)

e. Tropical islands usually have beautiful weather, but they are also prone to some of nature's most destructive forces. Look up information on an island or group of islands that suffered a strong hurricane, cyclone, tsunami, earthquake, or volcano. Write a report about this event and its aftermath. (1, 18)

f. Choose an island country and note some facts about modern life there. Include the island's main industries, educational system, type of government, name of ruler, sports and entertainment, agriculture, etc. How does this compare with the people's traditional way of life? What are some challenges or problems faced by the islanders? (4, 18, 21, 23, 25, 26, 27, 28, 29)

g. Many islands, such as those of the Caribbean, are populated by people whose ancestors came from a variety of other nations. Choose one island that has a multicultural background. Tell where its settlers came from and how this has influenced life on the island. Have people assimilated to the various cultures, or do problems arise? (4, 18, 21, 23, 25, 26, 27, 28, 29)

TOPICS FOR DISCUSSION

a. What are some holidays and festivals that are celebrated on island nations? When do they occur? (21, 27, 28)

b. What are some natural dangers to coral reefs? What are some ways that people are harming reefs? (5, 13, 16, 19)

c. Humans who have "discovered" and settled islands often upset the natural ecology of these places. Give some examples of how humans caused native plants and animals to become extinct or endangered. (9, 10, 15, 21, 27, 28)

d. Vacationers from all over the world like to visit tropical islands. Choose one or more tropical islands that cater to tourists. How does tourism affect the islands and the people who live there? (18, 21, 23, 25, 26, 27, 28, 29)

e. The Galápagos Islands were declared a national park by their owners, the people of Ecuador. Why was this done? Other islands have been named wildlife sanctuaries or refuges. What does this mean for the animals that live on these islands? (9, 10, 12)

f. Scientist Charles Darwin studied several islands in the 1800s while on a world-wide sea voyage on the HMS *Beagle*. From his observations, he developed some important scientific theories. What were some of his ideas? (1, 6, 10, 14)

g. Explorers, traders, and missionaries greatly influenced the lives of Pacific island natives, especially during the last two centuries. What were some of these lifestyle changes? Do you think the islanders are better off now, or before they were "civilized"? (4, 21, 23, 25, 26, 27, 29)

SUGGESTED RESOURCES

(1) Ballard, Robert D. *Exploring Our Living Planet.* National Geographic, 1988.
(2) Bender, Lionel. *Island* [The Story of the Earth]. Watts, 1989.
(3) Gelman, Rita Golden. *Dawn to Dusk in the Galápagos.* Little, 1991.
(4) Hereniko, Vilsoni, and Hereniko, Patricia. *South Pacific Islanders* [Original Peoples]. Rourke, 1987.
(5) Johnson, Rebecca L. *The Great Barrier Reef: A Living Laboratory* [Discovery!]. Lerner, 1991.
(6) Johnson, Sylvia A. *Coral Reefs* [Natural Science]. Lerner, 1984.
(7) Lambert, David, and McConnell, Anita. *Seas and Oceans* [The World of Science]. Facts on File, 1985.
(8) Lasky, Kathryn. *Surtsey: The Newest Place on Earth.* Hyperion, 1992.
(9) Laycock, George. *Islands and Their Mysteries.* Four Winds, 1977.
(10) McCormick, Maxine, and Root, Phyllis. *Galápagos* [National Parks]. Crestwood, 1989.
(11) Nixon, Hershell H., and Nixon, Joan Lowery. *Land Under the Sea.* Dodd, 1985.
(12) Rydell, Wendy. *All About Islands* [Question and Answer Book]. Troll, 1984.
(13) Sargent, William. *Night Reef: Dusk to Dawn on a Coral Reef* [New England Aquarium Books]. Watts, 1991.
(14) Stephens, William M. *Islands.* Holiday, 1974.

(15) Taylor, Dave. *Endangered Island Animals* [Endangered Animals]. Crabtree, 1993.
(16) Tayntor, Elizabeth, et al. *Dive to the Coral Reefs* [New England Aquarium Books]. Crown, 1986.
(17) Whitfield, Philip. *Why Do Volcanoes Erupt?* Viking, 1990.
(18) Winston, James. *The Caribbean* [Looking at Lands]. Macdonald, 1984.
(19) Wood, Jenny. *Coral Reefs: Hidden Colonies of the Sea* [Wonderworks of Nature]. Stevens, 1991.

GEOGRAPHY BOOKS SERIES: See titles of island countries and states

(20) [America the Beautiful] series. Childrens.
(21) [Countries of the World] series. Bookwright.
(22) [Easy Menu Ethnic Cookbooks] series. Lerner.
(23) [Enchantment of the World] series. Childrens.
(24) [From Sea to Shining Sea] series. Childrens.
(25) [Places and Peoples of the World] series. Chelsea.
(26) [Portraits of the Nations] series. Lippincott.
(27) [Visual Geography] series. Lerner.
(28) [We Live In...] series. Bookwright.
(29) [World in View] series. Steck-Vaughn.

LIBRARY SKILLS RESOURCES

Endangered Wildlife of the World. Cavendish, 1993.
Lands and Peoples. Grolier, 1993.
Rocks and Minerals of the World [Using and Understanding Maps]. Chelsea, 1993.
Wood, Jenny. *The Children's Atlas of People & Places.* Millbrook, 1993.
The World Almanac and Book of Facts. World Almanac, 1994.

ADDITIONAL READING – YOUNGER

Adams, Jeanie. *Going for Oysters.* Whitman, 1993.
Arnosky, Jim. *Near the Sea: A Portfolio of Paintings.* Lothrop, 1990.
Barrett, Norman. *Coral Reef* [Picture Library-Science]. Watts, 1991.
Bender, Lionel. *Life on a Coral Reef.* Watts, 1989.
[Children of the World] series. Stevens.
Cooney, Barbara. *Island Boy.* Viking, 1988.
Corwin, Judith Hoffman. *Latin American and Caribbean Crafts* [Crafts Around the World]. Watts, 1992.
Crespo, George. *How the Sea Began.* Clarion, 1993.
Gibbons, Gail. *Surrounded by Sea: Life on a New England Fishing Island.* Little, 1991.
[Islands in the Sea Discovery Library] Series. Rourke.
Jauck, Andrea, and Points, Larry. *Assateague: Island of the Wild Ponies.* Macmillan, 1993.
Joseph, Lynn. *A Wave in Her Pocket.* Clarion, 1991.
Krupinski, Loretta. *Celia's Island Journal.* Little, 1992.
McCloskey, Robert. *Time of Wonder.* Viking, 1957.
McGovern, Ann, and Clark, Eugene. *The Desert Beneath the Sea.* Scholastic, 1991.

Radlauer, Ruth, and Anderson, Henry M. *Reefs* [Radlauer Geo]. Childrens, 1983.

Shapiro, Irwin. *Darwin and the Enchanted Isles.* Coward, 1977.

Siegel, Beatrice. *Sam Ellis's Island.* Four Winds, 1985.

[Take a Trip] series. Watts.

Taylor, Barbara. *Coral Reef* [Look Closer]. Kindersley, 1992.

Wolf, Bernard. *Amazing Grace: Smith Island and the Chesapeake Watermen.* Macmillan, 1986.

ADDITIONAL READING – OLDER

Albyn, Carole Lisa, and Webb, Lois Sinaiko. *The Multicultural Cookbook for Students.* Oryx, 1993.

Behm, Barbara J., and Balouet, Jean-Christophe. *Endangered Animals of the Islands* [In Peril]. Stevens, 1994.

Branston, Brian. *Gods & Heroes from Viking Mythology* [World Mythologies]. Schocken, 1982.

Campbell, Andrew. *Seashore Life* [Nature Library]. Exeter, 1983.

[Cultures of the World] series. Cavendish.

Dorris, Michael. *Morning Girl.* Hyperion, 1992.

Engel, Leonard. *The Sea* [Life Nature Library]. Time, 1963.

Flaherty, Steven, and Ahrens, Lynn. *Once on This Island: A New Musical.* Astor, 1990.

Flint, David. *The Mediterranean and Its People* [People and Places]. Thomson, 1994.

Foster, Sally. *The Private World of Smith Island.* Cobblehill, 1993.

Gittins, Anne. *Tales from the South Pacific Islands.* Stemmer, 1977.

Goodman, Billy. *Natural Wonders and Disasters* [Planet Earth]. Little, 1991.

Lampton, Christopher. *Coral Reefs in Danger.* Millbrook, 1992.

Law, Felicia. *Darwin & the Voyage of the Beagle.* Deutsch, 1982.

[Let's Visit Places and Peoples of the World] series. Chelsea.

MacDonald, Robert. *Islands of the Pacific Rim and Their People* [People and Places]. Thomson, 1994.

Markl, Julia. *Living on Islands* [Cultural Geography]. Watts, 1987.

O'Dell, Scott. *Island of the Blue Dolphins.* Houghton, 1960.

Once on This Island (sound recording). BMG Music, 1990.

Park, Ruth. *My Sister Sif.* Viking, 1991.

Rodgers, Richard, and Hammerstein, Oscar. *South Pacific: A Musical Play.* Random, 1949.

South Pacific (sound recording). Columbia Records, 1973.

Stevenson, Robert Louis. *Treasure Island.* Holt, 1990.

See also: books in SEAS AND OCEANS unit.

FOR MORE INFORMATION ABOUT ISLANDS AND CORAL REEFS, WRITE TO:

Big Island Rainforest Action Group
Center for Marine Conservation
Charles Darwin Foundation for
   the Galápagos Isles

Global Coral Reef Alliance
Hawaii Volcanoes National Park
The Oceanic Society
Worldwatch Institute

THE SEASHORE

The seashore is where the land meets the sea. It is a beautiful but harsh environment. Powerful waves and other forces of nature are constantly acting to change the shape of Earth's coastal areas. Somehow, many forms of plant and animal life manage to thrive in these rocky, muddy, sandy, or coral habitats. But pollution is a major threat to seashores. They must be kept clean and healthy so that plants and animals can survive, and people can enjoy their natural splendor.

Note: In this unit, the terms "rock pool" and "tide pool" will be used interchangeably, as will "sea star" and "starfish."

LIBRARY SKILLS

a. Place a list of seashore plants in alphabetical order: violet, lichen, rockweed, kelp, wrack, horn-poppy, plankton, sea oats, marramgrass, algae, thistle, bayberry, oyster leaf, golden samphire.

b. Look in a world atlas. Make a list of major cities that are located near the shore.

c. Use *The Children's Atlas of Peoples & Places* to look up the capital and population of these coastal countries: Norway, Chile, South Africa, Vietnam, Ecuador, Portugal, Oman, Somalia, Suriname, Morocco.

d. In *The World Almanac and Book of Facts*, look up National Seashores. Locate these places on a map of the United States. What does the designation of "national seashore" mean?

e. Use *Reader's Guide to Periodical Literature* or an online data bank to locate an article about coastal or seashore conservation. Under what subject heading(s) did you look?

f. Consult a field guide to obtain answers to the following questions: 1) List five types of conch shells. 2) What is the largest scallop found near the east coast of the United States? How big is it? 3) Where are razor clams found? 4) Name a sea star that has more than five arms. How many arms does it have? 5) Name five types of sponges. 6) Where are horseshoe crabs found? 7) What is a Portuguese man-of-war? 8) What is kelp? What are some of its uses?

g. Use *The Guinness Book of World Records* to answer the following questions: 1) What is the heaviest species of starfish? 2) What was the weight of the largest concentration of crustaceans recorded? 3) Where was the oldest mollusk found? What was its size and weight? 4) What is the fastest snail? How fast is it? 5) How big is the largest jellyfish? 6) What and where is the largest coral reef in the world? What are its dimensions? 7) What is the smallest sponge?

ARTS AND CRAFTS

a. Look at some real sand dollars, then make your own clay models. What animal was a sand dollar originally? (7, 18, 29)

b. Cut out pictures of seashore plants and animals from old magazines. Glue these pictures onto construction paper to make a picture of an underwater habitat.

c. Color a series of pictures that show how coastal erosion can cause a rocky shore to become a cave or inlet. (8, 15, 17, 20, 21)

d. Use colored modeling clay to make a model of an anemone, starfish, coral, or other type of seashore animal. (7, 11, 16, 18, 23, 27, 28, 29)

e. Seashells can be used for a number of art projects. You can decorate a box by gluing small shells onto it. Shells can be made into necklaces and other types of jewelry. You can glue shells onto cardboard or wood to make a collage. Use some shells in an art project of your own design. (13)

f. *Group project:* Draw a mural of a coral reef. Include various types of coral and the sea plants and animals that live there. Label the different elements of your reef. (7, 14, 16, 28)

g. *Group project:* Draw a mural or make a diorama to illustrate the zones of a rocky, muddy, sandy, or coral seashore. Label the levels and each example of marine plants and animals shown. (7, 11, 17, 21, 22, 26, 29)

SPELLING/VOCABULARY

a. Complete a matching picture puzzle about things you can find at the seashore: egg case, sea glass, turtle, sun, ocean, coral, driftwood, seaweed, shell, sand dollar, starfish, pebble, sand, feather, dune, waves, mermaid's purse, anemone, tide pool, sea gull. (5, 6, 11, 13, 18, 22, 23, 24, 27)

b. Complete a word search puzzle of plants and animals that live in a rock pool: cockle, blenny, rockweed, periwinkle, sponge, plankton, algae, clam, crab, limpet, mussel, snail, barnacle, jellyfish, urchin, frog, seaworm, shrimp, fan worm, slug. (5, 6, 11, 12, 13, 18, 22, 23, 24, 26, 27)

c. Complete a word search puzzle of birds that live by the seashore: petrel, tern, plover, sanderling, blackbird, gull, sandpiper, turnstone, pelican, oystercatcher, godwit, kittywake, razorbill, gannet, albatross, cormorant, curlew, dunlin, puffin. (5, 7, 9, 11, 13, 17, 21, 22, 23, 24, 26, 29)

d. Complete a fill-in-the-blanks exercise of names of coastal land formations: estuary, geo, spit, cliff, bench, beach, bayhead bar, coral reef, tombolo, delta, ria, fjord, inlet, sand bar, peninsula, barrier beach. (8, 15, 17, 19, 20)

e. Complete a matching picture puzzle of types of seashells: saddle oyster, dogwinkle, razor clam, coquina, scallop, mussel, whelk, conch, abalone, periwinkle, limpet, spindle shell, cone, cockle, cowrie, nautilus, murex, winkle. (1, 5, 7, 9, 21, 23, 29)

f. Complete a crossword puzzle of terms that relate to the seashore environment: tides, detritus, erosion, shore, habitat, holdfast, limestone, kelp, salinity, wrack, sand dune, rocky beach, tide pool, zonation, beach, ecosystem, splash zone, seaweed, intertidal. (7, 16, 19, 21, 22, 26)

g. Match the following terms relating to corals to their meanings: polyp, coelenterata, anemone, tentacles, limestone, spicule, atoll, barrier reef, fringe reef, colony, calcium carbonate, lagoon, zooxanthellae, crown-of-thorns, planula, zooplankton. (7, 14, 28, 29)

GEOGRAPHY

a. The shape of a coastline changes as powerful ocean waves wear away the land. Look at pictures of rock formations caused by sea erosion. Find examples of a cove, stack, blow hole, arch. What might happen to the seashore after a big storm? (15, 17, 20, 21)

b. Seashores can be sandy, rocky, muddy, or coral. Make a chart to illustrate the differences among each type. Include what each area looks like, and some plants and animals that live there. Name a part of the United States where each type of shore is located. (11, 13, 15, 17, 18, 21, 22, 26)

c. Where in the United States can you find non-desert sand dunes? Where does the sand come from? (4, 16, 22)

d. What are the three types of coral coasts? Name one coral reef and note some geographical facts about it. Where is it located? (14, 16, 17, 28)

e. How are coastal caves formed? How are beaches made? Which one of these is an example of deposition? Which is erosion? Give some other examples of deposition and erosion. (8, 15, 16, 17, 20)

f. Many natural forces shape the Earth's coastlines and seashores. Name some of them. What are some human attempts to alter or protect the shape of the coast? (8, 10, 16, 17, 19, 20, 21, 26)

g. Some coastal features are unique to certain parts of the world. Other features are more common. For each of the following coastal features, name one country in which it occurs: fjord, dike, delta, chalk cliff, bayhead bar, spit, ria, raised beach, peninsula. What are submerged coastlines and emergent coastlines? What is reclaimed land? Where can these features be found? (8, 10, 17, 20)

MATH

a. What are bivalves? What does "bi" mean? Look at some sea shells. Identify the ones that are bivalves. How can you tell? (12, 18, 22, 24, 27, 29)

b. How many feet does a snail have? A crab? A sandpiper? Most types of starfish have how many arms? Make a list of several seashore creatures, grouped according to the number of legs (or arms) they have. Can you find any similarities among the animals in each set? (5, 7, 12, 24, 29)

c. Your teacher will provide several real seashells for you to measure. On a sheet of paper, write the name of each shell and its size. Then write down the size this type of shell can grow to. (1, 29)

d. Use the information found in the library skills exercise, item **d**, to complete this activity. List all the national seashores in the United States in descending order according to size. Then draw a chart to illustrate your answer.

e. Following are some facts about corals. Convert these numbers into metric terms. 1) Corals grow in waters that have a temperature of at least 61°F. 2) They grow about 2 or 3 inches per year. 3) The world's largest coral reef, Australia's Great Barrier Reef, is 1,260 miles long. 4) Parts of the Great Barrier Reef lie over 100 miles from the coast. 5) One reef-dwelling animal is the queen angelfish, which grows to 12 inches long. 6) The water in which coral reefs develop is usually not deeper than 150 feet. 7) The Great Barrier Reef is an exception. Its bottom lies more than 492 feet below the water surface.

f. Following are some facts about sea birds. Convert these metric terms into inches, gallons, pounds, or miles. 1) The bill of a pelican can hold up to 13.5 liters of water. 2) The largest albatross has a wing span of about 360 cm. 3) An emperor penguin may weigh up to 40 kg. 4) The least storm petrel is only 13 cm. long. 5) Gannets build their nests about 80 cm. apart from each other. 6) An arctic tern flies 18,000 km from its northern breeding grounds to spend the winter in Antarctica.

g. Every seashore experiences high tide and low tide twice a day. Low tide comes approximately 6 hours and 13 minutes after high tide. The day's second high tide comes 12 hours and 26 minutes after the first high tide. If, on Monday, the day's first high tide occurs at 6:13 AM, when will the first low tide occur? The second high tide? Make a chart to show all the high and low tides that occur from Monday morning until Friday evening (five days total).

MUSIC AND THEATER ARTS

a. Present a puppet show of a book about a seashore animal, such as *A House for Hermit Crab*, by Eric Carle.

b. Watch a film of waves crashing onto a beach. Then line up on one side of a room with your classmates. Hold hands and pretend to be a wave heading for the shore. Start out by crouching down low. Grow taller as the wave approaches the shore. How do you act when the wave pulls away from the shore?

c. Sing some popular songs about the beach or the seashore, such as "By the Sea."

d. Play a game of charades in which each person acts out a work-related or recreational activity that is done by the seashore.

e. Look at pictures or films of some seashore animals. Observe how they move. Using various musical instruments, create a sound that fits the movement of these creatures. Consider: does the animal move quickly or slowly? Does it scrabble, slither, swim, crawl? Should the music be fast or slow, loud or soft, high or low-pitched, silly or serious?

f. In the 1960s, teenagers watched beach movies, listened to surfer music, and did a dance called the Swim. Have the class stage a 1960s-type beach movie, and act out some of these roles.

g. Play a game of charades in which each person acts out the name of a coastal city.

ENGLISH COMPOSITION

a. Write a story or poem about a day at the beach. What do you see there? What do you like to do at the beach? (5, 11, 13, 21, 23, 27)

b. A popular tongue twister is "She sells seashells by the seashore." Create a new tongue twister about a scene at the beach, seashore, or other coastal area. Have a contest to see which tongue twisters are the longest, silliest and most difficult to say.

c. Pretend you are a blenny, limpet, or other animal that lives in a rock pool. How do the tides affect the way you live? Write a story about your day. Describe your activities during high and low tide. (6, 11, 12, 13, 18, 22, 23, 24, 27)

d. Write a science fiction story about a seashore animal that mutates. Does it become super strong, smart, large, or gain extraordinary powers? Is it a super hero ("Power Pelican") or a monster ("The Lobster That Ate Japan")?

e. Design a vacation brochure for a seaside resort. Describe some things people can do to have fun at the shore. Include pictures of your resort and the area around it.

f. Pretend an oil spill has occurred near a beach or a coastal city. You are a newspaper reporter assigned to write about this disaster. In your article, describe the extent of the damage and the clean-up effort. How will this tragedy affect plant and animal life in the area? How will it affect the people who live there? (3, 17, 19)

g. Pretend you are a naturalist or a marine biologist. Write an introduction to a Beginner's Guide to Exploring the Seashore. Give some safety tips for beginning explorers to follow. Also set some rules so that explorers do not harm the environment. (1, 7, 9, 17, 21, 22, 24, 29)

SCIENCE

Note: If you live near a seashore, you may want to take the class on a field trip. Students can observe life in a rock pool, identify sea birds, note high and low tide areas, and watch the action of the waves.

a. What happens to a crab or lobster if it loses a claw? What happens to a sea star if it loses an arm? What is the name for this occurrence? (9, 11, 12, 18, 27, 28, 29)

b. Look at some real seashells. Can you hear the waves when you place a large shell next to your ear? Use a book with pictures of shells to identify them. (1, 7, 9, 29)

c. What is molting? Which animals molt? What happens when they molt? (9, 22)

d. How are tide pools made? What animals and plants might you find in a tide pool? How do they survive there? (6, 11, 13, 18, 19, 21, 22, 23, 24, 28)

e. Following is a list of seashore animals. For each one, tell what it eats and how it eats: starfish, anemone, sponge, jellyfish, mussel, limpet, crab, snail, sea urchin, sea cucumber, clam. Which of these animals move around? How? (6, 7, 12, 16, 18, 21, 22, 23, 24, 27, 29)

f. Divide a sheet of paper into four columns. Label them: red seaweed, green seaweed, brown seaweed, and sea grasses. List at least five plants in each column. Which group of plants is found on land? In shallow water? Which group is in the deepest water? (3, 4, 7, 9, 13, 21, 22, 24, 29)

g. Scientists classify similar animals into a group called a phylum. For example, snails and clams belong to the phylum *Mollusca*. Give some examples of seashore animals of the following phyla: *Porifera, Coelenterata, Annelida, Arthropoda, Echinodermata, Mollusca*. What are the major characteristics of each phylum?   (7, 16, 18, 21, 26, 29)

HISTORY/SOCIOLOGY

a. Fishing is a major seaport industry. If you live near a seaport, discuss what goes on there. If you do not live near a seaport, choose one to learn about. What types of fish are caught there? Look at pictures of fishing boats. Discuss the life of a fisherman.

b. Look at some historical maps drawn by European explorers centuries ago. Compare them to current maps. How have the coastlines changed? What do you think caused these changes?   (25, 26)

c. Seashores are sometimes victims of litter, oil spills, or industrial pollution. Write an account of an actual coastal pollution incident. Where and when did it occur? How did it affect the community? What was done about it?   (2, 3, 17)

d. Many people live in coastal areas. Name some ways by which they earn a living. What types of jobs are common in seaports?   (3, 11, 17)

e. Life in a coastal community can vary greatly from life in a land-locked area. Read some books in which the main character lives on the coast, and some in which he/she lives inland. Write a paper comparing the lives of these characters. How does their environment affect their way of life?

f. Each state that borders the sea has its own policy about how to handle oceanfront property. Choose one East or West Coast American state. What is the government's policy on shoreline areas? How and why was this policy enacted? How does this affect the people who live near the shore?   (10, 17, 19, 24)

g. Violent acts of nature, such as a hurricane, tsunami, or earthquake, often occur along the coastline. Look up one coastal area that was affected by a natural disaster. What damage was done? How did the people who live there respond? How did the shape of the coastline change?   (10, 17, 25)

TOPICS FOR DISCUSSION

a. How do pollution and oil spills affect seashore life?   (2, 3, 6, 11, 13, 17)

b. Some of the largest cities around the world developed along the coast.

Why do you think this is so? What are the advantages to living near the seashore?   (17, 26)

c. How are seaweeds different from other plants? What are some ways that seaweed is used by seashore animals and people?   (6, 13, 18, 21, 22, 24, 29)

d. Name some sea birds and mammals that are in danger of becoming extinct. Why are they endangered? What is being done to protect them?   (3, 17, 19)

e. A variety of plants grow on coastal sand dunes. Name some of them. How can they grow on bare sand? How do these plants affect their environment? What are some threats to their survival?   (3, 11, 17, 19, 21, 29)

f. What are some human threats to the seashore environment? How can we protect it?   (3, 7, 16, 17, 19, 26, 28)

g. Why is the seashore a popular vacation spot? What are some benefits of the tourism industry to seaside communities? What are some of the disadvantages?   (7, 10, 17, 19)

SUGGESTED RESOURCES

(1) Abbott, R. Tucker. *Seashells of the World: A Guide to the Better-Known Species* [Golden Guides]. Western, 1991.
(2) Asimov, Isaac. *Why Are Some Beaches Oily?* [Ask Isaac Asimov]. Stevens, 1992.
(3) Baines, John. *Protecting the Oceans* [Conserving Our World]. Steck-Vaughn, 1991.
(4) Bannan, Jan Gumprecht. *Sand Dunes* [Earth Watch]. Carolrhoda, 1989.
(5) Behm, Barbara J., and Bonar, Veronica. *Exploring Seashores* [Eco-Journey]. Stevens, 1994.
(6) Bellamy, David. *The Rock Pool* [Our Changing World]. Potter, 1988.
(7) Campbell, Andrew. *Seashore Life* [Nature Library]. Exeter, 1983.
(8) Coburn, Doris K. *A Spit Is a Piece of Land* [Landforms in the U.S.A.]. Messner, 1978.
(9) Hansen, Judith. *Seashells in My Pocket: A Child's Guide to Exploring the Atlantic Coast from Maine to North Carolina*. Appalachian, 1988.
(10) Hecht, Jeff. *Shifting Shores: Rising Seas, Retreating Coastlines*. Scribner's, 1990.
(11) Hester, Nigel. *The Living Seashore* [Watching Nature]. Watts, 1992.
(12) Hidetomo, Oda. *Animals of the Seashore* [Nature Close-Ups]. Raintree, 1986.
(13) Jennings, Terry. *Sea and Seashore* [The Young Scientist Investigates]. Childrens, 1989.
(14) Johnson, Sylvia A. *Coral Reefs* [Natural Science]. Lerner, 1984.
(15) Knapp, Brian. *Beach* [Land Shapes]. Grolier, 1993.
(16) Lambert, David, and McConnell, Anita. *Seas and Oceans* [The World of Science]. Facts on File, 1985.
(17) Lye, Keith. *Coasts* [Our World]. Silver, 1987.
(18) Malnig, Anita. *Where the Waves Break: Life at the Edge of the Sea* [Nature Watch]. Carolrhoda, 1985.

(19) Miller, Christina G., and Berry, Louise A. *Coastal Rescue: Preserving Our Seashores*. Atheneum, 1989.
(20) Padget, Sheila. *Coastlines* [Planet Earth]. Bookwright, 1984.
(21) Parker, Steve. *Seashore* [Eyewitness Books]. Knopf, 1989.
(22) Pope, Joyce. *The Seashore* [Action Science]. Watts, 1985.
(23) Silver, Donald M. *One Small Square: Seashore* [Scientific American Books for Young Readers]. Freeman, 1993.
(24) Silverstein, Alvin, and Silverstein, Virginia. *Life in a Tidal Pool*. Little, 1990.
(25) Souza, D. M. *Powerful Waves* [Nature in Action]. Carolrhoda, 1992.
(26) Stone, Lynn M. *Seashores* [EcoZones]. Rourke, 1989.
(27) Watts, Barrie. *24 Hours on a Seashore* [24 Hours]. Watts, 1990.
(28) Wood, Jenny. *Coral Reefs: Hidden Colonies of the Sea* [Wonderworks of Nature]. Stevens, 1991.
(29) Zim, Herbert S. *Seashores* [Golden Guides]. Western, 1955.

LIBRARY SKILLS RESOURCES

The Guinness Book of World Records. Facts on File, 1994.
Reader's Guide to Periodical Literature. H.W. Wilson.
Wood, Jenny. *The Children's Atlas of People & Places*. Millbrook, 1993.
The World Almanac and Book of Facts. World Almanac, 1994.

ADDITIONAL READING – YOUNGER

Amos, William H. *Exploring the Seashore* [Books for Young Explorers]. National Geographic, 1984.
Arnosky, Jim. *Near the Sea: A Portfolio of Paintings*. Lothrop, 1990.
Berger, Melvin. *Oil Spill!* [Let's Read-and-Find-Out Science]. Scholastic, 1994.
Carle, Eric. *A House for Hermit Crab*. Picture Book, 1987.
Coldrey, Jennifer. *Shells* [Eyewitness Explorers]. Kindersley, 1993.
Cole, Sheila. *When the Tide Is Low*. Lothrop, 1985.
Florian, Douglas. *Discovering Seashells*. Scribner's, 1986.
Foreman, Michael. *One World*. Little, 1990.
Gibbons, Gail. *Surrounded by Sea: Life on a New England Fishing Island*. Little, 1991.
Godall, John S. *The Story of the Seashore*. Macmillan, 1990.
Gunzi, Christiane. *Tide Pool* [Look Closer]. Kindersley, 1992.
Sabin, Louis. *Wonders of the Sea*. Troll, 1982.
Shells [What's Inside?]. Kindersley, 1991.
Taylor, Barbara. *Shoreline* [Look Closer]. Kindersley, 1993.
Whitlock, Ralph. *On the Seashore* [Use Your Eyes]. Wayland, 1986.
Zolotow, Charlotte. *The Seashore Book*. HarperCollins, 1991.

ADDITIONAL READING – OLDER

Bat-Ami, Miriam. *Sea, Salt, & Air*. Macmillan, 1993.
Canada's Incredible Coasts. National Geographic, 1991.

Carson, Rachel. *The Edge of the Sea*. Houghton, 1955.

Connor, Judith. *Seashore Life on Rocky Coasts*. Monterey Bay Aquarium Foundation, 1994.

Crump, Donald J., editor. *The World's Wild Shores*. National Geographic, 1990.

Dixon, Dougal. *The Changing Earth* [Young Geographer]. Thomson, 1993.

Gowell, Elizabeth Tayntor. *Sea Jellies: Rainbows in the Sea* [New England Aquarium Books]. Watts, 1993. (Also other books in series.)

Hirschi, Ron. *Save Our Oceans and Coasts* [One Earth]. Bantam, 1993.

Holling, Holling Clancy. *Pagoo*. Houghton, 1957.

Kricher, John C., and Morrison, Gordon. *Peterson First Guide to Seashores*. Houghton, 1992.

Lazier, Christine. *Seashore Life* [Young Discovery Library]. Young Discovery, 1991.

McMillan, Bruce. *A Beach for the Birds*. Houghton, 1993.

Mason, Helen. *Life at the Seashore*. Durkin, 1990.

O'Dell, Scott. *The Cruise of the Arctic Star*. Houghton, 1973.

Patent, Dorothy Hinshaw. *Pelicans*. Clarion, 1992.

Streib, Sally. *Treasures by the Sea* [Starburst]. Pacific, 1991.

Swanson, Diane. *Safari Beneath the Sea: The Wonder of the North Pacific Coast*. Sierra, 1994.

See also: books in SEAS AND OCEANS, ISLANDS AND CORAL REEFS, and PONDS AND WETLANDS units.

FOR MORE INFORMATION ABOUT SEASHORES, WRITE TO:

American Shore and Beach Preservation Association

CAPE (Children's Alliance for Protection of the Environment)

Center for Coastal Studies

Coastal Conservation Association

Coastal States Organization

Friends of the Earth

National Audubon Society

National Wildlife Federation

Natural Resources Defense Council

Sierra Club

United Citizens Coastal Protection League

PONDS AND WETLANDS

Ponds and wetlands provide Earth with some of its richest habitats. A great variety of plant and animal life thrive in these fertile ecosystems. Yet, until recently, people did not realize how vital a role swamps, bogs, marshes, and ponds play in maintaining a healthy environment. We must do all we can to save our wetlands from being drained, filled in, or polluted.

LIBRARY SKILLS

a. Look in the subject section of the card or online catalog to find books about some of the animals listed in the spelling/vocabulary exercise, item **a**. Are your books fiction or nonfiction?

b. Look up Wetlands in *Scholastic Environmental Atlas of the United States* to answer the following questions: 1) What ratio of all endangered species live in wetlands? 2) How do wetlands protect our environment? 3) Which states have a lot of wetland area? 4) What is the Swampbusters Program?

c. Use *The Children's Animal Atlas* to color wetland areas on a map of the world. Color saltmarsh areas in blue, and mangrove swamps in red. Where do these areas overlap?

d. In *The New Book of Popular Science*, look up Succession. What does this environmental phenomenon mean in relation to ponds and wetlands?

e. Use *Atlas of Environmental Issues* to answer the following questions about drainage: 1) What areas are usually drained and why? 2) How has Britain encouraged drainage in the past? 3) What percent of lowland meadow, lowland bog, and lowland marsh have been lost in Britain since World War II? 4) Why is Sudd Swamp endangered? 5) How are environmentalists working to save Halvergate Marshes?

f. Use *The Information Please Environmental Atlas* to look up the procedure that must be followed in order to change a wetland. What can the public do to prevent this change?

g. Look up Mangroves in *Atlas of Endangered Species* to answer the following: 1) List four types of mangrove root. 2) Name five threatened or endangered mangrove animals and tell where they live. 3) How much annual rainfall is necessary for mangroves? What is the minimum temperature in these areas? 4) List five threats to mangrove trees. 5) List five ways that humans can benefit from managing and protecting mangroves. 6) What is the Ramsar Convention?

ARTS AND CRAFTS

a. Many wetland birds live in nests. Use cattails, grass, and twigs to make a bird's nest. (2, 7, 15, 19)

b. *Group project:* Make a pond diorama in a shallow, waterproof box. Place water in a container and set it in the box. Add rocks, dried plants, and small figures of pond animals to the diorama. (9, 14, 15, 18, 22, 24)

c. Create a slogan to encourage people to save our nation's wetlands. Draw a poster to illustrate your slogan.

d. Draw a picture that illustrates the food web of a pond, marsh, or swamp. (3, 6, 9, 14, 16, 17, 21)

e. Make a dried flower arrangement using dried pond grasses, cattails, and other wetland plants. (15)

f. In time, a pond may gradually become a marsh, swamp, then a forest. Make a series of four drawings or collages that illustrate this change. Include various plants, trees, and animals that are appropriate to each scene. At the bottom or on the back of each picture, list the plants and animals that are shown. (3, 6, 7, 16, 17, 19, 21, 22)

g. *Group project:* Make a diorama of a mangrove or cypress swamp in a shallow, waterproof box. Use modeling clay to create the trees. Add water, plants, and animal figures to simulate the swamp. (3, 6, 7, 17, 21)

SPELLING/VOCABULARY

a. Complete a word search puzzle of animals that live in ponds, marshes and swamps: mudskipper, goose, newt, duck, heron, coot, oyster, alligator, muskrat, damselfly, salamander, racoon, turtle, mosquito, snail, frog, flamingo, shrew, butterfly, otter. (1, 2, 4, 5, 6, 7, 9, 10, 13, 15, 17, 18, 19, 20, 23, 24)

b. Complete a crossword puzzle of wetland plants: sundew, bladderwort, sphagnum, cattail, reed, water lily, iris, duckweed, mangrove, marsh marigold, pondweed, crowfoot, hornwort, algae, cypress, cranberry, papyrus, sawgrass, moss, rice.   (2, 5, 6, 7, 9, 10, 15, 17, 18, 19, 20, 21)

c. Divide a piece of paper into six columns. Label them: bugs, birds, reptiles, amphibians, fish, and mammals. Your teacher will give you a list of pond and wetland animals. (See the library skills exercise, item **a.**) Place the names of each animal in the proper column.   (1, 2, 5, 6, 7, 9, 10, 13, 15, 16, 17, 18, 19, 20, 23)

d. Complete a word search puzzle of wetland habitats: bog, swamp, marsh, fen, pocosin, muskeg, Everglades, pond, saltmarsh, mangrove swamp, billabong, estuary, bayou, cypress swamp, tundra, bottomland, prairie pothole, riparian, delta, spring pool.   (2, 4, 6, 10, 13, 14, 21)

e. Complete these fill-in-the-blanks facts about ponds and wetlands: 1) An (amphibian) lives part of its life in the water, and part of its life on land. The term comes from a Greek word that means "two lives." 2) Early Spanish explorers named the (alligator) "el lagarto," which means "the lizard." 3) In their Native American language, the word (Seminole) means "people that choose to be free." 4) The (Okefenokee) Swamp is named after an Indian word that means "land of the trembling earth." 5) (Ecosystem) is derived from the Greek word "oikes" which means house. 6) Native Americans refer to small islands of trees that grow in the Everglades as (hammocks), which means "trees that float." 7) The name (Everglades) comes from the Old Saxon word "glyde," which means "bright, shimmering place in a forest." 8) The transparent, microscopic creatures that live in ponds and wetlands are called (zooplankton), which is Greek for "tiny, drifting organisms." 9) Many wetland animals are (nocturnal), which means they are active at night. Those that are active in the day are (diurnal). 10) Wetland animals that live in the water are (aquatic). 11) A living thing that eats detritus, or dead plants and animals, is called a (detritivore). 12) (Halophytes) are plants that grow in soil covered by salt water. 13) Female mosquitoes suck blood from animals and humans through a feeding tube called a (proboscis). 14) (Malaria) is a dangerous disease carried by mosquitoes.   (1, 2, 4, 6, 7, 11, 17, 22)

f. Following is a list of terms related to the food chain of ponds and wetlands. Match these terms to their definitions: photosynthesis, detritus, herbivore, carnivore, omnivore, ecosystem, invertebrate, vertebrate, algae, predator, scavenger, prey, parasite, decomposer, nutrients, larva, fungi, nymph, anaerobic bacteria, metamorphosis.   (3, 4, 5, 7, 13, 14, 16, 21)

g. Define these terms which relate to the wetlands environment: brackish, peat, niche, sedge, succession, water table, hammock, adaptation, aerated, salinity, water-logged, floating plants, submerged plants, free-floating plants, carnivorous plants, marginal plants, surface film, floodplain, freshwater, saltwater.   (3, 5, 13, 14, 21)

GEOGRAPHY

a. Over a period of many years, a wetland area may change until it becomes dry land. Put the following ecosystems in the order that this change would occur: marsh, forest, pond, swamp. Look at photographs of nature scenes. Identify pictures of marshes, forests, ponds, and swamps. How can you tell which is which? (3, 5, 6, 17, 19, 21)

b. On a map of your state, mark all the pond and wetland areas. If possible, also mark areas that used to be wetlands. What happened to them?

c. On a map of the United States, color in areas of inland and coastal bogs, marshes, and swamps. Label the Everglades, the Okefenokee Swamp, the Bear River Marshes, and other major wetlands. (3, 13, 21)

d. How did glaciers help to form some North American ponds and wetlands? What are some other natural and artificial origins of ponds and wetlands? (3, 14, 20, 21)

e. What is a national wildlife refuge? On a map of the United States, locate the refuges that are wetlands. Why were these refuges established? Also locate some bird and wildlife sanctuaries in the United States. (3, 10, 11, 13, 17, 21)

f. Make a list of ten pond or wetland animals and plants. Tell in what parts of the world each can be found. (5, 6, 10, 13, 23)

g. What does it mean to reclaim (or drain) a marsh or swamp? Which states and foreign countries have reclaimed wetland areas? How much wetland area has been reclaimed by these states and countries? Why have some areas stopped reclaiming wetlands? (5, 6, 10, 13, 21)

MATH

a. Pond life consists of plants, animals that eat plants (herbivores), and animals that eat other animals (carnivores). The life in a typical pond includes 87 percent plants, 10 percent herbivores, and 3 percent carnivores. Draw a chart to illustrate these numbers. (16)

b. Complete these fill-in-the-blanks math facts about pond and wetland animals. 1) The heron often flies (600) miles as it migrates. 2) A dragonfly can fly backwards, in place, or forward. Some can fly over (30) miles per hour. 3) More than (80) percent of Florida's alligators were killed before laws were made to protect them from hunters. 4) Of the (27) kinds of snakes in the Everglades, only four are poisonous. 5) The mother alligator lays between (30 and 40) eggs. 6) The loggerhead turtle may grow to be (500) pounds. 7) A female frog may lay between (5000 and 10000) eggs at a time. 8) Over (200) species of birds live in North American wetlands. (1, 17, 21)

    c. Look up the full-grown heights of the following pond birds: Great blue heron, common egret, ring-billed gull, Canada goose, gallinule, white pelican, common loon, osprey, killdeer, spotted sandpiper, pied-billed grebe, bobolink, mallard duck, whistling swan, coot. Then chart your answers on a graph. (6)

    d. Answer the following questions that relate to wetland animal population: 1) The number of birds in the Everglades has fallen from about 2.5 million to 250,000 in the last 100 years. What is the percentage of birds that are no longer present in the Everglades? 2) 400 years ago, an estimated 1,400 whooping cranes nested along the Gulf Coast during the winter. Because of habitat loss, there were only 25 cranes in the 1930s. What fraction of the original number were left? 3) About 400 million beavers once lived in North America. They were hunted almost to extinction for their fur. Now, there are about 9 million beavers. What fraction of their original population is this? 4) About 1,475,000 Florida alligators were killed for their skins between 1929 and 1938. How many alligators, on the average, were killed each year? 5) About 500,000 Louisiana alligators were hunted between 1940 and 1957, resulting in a 90 percent drop in their population. Approximately how many alligators lived in Louisiana before 1940? (5, 10, 13)

    e. In *The Information Please Environmental Atlas*, look up the State Ranking of Wetland Losses. What rank is your state, according to the number of acres lost? What rank is it according to percent lost? Approximately how many millions of wetland acres have been lost in the United States? What percentage of this total was lost in your state alone?

    f. Following is a list of pond and wetland insects. Convert their body sizes from inches to centimeters: saltmarsh mosquito, 0.2 inches; great diving beetle, 1.5"; horsefly, 0.9"; fisher spider, 0.7"; water scavenger beetle, 1.3"; giant water bug, 3.0"; green darner dragonfly, 2.5"; ephemera may fly, 1.0"; spiny-bellied orb weave, .5"; great silver water beetle, 2.0"; hawker dragonfly, body 2.75" and wingspan 3.75". Compare their sizes on a graph. (7, 9, 16, 22)

    g. Answer the following questions about wetland loss: 1) The biggest mangrove forest in the world is the Sundarbans, which grows along the banks of the Ganges River in India. About 600 square miles of mangrove trees have been cut down in the last 100 years. If there are 640 acres in a square mile, how many acres of mangroves were destroyed? 2) During the 1970s, the government of Bangladesh planted 62,000 acres of trees. How many acres were not replaced? 3) In the 1600s, the continental United States had about 200 million acres of wetlands. Now, there are approximately 95 million acres. What percent of the wetlands have been lost? 4) Of these 95 million acres,

95 percent are inland. How many acres of coastal wetlands remain? 5) The United States loses 500,000 acres of wetlands every year. At this rate, in how many years will the remaining 95 million acres be gone? 6) About 230 acres of the whooping crane's saltmarsh habitat in the Arkansas refuge have eroded due to boat traffic. At the rate of four acres per year, for how long has this destruction been going on? 7) Nebraska's Platte River wetland habitat has dwindled to an 80 mile stretch, from 300 miles, due to the river being diverted for irrigation. What fraction of the wetland remains?   (5, 10, 13)

MUSIC AND THEATER ARTS

a. Imitate the calls of some animals that live in a pond or wetland environment. When can you hear them?   (14, 17, 19, 20, 23)

b. Act out the movements of some wetland animals. Hop like a frog, crawl like an alligator, buzz around like a dragonfly, etc.   (14, 17, 19, 20, 23)

c. Play this memory game with your class. One person starts by saying: While exploring the Everglades, I saw an...(something that begins with the letter "a," such as alligator.) Each person, at his or her turn, repeats the list and adds an item that begins with the next letter of the alphabet. To make the game more challenging, make up a physical movement (such as a chomping motion with your arms) to go with each new word. See how many words and movements you can remember.   (7, 10, 17, 19, 20, 21, 23)

d. *Small group project:* Act out a scene of Seminole life in the Everglades, such as a hunt or the Green Corn Ceremony.   (12)

e. Present a puppet show of a Native American legend that takes place in a swamp or involves wetland creatures.   (3, 11)

f. The comic strip *Pogo* takes place in the Okefenokee Swamp. Create puppets of Walt Kelly's characters and present a Pogo puppet show.

g. Listen to *Peaceful Pond* (Soundings of the Planet), *Everglades* (Nature Recordings), or another nature soundtrack of a pond or wetlands environment.

ENGLISH COMPOSITION

a. Think about what you can see and do at a pond. Then write a story called "A Day at the Pond."   (2, 9, 14, 15, 18, 20, 22, 24)

b. Write a story about the adventures of a pond or wetland animal.   (1, 2, 4, 5, 7, 9, 15, 18, 22, 24)

c. Create your own field guide of ten or more plants and animals that live in ponds and wetlands. For each one, include a picture of it and a short description of its appearance and how it lives.   (4, 6, 7, 9, 14, 15, 16, 18, 22, 23)

d. Write a description of an insect, frog, or other wetland creature that starts its life as an egg. Tell how it changes until the animal grows into its adult form.   (1, 4, 5, 9, 15, 18, 22, 24)

e. Many folktales and legends have been written about wetlands and the animals that live there. Read some of these stories. Then create a legend of your own.   (3, 11)

f. Many tourists visit the Florida Everglades and other wetland areas that have been designated as national wildlife refuges or bird sanctuaries. Write a travel guide that explains what a visitor to one of these places might see. Specify which place you are describing. Include some pictures of the plants and animals that live there.   (3, 6, 10, 11, 13, 17)

g. Many wetland animals, such as the alligator, are endangered. Pretend you are a news reporter who can talk to animals. Write an imaginary interview with an endangered wetland animal. Have the animal explain its role in the ecosystem, why it is at risk, and what should be done to correct the problem.   (5, 11, 13, 23, 24)

SCIENCE

Note: You may want to set up an aquarium in the classroom so that students can observe pond life up close. Include some pond water, plants, and small animals or eggs. Students can help care for these pets and watch them grow while studying this unit.

a. What is the difference between a marsh and a swamp? How are they formed? What is a bog? Which of these has trees?   (5, 6, 10, 13, 19, 21)

b. What is a mangrove swamp? How is it different from a saltmarsh? Where are mangrove swamps located? Name some animals that live in each of these environments.   (2, 6, 7, 13, 17, 19, 21)

c. Collect a jar of water from a local pond or marsh. Carefully place a drop onto a slide and place it under a microscope or magnifying glass. What do you see? Try to identify some of these organisms.   (1, 4, 9, 14, 15, 16, 18, 22, 24)

d. Wetland creatures thrive in warm weather, but the winters are more difficult. Tell how three different types of pond or wetland animals manage to survive the winter or dry season.   (1, 3, 9, 15, 16, 17, 18, 20)

e. What is surface film (sometimes called pond scum)? Is it a sign of a healthy or unhealthy pond environment? Tell why.   (5, 9, 14, 16)

f. Name some of the different types of wetlands, and list the main characteristics of each. Are they inland or coastal? What types of plants or trees grow there? Do they contain salt or fresh water? (3, 7, 10, 13, 15, 21)

g. What is peat? Where and how does it form? How can it be used? What is sphagnum? Where does it grow? How is it different from other plants? What roles do peat and sphagnum play in wetland ecosystems? (3, 5, 6, 9, 10, 13, 21)

HISTORY/SOCIOLOGY

a. Many wetland animals have become extinct or endangered. Why? Tell how one wetland animal has struggled for survival. (4, 10, 13, 17, 20, 23)

b. Papyrus is one type of marsh plant. How did ancient Egyptians use papyrus? (5, 8)

c. Many ponds, past and present, have been made by people. Why? How have people used ponds in the past? How are they used now? (9, 14, 20)

d. The Seminole Indians have lived for a long time in parts of the Florida Everglades. Trace the history of this Native American tribe. How have they survived in the Everglades? Why did many Seminoles leave Florida? (11, 12, 17)

e. During the Revolutionary War, American General Francis Marion was known as "The Swamp Fox." Why? Read some historical accounts of the Swamp Fox. (3, 11)

f. Laws have been written to protect alligators, birds, and other endangered wetland animals. Conservation laws have been made to save wetlands. Write a report on one of these laws. (3, 5, 10, 11, 13, 17)

g. Look up information on a United States wetland area that is or was at risk. How did it become endangered? What, if anything, has been done to correct the problem? How have people's attitudes and actions harmed or helped the wetland? (3, 10, 11, 13, 17)

TOPICS FOR DISCUSSION

a. Discuss the food web in a pond, marsh, or swamp. How is nature "recycled" in these wetland ecosystems? (6, 7, 9, 14, 15, 19, 21)

b. Why do some ponds disappear? What can be done to preserve ponds? How can you make a pond? (5, 9, 14, 16, 20, 24)

c. Why are plants important to wetlands? Name some plants that grow only in wetland environments. (2, 3, 5, 6, 7, 9, 10, 13, 15, 16, 17, 19, 21, 23)

d. What is unique about mangrove trees? How do they grow? How is life in certain ecosystems dependent upon mangrove trees? Why are mangrove swamps in danger? (2, 3, 5, 7, 11, 13, 17, 21)

e. Why is the Florida Everglades a unique environment? How is it different from other swamps and marshes? (2, 3, 6, 10, 11, 13, 17, 21)

f. Why have many wetlands been destroyed? Why is it important to protect and restore wetlands? (2, 3, 4, 5, 6, 9, 10, 11, 13, 17, 21)

g. Why do people build dams, floodgates, canals, and reservoirs near wetland areas? What effect do they have on wetland the ecosystem? (3, 5, 6, 10, 11, 13, 17, 20, 21)

SUGGESTED RESOURCES

(1) *Animals in Rivers and Ponds* [Animals and Their Homes]. Raintree, 1988.
(2) Caitlin, Stephen. *Wonders of Swamps and Marshes*. Troll, 1990.
(3) Cowing, Sheila. *Our Wild Wetlands*. Messner, 1980.
(4) Downer, Ann. *Spring Pool: A Guide to the Ecology of Temporary Ponds* [New England Aquarium—Endangered Habitats Books]. Watts, 1992.
(5) Ganeri, Anita. *Rivers, Ponds and Lakes* [Ecology Watch]. Dillon, 1991.
(6) Gore, Sheila. *Swamps* [Our Planet]. Troll, 1994.
(7) Greenaway, Theresa. *Swamp Life* [Look Closer]. Kindersley, 1993.
(8) Harris, Geraldine. *Ancient Egypt* [Cultural Atlas for Young People]. Facts on File, 1990.
(9) Hester, Nigel. *The Living Pond* [Watching Nature]. Watts, 1990.
(10) Hirschi, Ron. *Save Our Wetlands* [One Earth]. Delacorte, 1994.
(11) Laycock, George. *Exploring the Great Swamp*. McKay, 1978.
(12) Lee, Martin. *The Seminoles* [First Books—Indians of the Americas]. Watts, 1989.
(13) Liptak, Karen. *Saving Our Wetlands and Their Wildlife* [First Books—Our Environment]. Watts, 1991.
(14) Milkins, Colin S. *Discovering Pond Life* [Discovering Nature]. Bookwright, 1990.
(15) Parker, Steve. *Pond & River* [Eyewitness Books]. Knopf, 1988.
(16) Reid, George K. *Pond Life* [Golden Guides]. Western, 1967.
(17) Rom, Christine Sotnak. *Everglades* [National Parks]. Crestwood, 1988.
(18) Schwartz, David M. *The Hidden Life of the Pond* [Hidden Life]. Crown, 1988.
(19) Stone, Lynn M. *Marshes and Swamps* [New True Books]. Childrens, 1983.
(20) _____. *Pond Life* [New True Books]. Childrens, 1983.
(21) _____. *Wetlands* [EcoZones]. Rourke, 1989.
(22) Taylor, Barbara. *Pond Life* [Look Closer]. Kindersley, 1992.
(23) Taylor, Dave. *Endangered Wetland Animals* [Endangered Animals]. Crabtree, 1992.
(24) Wyler, Rose. *Puddles and Ponds* [An Outdoor Science Book]. Silver, 1990.

LIBRARY SKILLS RESOURCES

Burton, John, ed. *The Atlas of Endangered Species*. Macmillan, 1991.
Lambert, David. *The Children's Animal Atlas*. Millbrook, 1992.

Mattson, Mark. *Scholastic Environmental Atlas of the United States.* Scholastic, 1993.
Middleton, Nick. *Atlas of Environmental Issues* [Issues Atlases]. Facts on File, 1989.
The New Book of Popular Science. Grolier, 1994.
World Resources Institute. *The Information Please Environmental Almanac.* Houghton, 1993.

ADDITIONAL READING – YOUNGER

Amsel, Sheri. *A Wetland Walk.* Millbrook, 1993.
Brown, Mary Barrett. *Wings Along the Waterway.* Orchard, 1992.
Carrick, Carol. *Dark and Full of Secrets.* Clarion, 1984.
————. *Swamp Spring.* Macmillan, 1969.
Cortesi, Wendy W. *Explore a Spooky Swamp* [Books for Young Explorers]. National Geographic, 1979.
Cutchins, Judy, and Johnston, Ginny. *Scoots the Bog Turtle.* Atheneum, 1989.
Dewing, Jennifer Owings. *At the Edge of the Pond.* Little, 1987.
George, William T., and George, Lindsey Barrett. *Beaver at Long Pond.* Greenwillow, 1988.
Grace, Theresa. *A Picture Book of Swamp and Marsh Animals* [A Picture Book of. . .] Troll, 1992.
Guiberson, Brenda Z. *Spoonbill Swamp.* Holt, 1992.
Hirschi, Ron. *Where Are My Swans, Whooping Cranes, and Singing Loons?* [One Earth]. Bantam, 1992.
Langley, Andrew. *Wetlands* [Nature Search]. Morris, 1993.
Lavies, Bianca. *Lily Pad Pond.* Dutton, 1989.
Mitgutsch, Ali. *From Swamp to Coal* [Start to Finish]. Carolrhoda, 1985.
National Wildlife Federation Staff. *Wading into Wetlands.* National Wildlife, 1991.
Reiser, Lynn. *Tomorrow on Rocky Pond.* Greenwillow, 1993.
Rood, Ronald. *Wetlands* [Nature Study Book]. HarperCollins, 1994.
Rosen, Michael J. *All Eyes on the Pond.* Hyperion, 1994.
Uchida, Yoshiko, reteller. *The Magic Purse.* McElderry, 1993.
Williams, Terry Tempest. *Between Cattails.* Scribner's, 1985.

ADDITIONAL READING – OLDER

Bloch, Marie Halun. *Footprints in the Swamp.* Atheneum, 1985.
Bulla, Clyde Robert. *Charlie's House.* Knopf, 1993.
Caduto, Michael J., and Bruchac, Joseph. *Keepers of the Animals: Native American Stories and Wildlife Activities for Children.* Fulcrum, 1991.
Carr, Archie. *The Everglades* [The American Wilderness]. Time-Life, 1973.
Challand, Helen J. *Disappearing Wetlands* [Saving Planet Earth]. Childrens, 1992.
Couffer, Jack, and Couffer, Mike. *Salt Marsh Summer.* Putnam, 1978.
DeFelice, Cynthia. *Lost Man's River.* Macmillan, 1994.
Duffy, Trent. *The Vanishing Wetlands* [Impact]. Watts, 1994.
Freshet, Berniece. *Year on Muskrat Marsh.* Scribner's, 1974.
Ganeri, Anita. *Ponds and Pond Life* [Nature Detective]. Watts, 1993.
Kelly, Walt. *Complete Pogo, Vols. 1 & 2.* Fantagraph, 1992.

Kudlinsky, Kathleen V. *Night Bird: A Story of the Seminole Indians* [Once Upon a Time in America]. Viking, 1993.

Lavies, Bianca. *Mangrove Wilderness: Nature's Nursery*. Dutton, 1994.

McClung, Robert M. *Black Jack: Last of the Big Alligators*. Shoe String, 1991.

Marsh, Carole. *The Great Dismal: America's Scariest Swamp*. Gallopade, 1993.

Maruska, Edward J. *Amphibians: Creatures of the Land and Water* [Cincinnati Zoo Books]. Watts, 1994.

Milne, Lorus J., and Milne, Margery. *Mystery of the Bog Forest*. Dodd, 1984.

Rockwell, Jane. *All About Ponds* [Question and Answer Book]. Troll, 1984.

Russell, Franklin. *The Okefenokee Swamp* [The American Wilderness]. Time-Life, 1973.

Sawyer, Kem Knapp. *Margery Stoneman Douglas: Guardian of the Everglades*. Discovery, 1993.

See also: books in THE SEASHORE and RIVERS AND LAKES units.

FOR MORE INFORMATION ABOUT PONDS AND WETLANDS, WRITE TO:

American Friends of the Wildfowl
  and Wetlands Trust
American Wildlands
Clean Water Action
Friends of the Everglades
National Audubon Society

National Wildlife Federation
The Nature Conservancy
Sierra Club
Walden Forever Wild
Wetlands Watch

RIVERS AND LAKES

Rivers and lakes contain a very small percentage of the total water on Earth, yet all plant and animal life is dependent upon them. Throughout history, people have used rivers and lakes for travel, recreation, farming, industry, and energy. But in doing so, we have also polluted these nourishing waters. We must strive to keep our rivers and lakes clean, so that they will serve us well into the future.

LIBRARY SKILLS

a. In the *Scholastic Environmental Atlas of the United States*, read Draining the Rivers. What has happened to the Colorado River? How does the river now compare to how it was in the past? Who is arguing over this river and why? In your opinion, who is right?

b. Your teacher will give you the name of a lake or river. Look it up in an atlas or encyclopedia. In what continent is it located? Name some cities and towns that are located along this lake or river.

c. Look up the following river and lake animals in *Children's Guide to Endangered Animals*. For each one, tell where it lives and the main threats to its survival: olm, boto, West African dwarf crocodile, wide-eyed river martin, river terrapin.

d. Use *Lands and People* to answer the following questions: 1) How much of Finland's area consists of lakes? How are the lakes important to that country? 2) What are wadis (in the Sahara Desert)? 3) Look up one country. List some of its major lakes and rivers.

e. Use *The Guinness Book of World Records* to answer the following questions about lakes. In each case, tell the name of the lake and where it is located. 1) What is the deepest lake in the United States? In the world? 2) What is the largest lake within a lake? 3) How high is the highest navigable lake? 4) How far underground is the largest underground lake? Answer these questions about rivers: 1) What is the true source of the Amazon? 2) What is the largest delta? 3) Through how many states do the Mississippi River and its tributaries flow?

f. Use *The World Almanac and Book of Facts* to complete the following questions about waterfalls: 1) Make a chart, in descending order, of the ten highest waterfalls in the world. List the elevation of each waterfall. 2) Which North American state has the most (listed) waterfalls? Where in the state are the majority of them located? 3) Which country has two waterfalls with a combined elevation of over 5,200 feet? 4) How many of the famous waterfalls listed are falls of more than one leap? 5) Name the cascade with the highest elevation. 6) Which waterfall has the greatest mean annual flow? 7) Not including the United States, which country has the greatest combined elevation of famous waterfalls? 8) Which country's waterfalls have the greatest annual flow of water? To which river system do these waterfalls belong?

g. Use *The Information Please Environmental Almanac* to make a list of 25 threatened and endangered rivers. Why are these rivers at risk? What is being done to save them?

ARTS AND CRAFTS

a. Make a collage of pictures of river animals. (2, 17, 24, 25, 26)

b. Water from a river can be used to turn a water wheel. When the wheel turns, it can be used to drive machinery in a mill. As a group project, create a working model of a water wheel. (1, 7, 27)

c. Draw a picture or build a diorama that shows the different stages (ages) of a river. Show how the water flows quickly from high ground, slows down and meanders in the middle, and flows into the sea. Label the stages of your river. (1, 5, 17, 22, 24, 26)

d. Create a poster to make people aware of river or lake pollution. Tell what they can do to clean up the water. (13, 18, 23, 26)

e. Draw a diagram or build a model of a dam. Label each feature, such as the water wheel and sluice gate, and the direction of the water flow. You may choose to add a canal to your dam. (6, 18, 26)

f. Water that has been soiled should be cleaned in a wastewater treatment plant before it is allowed to re-enter a lake or river. Draw a diagram or build a model of a wastewater treatment plant. Label each part of the process and tell how it works. (18)

g. Do one of the following: 1) Build a model of a boat that may be used on a river or lake. 2) Build a model of a bridge that would cross over a river. (7, 8, 13, 24, 26)

SPELLING/VOCABULARY

a. Complete a matching exercise of bodies of water: river, waterfall, spring, stream, brook, lake, pond, pool, creek, sea, swamp, reservoir, lagoon, ford, estuary. (1, 5, 9, 10, 13, 17, 19, 22)

b. Complete a matching picture puzzle of animals that live in or near lakes and rivers: heron, frog, otter, beaver, eel, carp, kingfisher, trout, dragonfly, swan, duck, anaconda, flamingo, salmon, shrimp, newt, snail, crayfish, leech, goose. (1, 2, 3, 13, 17, 19, 26)

c. Complete a crossword puzzle of river system terms: watershed, basin, tributary, mouth, delta, glacier, channel, oxbow lake, canyon, floodplain, gorge, valley, meander, mudflats, rapids, riverbank, silt, bed, source, current. (1, 2, 5, 7, 9, 10, 13, 17, 19, 22, 24, 26)

d. Define each of these man-made structures and explain their uses: dam, canal, lock, dike, embankment, ditch, levee, reservoir, barrage, bridge, waterworks, water mill. Explain these different types of bridges: pontoon, girder, draw bridge, suspension, arch, truss, cantilever. (1, 8, 13, 19, 26)

e. Create a word puzzle of 15 or more plants found near rivers and lakes. (3, 10, 13, 17, 19, 24, 25, 26)

f. Define these terms that relate to river and lake pollution: eutrophication, PCBs, DDT, sewage, industrial waste, acid rain, water hyacinth, nitrates, pesticides, agricultural waste, mercury, lead, sediment, thermal pollution, bacteria. (13, 18, 23, 26)

g. Complete a crossword puzzle of terms related to the evolution of a lake: moraine, glacier, corrie, valley, sediment, overflow, shore, water table, marsh, peat, farmland, varves, meltwater, kame, kettle hole (or pothole), crater lake. (4, 21)

GEOGRAPHY

a. On a map of North America, label the Great Lakes. Also label some major rivers: the Mississippi, Columbia, Colorado, Yukon, Nelson, St. Lawrence, Mackenzie, Rio Grande, Missouri, Ohio. (16, 21, 22, 24, 26)

b. How do rivers change the shape of the land? Name some geographical formations, such as gorge, that are made by rivers. (2, 7, 9, 19, 22, 24, 26, 27)

c. On a map of the world, label these lakes: Great Bear Lake, Lake Chad, Caspian Sea, Lake Superior, Lake Titicaca, Lake Ontario, Lake Malawi, Dead Sea, Lake Winnipeg, Lake Torrens, Lake Victoria, Lake Huron, Lake Baikal, Lake Erie, Lake Eyre, Lake Michigan, Lake Tanganyika, Aral Sea, Great Slave Lake, Great Salt Lake. Which of these are salt water lakes? (21, 26)

d. On a map of the world, locate these rivers: Nile, Amazon, Rhine, Mississippi, Missouri, Yangtze, Ob, Irtysh, Amur, Zaire, Ganges, Hwang Ho,

Lena, Mackenzie, Tigris, Euphrates, Niger, Thames, Danube, Murray, Volga, Indus, Seine, Rhone, Yenisey, Mekong, Darling, Ohio, Brahmaputra. (1, 7, 22, 24, 26)

e. How are waterfalls formed? What is hard rock and soft rock, and what effect do they have on waterfalls? What are cataracts, cascades, and rapids? Where are these waterfalls located: Niagara Falls, Victoria Falls, Yosemite Falls, Sutherland Falls, Iguaçú Falls. (7, 19, 27)

f. Locate the Great Rift Lakes on a map of Africa. Find out some information about them, including their names, how they were formed, what rivers flow into them, how the people who live there use the lakes, their sizes, and other features of interest. (13)

g. On a map of the world, locate the 25 threatened and endangered rivers from the library skills exercise, item **g.** Locate them on a map of the world.

MATH

a. The Nile is the longest river in the world, but there are other rivers in Africa. Make a chart comparing the lengths of these African rivers (in miles): Limpopo, 1,000; Niger, 2,560; Nile, 4,170; Orange, 1,310; Sengal, 1,600; Volta, 940; Zaire, 2,920; Zambezi, 1,690. You may also want to make charts comparing the lengths of rivers in North America, South America, Asia, Europe, and Australia/New Zealand. (24)

b. Water flows down rivers at different speeds. If a sailboat floats 6 feet per second down a river, then how many feet will it travel in 12 seconds? 30 seconds? 57 seconds? 2½ minutes? 7 minutes? If a log travels 5 feet per second, then how many seconds did it take to travel 15 feet? 100 feet? 450 feet?

c. The Great Lakes, combined, form the largest body of fresh water in the world. To find out their total amount of surface water in square miles, add the following: Lake Superior, 31,700; Lake Huron, 23,000; Lake Michigan, 22,300; Lake Erie, 9,910; Lake Ontario, 7,550. (*The World Almanac and Book of Facts*)

d. What is the largest river on each continent? Write the length of each of these seven rivers, in miles and kilometers. What are the three largest river basins in the world? (12, 24)

e. The Colorado River has been carving a channel through the Grand Canyon for about 10 million years. In some places, the canyon is 2 km. deep. How many miles is that? At a rate of 1 cm. per every 70 years, how many years will it take for the Colorado River to cut into the rock another meter? Another kilometer?

f. The world's highest dams, measured in meters, are: The Rogun, 335 meters; Chirkei, 233, Inguri, 272, Sayano-Shushensk, 242, and Nurek, 300 (all in the former USSR); Mica, 242 (Canada); Mauvoisn, 237 (Switzerland); Tehri, 261, Kishau, 253, Bhakra, 226 (India); Chicoasen, 261 (Mexico); Chivor, 2,337; Guavio, 243 (Columbia); Ertan, 245 (China); Hoover, 221, and Oroville, 230 (United States); El Cajón, 2,334 (Honduras); and Mratinje, 220 (former Yugoslavia). Convert these heights from meters to feet. Then make a chart that lists all 20 dams, plus their heights in meters and feet, in descending order.

g. Answer the following questions: 1) The European eel is born in the Sargasso Sea, in the North Atlantic Ocean. Then it swims 3,750 miles to the rivers of Europe. If it takes three years to make this journey, how many miles does it swim, on the average, per day? 2) Lake Baikal in Siberia is home to many species of animals and plants. Three-quarters of these are not found anywhere else in the world. If there are 1,200 animal species and 500 plant species living there, how many of these are unique to Lake Baikal? 3) The shortest freshwater fish in the world is the dwarf pygmy goby of the Philippines. It is about .3 inch in length. One of the largest freshwater fish is the South American pirarucu, which averages 6.5 feet long. How many gobies would you have to line up, head to tail, to equal the length of one pirarucu? 4) The anaconda of the Amazon River is the heaviest snake in the world. A 30 foot snake can weigh 440 lbs. How many ounces would a dozen 30 foot anacondas weigh? 5) Full-grown Atlantic salmon weigh about 10 lbs. each, chinook salmon weigh 22 lbs., and pink salmon weigh 5 lbs. If 8 salmon weigh a total of 111 lbs., how many are there of each type? (13, *The Guiness Book of World Records*)

MUSIC AND THEATER ARTS

a. What is a canal? Why are canals built? Where is the Erie Canal? Sing the folk song, "The Erie Canal." (6, 16, 17)

b. In the mid–1800s, American composer Steven Foster wrote many popular songs. These were often sung on steamboats that traveled the Mississippi River, providing entertainment to the people that lived along it. Sing some of Foster's famous showboat tunes, such as "Oh Suzanna!," "Old Folks at Home," and "My Old Kentucky Home."

c. A Native American story about a Chippewa spirit named Nanabazhoo takes place along the shores of Lake Superior. The poet Henry Wadsworth Longfellow based his poem "Hiawatha," on Nanabazhoo. He referred to Lake Superior by its Indian name, Gitchee Goomee, which means "Great Water." Read Longfellow's poem as a readers' theater piece. Listen to *Honor the Earth Powwow: Songs of the Great Lakes Indians* (Rykodisc).

d. Some popular musical plays take place on a river. Listen to some songs from *Showboat, Big River,* or other musicals. On what river does the play take place? Act out a short scene from one of these plays.

e. Rivers and lakes have inspired many composers to write music about them. Listen to "The Blue Danube" by Johann Strauss or another orchestral piece. Try to identify the instruments that are played.

f. Listen to *Loons on Mirror Lake, Mountain Stream* (Nature Recordings), or another recording of nature sounds. What animals can you identify?

g. Many popular songs from the past 30 years have been written about lakes and rivers, such as "The Wreck of the Edmund Fitzgerald" by Gordon Lightfoot, and "Proud Mary" by John C. Fogerty. Listen to some of these songs. Identify the river or lake that the song is about.

ENGLISH COMPOSITION

a. Write a story using at least five of the terms from the spelling/vocabulary exercise, item **a.**

b. Write a story about a mammal, bird, or fish that lives near or in a river. What does the animal eat? How does it live?   (3, 13, 17, 25, 26)

c. Find out information about a lake or river in your state that is polluted. Write to your senator or congressman to protest this pollution. Ask that some action be taken to solve the problem.

d. Tell the story of a drop of water as it goes through the hydrological (or water) cycle. Have the drop of water be a part of a lake or river at some point in the story.   (1, 18, 19, 24, 26, 27)

e. Write a story about what happens to a river or lake when it becomes polluted. Make sure to tell what type of pollution is involved, and where it is coming from.   (13, 18, 19, 23, 26)

f. Write a description of a waterfall or estuary. Use colorful language to convey the sights and sounds of these forces of nature.   (19, 27)

g. American author Mark Twain took his name from a Mississippi River expression. What does his name mean? Read a story by Mark Twain which takes place on the river. Then write your own river adventure.

SCIENCE

Note: If you live near a lake or river, you may want to take the class on a field trip. Have students note the plants and animals they see, and any other interesting features.

a. What was the Ice Age? How do ice and glaciers cause lakes to form? (1, 4, 16, 21, 26)

b. What is a dam? Why do people build dams? How do they provide electricity? (9, 10, 18, 19, 26, 27)

c. Name some animals and plants that live in streams or rivers. How does the speed of the water flow affect the types of life that are found? (10, 13, 17, 24, 25, 26)

d. Trace the life cycle of a Pacific salmon. How does it depend on rivers for survival? How has man disrupted the salmon's migration patterns? (13, 17, 24, 25, 26, 27)

e. What effect do pesticides and fertilizers have on lakes, rivers, and the animals that live there? (7, 10, 13, 18, 19, 23, 26)

f. What causes acid rain? How does it enter lakes and rivers? What are the effects of acid rain? What can be done to prevent it? What effect does lime have on lakes affected by acid rain? (13, 18, 23, 26)

g. Why do lakes and rivers need a large supply of oxygen? How do some types of pollution use up oxygen? What happens if the oxygen supply in river and lakes is too low? (7, 13, 18, 23)

HISTORY/SOCIOLOGY

a. How was the Nile River important to the Ancient Egyptians? (1, 10, 13, 18, 19, 24, 26)

b. Name some rivers and lakes that have been severely polluted by humans. Are they still polluted, or have some been cleaned up? (13, 18, 23, 24, 26)

c. Why have so many cities developed near rivers and lakes? How does the construction of canals and bridges cause cities to grow? (2, 6, 7, 19, 26)

d. What is the importance of the Ganges River to people of the Hindu faith? How do they use the Ganges? (7, 13, 18)

e. Many important historical events occurred along the Great Lakes, such as the French and Indian War and the War of 1812. Write a report on one historical event that occurred in the Great Lakes area. (14)

f. There are many nonfiction books about river explorations. Read one book. Draw a map or timeline that lists the highlights of the exploration. (12, 14, 28)

g. Choose one river or lake, anywhere in the world, and trace its history. Who discovered it? How was it used in the past? How is it used now? What major cities, industries, etc. have developed on its banks? Discuss any problems, such as pollution or flooding.   (7, 11, 12, 13, 14, 15, 18, 19, 23, 26, 28)

TOPICS FOR DISCUSSION

a. What are some causes of river and lake pollution? How does this pollution affect animals and people?   (1, 10, 13, 16, 18, 19, 24, 26)

b. Name some ways that people use lakes.   (4, 13, 18, 26)

c. Name some ways that people use rivers.   (1, 5, 7, 9, 10, 13, 17, 18, 19, 24, 26)

d. People often use lakes and rivers for recreation, such as fishing or boating. Name some more recreational uses. How can these pastimes endanger the natural habitats of lakes and rivers?   (7, 13, 17, 24, 26)

e. How are rivers and lakes important for agriculture? For industry? How can industry and agriculture harm lakes and rivers?   (7, 10, 18, 19, 26)

f. Name some situations which may cause a river to flood. What can be done to prevent or decrease the chances of flooding? What are some advantages and disadvantages of living on a flood plain?   (7, 13, 15, 18, 19, 20, 24, 26)

g. Why are dams built? Do they help or harm the environment? Present your argument for one side of this debate.   (7, 10, 13, 15, 18, 19, 24, 26)

SUGGESTED RESOURCES

(1) Bailey, Donna. *Rivers* [Facts About]. Steck-Vaughn, 1990.
(2) Baker, Susan. *First Look at Rivers* [First Look]. Stevens, 1991.
(3) Behm, Barbara J., and Bonar, Veronica. *Exploring Lakeshores* [Eco-Journey]. Stevens, 1994.
(4) Bender, Lionel. *Lake* [The Story of the Earth]. Watts, 1989.
(5) _____. *River* [The Story of the Earth]. Watts, 1988.
(6) Boyer, Edward. *River and Canal*. Holiday, 1986.
(7) Browne, Tom. *Rivers and People* [Nature's Landscapes]. Silver, 1982.
(8) Carlisle, Norman, and Carlisle, Madelyn. *Bridges* [New True Books]. Childrens, 1983.
(9) _____. *Rivers* [New True Books]. Childrens, 1982.
(10) Costa-Pau, Rosa. *Protecting Our Rivers and Lakes* [The Junior Library of Ecology]. Chelsea, 1994.
(11) The Cousteau Society. *An Adventure in the Amazon*. Simon & Schuster, 1992.
(12) [First Books—Famous Rivers of the World] series. Watts.
(13) Ganeri, Anita. *Rivers, Ponds and Lakes* [Ecology Watch]. Dillon, 1991.
(14) Granfield, Linda. *All About Niagara Falls*. Morrow, 1988.
(15) Hecht, Jeff. *Shifting Shores: Rising Seas, Retreating Coastlines*. Scribner's, 1990.

(16) Henderson, Kathy. *The Great Lakes* [New True Books]. Childrens, 1989.

(17) Hester, Nigel. *The Living River* [Watching Nature]. Watts, 1991.

(18) Hoff, Mary, and Rodgers, Mary M. *Rivers and Lakes* [Our Endangered Planet]. Lerner, 1991.

(19) Jennings, Terry. *Rivers* [Exploring Our World]. Cavendish, 1987.

(20) Knapp, Brian. *Flood* [World Disasters]. Steck-Vaughn, 1990.

(21) _____. *Lake* [Land Shapes]. Grolier, 1993.

(22) _____. *River* [Land Shapes]. Grolier, 1993.

(23) Leggett, Dennis, and Leggett, Jeremy. *Troubled Waters* [Operation Earth]. Cavendish, 1991.

(24) Mariner, Tom. *Rivers* [Earth in Action]. Cavendish, 1990.

(25) Parker, Steve. *Pond & River* [Eyewitness Books]. Knopf, 1988.

(26) Rowland-Entwistle, Theodore. *Rivers and Lakes* [Our World]. Silver, 1986.

(27) Wood, Jenny. *Waterfalls: Nature's Thundering Splendor.* [Wonderworks of Nature]. Stevens, 1991.

(28) [The World Explorers] series. Chelsea.

LIBRARY SKILLS RESOURCES

Few, Roger. *Children's Guide to Endangered Animals.* Macmillan, 1993.

The Guinness Book of World Records. Facts on File, 1994.

Lands and Peoples. Grolier, 1993.

Mattson, Mark. *Scholastic Environmental Atlas of the United States.* Scholastic, 1993.

The World Almanac and Book of Facts. World Almanac, 1994.

World Resources Institute. *The Information Please Environmental Almanac.* Houghton, 1993.

ADDITIONAL READING – YOUNGER

Ancona, George. *Riverkeeper.* Macmillan, 1990.

Ayer, Elanor. *Our Great Rivers and Waterways* [I Know America]. Millbrook, 1993.

Bellamy, David. *The River* [Our Changing World]. Potter, 1988.

Bushey, Jerry. *The Barge Book.* Carolrhoda, 1984.

Cherry, Lynn. *A River Ran Wild.* Harcourt, 1992.

Gilliland, Judith Heide. *River.* Clarion, 1993.

Hartford, John. *Steamboat in a Cornfield.* Crown, 1986.

Hirschi, Ron. *Loon Lake.* Dutton, 1991.

Kovacs, Deborah. *Moonlight on the River.* Viking, 1993.

Locker, Thomas. *Where the River Begins.* Dial, 1984.

Longfellow, Henry Wadsworth. *Hiawatha.* Dial, 1983.

McCauley, Jane R. *Let's Explore the River* [Books for Young Explorers]. National Geographic, 1988.

Say, Allen. *The Lost Lake.* Houghton, 1989.

_____. *River Dream.* Houghton, 1988.

Stewart, Gail. *Rivermen* [The Wild West in American History]. Rourke, 1990.

Taylor, Barbara. *River Life* [Look Closer]. Kindersley, 1992.

_____. *Rivers and Oceans: Geography Facts and Experiments* [Young Discoverers]. Kingfisher, 1993.

Whitlock, Ralph. *By the River* [Use Your Eyes]. Wayland, 1986.
Williams, Vera B. *Three Days on the River in a Red Canoe*. Greenwillow, 1981.
Yolen, Jane. *Letting Swift River Go*. Little, 1992.

ADDITIONAL READING – OLDER

Big River (sound recording). MCI, 1985.
Bramwell, Martyn. *Rivers and Lakes* [Earth Science Library]. Watts, 1994.
Carter, Alden R. *The War of 1812: Second Fight for Independence* [First Books – War].
     Watts, 1992.
Cheripko, Jan. *Voices of the River: Adventures on the Delaware*. Boyds Mills, 1994.
Cohen, Peter Zachary. *The Great Red River Raft*. Whitman, 1984.
Collier, James Lincoln. *When the Stars Begin to Fall*. Delacorte, 1986.
Cumming, David. *The Ganges Delta and Its People* [People and Places]. Thomson,
     1994.
David, Andrew, and Moran, Tom. *River Thrill Sports* [Superwheels and Thrill Sports].
     Lerner, 1983.
Esbensen, Barbara Juster. *Playful Slider: The North American River Otter*. Little, 1993.
Foster, Stephen. *Stephen Foster Songbook*. Dover, 1974.
Hauptman, William, and Miller, Roger. *Big River: The Adventures of Huckleberry Finn*.
     Grove, 1986.
Hobbs, Will. *Downriver*. Atheneum, 1991.
Holling, Holling Clancy. *Minn of the Mississippi*. Houghton, 1951.
_____. *Paddle-to-the-Sea*. Houghton, 1941.
Kern, Jerome, and Hammerstein, Oscar. *Show Boat*. EMI, 1988.
Lambert, David, and the Diagram Group. *The Field Guide to Geology*. Facts on File,
     1988.
Leopold, Luna B., and Davis, Kenneth S. *Water* [Life Science Library]. Time, 1960.
McNeese, Tim. *America's Early Canals* [Americans on the Move]. Crestwood, 1993.
_____. *Early River Travel* [Americans on the Move]. Crestwood, 1993.
[Rivers of the World] series. Raintree, 1993.
Rounds, David. *Cannonball River Tales*. Sierra, 1992.
Shepard, John. *The Stream Team on Patrol* [Target Earth]. Abdo, 1993.
Stein, R. Conrad. *The Story of the Erie Canal* [Cornerstones of Freedom]. Childrens
     1985.
Twain, Mark. *The Adventures of Huckleberry Finn*. Morrow, 1994.

See also: books in WATER and PONDS AND WETLANDS units.

FOR MORE INFORMATION ABOUT RIVERS AND LAKES, WRITE TO:

American Rivers
American Water Works Association
American Wildlands
The Cousteau Society
The Freshwater Foundation
Friends of the River Foundation

Great Lakes United
Save Our Streams
Upper Mississippi River Conservation
     Commission
Worldwatch Institute

RAINFORESTS

Rainforests cover only a small portion of our Earth, yet they are vital to our survival. They are home to over half of all the plant and animal species on Earth. Their dense and diverse vegetation greatly affects the weather and air we breathe. But the rainforests are being destroyed at an alarming rate. The health of the entire planet will suffer unless these lush and beautiful habitats are saved.

LIBRARY SKILLS

a. Choose a nonfiction book about rainforests. Answer the following questions: Who is the author? Is this book part of a series? If so, what is the name of the series? In what year was the book published? On what page will you find information about rainforest animals? Plants? Weather? Does the book have a Table of Contents? An Index?

b. In the *Atlas of Environmental Issues,* look up Deforestation to answer the following questions: 1) How many acres of Brazilian rainforest are destroyed each year? What percent is that? 2) What is the percent of destruction of rainforests in the Ivory Coast? 3) How does the building of roads in Brazil lead to further rainforest destruction?

c. Use *The Children's Atlas of People & Places* to look up the capital and population of the following rainforest countries: Brazil, Gabon, Singapore, Madagascar, Liberia, Philippines, French Guiana, Congo.

d. Use the *Children's Guide to Endangered Animals* to look up the following endangered animals that live in rainforests. For each animal, tell where it lives and the main threats to its survival: Congo peacock, emperor tamarin, orangutan, Rodrigues flying fox, Queen Alexandria's birdwing, toucan barbet, helmeted hornbill, kauai o-o, giant armadillo, aye-aye.

e. In *The Guinness Book of World Records,* under The Living World, look up Insects, Reptiles, Birds, and Plant Kingdom. Find five facts about animals or plants that live in a tropical rainforest.

f. In *Lands and Peoples,* look up countries in which there are tropical rainforests. Then make a list of tribes that inhabit these lands.

g. Use *The Information Please Environmental Almanac* to answer the following: 1) What is ecotourism? Why is it becoming popular? What is the effect of ecotourism on rainforests? 2) By their estimate, in how many years will all tropical rainforest be destroyed if deforestation continues at current rates? 3) What is the top country for flowering plants? Approximately how many species of plants grow there? What is the top country for mammals, birds, reptiles, and amphibians, and approximately how many species live there?

ARTS AND CRAFTS

a. *Group project:* One tree that grows in tropical rainforests is the cacao tree, from which chocolate is made. Make a pretend cacao fruit from a brown paper bag and stuff it with cardboard cacao beans. Attach these pods to a paper cacao tree. (5, 19)

b. Use modeling clay to make an emergent tree. Give it several large buttresses so the tree will stand up. (5, 10, 16)

c. Make a collage of rainforest plants or animal life.

d. *Group project:* Turn the classroom into a tropical rainforest. Cut out construction paper trees, plants, and animals to decorate the walls. Hang paper birds from the ceiling.

e. Design a poster to make people aware of the destruction of the rainforests. (16, 22, 27, 29)

f. People of the tropical rainforest build simple homes. Create a model of one such dwelling. Which tribe might live there? (13, 17, 21, 29)

g. Use twigs, ferns, and small plants to make a diorama of a tropical or temperate rainforest.

SPELLING/VOCABULARY

a. Complete a word search puzzle of tropical rainforest birds and insects: cassowary, peacock, quetzal, katydid, army ant, butterfly, hummingbird, parrot, macaw, termite, grasshopper, currasow, toucan, kite, parakeet, harpy eagle, mosquito, magpie, beetle, tityra. (3, 4, 6, 8, 16, 22, 24, 25)

b. Complete a word search puzzle of tropical rainforest animals: anaconda, monkey, sloth, jaguar, armadillo, peccary, tapir, anteater, tree frog, gorilla, kinkajou, caiman, tamarin, lemur, coral snake, bat, mountain lion, orangutan, chimpanzee, ocelot. (2, 3, 4, 6, 7, 16, 24, 25, 29)

c. On a drawing of a tropical rainforest, label these terms: understory, canopy, soil, sunlight, bromelaid, sapling, emergent tree, seed, canopy hole, stream, water lily, buttress, climber, jungle floor, stilt root, epiphyte, liana, clearing. (2, 5, 6, 7, 16, 24, 29)

d. What is deforestation? Complete a fill-in-the-blanks exercise of related terms: slash-and-burn, greenhouse effect, endangered species, global warming, shifting cultivation, smelting, plantation, clear-cut, open-cast mining, topsoil, exploitation, logging, carbon dioxide, erosion, desertification. (1, 2, 3, 15, 16, 22, 25, 27, 29)

e. Following is a list of rainforest trees. For each one, tell whether it grows in a temperate or tropical rainforest. Also tell what food or other product comes from each tree (if applicable): mahogany, cacao, hemlock, mango, spruce, cedar, coffee, Brazil nut, sapele, hickory, Douglas fir, giant sequoia, nutmeg, African oil palm, ebony, oak, maple, cinchona, redwood, beech. (5, 7, 26)

f. Compile a glossary of terms that relate to medicines and other products that can be derived from rainforest plants and trees. (3, 5, 17, 18, 22, 26, 27)

g. What is a deciduous tree? A palm? A conifer? Complete a matching puzzle of plant-related rainforest terms: evergreen, fungi, biodiversity, infertile, dormant, succession, colonizer, photosynthesis, pollination, stranglers, detritus, emergent, transitional forest, nutrients, strata, parasite, saprophyte, drip-tip, transpire. (1, 2, 5, 15, 16, 18, 22, 25, 27, 29)

GEOGRAPHY

a. Tropical rainforests lie between the Tropic of Cancer and the Tropic of Capricorn. Locate these lines on a world map or globe. Where is the equator? What is the latitude of the tropics and the equator? (1, 2, 22, 25, 29)

b. On an outline of a world map, color the areas where there are rainforests. Color the tropical rainforests green, and the temperate rainforests red. (1, 2, 7, 11, 15, 24, 29)

c. List the names of countries in which there are rainforests. Locate on a map some rivers that flow through rainforests. (3, 11, 16, 18, 22, 24, 25, 29)

d. Compare tropical rainforests to temperate rainforests. What are their seasons like? How do their plants and animals adapt to the weather? (7, 11, 22, 26, 27, 29)

e. The Amazon Basin is the largest river system in the world. Look up some facts about it. Where is it located? Where does its water come from and where does it go? About how long is the Amazon River? How do the people near the Amazon use the water? (17, 24, 27)

f. In a tropical rainforest, there are four layers of plant life: the emergent tree layer, canopy, understory, and floor. List some characteristics of each layer, such as plants and animals that live there, amount of light and rain received, and humidity level.   (3, 5, 9, 16, 18, 24, 27, 29)

g. Scientists distinguish among the different types of temperate and tropical rainforests. What are the characteristics of a cloud or montaine forest? An ancient or old-growth forest? A mangrove forest? Which of these is a lowland forest? Highland? Coastal? What is a transitional forest?   (11, 22, 25, 26, 27, 29)

MATH

a. Tropical rainforests have year-round temperatures of 70–90°F (21–32°C). What is the temperature range (low to high) where you live? Locate these temperatures on a thermometer.

b. Tropical rainforests in Central and South America cover about 2 million square miles. Possibly a million types of plants and animals live there. Rainforest land in Africa amounts to about 700,000 square miles and supports 330,000 types of plants and animals. Mainland Asia and its islands have 800,000 square miles of rainforest, with 750,000 different plants and animals. Draw up a chart to illustrate these numbers.   (5)

c. Make a chart showing the full-grown heights of several rainforest trees. Include trees from the understory and canopy, plus emergent trees and some trees from temperate rainforests. Label each tree with its approximate height.   (5, 11, 27, 29)

d. Make a graph showing the average temperature and rainfall in a tropical and a temperate rainforest. Compare this to a chart of average temperature and rainfall where you live.   (10, 16, 22, 27, 29)

e. Answer these questions about habitat destruction: 1) As the tropical rainforests are destroyed, the populations of native people are declining. In 1500, approximately 6 million natives lived in the Amazon River Basin. In 1900, there were 1 million, and by 1990 there were about only 200,000. Make a graph to illustrate this decrease in population. 2) Animal and plant species are becoming extinct at the rate of 4,000 per year. About how many species have been lost in your lifetime?   (22)

f. Compile a list of ten or more interesting math facts about tropical and temperate rainforests.   (5, 9, 24, 27)

g. Answer these questions about rainforest destruction: 1) Estimates vary, but experts believe that every minute between 50 and 250 acres of rainforest are destroyed. At each of these rates, how much would be destroyed in a day? A week? A year? 2) At one time, there were approximately 4 billion acres of rainforest on Earth. Convert this number to square miles. (1 sq. mile = 640 acres.) About half of this amount has already been destroyed. How many square miles is that? 3) About 250 million slash-and burn farmers cut down up to 50 million acres of tropical rainforest each year. How many acres is that per farmer? 4) Tropical rainforests on the islands of Southeast Asia are being deforested at the rate of 6 million acres per year. How many acres have been destroyed during your lifetime? (22)

MUSIC AND THEATER ARTS

a. Sing and dance along to music from the soundtrack to Walt Disney's *The Jungle Book*.

b. *Group project:* Create some puppets of rainforest creatures. Present a puppet show about life in a rainforest. (1, 4, 6, 7, 8, 10, 16, 23)

c. Pretend you are a rainforest animal. Act out its movements. Tell what it is thinking. (4, 6, 7, 10, 16, 28)

d. Act out a picture book story that takes place in a tropical rainforest, or a folktale told by rainforest natives.

e. *Group project:* The ecology of a rainforest thrives because of the interdependence of the plants and animals that inhabit it. Create a movement exercise that illustrates the concept of interdependence. (1)

f. Listen to a recording of rainforest sounds from Rykodisc's *A Month in the Brazilian Rain Forest,* or to *Jungle* by Nature Recordings. Try to identify the animals you hear.

g. Listen to some music of people who live in a tropical rainforest, such as Rykodisc's *Voices of the Rainforest* or *Heart of the Forest*. How does it differ from American music? How is it similar?

ENGLISH COMPOSITION

a. Read some stories from tropical rainforest peoples. Choose one of them. Give a brief description of the plot and your opinion of the story. (2)

b. Write a description of a rainforest from the point of view of an animal that lives there. Tell about how you live, and what you see. How do you hide from your enemies? (2, 7, 10, 24, 25, 28)

c. There are many organizations that are dedicated to saving the rainforests. Write to one of them. Ask for information on how you can help. (See list at end of unit. Also: 3, 7, 17, 18, 22, 25, 29)

d. Pretend you are an explorer on an expedition through a rainforest. Write a story about your adventures. (7, 8, 9, 16, 24, 28, 29)

e. Compile a list of facts about rainforests. Pretend you are a newspaper reporter and use ten of these facts in a news story. (3, 4, 9, 11, 15, 16, 22, 23, 24, 25, 29)

f. Write an essay telling what might happen to the world if the destruction of the rainforests continues. Base your article on factual information. (2, 3, 9, 11, 16, 17, 21, 25, 29)

g. Pretend you are a native of a tropical or temperate rainforest. Write a diary of a typical week in your life. Tell where you live, what the climate is like, and how you and your family survive. (12, 14, 15, 17, 21, 24, 29)

SCIENCE

a. Make a terrarium. A small green plant and soil in a clear drinking glass or bottle will do. Water it well, seal the top with plastic wrap, and place it in a warm, sunny spot. Observe how the plant creates its own "rain" as it grows in the terrarium. Compare this to the ecology of a rainforest.

b. List some characteristics of tropical rainforests, such as temperature between 70° and 90°F, high humidity, location near the equator, etc. (3, 6, 7, 10, 16, 24, 25, 28, 29)

c. What is photosynthesis? What is the role of rainforests in this process? (5, 14, 22)

d. Some mammals of the tropical rainforest are terrestrial, and others are arboreal. What does this mean? List several of each type of animal. Also note whether they are herbivores, carnivores, or insectivores. (3, 18, 24, 25, 27, 29)

e. What is adaptation? Name some ways in which plants and animals of tropical rainforests have adapted to their environment. What is biological diversity? Give some examples of biodiversity in a tropical rainforest. (1, 3, 9, 16, 27, 29)

f. Make a chart that explains the correlation between the destruction of rainforests and the spread of hot deserts. How do population growth and exploitation affect this phenomenon? (2, 9, 11, 16, 29)

g. The soil of the tropical rainforest is thin and poor in nutrients. So how can it support an abundance of plant life? What happens when people try to farm there? Why? (1, 2, 5, 9, 15, 16, 18, 22, 25, 29)

HISTORY/SOCIOLOGY

a. Explain the difference between two types of tropical rainforest peoples: hunter-gatherers and farmers.   (1, 3, 10, 15, 17, 29)

b. Many tropical rainforest natives know how to use various plants as medicines. Give some examples.   (1, 3, 13, 22, 24, 29)

c. Look up information about a tribe of people that lives in a rainforest. What is their relationship to their environment? Why is their traditional way of life threatened?   (1, 3, 9, 12, 17, 18, 21, 22)

d. Several organizations and individual people have worked hard to save tropical and temperate rainforest lands, animals, and people. Write a report on one of these conservationists, from the past or present.   (3, 5, 17, 18, 22, 25, 27, 29)

e. How has the destruction of rainforest lands affected the tribes who live there? What is the role of the government in some of these countries?   (3, 9, 16, 18, 22, 29)

f. What role has the United States played in the destruction of Central American and Amazonian rainforests? How is public opinion changing that role?   (9, 17, 18, 25, 29)

g. How have the logging and cattle ranching industries of the United States, Japan, and western Europe affected the rainforests and their inhabitants?   (1, 3, 9, 17, 18, 22, 27, 29)

TOPICS FOR DISCUSSION

a. Give some reasons why our Earth needs rainforests.   (1, 2, 3, 6, 7, 15, 16, 22, 24, 28)

b. Name some foods and other products we get from rainforests.   (2, 3, 4, 5, 7, 15, 16, 17, 19, 20, 22, 24)

c. What do you think is the best way to alert people to the tragedy of rainforest destruction? What can you do on a local level?   (2, 3, 11, 17, 18, 22, 27, 29)

d. Money and survival are the two main reasons for rainforest destruction. List some ways that people make money from exploiting rainforests. Explain why some rainforest natives destroy their homeland.   (1, 2, 3, 6, 9, 16, 17, 18, 22, 25, 27, 29)

e. Discuss how the burning of rainforests contributes to global warming. What is the "greenhouse effect" and why is it bad?   (1, 3, 5, 9, 10, 11, 14, 16, 22, 24, 27, 29)

f. Farmers argue that slash-and-burn clearing of jungle is necessary to their survival. Conservationists disagree. Take one side of this argument, and let a classmate take the other. Debate this issue, citing facts you have found. (1, 3, 5, 11, 18, 22, 27, 29)

g. What are some ways that people can make a living from rainforests without damaging them? (1, 3, 15, 16, 17, 18, 22, 24, 25, 27, 29)

SUGGESTED RESOURCES

(1) Aldis, Rodney. *Rainforests* [Ecology Watch]. Dillon, 1991.

(2) Baker, Lucy. *Life in the Rainforests* [Life in]. Watts, 1990.

(3) Banks, Martin. *Conserving Our Rain Forests* [Conserving Our World]. Steck-Vaughn, 1989.

(4) Catchpole, Clive. *Jungles* [The Living World]. Dial, 1984.

(5) Cochrane, Jennifer. *Trees of the Tropics* [Green World]. Steck-Vaughn, 1990.

(6) Dixon, Dougal. *Jungles* [A Closer Look At]. Gloucester, 1984.

(7) Dorros, Arthur. *Rainforest Secrets*. Scholastic, 1990.

(8) Forsyth, Adrian. *Journey Through a Tropical Jungle*. Simon & Schuster, 1988.

(9) Gallant, Roy A. *Earth's Vanishing Forests*. Macmillan, 1991.

(10) Hamilton, Jean. *Tropical Rainforests*. Blake, 1990.

(11) Hare, Tony. *Rainforest Destruction* [Save Our Earth]. Gloucester, 1990.

(12) Hintz, Martin. *Living in the Tropics: A Cultural Geography*. Watts, 1987.

(13) James, Alan. *Homes in Hot Places* [Houses and Homes]. Lerner, 1989.

(14) Johnson, Rebecca L. *The Greenhouse Effect: Life on a Warmer Planet* [Discovery!]. Lerner, 1990.

(15) Knapp, Brian. *What Do We Know About Rainforests?* [Caring for Environments]. Bedrick, 1991.

(16) Landau, Elaine. *Tropical Rain Forests Around the World* [First Books—Our Environment]. Watts, 1990.

(17) Lewington, Anna. *Rain Forest Amerindians* [Threatened Cultures]. Steck-Vaughn, 1993.

(18) Miller, Christina G., and Berry, Louise A. *Jungle Rescue: Saving the New World Tropical Rain Forest*. Atheneum, 1991.

(19) Mitgutsch, Ali. *From Cacao Bean to Chocolate* [Start to Finish]. Carolrhoda, 1981.

(20) _____. *From Rubber Tree to Tire* [Start to Finish]. Carolrhoda, 1985.

(21) Morgan, Gillian. *Jungles and People* [Nature's Landscapes]. Wayland, 1982.

(22) Mutel, Cornelia F., and Rodgers, Mary M. *Tropical Rain Forests* [Our Endangered Planet]. Lerner, 1991.

(23) Nations, James D. *Tropical Rainforests: Endangered Environment* [Environmental Issues]. Watts, 1988.

(24) Razon, Mark J. *Jungles*. Doubleday, 1992.

(25) Stone, Lynne M. *Rain Forests* [EcoZones]. Rourke, 1989.

(26) Tesar, Jenny. *Endangered Habitats* [Our Fragile Planet]. Facts on File, 1992.

(27) _____. *Shrinking Forests* [Our Fragile Planet]. Facts on File, 1991.

(28) Wilkes, Angela. *Jungles*. Usborne, 1980.

(29) Williams, Lawrence. *Jungles* [Last Frontiers for Mankind]. Cavendish, 1990.

LIBRARY SKILLS RESOURCES

Few, Roger. *Children's Guide to Endangered Animals*. Macmillan, 1993.
The Guinness Book of World Records. Facts on File, 1994.
Lands and Peoples. Grolier, 1993.
Middleton, Nick. *Atlas of Environmental Issues* [Issues Atlases]. Facts on File, 1989.
Wood, Jenny. *The Children's Atlas of People & Places*. Millbrook, 1993.
World Resources Institute. *The Information Please Environmental Almanac*. Houghton, 1993.

ADDITIONAL READING – YOUNGER

Amsel, Sheri. *Rain Forests* [Habitats of the World]. Steck-Vaughn, 1993.
Asimov, Isaac. *Why Are the Rain Forests Vanishing?* [Ask Isaac Asimov]. Stevens, 1993.
Bright, Michael. *Tropical Rainforest* [World About Us]. Watts, 1991.
Cherry, Lynne. *The Great Kapok Tree*. Harcourt, 1990.
Cobb, Vicki. *This Place Is Wet* [Imagine Living Here]. Walker, 1989.
Coucher, Helen. *Rain Forest*. Farrar, 1988.
Explore a Tropical Forest [National Geographic Action Book]. National Geographic, 1989.
Fischetto, Laura. *The Jungle Is My Home*. Viking, 1991.
George, Jean Craighead. *One Day in the Tropical Rain Forest*. Crowell, 1990.
Gilliland, Judith Heide. *River*. Clarion, 1993.
Greenburg, Judith E., and Carey, Helen H. *The Rain Forest* [Science Adventures]. Raintree, 1990.
Hogan, Paula. *Vanishing Rain Forests* [Environment Alert!]. Stevens, 1991.
Huntley, Beth. *Amazon Adventure* [Young Explorers]. Stevens, 1989.
The Jungle Book (sound recording). Disney, 1990.
Lewington, Anna. *Antonio's Rain Forest* [Photo Books]. Carolrhoda, 1993.
Morris, Ting, and Morris, Neil. *Rain Forest* [Sticky Fingers]. Watts, 1994.
Palmer, Joy. *Rain Forests* [First Starts]. Raintree, 1993.
Pratt, Kristin Joy. *A Walk in the Rainforest*. Dawn, 1992.
Reynolds, Jan. *Amazon: Vanishing Cultures*. Harcourt, 1993.
Ross, Suzane. *What's in the Rainforest? One Hundred Six Answers from A to Z*. Enchanted Rainforest, 1991.
Silver, Donald M. *Why Save the Rainforest?* Messner, 1993.
Taylor, Barbara. *Rain Forest* [Look Closer]. Kindersley, 1992.
Yolen, Jane. *Welcome to the Green House*. Putnam, 1993.
Zak, Monica. *Save My Rainforest*. Volcano, 1992.

ADDITIONAL READING – OLDER

Baker, Jeannie. *Where the Forest Meets the Sea*. Greenwillow, 1988.
Bosse, Malcolm. *Deep Dream of the Rain Forest*. Farrar, 1993.
de Larramendi, Alberto Ruiz. *Tropical Rain Forests of Central America* [World Heritage]. Childrens, 1993.
DeStefano, Susan. *Chico Mendes: Fight for the Forest* [Earth Keepers]. Twenty-First Century, 1992.

The Emerald Rim: Earth's Precious Rain Forests. National Geographic, 1990.

Farb, Peter. *The Forest* [Life Nature Library]. Time, 1963.

Goodman, Billy. *Rain Forest* [Planet Earth]. Little, 1992.

Kipling, Rudyard. *Jungle Book.* Putnam, 1950.

Liptak, Karen. *Endangered Peoples* [Impact]. Watts, 1993.

Lourie, Peter. *Amazon: A Young Reader's Look at the Last Frontier.* Boyds Mills, 1991.

Mallory, Kenneth. *Water Hole: Life in a Rescued Tropical Forest* [New England Aquarium—Endangered Habitats Books]. Watts, 1992.

Marsh, Carole. *Jungle Gym: A Monkey's Eye View of the World's Jungles, Yesterday, Today, and Tomorrow?* Gallopade, 1993.

Meyer, Carolyn, and Gallencamp, Charles. *The Mystery of the Ancient Maya.* Macmillan, 1985.

Morrison, Marion. *The Amazon Rain Forest and Its People* [People and Places]. Thomson, 1994.

Ransome, Arthur. *Swallows and Amazons.* Godine, 1985.

Siy, Alexandra. *The Brazilian Rain Forest* [Circle of Life]. Dillon, 1991.

_____. *The Penan: People of the Borneo Jungle* [Global Villages]. Dillon, 1993. (Also other books in series.)

Twist, Clint. *Jungles and Forests: Projects with Geography* [Hands On Science]. Gloucester, 1993.

See also: books in FORESTS AND WOODLANDS unit.

FOR MORE INFORMATION ABOUT RAINFORESTS, WRITE TO:

Big Island Rainforest Action
  Group
The Children's Rainforest
Conservation International
Environmental Defense Fund
Forest Ecosystem Rescue Network

Friends of the Earth
Global ReLeaf Through Learning
Rainforest Action Network
Rainforest Alliance
Tree Amigos Project
World Wildlife Fund

FORESTS AND
WOODLANDS

At one time, forests covered a third of the land on Earth. But they are disappearing as trees are cut down for wood, and land is cleared for farming or development. When people destroy forests, it affects the survival of millions of plants and animals. It also has a great impact on climate and the quality of life on Earth. A forest may take hundreds, or even thousands, of years to grow, but it can be destroyed in just a few hours. We must conserve and protect this most valuable natural resource.

LIBRARY SKILLS

a. Use *The Holiday Handbook* or another book about holidays or celebrations to look up Arbor Day. When was it first observed? What is the purpose of celebrating it?

b. Use *Facts About the Fifty States* to compile a list of the 50 state trees.

c. In an encyclopedia, look up Forestry. What is it? What do foresters do?

d. Use *The World Almanac and Book of Facts* to answer the following questions about giant trees: 1) What and where is the world's largest living thing? How big is it? 2) Which giant tree is located in Siskiyou National Forest, Oregon? 3) Which giant trees are located in Texas? 4) How tall is the biggest Arizona walnut tree? 5) Which tallest tree is only eight feet tall? 6) In what year was the umbrella magnolia in Bucks County, Pennsylvania, judged to be the tallest of its kind? 7) Where is the Nisqually Wildlife Refuge? 8) About how many different types of trees grow in the United States?

e. Use *The Information Please Environmental Almanac* to answer the following questions: 1) What is timberland? 2) Why has the United States Forest Service come under fire for its management of timberland? 3) What percent of America's forests have never been cut?

f. Use *Famous First Facts* to answer the following questions: 1) What and where was the first national forest? When was it established? 2) When did the first federal planting of forests begin? Where? What was planted? 3) What was the first national forestry association? 4) What was the purpose of the first colonial forestry legislation? 5) When and where was the first college level school of forestry established? 6) Name the title, author, publisher, and date of publication of the first book on forestry. 7) How many acres of timberland were destroyed in the first major United States forest fire?

g. Find an index to folktales, fairy tales, or legends. List some stories that have been told or written that involve forests. Then find an index to children's poetry and list some poems about forests. Look in anthologies to locate three of the stories or poems on your list.

ARTS AND CRAFTS

a. Draw a deciduous tree or forest scene as it would look in summer. Then draw the same scene as it would look in autumn, winter, and spring. (12, 14, 15, 17)

b. Glue acorns, leaves, pine cones and needles, and other bits of woodland plants onto heavy paper to make a collage.

c. Draw a picture or make a model of a woodland animal's home, such as a bird nest, the underground home of a vole, or an owl living in a tree.   (3, 4, 6, 7, 13, 14, 17, 20, 21)

d. Pick a country or a particular part of the world. Make a list of ten or more trees that grow there. Draw or cut out pictures of these trees and label them. Make a picture book or mural of trees from your country.   (5, 12, 15, 21, 22, 23)

e. Draw a series of pictures that illustrates the rebirth of a forest after it has been destroyed in a forest fire. Tell what is happening in each picture.   (18, 19, 23)

f. Make a diorama of a forest scene. Tell the type of forest it is, and the season. Identify the plants and animals depicted in your diorama.

g. Draw a picture or diagram that explains the carbon cycle as it relates to forests. In your picture, show how pollution and deforestation add to the carbon dioxide level in the atmosphere, and the effects of this.   (8, 9, 16, 21, 23)

SPELLING/VOCABULARY

a. Complete a matching picture puzzle of temperate forest animals: butterfly, earthworm, badger, chipmunk, ant, mole, mouse, shrew, fox, deer, owl, rabbit, weasel, vole, bobcat, squirrel, falcon, wolf, bear, eagle. (3, 6, 7, 9, 10, 13, 14, 17, 20, 22)

b. Complete a word search puzzle of temperate forest plants: lichen, fern, mushroom, moss, bluebell, holly, ivy, honeysuckle, violet, mistletoe, grass, liverwort, clover, lady's slipper, pussywillow, sumac, skunk cabbage. (4, 6, 7, 14, 17, 22)

c. Label the parts of a tree: leaf, crown, trunk, blossom, fruit, sap, branch, twig, roots, taproot. Label a cross-section of a tree trunk: heartwood, sapwood, growth ring, bark, cambium, phloem. (4, 5, 12, 14, 23, 25, 26)

d. Complete a crossword puzzle of tree terms: deciduous, frond, evergreen, broad-leaf, hardwood, conifer, tree line, palm, fern, foliage, forest floor, arboreal, canopy, understory, herbaceous, tropical forest, temperate forest. (5, 9, 10, 12, 14, 22, 23, 24, 25, 26)

e. Complete a matching puzzle of terms related to the life cycle of a tree: seedling, parasite, sapling, spores, saprophyte, litter, boreal, pollinate, chlorophyll, photosynthesis, pioneer tree, compost, catkin, lichen, fungi, deadwood, succession, climax forest, old growth, decompose. (8, 12, 14, 21, 22, 23, 24, 25)

f. For each of these environmental terms, give an example pertaining to forests: biome, ecosystem, climate, habitat, niche, biological or species diversity, interdependent, natural resource, greenhouse effect, biomass, ecosystem, watershed, extinction, recycling, carbon cycle. (8, 9, 11, 21, 23)

g. Define these terms that relate to forest conservation: clear cut, defoliate, selective cutting, virgin woodland, deforestation, second growth forests, coppicing, reseeding, plantation, erosion, sustainable forestry, monoculture, agroforestry, selective breeding, reforestation, fragmentation. (8, 11, 12, 15, 16, 22, 23, 24)

GEOGRAPHY

a. On a map of the world, color temperate forests (also called deciduous or mixed forests) red, coniferous forests brown, and tropical forests green. (5, 10, 12, 15, 16, 24)

b. Use the information you found for the library skills exercise, item **b**, to complete this activity. On a map of the United States, write the names of the 50 state trees in their corresponding states.

c. Following are some descriptions of trees. Match each one to its name: 1) The sap that flows from this tree can be made into a sweet syrup. 2) This conifer is the tallest tree in the world. 3) Koala bears live in this evergreen. 4) The latex that is gathered from this tree is used to make tires, balloons, and plastic. 5) The longest-lived tree in the world, this conifer can live over 4,500 years. 6) This tree bears a prickly fruit which contains a large, edible seed. Unfortunately, many trees have died from a disease called blight. 7) Silk worms eat the leaves of this tree. 8) The fruit of this family of trees is called an acorn. Their sturdy wood is made into furniture. 9) This short evergreen has ferny leaves and clusters of yellow flowers. 10) This tree grows quickly in waterlogged soil. Names of trees: chestnut, white mulberry, redwood, kowhai, rubber tree, sugar maple, eucalyptus, bristlecone pine, English oak, alder. (5, 12, 15, 26)

 d. For each of the following trees, tell where it grows (some may grow in more than one place): Antarctic beech, sycamore maple, birch, pagoda, cottonwood, aspen, giant sequoia, katsura, olive, Jarrah, Yoshino cherry, Douglas fir, mahogany, bamboo, balsa, cypress. (5, 12, 15, 26)

 e. How do climate, altitude, rainfall, wind and other geographic factors determine which trees will be able to grow in a certain location? Make a list of twenty trees from various parts of the world. Tell how each is adapted to its particular environment. (9, 10, 12, 23)

 f. Deforestation has caused problems with erosion and flooding in many parts of the world. On a map of the world, locate some of these areas and mark them in blue. Deforestation has also led to desertification in some parts of the world. Mark these areas in red. (8, 11, 16, 23)

 g. Prepare a report on a forest in a continent other than North America. Locate it on a map. Describe its climate, elevation, latitude, and the country(ies) in which it is located. Make a list of plants and animals that live there. If possible, include pictures of your forest in your report. (10)

MATH

 a. The northern coniferous forests may receive about 8 to 20 inches of rain per year. Temperate deciduous forests get between 20 and 60 inches of rain annually. Anywhere from 70 to 200 inches of rain may fall in a tropical rainforest in one year. Draw up a chart or graph to illustrate these rainfall facts.

 b. Trees have long lifespans. Douglas firs may live 400 years; redwoods 3,000 years; maples 200 years; English oak 800 years; bristlecone pines 4,500 years. How old are you? Divide the age of each of these trees by your age.

 c. In Canada, only 3 new trees are planted for every 10 that are cut down. What fraction is that? If 50 trees are cut, how many new ones will be planted? If 80 trees are cut? 120? 200? 1,000? If 12 trees are planted, how many were cut? If 27 are planted? 48? 72? (16)

d. Old growth forests of the Pacific Northwest once covered 15 million acres. Now, only 15 percent of these forests remain. How many millions of acres were cut down? Draw a bar graph to illustrate your answer.

e. In 1990, the Earth's forests were being destroyed at an average rate of 100 acres per minute. How many acres is that per hour? Per day? Per year? If this rate continues, how many acres of trees will be destroyed during this decade?

f. Trees vary greatly in height. The bristlecone pine grows to approximately 33 feet, chestnut to 110 feet, aspen to 66 feet, balsam poplar to 140 feet, redwood to 360 feet, eucalyptus to 330 feet, mountain laurel to 25 feet, poison sumac to 16 feet, Oregon crab apple to 79 feet, Carolina ash to 48 feet, giant sequoia to 275 feet. Change these measurements to inches, then to meters.

g. Answer these recycling problems: 1) Americans used 86 million tons of paper in 1989. About 27.6 million tons were recycled. What percentage is that? 2) Of this 27.6 million tons in recycled paper, 40 percent was corrugated boxes. How many tons is that? 3) It takes one 15-year-old tree to make 700 large paper bags. How many trees would have to be cut to produce one bag for every person in the United States (rounding the population to 250 million)? How many years' worth of trees is that? 4) Americans use, on the average, about 332 pounds of paper per person each year. In one year, how many total pounds of paper are used in America? 5) About 500,000 trees must be cut to produce enough paper for the Sunday editions of America's newspapers. How many trees is that in one year? 6) At an average of 300 trees per acre, how many acres of forest must be cut each week to produce Sundays' newspapers? How many acres in one year? (16, 21)

MUSIC AND THEATER ARTS

a. Experiment with a variety of wooden percussion instruments to hear the different sounds they make.

b. Companies such as Soundings of the Planet and Nature Recordings produce sound recordings of woodland birdsong and animal calls. Listen to one of these recordings and try to identify the animal sounds.

c. Many musical instruments are made of wood. Make a list of them. Listen to a violin, cello, some woodwinds, etc. Try to identify each one while listening to a piece of music. How does the sound of a (wooden) acoustic guitar compare to the sound of an electric guitar?

d. Pretend you are camping in the woods. Act out how you would set up camp, pitch a tent, build a fire, cook food, etc.

e. Act out a scene showing one example of how people use trees, such as collecting and refining maple sugar, building a house with wood, making paper, etc. (1, 2, 5, 12, 16, 23)

f. Present a puppet show that illustrates the food web in a forest ecosystem. (8, 21, 23)

g. Act out a scene from *Into the Woods*, or another play or story that takes place in a forest.

ENGLISH COMPOSITION

a. Read some poems about trees, forests, or woodland animals. Then write your own poem about one of these topics.

b. Write a story about a year in the life of an insect, bird, or mammal that lives in a deciduous forest. Tell how it adapts to the four seasons. Where is its home? What does it eat? What enemies does it have? How does it survive the winter? (3, 6, 7, 17, 20, 23)

c. Write a story about exploring or going camping in a forest. What equipment do you take along? What do you see in there?

d. Write an essay on what people can do to conserve wood and save Earth's forests. (8, 15, 16, 21, 23)

e. Write a journal of one week in the life of a logger or a related occupation, past or present. What is the job like? What are some dangers or other concerns of this occupation? (1, 2, 15, 21)

f. Create a picture book to give children an appreciation of forests and woodlands. You may write about forest plants or animals, conservation, preventing forest fires, a specific national forest, or any other related topic. Make sure your words are simple enough for young children to read.

g. Write a first person narrative from the point of view of a forest animal that is losing its habitat. Is its home threatened by logging, slash and burn farming, acid rain, fire, or something else? What is happening to the animal's food supply? Will it survive? (8, 16, 21, 23)

SCIENCE

a. Make a collection of leaves, seeds, pine cones, and berries from various woodland trees and shrubs. Mount each one together with a picture of the tree or bush from which it came. Label your collection and display it in the classroom. (4, 12, 14, 26)

b. Divide a piece of paper into four columns. Label them: canopy (tree tops), understory (shrub layer), forest floor (field layer), soil (underground). In each column, list some birds, animals, and insects you might find in one type of forest (such as Northeastern United States or Brazilian rainforest). Only include animals that are native to the part of the world in which your forest is located. (7, 10, 12, 14, 15, 23, 24)

c. Divide a piece of paper into three columns. Label them: conifers, palms and ferns, broad-leaf. Give a brief explanation of the main characteristics of each type of tree. Then list as many names of trees as you can in each column. (4, 5, 10, 12, 14, 26)

d. What are some ways by which the seeds of forest plants and trees are spread? How are they pollinated? (5, 12, 14, 19, 26)

e. Answer these questions about tree life: 1) What is photosynthesis? 2) What is chlorophyll? 3) Why do the leaves of deciduous trees change color and fall off in autumn? 4) How can you tell the age of a tree? (8, 12, 14, 15, 20, 22, 23, 25)

f. How do acid rain and air pollution affect forests? (8, 9, 10, 16, 23, 24)

g. How does a tree grow? What are the functions of the leaves, roots, bark, phloem, cambium, xylem, and heartwood? What can you learn about the life of a tree by studying its annual rings? (9, 12, 23, 25, 26)

HISTORY/SOCIOLOGY

a. How did the early settlers of America clear the forest land they wanted to live on? What is the difference between a logger and a lumberman? What are some other related jobs? (1, 2)

b. What are some ways that early settlers used wood? Why was having a sawmill important to the community? (2)

c. How do some natives of tropical rainforests make a living off their land? How do some people use the northern coniferous forests to make a living? (5, 10, 15)

d. Some trees and forests have been nearly wiped out due to an insect (such as the gypsy moth) or a disease (such as chestnut blight). Give an example of one such incident. When and where did it occur? What tree(s) or area did it affect? What was the cause, and how much damage was done? Why does disease spread more easily in a temperate forest than in a tropical forest? (12, 22, 23)

e. What has happened to the temperate forests of Eastern Europe, Africa, China, and Asia? What has happened to the tropical forests in South America, Africa, and Asia? (8, 10, 11, 15, 23, 24)

f. Look up some information on a particular forest fire. When did it happen? How did it start? How much area burned? How did the fire affect the forest? (8, 18, 19, 23)

g. Look up information on a person, conservation group, or program that is committed to saving forests. Tell how this person, group or program works and which forest(s) or trees it is trying to protect. How effective has it been in reaching its goal? (8, 11, 16, 23)

TOPICS FOR DISCUSSION

a. How do people use trees? What can be made from their wood, sap, bark, and leaves? (1, 2, 5, 12, 15, 16)

b. What are some dangers for forests? What do you think can cause the most harm to a forest: animals, humans, or acts of nature? Why? (5, 9, 12, 15, 16, 19, 24)

c. How can a dead tree be an important part of the forest ecosystem? (4, 14, 15, 21, 23)

d. How can periodic fires benefit the forest ecology? How might preventing all forest fires be harmful? (8, 18, 19, 23, 24)

e. Why are forests a valuable resource? Why are they worth preserving? (1, 8, 11, 16, 21, 23, 24)

f. Should the United States government continue to allow loggers to cut down the old-growth forests of the Pacific Northwest? Argue this issue from the point of view of the timber industry, the United States government, or an environmental group. Can a compromise be reached that would satisfy all the parties involved? (8, 11, 21, 23)

g. What are the main causes of deforestation? How does deforestation affect plants and wildlife in the immediate area? How does it affect the local human population? What are the worldwide effects? (8, 11, 16, 19, 21, 23)

SUGGESTED RESOURCES

(1) Abrams, Kathleen, and Abrams, Lawrence. *Logging and Lumbering*. Messner, 1980.
(2) Adams, Peter D. *Early Loggers and the Sawmill* [The Early Settler Life Series]. Crabtree, 1981.
(3) *Animals in the Forest* [Animals and Their Homes]. Raintree, 1988.
(4) Arnosky, Jim. *Crinklefoot's Guide to Knowing Trees*. Bradbury, 1992.
(5) Bailey, Donna. *Forests* [Facts About]. Steck-Vaughn, 1990.

(6) Behm, Barbara J., and Bonar, Veronica. *Exploring Forests* [Eco-Journey]. Stevens, 1994.

(7) _____. *Exploring Woodlands* [Eco-Journey]. Stevens, 1994.

(8) Challand, Helen J. *Vanishing Forests* [Saving Planet Earth]. Childrens, 1991.

(9) Costa-Pau, Rosa. *Protecting Our Forests* [The Junior Library of Ecology]. Chelsea, 1994,

(10) Dixon, Dougal. *Forests* [Franklin Watts Picture Atlas]. Watts, 1984.

(11) Gallant, Roy A. *Earth's Vanishing Forests*. Macmillan, 1991.

(12) Greenaway, Theresa. *Woodland Trees* [Green World]. Steck-Vaughn, 1990.

(13) Greenway, Shirley. *Animal Homes: Forests* [Oxford Scientific Films]. Newington, 1991.

(14) Hester, Nigel. *The Living Tree* [Watching Nature]. Watts, 1990.

(15) Jennings, Terry. *Temperate Forests* [Exploring Our World]. Cavendish, 1987.

(16) Leggett, Jeremy. *Dying Forests* [Operation Earth]. Cavendish, 1991.

(17) Lerner, Carol. *A Forest Year*. Morrow, 1987.

(18) Patent, Dorothy Hinshaw. *Yellowstone Fires: Flames and Rebirth*. Holiday, 1990.

(19) Pringle, Laurence. *Natural Fire: Its Ecology in Forests*. Morrow, 1979.

(20) Schwartz, David M. *The Hidden Life of the Forest* [Hidden Life]. Crown, 1988.

(21) Siy, Alexandra. *Ancient Forests* [Circle of Life]. Dillon, 1991.

(22) Stone, Lynn M. *Temperate Forests* [EcoZones]. Rourke, 1989.

(23) Tesar, Jenny. *Shrinking Forests* [Our Fragile Planet]. Facts on File, 1991.

(24) Tompkins, Terry. *Ravaged Temperate Forests* [Environment Alert!]. Stevens, 1993.

(25) *Woodland Life* [Science in Our World]. Grolier, 1991.

(26) Zim, Herbert T. *Trees* [Golden Guides]. Western, 1991.

LIBRARY SKILLS RESOURCES

Barkin, Carol, and James, Elizabeth. *The Holiday Handbook: Activities for Celebrating Every Season of the Year and More*. Clarion, 1994.

Brandt, Sue R. *Facts About the 50 States* [First Books — American History]. Watts, 1988.

Kane, Joseph Nathan. *Famous First Facts*. H.W. Wilson, 1981.

The World Almanac and Book of Facts. World Almanac, 1994.

World Resources Institute. *The Information Please Environmental Almanac*. Houghton, 1993.

ADDITIONAL READING — YOUNGER

Arnosky, Jim. *Crinklefoot's Book of Animal Tracks and Wildlife Signs*. Putnam, 1979. (Also other Crinklefoot books.)

Bellamy, David. *Our Changing World: The Forest*. Crown, 1988.

Brooks, F. *Protecting Trees and Forests* [Conservation Guides]. Usborne, 1991.

Burns, Diane L. *Arbor Day* [On My Own]. Carolrhoda, 1989.

Butler, Daphne. *First Look in the Forest* [First Look]. Stevens, 1991.

Chiefari, Janet. *Logging Machines in the Forest*. Dodd, 1985.

Davol, Marguerite W. *The Heart of the Wood*. Simon & Schuster, 1992.

Eugene, Toni. *Creatures of the Woods* [Books for Young Explorers]. National Geographic, 1985.

George, Jean Craighead. *One Day in the Woods*. Crowell, 1988.
James, Simon. *The Wild Woods*. Candlewick, 1993.
Lavies, Bianca. *Tree Trunk Traffic*. Dutton, 1989.
McCauley, Jane R. *Animals That Live in Trees* [Books for Young Explorers]. National Geographic, 1986.
Mitgutsch, Ali. *From Tree to Table* [Start to Finish]. Carolrhoda, 1981.
_____. *From Wood to Paper* [Start to Finish]. Carolrhoda, 1986.
Newton, James R. *A Forest Is Reborn*. Crowell, 1982.
Sabin, Francene. *Wonders of the Forest*. Troll, 1982.
Taylor, Barbara. *Forest Life* [Look Closer]. Kindersley, 1993.
Taylor, Dave. *Endangered Forest Animals* [Endangered Animals]. Crabtree, 1992.
Thornhill, Jan. *A Tree in a Forest*. Simon & Schuster, 1992.
Viera, Linda. *The Ever-Living Tree: The Life and Times of a Coast Redwood*. Walker, 1994.
Whitlock, Ralph. *In the Woods* [Use Your Eyes]. Wayland, 1986.

ADDITIONAL READING—OLDER

Applebaum, Diana. *Giants in the Land*. Houghton, 1993.
Booth, Basil. *Temperate Forests* [Our World]. Silver, 1989.
Farb, Peter. *The Forest* [Life Nature Library]. Time, 1963.
Ganeri, Anita. *Trees* [Focus on—Science]. Watts, 1993.
Harlow, Rose, and Morgan, Gareth. *Trees and Leaves* [Fun with Science]. Watts, 1991.
Hirschi, Ron. *Save Our Forests* [One Earth]. Bantam, 1992.
Holling, Holling Clancy. *Tree in the Trail*. Houghton Mifflin, 1942.
Into the Woods (sound recording). RCA, 1988.
Kudlinsky, Kathleen V. *Animal Tracks and Traces*. Watts, 1991.
Lauber, Patricia. *Summer of Fire: Yellowstone, 1988*. Orchard, 1991.
Lisle, Janet Taylor. *Forest*. Orchard, 1993.
Marsh, Carole. *The Giant Sequoia and Kings Canyon National Parks*. Gallopade, 1993.
Schoonmaker, Peter K. *The Living Forest* [Living World]. Enslow, 1990.
Sondheim, Stephen, and Lapine, James. *Into the Woods*. Crown, 1988.
Spenser, Guy. *An Ancient Forest* [Let's Take a Trip]. Troll, 1988.
Staub, Frank. *Yellowstone's Cycle of Fire* [Earth Watch]. Carolrhoda, 1994.
Stewart, Gail. *Smokejumpers and Forest Firefighters* [At Risk]. Crestwood, 1988.
Stone, Lynn M. *Timber Country* [Back Roads]. Rourke, 1993.
Weber, Michael. *Our National Parks* [I Know America]. Millbrook, 1993.
Wilkins, Marne. *The Long Ago Lake: A Child's Book of Nature Lore and Crafts*. Sierra Club, 1978.
Zuckerman, Seth. *Saving Our Ancient Forests*. Living Planet, 1991.

See also: books in RAINFOREST unit.

FOR MORE INFORMATION ABOUT FOREST AND WOODLANDS, WRITE TO:

American Forestry Association   Forest Ecosystem Rescue Network
American Wildlands   Global ReLeaf Through Learning

National Arbor Day Foundation
National Audubon Society
National Parks and Conservation
  Association
National Wildlife Federation

Natural Resources Defense Council
The Nature Conservancy
Save-the-Redwoods League
Sierra Club
Tree Amigos Project

MOUNTAINS

Mountains dominate a landscape like no other feature on Earth. Their rocky ledges, forested slopes, and jagged snow-capped peaks seem to personify strength and permanence. But mountains are constantly changing. Weathering and erosion are gradual changes. Others, such as volcanic eruptions, are more dramatic. The actions of people also affect the appearance and environment of mountains. Proper management of mountain resources is necessary to protect these majestic but fragile landforms.

LIBRARY SKILLS

a. Look in *The Facts on File Children's Atlas* or another source to find a topographical map of the world. How are mountains shown? Where are some of the major mountain ranges in the world?

b. Use *How the Earth Works* to answer these questions: 1) Look up Mountains. What caused the Himalayas to form? 2) Look up Rocks in Mountains. What are two types of rocks made by mountains? How are they made? 3) Look up The Rock Cycle. What is a third type of rock made by mountains? How is it made?

c. Use *The Physical World* to answer the following: 1) Name the world's five longest mountain ranges. Tell where they are and their approximate lengths in miles. 2) What mountain ranges surround Africa's Great Rift Valley? 3) The Amazon River begins on what mountain chain? 4) The Himalayas are still growing. What is their rate of growth? 5) List the mountain ranges of the Middle East.

d. Look up Mountains in *World Book Encyclopedia* or another encyclopedia to answer these questions: 1) The Mid-Atlantic Ridge is the world's largest mountain system. How long is it and where is it located? How was it formed? 2) What mountain ranges are part of the Pacific Mountain System? 3) Where is the Tethyan Mountain System and what mountains does it include? 4) How old are the Appalachian Mountains? 5) What is K2? 6) How are mountains measured?

e. Look up Mountaineering in *The Guinness Book of World Records* to answer the following: 1) How old was the oldest mountain climber and what mountain did he conquer? 2) Who climbed Mt. Everest the most number of times, and when? 3) From what country does Reinhold Messner come? What are some of his accomplishments? 4) What is the highest mountain on each of the seven continents? Who was the first to climb them all? 5) What was the greatest number of people to conquer Mt. Everest together? What countries did they represent? 6) What is the fastest time recorded for climbing and descending Mt. Cameroon? 7) What are the most demanding free climbs in the world? 8) How long has mountaineering been a recognized sport?

f. Look up a topographical map of North America in an atlas. Locate these mountain ranges: Cassiar Mtns., Chugach Mtns., San Juan Mtns., Brooks Range, Alaska Range, Mackenzie Mtns., Rocky Mtns., Coastal Mtns., Cascade Mtns., Sierra Nevada, Bitterroot Range, Uinta Mtns., Selkirk Mtns., Big Horn Mtns., Appalachian Mtns., Smoky Mtns., Alleghany Mtns., Ozark Mtns., Sangre de Cristo Range, Sierra Madre Occidental, Sierra Madre del Sur, Adirondak Mtns., Coast Ranges, Catskill Mtns., Blue Ridge. How many smaller ranges, including the following, can you find? Red Hills, Green Mtns., Blue Mtns., White Mtns., Black Hills.

g. Use *Webster's New Geographical Dictionary* and other sources such as almanacs, atlases, and encyclopedias to complete this mountain scavenger hunt. For each mountain or mountain range, write down its location and its claim to fame: Mt. Olympus, Mt. Rushmore, the Old Man in the Mountains (or the Great Stoneface), Mount Sinai, Mt. Nebo, Mount of Olives (or Mt. Olivet), Mount Wilson, Mount Mazama, Katmai, Mount Athos, Manzano Peak, Mount Greylock, Alaska Range, Mount Ndikeva, Ajanta Range, Albert Mountains, Moldavian Carpathian Mountains, Macdonnell Ranges, Duckwater Peak, Stone Mountain, Devil's Tower, Ararat, Popocatepetl, Manaslu, Mount Vesuvius, Sri Pada, Carstensz, Huascaran, Pelée, Aconcagua.

ARTS AND CRAFTS

a. Mining, logging, pollution, and other human activities are destroying mountains in many parts of the world. Create a poster to draw attention to this problem and offer a possible solution. (1, 8, 11, 15, 16, 19, 27)

b. Make a collage of mountain animals and plants from around the world. (1, 6, 8, 11, 12, 16, 19, 21, 25)

c. Use modeling clay to create a mountain sculpture. Your mountain may be jagged, rounded or volcanic, and may have a crater or other features. After the clay hardens, paint your mountain.

d. *Group project:* Make a bulletin board display of mountain sports and activities. Include winter and summer activities. Identify any equipment that is shown.

e. Collect pictures of animals that live on a mountain range of your choice. Mount and label the pictures on sheets of paper. Include facts such as the full-grown size of each animal and what it eats. Bind the pages into an illustrated fact book of mountain wildlife. (1, 8, 11, 12, 16, 19, 21, 25)

f. Create a diorama of a mountain range and the surrounding landscape. You can include such features as volcanoes, glaciers, streams, valleys, etc. (7, 12, 16, 19, 27)

g. Use a topographical map as a guide for making a three-dimensional relief map of a country or continent. Use clay or papier-mâché to build mountain ranges. Remember that mountains have different characteristics. For example, a map of the United States would include tall, jagged peaks for the Rockies and shorter, rounded peaks for the Appalachians, while the Cascade Mountains would be volcanoes.

SPELLING/VOCABULARY

a. Complete a matching picture puzzle of animals that live in mountains: grizzly bear, cougar, peregrine falcon, panda, takin, mountain goat, elk, bald eagle, bighorn sheep, chinchilla, snow leopard, marmot, llama, yak, coyote, red grouse, chamois, vole, gorilla, vicuña. (1, 3, 7, 8, 9, 11, 12, 16, 19, 21, 25, 27)

b. Complete a matching activity of mountain features and descriptions: plateau, cordilla, ledge, summit, forest, gorge, cliff, slope, upland, foothill, steep, peak, range, snow-capped, rocky, jagged, crater, cone, cirque, arete. (1, 8, 12, 19, 21, 23, 27)

c. Complete a word search puzzle of mountain plants: lupine, bitterroot, azalea, bamboo, rhododendron, oak, mahogany, lobelia, pine, heather, moss, grass, edelweiss, lichen, spruce, fireweed, huckleberry, gentian, beech, redwood. (1, 3, 6, 8, 11, 18, 19, 21, 25, 28)

d. Complete a crossword puzzle of terms related to the formation of mountains: crust, glacier, volcano, earthquake, limestone, collision, plates, fold, block, ocean ridge, magma, ocean trench, anticline, nappe, recumbent, syncline, strata, dome, erode, caldera. (1, 2, 3, 4, 8, 9, 16, 18, 19, 20, 21, 22, 23, 26, 27, 28)

e. Define these terms that relate to mountain environments: alpine, altitude, rain shadow, elevation, rift valley, habitat, treeline (or timberline), snowline, continental divide, foliage, deciduous, coniferous, latitude, ground level, topsoil, terrace, temperate, lowlands, highlands, precipitation. (1, 6, 8, 10, 12, 21, 28)

f. Complete a fill-in-the-blanks exercise of geological terms: isostatic rebound, continental plate, metamorphic rock, igneous rock, sedimentary rock, fault, plate tectonics, subduction zone, seamount, plateau, fjord, Pangaea, oceanic plate, asthenosphere, continental drift, inner core, mantle, outer core, Laurasia, Gondwanaland.   (4, 16, 19, 20, 21, 23, 26)

g. Compile your own glossary of terms related to volcanoes. List at least 20 terms alphabetically, and give their definitions.   (2, 4, 9, 14, 18, 19, 20, 21, 22, 23, 26, 27, 28)

GEOGRAPHY

a. Many mountains form along geologic plates. What are geologic plates? On a map of the world, draw lines to show the borders of these plates. What is the Ring of Fire? How does it compare to your map?   (3, 4, 8, 16, 19, 21, 26, 27)

b. On a map of the world, color in these mountain ranges: Andes, Pyrenees, Rocky Mtns., Ethiopian Highlands, Great Dividing Range, Ural Mtns., Scottish Highlands, Altai Mtns., Alps, Drakensberg Mtns., Himalayas, Atlas Mtns., Caucasians, Appalachian Mtns., Tien Shan, Zagros Mtns., Cascades, Ruwenzori, Ellsworth Highlands, Mackenzie Mtns.   (5, 8, 11, 12, 15, 19, 20, 21, 27)

c. How are mountains measured? How high does a land mass have to be to be considered a mountain? What is the difference among mountains, highlands, and hills? Are mountains found only above sea level?   (4, 9, 11, 16, 21, 25, 27)

d. Following is a list of volcanoes. For each one, tell if it is active or extinct, and in which country it is located: Vesuvius, Citlaltépetl (also called Orizaba), Ruapehu, Kenya, Paricutin, Etna, Kilimanjaro, Ngauruhoe, Fuji, Pelée, Eldfell, Mount St. Helens, Erebus, Mauna Loa, Ben Nevis, Ararat, Chimborazo, Stromboli, Klyuchevskaya, Surtsey, Nevado del Ruiz, Krakatoa, Pinatubo. Which of these are along the Ring of Fire?   (3, 12, 14, 20, 21, 26, 27)

e. Match each of the following mountains to the mountain range in which it is located: Everest, Narodnaya, Ranier, Jungfrau, Vinson Massif, McKinley, Mont Blanc, Whitney, Elbrus, Kosciusko, Elbert, Godwin Austen (K2), Cayambe, Logan, Mitchell, Cotopaxi, Matterhorn, Jebel Toubkal, Margherita, Annapurna.   (12, 21)

f. Divide a sheet of paper into five columns and label them: Rockies, Himalayas, Ruwenzori, and Alps. In each column, list some animals that live on that mountain range.   (3, 9, 11, 12)

g. What geological changes do scientists predict will happen to mountain ranges in Earth's future? Within the next few million years, which mountains are expected to wear down? Where will new mountains probably form? How will continental drift cause these changes?   (2, 4, 7, 12, 19, 20, 23)

MATH

Note: Heights of mountains may vary, according to the sources used.

a. Following is a list of mountains, their locations, and the years of their first recorded climbs. Place these years in chronological order: Matterhorn, Switzerland, 1865; Washington, New Hampshire, 1642; Logan, Canada, 1925; Cook, New Zealand, 1894; McKinley, Alaska, 1913; Mont Blanc, France, 1786; Vinson Massif, Antarctica, 1966; Gunnbjorn, Greenland, 1935; Ararat, Turkey, 1829; Toubkal, Morocco, 1923.

b. Following is a list of the largest mountain on each continent and its height in feet. Round off these numbers to the nearest hundred, and to the nearest thousand. Then place these numbers in ascending order: Asia— Everest 29,028; Australasia—Djaja 16,503; North America—McKinley 20,320; Antarctica—Vinson Massif 16,864; Europe—Mont Blanc 15,771; South America—Aconcagua 22,834; Africa—Kilimanjaro 19,340.

c. On February 20, 1943, smoke began pouring out of a hole in the ground in the village of Paricutin, Mexico. On February 21, a cinder cone had grown from the hole to a height of 100 feet. In two weeks, the young volcano was 450 ft. tall. In 8 months, it was 930 ft., and in 2 years it reached 1,020 ft. Nine years after its birth, the volcano had risen to an altitude of 1,350 ft. Make a graph to illustrate the growth of this volcano.

d. In tropical Africa, mountains such as Kilimanjaro have 6 distinct ecological zones. On a mountain that is about 19,000 ft. high, the zones are: 1) grasslands (called savanna) from ground level to 6,500 ft.; 2) dense rainforest to 9,500 ft.; 3) dense bamboo forest to 10,000 ft.; 4) heath forest to 13,000 ft.; 5) alpine zone to 16,000 ft.; 6) permanent snow beyond 16,000 feet. Draw a chart that illustrates these numbers.

e. It is colder at the top of a mountain than at its base. The air temperature drops about 4°F for every 1,000 feet of altitude. Use this information to calculate the temperature at the top of the mountain in the following cases: 1) It is 50° at the base of a mountain, and the mountain is 19,000 ft. high; 2) 84°F at the base and 1,400 ft. high; 3) 72°F at the base and 25,000 ft. high; 4) 47°F at the base and 16,500 ft. high; 5) 65°F at the base and 29,000 ft. high; 6) 98°F at the base and 7,200 ft. high; 7) 32°F at the base and 1,800 ft. high; 8) 55°F at the base and 21,200 ft. high; 9) 105°F at the base and 5,400 ft. high; 10) 87°F at the base and 21,400 ft. high.

f. Convert the following mountain heights to meters: 1) Aconcagua in the Andes is the highest extinct volcano at 22,835 ft. 2) The tallest mountain above sea level is Mt. Everest on the Nepal/China border at 29,028 ft. 3) The sheerest mountain wall is that of Mt. Rakaposhi in Pakistan, which is 25,498 ft. 4) The highest mountain in North America is Mt. McKinley at 20,320 ft. 5) The highest altitude in Florida is 345 ft.

g. Use a calculator to answer the following questions: 1) The Himalayan/Karakoran mountain range contains 96 of the 109 mountains in the world that are over 24,000 ft. tall. What percent is that? 2) The normal speed for a glacier to move is about 15 feet in one year. How many years would it take for a glacier to move one mile? 3) The greatest mountain range on Earth is the underwater Mid-Atlantic Range, which is about 10,000 miles long and 500 miles wide. What is the area in square miles of the Mid-Atlantic Ridge? 4) Hawaiian volcano Mauna Loa is the tallest mountain on Earth, at a total height of 33,476 ft. (19,678 ft. of this is underwater). How many feet are above sea level? What percent of the mountain's total height is above sea level? 5) The Los Angeles, California, San Gabriel Mtns. are about 10,000 ft. high. In 1977, an unusually heavy rainfall caused a debris flow of water, land and rock. It poured down at 550 ft. per minute, causing major destruction in the city. How long would it have taken the debris flow to travel halfway down a mountain?

MUSIC AND THEATER ARTS

a. Sing songs about mountains, such as "She'll Be Coming Around the Mountain," or "On Top of Old Smokey."

b. *Group project*: Act out these geological scenes: 1) The entire class should stand bunched up together on one side of the room. Pretend to be a glacier, moving oh-so-slowly across the room. 2) Now the group is a landslide, roaring down a mountainside. How do you move? 3) Act out the birth of a volcano. Some children can form the growing cone of the volcano, while others can represent rocks and lava erupting from it.

c. There are many folktales and legends that take place in the mountains, such as the Native American tale "When Coyote Stole Fire." Choose one mountain story from any culture. Perform a puppet show of this tale.   (8)

d. *Group project*: Decide which mountain you would like to visit and take part in an imaginary guided tour of that mountain. Point out plants, animals, and other things of interest that would be found on your mountain.   (12, 16)

e. *Group project*: Many mountain sports require the use of special equipment. Choose one sport and demonstrate how to use the equipment involved. You can use simulated items (such as skis made out of cardboard). Each member of the group can show a different aspect of its use. For example, one person can demonstrate how to put on skis, another can show how to walk in them, someone else can simulate skiing down a slope, etc.

f. Listen to the music of people who live in mountains, such as *Malkuri: Traditional Music of the Andes* by Soundings of the Planet, *Mountain Music of Peru* by Smithsonian/Folkways, or *Cumbre* produced by Sukay. Compare the music of these Andes people to what you have read about their culture.

g. The play *Foxfire* takes place on a mountain in the Appalachians. Act out a scene from this play, or another play set in or near mountains.

ENGLISH COMPOSITION

a. Write a story or poem about a visit to a mountain. What do you do there? What do you see? (1, 3, 5, 6, 8, 12, 19, 25)

b. The song "America the Beautiful" describes mountains as "purple mountain majesties above the fruited plains." Look at pictures of mountains and create several picturesque phrases to describe how they look to you.

c. Many mountain animals are endangered. Choose one mountain animal and write a report about it. Tell what it looks like, where and how it lives, and why it is endangered. (11, 12, 16, 25)

d. The Abominable Snowman, or Yeti, is a creature that is rumored to live in the Himalayas. Look up some information about this creature. Then write a fiction or nonfiction story about a sighting of the Abominable Snowman. (16, 17)

e. Do one of the following writing exercises: 1) Write an adventure story about a mountain-climbing expedition. Include descriptions of your clothing and equipment, and tell what you did on the climb. 2) Write a report about an actual mountain-climbing expedition. Tell who was involved, what mountain was attempted, and whether or not the climb was successful. (16, 19)

f. Mountains are often the sites of natural disasters, such as avalanches, volcanic eruptions, earthquakes, and landslides. Write a fictitious eyewitness account of a natural disaster as it occurs on or near a mountain. Describe what happens to the mountain and how it affects the animals, people, and area around it. (4, 11, 13, 14, 18, 19, 23, 26, 27)

g. Choose a specific mountain or mountain range and write a travel guide about it. Include pictures and descriptions of the area, some plants and animals that live there, things to do, any events of note that happened there, the best time to visit, etc. (12, 16, 17)

SCIENCE

a. Mountains form on the outer layer of the Earth, called the crust. What are Earth's other layers? What are they like? (3, 4, 7, 8, 16, 19, 20, 23, 28)

b. How do mountains affect the climate of the surrounding area? How can the eruptions of volcanoes affect weather? (3, 5, 9, 10, 11, 16, 18, 21, 27)

c. What is erosion? What are some of the ways mountains are eroded? What can slow down erosion? What is weathering? How does weathering wear away mountains? (3, 4, 7, 8, 9, 10, 11, 13, 14, 15, 16, 19, 21, 22, 23, 27)

d. What is a volcano? How can a dormant volcano become active? Name the different forms of volcanoes and ways they might erupt. What are the various forms escaping lava may take? (2, 3, 4, 14, 16, 18, 19, 20, 21, 22, 23, 26, 27, 28)

e. How are fold, block, dome and undersea mountains formed? Name some mountains that are examples of each type. (2, 4, 5, 7, 9, 10, 12, 14, 16, 18, 19, 20, 21, 22, 23, 27, 28)

f. How can mountains provide energy? Give some examples of how mountain resources are harnessed or mined by humans to supply energy. (8, 9, 11, 12, 19)

g. How does the temperature on a mountain vary according to altitude? What plants and animals can survive at the various altitudinal zones? How do factors such as the shape of the mountain and access to light, wind, ice, and soil conditions determine the type of plants and animals that live on a mountain? (3, 5, 9, 11, 12, 16, 19, 21, 27)

HISTORY/SOCIOLOGY

a. Name some disasters, such as volcanic eruptions or avalanches, that involved mountains. Choose one of these events and find out some information about it. What was the nature of the disaster? When and where did it occur? What happened? (3, 4, 16, 18, 28)

b. Who were the Incas? Where did they live? What did they accomplish? What happened to them? (3, 11, 12, 19)

c. Choose one mountain sport, such as skiing, sledding, or mountain-climbing. Find out about the history of the sport and one or more persons who have excelled at it. (3, 16, 19, 21, 27)

d. Few people live in the mountains. What factors make living in mountains so difficult? How have mountain-dwellers adapted to life at high altitudes?

Note some interesting facts about a group of people who live on a particular mountain range.   (3, 9, 11, 12, 16, 19, 21, 24, 25, 27)

e. List, in chronological order, the eras and periods of geologic time. Then tell what type of mountain-building activity happened during each time. Name specific mountain ranges whenever possible. For example, when were the Appalachian Mountains formed? Which mountain ranges are forming now?   (9, 12, 23, 27)

f. Look up information about a famous mountain climber, such as Edmund Hillary, or a noteworthy mountain-climbing expedition. Write a report about your subject.   (16, 17, 19, also *The Guinness Book of World Records*)

g. Write a report on how logging, air pollution, mining, tourism, damming, or another human interference has caused destruction on one particular mountain or mountain system. How much damage has been done to the mountain and its environment? What effect has this had on the surrounding area? What is being done to repair the damage?   (9, 11, 15, 19, 27)

TOPICS FOR DISCUSSION

a. Mountains are beautiful, but they can also be dangerous. Give some examples of possible mountain dangers. Why do people live near mountains or visit them if they are dangerous?   (5, 13, 14, 16, 18, 26)

b. What are some forces in nature that erode mountains? What are some human activities that damage mountains and upset mountain habitats? (4, 7, 8, 9, 10, 11, 12, 13, 15, 16, 21, 22, 23, 25, 27)

c. What are some natural resources contained in and on mountains? How do people use these resources?   (3, 7, 8, 9, 12, 16, 19, 21, 22, 23, 27)

d. In the past, mountains were considered barriers to people. Why? How has modern technology allowed people to overcome these barriers? How has this affected mountain habitats?   (9, 12, 19)

e. What is deforestation and what are some causes? How does mountain deforestation destroy animal habitats? How does it harm the environments surrounding the mountains and beyond?   (9, 11, 15, 16, 19, 27)

f. Why are mountain environments fragile? How do humans exploit mountains? What can be done to conserve mountain resources and protect mountain environments?   (9, 11, 12, 13, 16, 19, 27)

g. How does the exploitation of mountain environments increase the possibility of avalanches, landslides, and flooding? What conservation measures can be taken to lessen the frequency and severity of these disasters? (11, 13, 15, 21, 27)

SUGGESTED RESOURCES

(1) Amsel, Sheri. *Mountains* [Habitats of the World]. Raintree, 1993.
(2) Aylesworth, Thomas G. *Moving Continents: Our Changing Earth* [Earth Processes]. Enslow, 1990.
(3) Bailey, Donna. *Mountains* [Facts About]. Steck-Vaughn, 1990.
(4) Bain, Iain. *Mountains and Earth Movements* [Planet Earth]. Bookwright, 1984.
(5) Barrett, Norman. *Mountains* [Picture Library]. Watts, 1989.
(6) Behm, Barbara J., and Bonar, Veronica. *Exploring Mountains* [Eco-Journey]. Stevens, 1994.
(7) Bender, Lionel. *Mountain* [The Story of the Earth]. Watts, 1988.
(8) Bradley, Catherine. *Life in the Mountains* [Life in]. Scholastic, 1993.
(9) Bramwell, Martyn. *Mountains* [Earth Science Library]. Watts, 1994.
(10) Brandt, Keith. *Mountains*. Troll, 1985.
(11) Collinson, Alan. *Mountains* [Ecology Watch]. Dillon, 1991.
(12) Dixon, Dougal. *Mountains* [Franklin Watts Picture Atlas]. Watts, 1984.
(13) Facklam, Howard, and Facklam, Margery. *Avalanche!* [Nature's Disasters]. Crestwood, 1991.
(14) Goodman, Billy. *Natural Wonders and Disasters* [Planet Earth]. Little, 1991.
(15) Hogan, Paula. *Fragile Mountains* [Environment Alert!]. Stevens, 1991.
(16) Jennings, Terry. *Mountains* [Exploring Our World]. Cavendish, 1987.
(17) Landau, Elaine. *Yeti: Abominable Snowman of the Himalayas* [Mysteries of Science]. Millbrook, 1993.
(18) Lauber, Patricia. *Volcano: The Eruption and Healing of Mount St. Helens*. Bradbury, 1986.
(19) Lye, Keith. *Mountains* [Our World]. Silver, 1987.
(20) Mariner, Tom. *Continents* [Earth in Action]. Cavendish, 1990.
(21) _____. *Mountains* [Earth in Action]. Cavendish, 1990.
(22) Markle, Sandra. *Digging Deeper: Investigations into Rocks, Shocks, Quakes, and Other Earthly Matters*. Lothrop, 1987.
(23) Silver, Donald M. *Earth: The Ever-Changing Planet* [Random House Library of Knowledge]. Random, 1989.
(24) Stewart, Gail. *In the Mountains* [Living Spaces]. Rourke, 1989.
(25) Stone, Lynne M. *Mountains* [New True Books]. Childrens, 1983.
(26) Thomas, Margaret. *Volcano!* [Nature's Disasters]. Crestwood, 1991.
(27) Williams, Lawrence. *Mountains* [Last Frontiers for Mankind]. Cavendish, 1990.
(28) Wood, Jenny. *Volcanoes: Fire from Below* [Wonderworks of Nature]. Stevens, 1990.

LIBRARY SKILLS RESOURCES

The Guinness Book of World Records. Facts on File, 1994.
How the Earth Works [Science in Our World]. Grolier, 1992.
Rocks and Minerals of the World [Using and Understanding Maps]. Chelsea, 1993.
Webster's New World Pocket Geographical Dictionary. Prentice Hall, 1994.
World Book Encyclopedia. World Book, 1994.
Wright, David, and Wright, Jill. *The Facts on File Children's Atlas*. Facts on File, 1993.

ADDITIONAL READING – YOUNGER

Animals in the Mountains [Animals and Their Homes]. Raintree, 1988.

Baker, Susan. *Mountains* [First Look]. Stevens, 1991.

Berger, Melvin. *As Old as the Hills* [Discovering Science]. Watts, 1989.

Catchpole, Clive. *Mountains* [The Living World]. Dial, 1985.

Cobb, Vicki. *This Place Is High* [Imagine Living Here]. Walker, 1989.

George, Jean Craighead. *The Moon of the Mountain Lions* [Thirteen Moons]. Crowell, 1991.

_____. *One Day in the Alpine Tundra.* Crowell, 1984.

Hargrove, Jim, and Johnson, Sylvia A. *Mountain Climbing* [Superwheels and Thrill Sports]. Lerner, 1983.

Hyden, Tom, and Anderson, Tim. *Rock Climbing Is for Me* [Sports for Me Books]. Lerner, 1984.

Kramer, S. A. *To the Top!* [Step into Reading]. Random, 1993.

Lye, Keith. *Mountains* [First Starts]. Raintree, 1993.

Magley, Beverly. *The Fire Mountains: The Story of the Cascade Volcanoes* [Interpreting the Great Outdoors]. Falcon, 1989.

Morgan, Patricia G. *A Mountain Adventure* [Let's Take a Trip]. Troll, 1988.

Morrison, Marion. *An Inca Farmer* [How They Lived]. Rourke, 1988.

Reynolds, Jan. *Himalaya* [Vanishing Cultures]. Harcourt, 1991.

Rylant, Cynthia. *Appalachia: The Voices of Sleeping Birds.* Harcourt, 1991.

_____. *When I Was Young in the Mountains.* Dutton, 1982.

Schachtel, Roger. *Caught on a Cliff Face.* Raintree, 1980.

Siebert, Diane. *Sierra.* HarperCollins, 1991.

Simon, Seymour. *Mountains.* Morrrow, 1994.

Taylor, Barbara. *Mountains and Volcanoes* [Young Discoverers]. Kingfisher, 1993.

ADDITIONAL READING – OLDER

Allen, Linda B. *High Mountain Challenge: A Guide for Young Mountaineers.* Appalachian, 1989.

Bain, Iain. *Mountains and People* [Nature's Landscapes]. Silver, 1982.

Barnes-Svarney, Patricia L. *Born of Heat and Pressure: Mountains and Metamorphic Rocks* [Earth Processes]. Enslow, 1991.

Blue Ridge Range: The Gentle Mountains. National Geographic, 1992.

Bullen, Susan. *The Alps and Their People* [People and Places]. Thomson, 1994.

Christian, Mary Blount. *Bigfoot* [The Mystery of. . .]. Crestwood, 1987.

Cooper, Susan, and Cronyn, Hume. *Foxfire: A Play Based on Materials from the Foxfire Books.* French, 1983.

George, Jean Craighead. *My Side of the Mountain.* Dutton, 1988.

Glass, Paul, and Singer, Louis C. *Songs of Hill and Mountain Folk.* Grosset, 1967.

Gonzalez, Christina. *Inca Civilization* [World Heritage]. Childrens, 1993.

Haley, Gail E. *Mountain Jack Tales.* Dutton, 1992.

Hirschi, Ron *Who Lives in the Mountains?* [Who Lives in. . .] Putnam, 1989.

Horwitz, Elinor Lander. *Mountain People, Mountain Crafts.* Lippincott, 1974.

Knapp, Brian. *Volcano* [World Disasters]. Steck-Vaughn, 1990.

Lambert, David, and The Diagram Group. *The Field Guide to Geology.* Facts on File, 1988.

Lasky, Kathryn. *Surtsey: The Newest Place on Earth.* Hyperion, 1992.

Milne, Lorus J., and Milne, Margery. *The Mountains* [Life Nature Library]. Time, 1962.

Morrison, Marion. *Indians of the Andes* [Original Peoples]. Rourke, 1987.

Rinard, Judith E. *Animals of the High Mountains* [Books for Young Explorers]. National Geographic, 1989.

Tilling, Robert I. *Born of Fire: Volcanoes and Igneous Rocks* [Earth Processes]. Enslow, 1991.

Wakefield, Celia. *High Cities of the Andes.* Wide World-Tetra, 1988.

See also: books in OUR EARTH unit.

FOR MORE INFORMATION ABOUT MOUNTAINS, WRITE TO:

Alliance for the Wild Rockies
Council of the Alleghanies
Hawaii Volcanoes National Park
Institute of Andean Studies
International Mountain Society
Mountaineers

National Parks and Conservation
 Association
Ozark Society
Sierra Club
World Wildlife Fund

GRASSLANDS

Grasslands are one of the most important ecosystems on Earth. It was on these fertile plains that early humans first learned to cultivate the land and domesticate animals. But as humans developed these skills, they upset the balance of nature. Today, natural grasslands, along with their plants and wildlife, are shrinking due to overpopulation, over-farming, and overgrazing. We must strive to repair the damage done to grasslands and to encourage the preservation of plants and animals that originally inhabited these lands.

LIBRARY SKILLS

a. Use a dictionary or encyclopedia to answer the following: What is the difference between a bison and a buffalo? Where does each animal live?

b. Following is a list of grassland terms. Place them in alphabetical order. Then look up each word in a dictionary and divide it into syllables: baobab, wildebeest, Serengeti, acacia, hyena, marsupial, decomposer, kangaroo, capybara, nomadic, hippopotamus, elephant.

c. Use *Children's Guide to Endangered Animals* or a similar source to look up information about the following endangered grassland animals. Write a sentence about each one: African elephant, bridled nail-tail wallaby, black-footed ferret, pampas deer, corncrake, great bustard, European bison, pronghorn, volcano rabbit, Przewalski's horse.

d. Use the *Young Scientist* series to answer the following questions: 1) Give a brief definition of grasslands. 2) Grass is eaten, cut, and burned. Why does it keep growing in spite of this? 3) The Sahel in Africa was once fertile grassland. Now it is desert. How did the Sahel become a desert?

e. Use the *Lands and Peoples* series to answer the following: 1) What are the three Canadian prairie provinces? Where are they located? 2) Where does the word "prairie" come from and what does it mean? 3) When were the prairie provinces settled? By whom? How much did it cost the settlers to acquire land? 4) What is the climate of this area? 5) What tragedy occurred in the 1930s and why? 6) In addition to farming and ranching, what are some other industries and resources of these Canadian provinces?

f. Many grassland animals, such as wildebeests, zebras, elephants and bison, regularly migrate across large expanses of land. Choose one migratory grassland animal. Use the *Atlas of Animal Migration* to write a summary of the animal's migration habits and route.

g. In *The Information Please Environmental Almanac,* look up Wildlife. 1) What are some grassland animals that are legally hunted in United States wildlife refuges? What are some arguments for and against this practice? 2) How has poaching affected the populations of African elephants and rhinoceros? 3) What is CITES? What is the CITES position on legal hunting of these animals?

ARTS AND CRAFTS

a. Many grassland animals are endangered. Draw a poster to encourage people to protect one or more grassland animals from extinction. (1, 3, 4, 5, 8, 16, 22, 24, 25, 26)

b. Make a collage of grassland scenes. Include various types of grassland plants as well as wildlife.

c. Many staple foods are made of grasses. Glue dried corn kernels, rice, barley, oat flakes, macaroni and bran on paperboard to make a mosaic design with grass foods.

d. Draw a picture that illustrates the food web of a savannah or prairie ecosystem. (10, 11, 16, 23, 24, 27)

e. Make a diorama of a grassland habitat. Label your work to show what part of the world the diorama represents. Be careful to include only the plants, animals, and landscape that are specific to the area you have chosen.

f. Some examples of simple grassland homes of the past and present include the "soddies" of the American pioneers, tepees of the Plains Indians, and yurts of the Mongols of the Central Asian steppes. Make a model of one of these, or another grassland home. Label your model telling what it is, who lived there, and the materials that were used to make it. (6, 10, 15, 21)

g. *Group project:* Make a bulletin board or mural of extinct and endangered grassland animals. Label each animal with its name, physical characteristics, feeding and migration habits, and where it lives or lived. If extinct, tell when the species died out.

SPELLING/VOCABULARY

a. Complete a matching picture puzzle of African and Eurasian grassland animals: zebra, cheetah, giraffe, lion, gazelle, hyena, jackal, vulture, wildebeest, ostrich, elephant, secretary bird, locust, weaverbird, leopard, rhinoceros, saiga, Przewalski's horse, aardvark, bustard.   (1, 3, 4, 7, 10, 11, 12, 16, 17, 22, 25, 26, 27)

b. Complete a matching picture puzzle of North and South American grassland animals: bison, pronghorn, prairie dog, coyote, black-footed ferret, prairie chicken, jackrabbit, rattlesnake, armadillo, elk, skylark, badger, grasshopper, gray fox, pampas deer, rhea, llama, anteater, capybara, scarlet ibis. (1, 3, 4, 7, 10, 11, 17, 18, 20, 23, 24, 25)

c. Complete a word search puzzle of grassland plants: cattail, poppy, iris, steppe thistle, legumes, bluebonnet, aster, pasque, bluestem, cordgrass, baobab, acacia, indigo, milkweed, phlox, coneflower, sunflower, clover, gentian, goldenrod.   (1, 7, 10, 13, 18, 23)

d. Complete a crossword puzzle of terms that relate to grassland animals: graze, migrate, herbivore, carnivore, browse, fossorial, trample, predator, scavenger, lek, burrow, adaptation, herd, pride, omnivore, colony, camouflage, rodent, marsupial, kopje.   (4, 7, 11, 16, 23, 24, 26, 27)

e. Complete a crossword puzzle of terms that relate to grassland vegetation: forb, perennial, annual, rhizome, tiller, sod, pollinate, herb, dormant, decompose, tussock, blade, stolan, spikelet, stamen, shoots, humus, topsoil, litter, chernozems.   (5, 7, 10, 11, 12, 13, 20, 23)

f. Define the following terms that relate to the grassy areas of the world. Tell how each type is different from the others: steppe, meadow, veldt (or veld), puszta, downs, pampas, pamir, scrubland, pasture, llanos, plain, savannah, field, puna, patana, farmland, tallgrass prairie, middle grass prairie, short grass prairie, campos.   (4, 5, 7, 10, 12, 17, 20)

g. Choose a grassland area anywhere in the world. Create a word puzzle using at least twenty terms related to that area.

GEOGRAPHY

a. On a map of the world, color in the grassland areas.   (1, 3, 4, 5, 7, 10, 11, 12)

b. Grasslands are called various names in different parts of the world. Match each of the following terms to the correct continent: savannah, pampas, prairie, veldt, llanos, steppe.   (1, 4, 5, 7, 10, 11, 25)

c. Divide a sheet of paper into five columns. Label them: North America, South America, Africa, Eurasia, Australia. In each column, list some animals and plants that live in grasslands there.   (1, 2, 4, 5, 7, 10, 12, 16, 22, 25, 26)

d. Much of the world's grasslands are cultivated for farming or fenced in for ranching. Name some crops grown and animals raised for food on grasslands in each continent (except Antarctica). (5, 10, 11, 12)

e. Where are the temperate grasslands? Where are tropical grasslands? What are these grasslands called? List some specific differences between them, such as amount of rainfall, climate, vegetation, etc. (5, 10, 11, 12)

f. Divide a sheet of paper into five columns and label them: Eurasian steppe, African savannah, African veldt, South American pampas, Australian grassland. Compare geographical features of these areas, including climate, rainfall, seasons, terrain, size of areas, etc. (5, 10, 11, 12, 16)

g. On a map of the United States, draw the areas of the three types of prairie: tallgrass, middle grass, and short grass. Explain some of the differences among them, such as amount of rainfall and the types of vegetation that grow in each one. Before the arrival of the Europeans, what area of North America was covered by grasslands? For what purpose is most of this area now used? (11, 12, 20, 23)

MATH

a. Following are the top speeds in miles per hour of several grassland animals: Red kangaroo 25; ostrich 45; cheetah 70; rhinoceros 25; pronghorn 60; rhea 40; cape buffalo 13; hyena 40; emu 30; Przewalski's horse 30; Dorcas gazelle 50; bison 35; saiga 50; jackrabbit 45; African elephant 25; coyote 43. Make a chart to compare the speeds of these animals. (3, 4, 8)

b. America's prairie is of three types. The short grass prairie receives 10 to 15 inches of rain per year, and the grasses grow about 12 to 15 inches high. The middle grass prairie gets from 20 to 23 inches of rain per year, and the grasses grow from 2 to 4 feet high. The tallgrass prairie receives about 40 inches of rain annually. These grasses range in height from 5 to 12 feet tall. Make two charts that compare the rainfall and growth of these prairie areas.

c. Answer these questions about the African savannah: 1) Each month during Africa's rainy season, a half square mile of grassland produces about 450 tons of grass. At that rate, how much grass would be produced during one month in an area of one square mile? 6 square miles? 25 square miles? 2) With 450 tons of grass being a day's worth of food for about 30 antelope, how many antelope will 6 square miles of grass feed? 25 square miles? 3) New grass in the Serengeti can grow an inch in 24 hours. At that rate, how long will it take to grow one foot? Some grasses can reach 6 feet. How many days would that take? (4)

d. Grassland animals include insects, birds, large mammals, small mammals, and amphibians/reptiles. Choose ten grassland animals from one of these categories. Make charts or graphs to compare their weights, sizes, and natural lifespans.   (2, 5, 8, 10, 12, 16, 17, 18, 20, 23, 25)

  e. Answer these questions about endangered grassland animals. If your answer is a fraction, round it off to the next whole number. 1) An estimated 2,500,000 bison were killed by white hunters in the United States between 1870 and 1875. On the average, how many bison were killed per year? Buffalo Bill Cody alone reportedly killed 400 bison in 17 months. What was his average kill per month? 2) Each year, poachers kill about 100,000 African elephants for their tusks. What is the average number of elephants killed per month? 3) About 50,000,000 pronghorns were living in North America when the Europeans arrived. By 1920, there were only 13,000 left. What percent were killed? Conservationists were able to rescue the pronghorns from extinction. By 1985, there were about 450,000 animals. What percent of an increase is the 1985 figure over the 1920 figure? What percent is the 1985 number from the original number? 4) Because of poaching, the rhinoceros population has dropped by 85 percent. Only about 5,000 remain in African wildlife reserves. What was the former rhinoceros population?   (10, 22, 25)

  f. Answer these math questions about the North American prairies: 1) North America once had 400,000 square miles of tallgrass prairie. Now, less than 4,000 square miles of natural tallgrass remains. What percent was destroyed? 2) When American explorers Lewis and Clark first crossed the continent in 1805, there were 1,400,000 square miles of prairie land. How many square miles were the middle and short grass prairies combined? What percent of the total prairie area did this represent? 3) Illinois alone once had 38,600 square miles of tallgrass prairie. Now there are only about 4 square miles left. What percent was lost? 4) Big bluestem grass can grow a half inch per day. At that rate, how many days would it take to reach its greatest height of 12 feet? 5) At its greatest width, the North American prairie extends north and south for 2,400 miles. How many feet is that?   (5, 23)

  g. Answer these questions about grassland animals: 1) The cheetah's top speed is 70 miles per hour, but it can only sustain this speed for about 1,300 feet. Then it slows down to about 45 mph. Some gazelles can sustain a speed of 50 mph for longer distances. A cheetah is 100 feet from a gazelle. If they both run at their top speeds, will the cheetah catch the gazelle? What if they start running at 150 feet apart? 200 feet? 2) A male African elephant eats about 300 pounds of food during a period of 16 hours each day. At that rate, how many pounds of food does it eat per minute? 3) A locust swarm may contain a billion insects. They can eat 3 million pounds of food in one day. How much food does each locust consume in a day? 4) The three largest grassland birds are swift runners. The emu can run 30 mph, the rhea 40 mph, and the ostrich 45 mph. If they were to run a 20 mile race against each other, how many minutes would it take for each bird to run the course?   (8, 10)

MUSIC AND THEATER ARTS

a. Sing songs of the American prairie, such as "Home on the Range" and "Sweet Betsy from Pike."

b. Grassland animals have different characteristics. Elephants are slow and heavy, gazelles are swift and graceful, etc. How would you use music to describe each animal? For example, which animal could be represented by two low notes repeated on a tuba? A speedy trill on a flute? Try to match different types of music to several grassland animals.

c. People that live in grasslands, such as the Masai people in Africa or the North American Plains Indians, tell many folktales and legends. Choose one story and perform a puppet show of it.

d. Some children's books about prairie life, such as *Little House on the Prairie* or *Sarah, Plain and Tall,* have been made into television shows or movies. Act out a scene from one of these books.

e. Life on the prairie was difficult in the 1800s. An old American folksong, "Starving to Death on a Government Claim," describes the feelings of one of these early pioneers. Listen to the words of this song. Is the song serious or humorous? Try making up your own verse to this song.

f. The American buffalo, or bison, was very important to the livelihood of the Plains Indians. Act out a scene from a buffalo hunt, such as a dance in preparation of a hunt, stalking a buffalo on horseback or on foot, etc. (9, 14, 15)

g. Around the world, there are debates over how to manage grasslands. Act out one of these scenes, or make up one of your own: 1) Australian ranchers think of kangaroos as pests that should be exterminated to make room for their animals to graze; conservationists think the ranchers' sheep and cattle are destroying the land. 2) American farmers want to plant corn in the last of the fertile tallgrass prairie; naturalists want to preserve the area. 3) Keepers of the Serengeti want to save elephants, lions, and rhinoceros from extinction; people living nearby argue that these animals are destructive and should be hunted. (5, 10, 11, 12, 16, 20)

ENGLISH COMPOSITION

a. Write a letter to one of the addresses listed below to ask for more information about grasslands.

b. Read some stories, such as Rudyard Kipling's "How the Leopard Got His Spots" from *Just So Stories,* or folktales about some grassland animals.

Then make up your own story to explain why another grassland animal looks or acts the way it does.

   c. The tallgrass prairie has often been described as "a sea of grass." The African baobab tree has been called "the tree of life." Write a poem about either topic. (2, 7, 11, 13, 18, 21, 23)

   d. Look at some photographs or paintings of American pioneers or Plains Indians of the 1800s. Write a story or essay based on what you see in one of these pictures. (6, 9, 15)

   e. Write a true story about a grassland animal. Tell where and how it lives. What is its role in the grassland food web or ecosystem? (1, 2, 4, 5, 8, 10, 12, 16, 22, 24, 25, 26, 27)

   f. The pioneers and frontiersmen that homesteaded the American prairie in the 1800s led difficult lives. Write several diary entries from the point of view of one of these people. Describe the land, your home, how you live, and some of the difficulties you encounter. Do you enjoy your life on the prairie, or do you long to move back to your former home? (6, 21)

   g. North American Plains Indians lived on the prairie for many years before the pioneers settled the area. With the white man's arrival, the Indians' way of life changed drastically. Write a story or essay from the point of view of a Plains Indian. Tell your reaction to these changes and how you think your future will be affected. (1, 4, 9, 12, 14, 15, 21, 23, 25)

SCIENCE

   a. What important foods are from the grass family? Look at seeds of these grasses. Plant some seeds and see how they grow. (7, 10, 11, 12, 18, 20, 23, 25)

   b. How do water and fire help to form grasslands? In what type of climate do grasslands thrive? Why? (5, 7, 11, 13, 17, 18, 20, 23)

   c. Divide a sheet of paper into four columns. Label them: Rodents, Insects and Bugs, Reptiles and Amphibians, Birds. List some grassland animals in each column. (2, 5, 8, 10, 12, 16, 17, 18, 20, 23, 24)

   d. What are some factors that caused grasslands to develop and grow hundreds of thousands of years ago? How can grasses grow in places that forests cannot? (5, 10, 11, 12, 16, 18, 24)

   e. Divide a sheet of paper into four columns. Label them: Browsers and Grazers, Scavengers, Predators, and Decomposers. In each column, list several grassland animals of that type. (1, 3, 4, 5, 7, 8, 10, 11, 12, 16, 20, 23, 24, 25, 26, 27)

f. What is biological diversity? Explain this in the context of a grasslands ecosystem. (5, 10, 11, 12, 18, 20)

g. Choose one animal and one plant from the same grassland ecosystem. Tell how they are both adapted to their environment. Then choose a plant and animal from a different grassland ecosystem and explain their adaptations. What are some similarities and differences between the plants and animals you chose? (5, 8, 10, 11, 12, 22, 24, 27)

HISTORY/SOCIOLOGY

a. The pioneers who settled America's prairies in the 1800s usually did not have wood or stone available for building homes. What did they use instead? How were these homes built? What were some problems of living in these homes? (6, 17, 21)

b. What happened to the American bison during the 1800s? How did this affect the ecology of the prairie and the Plains Indians who lived there? (4, 7, 9, 12, 14, 15, 20, 23, 24, 25)

c. Name some tribes that lived in grasslands years ago. Which tribes were hunter-gatherers or herders-shepherds? What did they eat? (9, 10, 11, 12, 14, 15, 19)

d. What was the Homestead Act? How did the pioneers during this time change the American prairie? (6, 10, 11, 20, 21, 23, 24)

e. Look up some information about a grasslands people, such as the Masai people of East Africa or the North American Plains Indians. Compare their lives now to how they lived in the past. How has it changed? Why? (5, 10, 11, 12, 14, 15, 16, 19, 20)

f. Humans have caused many ecological disasters on Earth's grasslands. Some have had far-reaching effects on the land, wildlife, habitats, and people. Name some of these disasters. Tell when, where, and why they occurred. (5, 10, 11, 12, 18, 20)

g. Scientists believe that the first humans evolved from apes that lived on the African savanna. Trace the history of these early humans. When did they live? What knowledge helped them to control their environment? Why was this part of the world favorable for the advancement of this species? How did humans spread to all parts of the world? (5, 10, 12)

TOPICS FOR DISCUSSION

a. What effects have farming and ranching had on the world's grasslands? (1, 4, 5, 7, 10, 11, 12, 13, 17, 23, 25)

b. What is the difference between natural grasslands and cultivated grasslands? Why are natural grasslands important? What are some problems that occur when natural grasslands are destroyed?   (5, 7, 10, 11, 12, 17, 23, 25)

c. What are some causes of grassland destruction? What is being done to save grasslands?   (4, 5, 7, 11, 12, 13, 17, 23)

d. What is poaching? Why is it done? How does poaching affect the grasslands' ecosystem? Why is it difficult to prevent poaching?   (5, 16, 25, 26, 27)

e. How much of Earth's land surface was once grassland? How much is grassland today? What has happened to much of Earth's temperate grasslands? What is happening to much of the tropical grasslands? Why?   (5, 10, 11, 12, 20)

f. Name some grassland animals that are extinct or endangered. What are some of the reasons this has happened? Give examples of animals from different parts of the world.   (5, 8, 9, 12, 15, 16, 22, 24, 25)

g. For hundreds of thousands of years, humans have been altering the ecology of the world's grasslands. Why and how have they changed grasslands? Give some specific examples from various parts of the world. Humans' interference never seriously upset the balance of nature until a few hundred years ago. Why did humans suddenly have greater control over grassland areas? Has this power been used wisely?   (5, 11, 12, 20)

SUGGESTED RESOURCES

(1) Amsel, Sheri. *Grasslands* [Habitats of the World]. Raintree, 1993.
(2) Bash, Barbara. *Tree of Life: The World of the African Baobab* [Tree Tales]. Sierra Club, 1989.
(3) Catchpole, Clive. *Grasslands* [The Living World]. Dial, 1984.
(4) Chinery, Michael. *Grassland Animals* [Tell Me About It]. Random, 1992.
(5) Collinson, Alan. *Grasslands* [Ecology Watch]. Dillon, 1992.
(6) Conrad, Pam. *Prairie Visions: The Life and Times of Solomon Butcher*. Harper-Collins, 1991.
(7) Cook, Kevin J. *Disappearing Grasslands* [Environment Alert!]. Stevens, 1993.
(8) Cuisin, Michel. *Animals of the African Plains* [Nature's Hidden World]. Silver, 1980.
(9) Freedman, Russell. *Buffalo Hunt*. Holiday, 1988.
(10) Horton, Casey. *Grasslands* [Franklin Watts Picture Atlas]. Watts, 1984.
(11) Knapp, Brian. *What Do We Know About Grasslands?* [Caring for Environments]. Bedrick, 1992.
(12) Lambert, David. *Grasslands* [Our World]. Silver, 1987.
(13) Lerner, Carol. *Seasons of the Tallgrass Prairie*. Morrow, 1980.
(14) May, Robin. *A Plains Indian Warrior* [How They Lived]. Rourke, 1988.
(15) _____. *Plains Indians of North America* [Original Peoples]. Rourke, 1987.

(16) Peters, Lisa Westberg. *Serengeti* [National Parks]. Crestwood, 1989.

(17) Rowan, James P. *Prairies and Grasslands* [New True Books]. Childrens, 1983.

(18) Sabin, Louis. *Grasslands*. Troll, 1985.

(19) Shachtman, Tom. *Growing Up Masai*. Macmillan, 1981.

(20) Siy, Alexandra. *Native Grasslands* [Circle of Life]. Dillon, 1991.

(21) Stein, R. Conrad. *The Story of the Homestead Act* [Cornerstones of Freedom]. Childrens, 1978.

(22) Stidworthy, John. *The Large Plant-Eaters* [Encyclopedia of the Animal World: Mammals]. Facts on File, 1988.

(23) Stone, Lynne M. *Prairies* [Ecozones]. Rourke, 1989.

(24) Taylor, Dave. *The Bison and the Great Plains* [Animals and Their Ecosystems]. Crabtree, 1990.

(25) _____. *Endangered Grassland Animals* [Endangered Animals]. Crabtree, 1992.

(26) _____. *Endangered Savannah Animals* [Endangered Animals]. Crabtree, 1993.

(27) _____. *The Lion and the Savannah* [Animals and Their Ecosystems]. Crabtree, 1990.

LIBRARY SKILLS RESOURCES

Few, Roger. *Children's Guide to Endangered Animals*. Macmillan, 1993.

Jarman, Cathy. *Atlas of Animal Migration*. John Day, 1972.

Lands and Peoples. Grolier, 1993.

World Resources Institute. *The Information Please Environmental Almanac*. Houghton, 1993.

Young Scientist. World Book, 1993.

ADDITIONAL READING — YOUNGER

Bannatyne-Cugnet, Jo. *A Prairie Alphabet*. Childrens, 1993.

Brusca, Maria Cristina. *My Mama's Little Ranch on the Pampas*. Holt, 1994.

Dvorak, David. *A Sea of Grass: The Tallgrass Prairie*. Macmillan, 1994.

George, Jean Craighead. *One Day in the Prairie*. Crowell, 1986.

Harvey, Brett. *My Prairie Year*. Holiday, 1986.

Lindblad, Lisa. *The Serengeti Migration: Africa's Animals on the Move*. Hyperion, 1994.

McGogan, Jim. *Josepha: A Prairie Boy's Story*. Chronicle, 1994.

Margolies, Barbara A. *Olbalbal: A Day in Masai Land*. Four Winds, 1994.

May, Robin. *An American Pioneer Family* [How They Lived]. Rourke, 1988.

Mitgitsch, Ali. *From Grain to Bread* [Start to Finish]. Carolrhoda, 1981.

[Nature's Children] series. Grolier.

Patent, Dorothy Hinshaw. *Prairie Dogs*. Clarion, 1993.

Prairie Animals [Treasury of American Wildlife]. Encyclopaedia Britannica, 1979.

Purcell, John Wallace. *African Animals* [New True Books]. Childrens, 1982.

Schmidt, Jeremy. *In the Village of the Elephants*. Walker, 1994.

Selley, Lyndsey. *Grasslands and Deserts* [Vanishing Animal Pop- Ups]. HarperCollins, 1993.

Taylor, Barbara. *Meadow* [Look Closer]. Kindersley, 1992.

Turner, Ann. *Dakota Dugout*. Macmillan, 1985.
_____. *Grasshopper Summer*. Macmillan, 1989.
Watts, Barrie. *24 Hours in a Game Reserve* [24 Hours]. Watts, 1992.
Welch, Catherine A. *Clouds of Terror*. Carolrhoda, 1994.

ADDITIONAL READING – OLDER

Conrad, Pam. *Prairie Songs*. HarperCollins, 1985.
Flint, David. *The Prairies and Their People* [People and Places]. Thomson, 1994.
Grasslands and Tundra [Planet Earth]. Time, 1985.
Hirschi, Ron. *Save Our Prairies and Grasslands* [One Earth]. Delacorte, 1994.
Johnson, Sylvia A. *Wheat* [Natural Science]. Lerner, 1990.
Kurelek, William. *A Prairie Boy's Summer*. Houghton, 1975.
_____. *A Prairie Boy's Winter*. Houghton, 1973.
Landau, Elaine. *The Sioux* [First Books – Indians of the Americas]. Watts, 1989.
Langley, Andrew. *Grasslands* [Nature Search]. Silver, 1989.
Lawler, Laurie. *Addie Across the Prairie*. Whitman, 1986.
MacLachlan, Patricia. *Sarah, Plain and Tall*. Harper, 1985.
_____. *Skylark*. HarperCollins, 1994.
Masey, Mary Lou, reteller. *Stories of the Steppes: Kazakh Folklore*. McKay, 1968.
Mbugua, Kioi wa, adapter. *INKISHU: Myths and Legends of the Maasai*. Jacarunda, 1994.
Sandler, Martin W. *Pioneers* [Library of Congress]. Scholastic, 1994.
Stone, Lynne M. *Autumn of the Elk* [Animal Odysseys]. Rourke, 1991. (Also other books in series.)
Turner, Ann. *Grass Songs: Poems*. Harcourt, 1993.
Wilder, Laura Ingalls. *Little House on the Prairie*. HarperCollins, 1993.

See also: books in ENDANGERED SPECIES AND HABITATS and FOOD AND FARMING units.

FOR MORE INFORMATION ABOUT GRASSLANDS, WRITE TO:

African Wildlife Foundation
Association of National Grasslands
Defenders of Wildlife
Grassland Heritage Foundation
Great Plains Agricultural Council

The Land Institute
National Wildlife Federation
The Nature Conservancy
Sierra Club
World Wildlife Fund

DESERTS

Deserts cover about a quarter of the Earth's surface, and they are spreading. Temperatures vary from scorchingly hot to frigidly cold and there is very little rain or water. Yet, some especially rugged animals and plants manage to survive in the desert. Life is uncertain, however, for the 5 percent of Earth's human population who inhabit these harsh environments.

LIBRARY SKILLS

a. Choose a book about deserts and find out the following information: Title of book, author, illustrator/photographer, number of pages, publisher, date of publication. Is there a Table of Contents? Glossary? Index? Is the book part of a series? If so, what is the name of the series?

b. Use *The Children's Atlas of People & Places* to look up the capitals and populations of the following desert countries: Mauritania, Algeria, Saudi Arabia, Yemen, Iran, Namibia, Pakistan, Israel, Western Sahara, Egypt.

c. Look up North Africa in *The Facts on File Children's Atlas* to answer the following: 1) What is the Suez Canal? 2) What North African country has the largest population? 3) Why is Libya rich? 4) How much of the Sahara Desert is sand dunes? What type of terrain is the rest of the desert? 5) How large is the Sahara?

d. Look up The Increasing Desert in *Atlas of World Issues* to answer the following: 1) To what percent of Earth's land and population is desertification a threat? 2) Where does desertification first occur? 3) What are some reasons for the desertification of the Sahel? 4) How does desertification change the local climates? 5) How many acres of range land are affected by desertification? How many acres of irrigated lands?

e. Look up Desert in *Lands and Peoples*. What kind of information do you find? Draw up a graph to show the number of deserts located on each continent based on this information.

f. Consult *The Guinness Book of World Records* to answer the following: 1) Where are the world's highest sand dunes? What are their measurements?

2) What was the highest shade temperature ever recorded? 3) When was the longest heat wave of consecutive days over 120°F in the United States? 4) How high was the tallest cactus? 5) What is the largest desert in the United States and what is its area in square miles? 6) About how many years was the longest drought? Where was it?

g. In *The New State of the World Atlas,* look up The Dying Earth. Use this information to color a map of the world. Color in orange the areas that are deserts. Color in purple the areas that are at risk of becoming deserts.

ARTS AND CRAFTS

a. Look at some pictures of Bedouin rugs. Glue pieces of yarn, felt, and beads onto squares of burlap to create your own Bedouin-design rugs. (1, 6, 13, 26)

b. Desert sand comes in many different colors. It can be used to make beautiful works of art. To make your own sand art, carefully spoon layers of different colors of sand into a clear plastic cup. You can poke a popsicle stick through the layers to make wavy lines. Cover your finished art work with plastic wrap. Be careful not to shake the cup.

c. Make replicas of some homes used by desert people, such as the grass hut of the Bushmen of the Kalahari Desert, the cave-like dwellings of the Troglodytes of the Sahara Desert, a Bedouin tent, the yurt of the Mongols, and the mud-brick buildings of the Pueblo. (1, 8, 10, 11, 13, 15)

d. Draw a desert scene on a large sheet of paper. Then draw or paste on pictures of desert plants and animals that live in that landscape. (1, 4, 17, 19, 24, 28, 29)

e. The desert landscape may take many forms. It can have sand dunes, an oasis, rock formations, cactus, etc. Use sand, rocks, clay, paper flowers, or other materials to make a diorama of a desert landscape. Label your diorama to indicate which desert it represents. (14, 15, 16, 17, 19, 22, 24, 28)

f. The Navajo Indian tribe of the American Southwest produces many beautiful works of art. These include silver and turquoise jewelry, and patterned beadwork. String together a strand of beads in a style that is similar to the work of the Navajo tribe.

g. Arab mosques are among the most beautiful buildings in the world. Look at pictures of Arabian structures, noting the style of architecture and the elaborate patterns. As a group project, design and build a model of an Arabian mosque. (8)

SPELLING/VOCABULARY

a. Complete a matching picture puzzle of plants and animals from Asian, African, and Australian deserts: viper, sand grouse, sheep, gerbil, ostrich, puff adder, frilled lizard, camel, oryx, goat, jerboa, addax, locust, gecko, fennec fox, rat kangaroo, baobab, date palm, millet, sorghum. (1, 4, 7, 12, 15, 16, 25, 26, 28)

b. Complete a word search puzzle of plants and animals from the North American deserts: cactus, prickly pear, aloe, desert poppy, bobcat, jackrabbit, spadefoot toad, kit fox, tarantula, conenose bug, iguana, sage grouse, roadrunner, whipsnake, sidewinder, elf owl, centipede, Harris' hawk, horned lizard. (1, 3, 7, 9, 12, 16, 17, 24, 28)

c. Label pictures of these geographical features of hot and semi-hot deserts: sand dunes, wadi, mesa, oasis, mountain, pedestal, butte, canyon, plateau, alluvial fan, hamada, watering hole, reg, pillar, arroyo, playa lake, mushroom rock, yardang. (2, 5, 10, 15, 17, 29)

d. Complete a fill-in-the-blanks exercise of terms which relate to the formation and spread of deserts: arid, erosion, friable, desertification, overcropping, savannah, salt-saturated, irrigation, dust storm, climatic change, overpopulation, intensive farming, sandstorms, drought, deforestation, overfarming, overgrazing, weathering, barren, rain shadow. (2, 10, 15, 16, 26, 29)

e. Define some terms which relate to the North American Desert: gila monster, javelina pig, mesquite, creosote bush, joshua tree, playa, Death Valley, Pueblo, saguaro cactus, arroyo, sagebrush, coyote, Dust Bowl, peccary, diamond back, palo verde tree, Navajo, scorpion. Note the Spanish pronunciation of many of these terms. What are the four regions of the North American Desert? (10, 15, 16, 21, 22, 24, 26, 28)

f. Complete a crossword puzzle of terms that relate to reclaiming desert lands: anchored, stabilize, humus, shelter belt, education, regenerate, new crops, settled farming, water management, greenhouse, crop rotation, terracing, resettlement, double cropping, nutrients, hydroponics, fertilizer, agroforestry. (10, 15, 16, 26, 29)

g. Complete a matching exercise of terms related to desert plants: dormant, transpiration, succulent, lateral root, spine, ephemeral, germinate, perennial, pioneer species, nectar, pollinate, climax community, fertilize, stamen, ovary, stigma, xerophyte, Euphorbia, style, saguaro boot. (3, 4, 24, 26, 29)

GEOGRAPHY

Note: Names of deserts may vary, according to the source used.

a. Sand is a major feature of many deserts. The strong desert winds shift the sand into different formations. Fill a box with sand. Look at pictures of sand dunes and shape the sand in your box to match the pictures. Some types of dunes you can form are: seif dunes, barchan dunes, star dunes, longitudinal dunes, and transverse dunes. (10, 14, 15, 17)

b. Locate the polar lands on a world map. Are they deserts? Why or why not? (1, 10, 15, 17, 22)

c. Fold a piece of paper into four sections. Label the sections of both sides: North American Desert, Cold Deserts, Great Australian Desert, and Sahara/Arabian Deserts. On one side of the paper, list some plants that grow in each of these deserts. List some animals that live in these deserts on the other side of the paper. (3, 9, 10, 16, 17, 25, 26, 28)

d. On a map of the world, color in the areas that are hot desert (red), semi-hot desert (yellow), and cold desert (blue). Label these deserts: Atacama, Great Australian, Turkistan, Thar, North American, Kalahari, Gobi, Patagonia, Somali, Sahara, Negev, Arabian, Takla Makan, Iranian, Namib, and Antarctic. What is the largest desert on Earth? (1, 2, 6, 12, 15, 16, 17, 26, 28)

e. Many countries are made up entirely or partially of desert land. Name the countries associated with each of the following deserts: Sahara, Gobi, Kalahari, Atacama, Takla Makan, Namib, Patagonia, Thar, Negev, and Arabian. What rivers or seas flow through or nearby these deserts? (6, 15, 16, 24, 29)

f. People who live in the desert must be able to adapt to the harsh conditions of their land. For each of the following tribes, name the desert they inhabit, and their method of survival. Are they oasis dwellers, herders, or hunter-gatherers? Bushman, Bedouin, Navajo, Mozabite, Aborigine, Tuareg, Baluchi, Beja, Somali, Mongol, Pueblo, Troglodyte. (6, 8, 10, 12, 13, 15, 20, 23, 26)

g. What are subtropical deserts? What are rain shadow deserts? How are they different? Which type is near the equator, and which type is at higher latitudes? Give examples of each of these deserts, and tell where they are located. (12, 15, 17, 19, 22, 26)

MATH

a. Desert creatures move around on 2 legs, 4 legs, 6 legs, 8 legs, or no legs. Name at least two examples of each type of animal. (1, 3, 4, 10, 25, 28)

b. About 6 to 10 inches of rain falls per year in a desert. Find out what the annual rainfall is where you live. Compare these measurements on a ruler.

c. An average daytime temperature in the Sahara is about 95°F (35°C).

Some parts of the Sahara can get as high as 185°F (85°C). Look up the average summer temperature where you live, and the temperature of the hottest day within the last year. Make up a chart that compares these four temperatures.

d. Overpopulation is a major problem for many desert nations. The populations of some countries of the Sahara Desert are doubling approximately every 25–30 years. At this rate, compute how many people will live in the following countries by the year 2020, based on their current populations: Chad, 5,000,000; Niger, 8,154,000; Libya, 4,350,000; Egypt, 54,451,000.

e. What is the total number of square miles for the following deserts? In Africa: Kalahari, 200,000; Sahara, 3,240,000; Somali, 100,000. In North and South America: Atacama, 70,000; Great Basin, 200,000; Mojave, 25,000; Patagonia, 300,000. In Asia: Arabian, 500,000; Gobi, 400,000; Kara Kum, 200,000; Takla Makan, 175,000. In Australia: 600,000. Based on these figures, which land mass (Africa, Americas, Asia, or Australia) has the most desert area? (17)

f. Answer the following questions about desert areas: 1) Deserts cover about a fourth of the land surface of the Earth. What percentage is this? 2) What is the total land surface of the Earth, in square miles? Calculate the total land area, in square miles, that is made up of deserts. 3) Only 20 percent of the world's deserts consist of sand. How much is that in square miles? 4) What percentage of the total land surface of the Earth is desert sand?

g. The daytime surface temperature of the Sahara is commonly about 35°C, but it has been known to reach as high as 65°C or even 85°C. Yet at night, the temperature drops to 20°C, and may sometimes plummet to 2°C. Convert these Celsius temperatures to Fahrenheit temperatures. Draw a thermometer and plot Celsius temperatures on the left and Fahrenheit temperatures on the right. Note the above temperatures on your thermometer.

MUSIC AND THEATER ARTS

a. Pretend to be various desert creatures. Hop like a kangaroo, slither across the ground like a snake, walk slowly using a rocking motion like a camel, etc. (1, 3, 9, 12, 25, 29)

b. Listen to sounds from a desert environment, such as *Desert Moon Song* produced by Soundings of the Planet, or *Africa: Desert Solitude at Bushman Fountain* by Nature Recordings. What do you hear?

c. Present a puppet show of a story from *Arabian Nights* or a traditional folktale from a desert culture.

d. What kind of music is played in desert lands? Listen to recordings of music from different desert cultures. (Several can be found in the Smithsonian/Folkways Recordings Catalog.) Identify the musical instruments that are used.

e. With some friends, act out a scene about the life of a desert people, such as: Bushmen hunting, a Bedouin family welcoming guests to their tent, Mongols building a yurt, etc. (1, 6, 12, 13, 15, 20, 23)

f. The Israeli people of the Negev do a line dance called the horah. Do this dance to an Israeli song with your teacher.

g. *Small group project:* Choose one desert tribe. Find out how they lived in the past and how they live now. Then think about their future. Act out a skit about how the tribe may be living ten or twenty years from now. What changes, if any, will there be in their lifestyle, dress, homes, education, etc.? (6, 12, 13, 15, 16, 20, 23, 26, 29)

ENGLISH COMPOSITION

a. Write a poem about the desert. It can be about a desert plant, animal, tribe of people, geographical feature, or any other desert subject.

b. Write a story about a desert animal. (2, 3, 4, 9, 10, 12, 16, 28)

c. Pretend you are a cactus-seller. Write an advertisement that will make people want to buy your cactus. Tell how the cactus looks, how it can be used, what it costs to buy and keep, and anything else you can think of to sell your product. (3, 15, 19, 24, 26, 28)

d. Pretend you are in the Mojave Desert after it has rained. Write a description of how the desert flowers suddenly bloom. What does the desert look, smell, sound like? What animals do you see? How long does it last? (16, 22, 24, 26, 28)

e. Write a description of a hot or semi-hot desert during a flash flood or a sandstorm. How are you alerted to the danger? How do you protect yourself? How long does it last? What happens during the storm? Is the land changed? (12, 14, 15, 17, 22)

f. Millions of Africans who live in the desert are starving. Trace one of the causes of this tragedy, such as overgrazing, poor farming techniques, or overpopulation. Write an essay explaining the problem, and suggest some actions that can be taken to correct the situation. (6, 15, 16, 27, 29)

g. Pretend you are a native of one of the Earth's deserts. Write a diary of one week in your life. Do you live in a traditional tribe, or have you begun to assimilate into modern society? What challenges do you face? (6, 12, 13, 15, 16, 20, 23, 29)

SCIENCE

a. The date palm is an important plant that grows in a desert oasis.

Draw a picture of a date tree. Taste some dates. What are some uses of the date palm?   (6, 12, 15, 17, 26)

b. Explain why deserts are so hot during the day, but so cold at night. (12, 15, 17, 22, 26)

c. What is weathering? How do heat, wind, and rain change the desert landscape?   (2, 5, 10, 12, 14, 15, 17, 22, 29)

d. What is an oasis? How is it formed? How can it be destroyed? Why are oases important?   (12, 15, 16, 17, 29)

e. Choose a desert plant. Explain how it has adapted to its environment. Choose a desert animal and explain how it survives.   (1, 3, 6, 12, 16, 21, 22, 24, 26, 28)

f. What causes deserts to occur? What causes them to spread?   (12, 15, 16, 17, 26, 29)

g. Improved agricultural methods and other scientific approaches may help to reclaim desert land. Describe some of these possible solutions.   (6, 12, 15, 16, 17, 29)

HISTORY/SOCIOLOGY

a. What are hunters/gatherers? What are herders? Name three examples of each type of desert tribe.   (1, 2, 13, 15, 23)

b. Read about the aborigines of Australia and the bushmen of Africa who still live in the traditional way of their tribes. Tell how they have adapted to desert life. How are they similar to Stone Age man?   (6, 10, 12, 15, 16, 23, 26)

c. What are nomads? How do they live? How has their lifestyle contributed to desertification?   (10, 12, 15, 16, 17, 26, 29)

d. Choose one tribe of desert people to study. Note some facts about them, such as where they live, how they survive, what they wear, some of their customs, their religion, their language and alphabet, the jobs of men and women, how children are raised, and the architecture of their buildings.   (6, 10, 11, 12, 13, 15, 17, 23, 26)

e. The traditional way of life of many desert tribes is threatened. Choose one tribe and tell what has happened to their culture. What has forced this change? How are these people treated by their government?   (6, 13, 16, 20, 23, 29)

f. An area of the North American Desert is known as the Dust Bowl. Trace its history. How did it become a desert? How is it changing now? What was man's role in this process?   (6, 15, 16, 21, 27)

g. Religion has played an important role in the civilizations of some desert nations, especially those of the Middle East. Explore the religious background of one nation or tribe, past or present. How did/does their religious beliefs affect their dress, art, lifestyle, customs, diet, relationships with other nations, etc.?   (6, 8, 13)

TOPICS FOR DISCUSSION

a. Why are camels so important to the people of the Sahara and Arabian Deserts?   (2, 12, 16, 17)

b. Sand is the most plentiful resource in the desert. What are some products that can be made from sand? Can you think of any more uses for sand?   (6, 18)

c. What is a drought? How has it affected people and land in Africa? Have droughts ever been a problem in the United States?   (1, 15, 16, 27, 29)

d. How has the discovery of oil and minerals changed the lives of desert people?   (1, 6, 12, 15, 29)

e. What is desertification? What are some causes of desertification?   (2, 15, 16, 26, 29)

f. Does food aid solve the problem of starvation in the desert? Or does it add to the problem? What type of aid do you think would work best?   (16, 27, 29)

g. Many areas that were once fertile land are now deserts. Discuss some ways in which changes in climate and the actions of people have caused some areas to become deserts. How can educating people help?   (6, 10, 15, 16, 21, 26, 29)

SUGGESTED RESOURCES

(1) Bailey, Donna. *Deserts* [Facts About]. Steck-Vaughn, 1989.
(2) Baker, Lucy. *Life in the Deserts* [Life in]. Watts, 1990.
(3) Bash, Barbara. *Desert Giant: The World of the Saguaro Cactus* [Tree Tales]. Sierra Club, 1989.
(4) Behm, Barbara J., and Bonar, Veronica. *Exploring Deserts* [Eco-Journey]. Stevens, 1994.
(5) Bender, Lionel. *Desert* [The Story of the Earth]. Watts, 1989.
(6) Carson, James. *Deserts and People* [Nature's Landscapes]. Silver, 1982.
(7) Catchpole, Clive. *Deserts* [The Living World]. Dial, 1985.
(8) *Civilizations of the Middle East* [History of the World]. Raintree, 1986.
(9) Dewey, Jennifer Owings. *A Night and Day in the Desert*. Little, 1991.

(10) Dixon, Dougal. *Deserts and Wastelands* [Franklin Watts Picture Atlas]. Watts, 1984.

(11) James, Alan. *Homes in Hot Places* [Houses and Homes]. Lerner, 1987.

(12) Jennings, Terry. *Deserts* [Exploring Our World]. Cavendish, 1987.

(13) King, John. *Bedouin* [Threatened Cultures]. Steck-Vaughn, 1993.

(14) Knapp, Brian. *Dune* [Land Shapes]. Grolier, 1993.

(15) Lye, Keith. *Deserts* [Our World]. Silver, 1987.

(16) McLeish, Ewan. *The Spread of Deserts* [Conserving Our World]. Steck-Vaughn, 1989.

(17) Mariner, Tom. *Deserts* [Earth in Action]. Cavendish, 1990.

(18) Mitgutsch, Ali. *From Sand to Glass* [Start to Finish]. Carolrhoda, 1981.

(19) Newton, James R. *Rain Shadow*. Crowell, 1983.

(20) Nile, Richard. *Australian Aborigines* [Threatened Cultures]. Steck-Vaughn, 1993.

(21) Pringle, Laurence. *The Gentle Desert: Exploring an Ecosystem*. Macmillan, 1977.

(22) Simon, Seymour. *Deserts*. Morrow, 1990.

(23) Steyn, H. F. *The Bushman of the Kalahari* [Original Peoples]. Rourke, 1989.

(24) Stone, Lynn M. *Deserts* [EcoZones]. Rourke, 1989.

(25) Taylor, Barbara. *Desert Life* [Look Closer]. Kindersley, 1992.

(26) Twist, Clint. *Deserts* [Ecology Watch]. Dillon, 1991.

(27) Walker, Jane. *Famine, Drought and Plagues* [Natural Disasters]. Gloucester, 1992.

(28) Wiewandt, Thomas. *The Hidden Life of the Desert* [Hidden Life]. Crown, 1990.

(29) Williams, Lawrence. *Deserts* [Last Frontiers for Mankind]. Cavendish, 1990.

LIBRARY SKILLS RESOURCES

The Guinness Book of World Records. Facts on File, 1994.

Kidron, Michael, and Segal, Ronald. *The New State of the World Atlas*. Simon & Schuster, 1991.

Lands and Peoples. Grolier, 1993.

Middleton, Nick. *Atlas of World Issues* [Issues Atlases]. Facts on File, 1989.

Wood, Jenny. *The Children's Atlas of People & Places*. Millbrook, 1993.

Wright, David, and Wright, Jill. *The Facts on File Children's Atlas*. Facts on File, 1993.

ADDITIONAL READING — YOUNGER

Aardema, Verna, reteller. *Bringing the Rain to Kapiti Plain: A Nandi Tale*. Dial, 1981.

Albert, Richard E. *Alejandra's Gift*. Chronicle, 1994.

Amsel, Sheri. *Deserts* [Habitats of the World]. Steck-Vaughn, 1993.

Bailey, Donna. *Nomads* [Facts About]. Steck-Vaughn, 1990.

Bayler, Byrd. *The Desert Is Theirs*. Macmillan, 1986.

————. *Desert Voices*. Scribner's, 1975.

Brandenberg, Jim. *Sand and Egg: Adventures in Southern Africa*. Walker, 1994.

Cobb, Vicki. *This Place Is Dry* [Imagine Living Here]. Walker, 1989.

George, Jean Craighead. *One Day in the Desert*. Crowell, 1983.

Hogan, Paula. *Expanding Deserts* [Environment Alert!]. Stevens, 1991.

Hughes, Jill. *A Closer Look at Deserts* [A Closer Look]. Watts, 1987.

Lerner, Carol. *A Desert Year*. Morrow, 1991.

Milner, Cedric. *Desert Trek* [Young Explorers]. Stevens, 1989.
Palmer, Joy. *Deserts* [First Starts]. Raintree, 1993.
Posell, Elsa. *Deserts* [New True Books]. Childrens, 1982.
Reynolds, Jan. *Sahara* [Vanishing Cultures]. Harcourt, 1991.
Sabin, Louis. *Wonders of the Desert*. Troll, 1982.
Siebert, Diane. *Mojave*. Harper, 1988.

ADDITIONAL READING — OLDER

Andryszewski, Tricia. *The Dust Bowl: Disaster on the Plains* [Spotlight on American History]. Millbrook, 1993.
Bernard, Alan. *Kalahari Bushmen* [Threatened Cultures]. Thomson, 1994.
Carter, Alden R. *The Shoshoni* [First Books — Indians of the Americas]. Watts, 1989.
Farris, John. *The Dust Bowl* [World Disasters]. Lucent, 1989.
Graham, Ada, and Graham, Frank. *The Changing Desert*. Sierra Club, 1981.
Greenaway, Theresa. *Cacti and Other Succulents* [Green World]. Steck-Vaughn, 1990.
Ingrams, Doreen. *Mosques and Minerets*. EMC, 1974.
James, J. Alison. *Sing for a Gentle Rain*. Atheneum, 1990.
Johnson, Annabel. *I Am Leaper*. Scholastic, 1990.
Knapp, Brian. *Drought* [World Disasters!]. Steck-Vaughn, 1990.
Lewis, Naomi, and Pieck, Anton. *Stories from the Arabian Nights*. Holt, 1987.
Liptak, Karen. *Endangered Peoples* [Impact]. Watts, 1993.
Marsh, Carole. *Death Valley: A(lluvial) Fans-to-Z(abriske) Quartzite*. Gallopade, 1993.
_____. *The Fantastic Painted Desert & the Phenomenal Petrified Forest*. Gallopade, 1993.
Moore, Randy, and Vodopich, Darrell S. *The Living Desert* [The Living World]. Enslow, 1991.
Reading, Susan. *Desert Plants* [Plant Life]. Facts on File, 1990.
Scoones, Simon. *The Sahara and Its People* [People and Places]. Thomson, 1993.
Stanley, Jerry. *Children of the Dust Bowl: The True Story of the School at Weedpatch Camp*. Crown, 1992.
Staples, Suzanne Fisher. *Shabanu, Daughter of the World*. Knopf, 1989.
Stewart, Gail. *In the Desert* [Living Spaces]. Rourke, 1989.
Timberlake, Lloyd. *Famine in Africa* [Issues]. Watts, 1986.

See also: books in FOOD AND FARMING unit.

FOR MORE INFORMATION ABOUT DESERTS, WRITE TO:

Chihuahuan Desert Research Institute
Children of the Green Earth
Desert Fishes Council
Desert Protective Council
Friends of the Earth

National Geographic Society
Sierra Club
World Nature Association
Worldwatch Institute

POLAR REGIONS

The Arctic and Antarctica—homes to the North Pole and the South Pole, where day or night lasts for months at a time. Cold, wind, ice, and snow are constant challenges, yet animals, plants, and even humans have adapted to the harsh conditions of these ruggedly beautiful regions. But even these "ends of the Earth" are not immune to pollution and human exploitation. We must take care to preserve the fragile environments of these foreboding, yet fascinating, poles.

LIBRARY SKILLS

a. In *Scholastic Environmental Atlas of the United States*, look up The Ozone Layer to answer to following questions: 1) How does the ozone layer protect life on Earth? 2) What human health problems could happen if the ozone layer were damaged? 3) What is the United States doing to prevent further damage? 4) Where is the biggest ozone hole?

b. Look up Antarctica in *The Physical World* to answer the following: 1) Write three facts about icebergs. 2) What would happen if the Antarctic ice cap melted? 3) Name ten mountain ranges in Antarctica. 4) Name ten coasts.

c. In *Famous First Facts*, look up Submarines. Find information on the first submarine to travel under the North Pole. What was the name of the submarine? Who was the commander? When did the event occur?

d. In *The New Book of Popular Science*, look up Glaciers. Answer the following questions: 1) What are the two types of glaciers? Which type is found near the polar regions? 2) When does a sheet of ice become an iceberg? 3) How much of an iceberg is below the surface of the water? 4) During which months are icebergs most dangerous to ships?

e. In *The World Almanac and Book of Facts*, look up Important Islands and Their Areas. Make a chart that lists, in descending order, the islands located within the Arctic Circle. Include the area in square miles and the country of ownership for each island. How is Greenland represented in the book?

f. In *The Information Please Almanac*, look up: 1) The place and date of the Earth's lowest recorded temperature. 2) The lower and upper limits of an aurora. 3) The name of the first person to fly solo over the North Pole, and the date this was accomplished. 4) The number of active volcanoes in Antarctica. 5) The area, in square miles, of the Arctic Ocean, and the latitude and longitude of its greatest known depth.

g. Use *The Information Please Environmental Almanac* to look up information on ozone layer depletion, in relation to the polar regions. What is the extent of the ozone holes? What factors have contributed to the problem?

ARTS AND CRAFTS

a. Create a poster that tells of a problem that threatens the Arctic or Antarctic environment. Tell what people can do to protect the region. (3, 4, 9, 10, 11, 16, 26)

b. Use modeling clay to make figures of a penguin, seal, polar bear, whale, or other polar animal. Paint your model when the clay has dried.

c. Make a collage of Arctic or Antarctic scenes. You may include pictures of polar animals or plants, ice formations, people who live there, the auroras, etc.

d. Use pieces of clay or styrofoam to make replicas of the various ice formations mentioned in the spelling/vocabulary exercise, item **d.** (1, 10, 11, 12, 18, 24, 25)

e. Build a model of an igloo or another traditional dwelling used by people in polar or tundra climates. (2, 4, 7, 8, 11, 12, 27)

f. Create a diorama of an Arctic or Antarctic landscape. If you choose an Arctic scene, consider: What type of people live there? Do they live in the traditional or modern way? How does this affect their homes and the surrounding landscape?

g. Make paper doll cut-outs or drawings, or sew doll clothes out of material scraps to represent a type of traditional clothing worn by the Inuit or Lapp people. (2, 6, 8, 13, 27)

SPELLING/VOCABULARY

a. Match the names of these Arctic animals to their pictures: Arctic fox, caribou, musk ox, snowy owl, walrus, Canada geese, wolf, polar bear, Arctic hare, lemming, ptarmigan, puffin. Match the names of these animals from the Antarctic to their pictures: krill, penguin, blue whale, seal, albatross, orange sea spiders. (1, 4, 6, 9, 10, 11, 12, 16, 21, 22)

b. Complete a word search puzzle of Arctic plants: bilberry, tussock grass, tundra shrub, Arctic willow, saxifrage, Arctic buttercup, dwarf birch, rosebay, crowfoot, willowherb, lousewort, purple fireweed, lichen, sedge, cloudberry, mountain aven, crowberry, moss, poppy.   (1, 6, 10, 11, 12, 16, 21, 22, 23)

c. Complete a fill-in-the-blanks exercise of Arctic terms: Northern lights, Baffin Island, permafrost, circumpolar, polygon, esker, hummock, pingo, taiga, archipelago, alpine, Barren Grounds, tundra, Land of the Midnight Sun, aurora borealis, tree line, thaw, magnetic north pole, Arctic summer, Arctic winter.   (1, 3, 4, 6, 10, 12, 22, 23)

d. Complete a matching puzzle of ice formation terms: glacier, ice sheet, crevasse, meltwater, iceberg, calving, pack ice, ice shelf, pancake ice, ice floe, bergy bits, growlers, fast ice, polynya, ice cap, ice age, shore lead, whiteout, sastrugi, pressure ridge.   (1, 3, 4, 10, 11, 12, 18, 24, 26)

e. Complete a word search puzzle of terms that relate to polar animals: hibernate, migrate, molt, camouflage, breeding grounds, herd, hooves, antlers, scavenger, herbivore, carnivore, blubber, undercoat, prey, burrow, reproduce, interdependent, habitat, adaptation, predator.   (1, 3, 4, 5, 6, 10, 19)

f. Many scientists do research in Antarctica. Define the area of study of each of the following: geologist, marine biologist, paleontologist, glaciologist, geochemist, medical scientist, biologist, ornithologist, conservationist, geographer, meteorologist, oceanographer, environmentalist.   (6, 12, 25)

g. Compile a glossary of native terms used by the Inuit or another Arctic native people.   (2, 8, 12, 13, 15, 19, 20)

GEOGRAPHY

Note: Some maps refer to the waters surrounding Antarctica as the Antarctic Ocean or the Southern Ocean, while other sources do not use a special name for that area.

a. On a globe, locate the Antarctic Circle. Which oceans touch Antarctica? Then locate the Arctic Ocean. Which countries border it? Which region is north? Which is south?   (1, 3, 4, 6, 10, 12, 21, 22, 25)

b. On a map of the world, color in the areas that have a polar climate (violet) and a tundra climate (orange).   (6, 7, 20, 25)

c. Note these places on a map of Antarctica: South Pole, Ronne Ice Shelf, McMurdo Station, Ross Sea, Ross Ice Shelf, Weddell Sea, Antarctic Peninsula, Transantarctic Mountains, Vinson Massif, Mount Erebus. Label the Indian, Atlantic, and Pacific oceans. Name some countries that have exploratory stations on Antarctica. What is the Antarctic Convergence? (12, 14, 17, 26)

d. Locate the Arctic and Antarctic circles on a globe. What are their latitudes? Geographers prefer to define the Arctic area according to the tree line, and the Antarctic by the convergence of polar and tropical waters. On the globe, locate the polar lands as defined by geographers. How do they compare to the latitudinal areas? (1, 5, 9, 12, 25)

e. There are many striking contrasts and similarities between the Arctic and Antarctic. Divide a sheet of paper in half. Label one side "Arctic" and the other "Antarctic." Compare the physical properties of these regions in regard to land area, highest and lowest points, seasons, amount of ice, etc. (1, 9, 12, 17, 21, 22, 25)

f. What role did continental drift and changing world temperatures play in forming the polar regions? (4, 12, 17)

g. Compile a list of geographic facts about Antarctica, Greenland, Arctic Canada, Alaska, Lapland, or Siberia. Note facts such as the land's area in square miles, major cities or settlements, native people or other inhabitants, climate, plant and animal life. (5, 10, 12, 13, 17, 19, 26)

MATH

a. Antarctica is covered year-round with ice and snow. In some places it is two miles deep. On a local map, mark a distance that is two miles apart. Make a list of places that are two miles from your school.

b. About 3 percent of all the water on Earth is fresh water. Antarctica alone contains about 70 percent of this fresh water in its ice cap. The Antarctic also contains about 90 percent of all the world's ice. Make charts to illustrate these facts. (3)

c. Compile a list of interesting math facts about glaciers and icebergs. (12, 13, 17, 18, 24)

d. What is the average winter-summer temperature range where you live? The average winter-summer temperature range in the Arctic Circle is approximately $-40°F$ to $+50°F$. The average Antarctic temperature range is about $-58°F$ to $+5°F$. Draw a graph or chart that compares these temperature ranges. Also note the freezing point.

e. Lemmings are rodents that live in the Arctic region. They multiply rapidly. A female lemming may have 2 to 5 litters a year, with 2 to 11 young per litter. How many babies will be born to a lemming that has: 1) 8 babies for each of 2 litters, 6 babies in each of 2 litters and 5 babies in 1 litter? 2) 3 babies in 1 litter, twice that amount each time in 2 more litters, and 3 times the original amount each time in 3 more litters? 3) If a lemming has 3 litters a year, with 9 babies per litter, for 5 years, how many babies will she produce?

f. Vinson Massif, at 16,860 feet above sea level, is the highest land formation in Antarctica. Alaska's Mt. McKinley is the Arctic's highest peak at 20,320 feet. 1) What percent of Mt. McKinley's height is Vinson Massif? 2) Convert the heights of both mountains to inches, yards, and miles.

g. Change these math facts about Antarctica to metric terms: 1) Antarctica is 5,100,000 square miles in area. 2) It contains about 7 million cubic miles of ice. 3) The greatest thickness of ice is 2.97 miles. 4) The South Pole is situated atop 9,200 feet of glacial ice. 5) The lowest temperature ever recorded in the world was −128.6°F at Vostok Station on July 21, 1983. 6) Winds in Antarctica can reach up to 200 miles per hour, making it the windiest place on Earth. 7) In 1956, an iceberg was found near the Ross Ice Shelf measuring 201 miles long and 58 miles wide.

MUSIC AND THEATER ARTS

a. Read a folktale of the Inuit or Lapp people. Then create a puppet show based on the story.

b. Pretend to be an animal of the Arctic or Antarctic. Act out a scene from the animal's life.

c. *Group project*: Act out an Arctic hunting expedition. How would a modern hunt differ from a traditional one?   (1, 2, 10, 27)

d. *Group project*: Act out a scene that depicts some aspect of Lapp or Inuit culture, such as building an igloo, herding reindeer, or playing a game.   (2, 8, 10, 19, 27)

e. Listen to the soundtrack *Antarctica Vangelis*, by Vangelis. How does the music reflect this land?

f. *Group project*: Samuel Taylor Coleridge's epic poem "The Rime of the Ancient Mariner" takes place in the waters of Antarctica. Perform this poem as a readers' theater piece.

g. Choose 12 students to represent the 12 countries that originally signed the Antarctic Treaty. Let them act out this historic scene. Then have all the students, each representing a different country, act out the negotiations of 1991 that led to the next international agreement about Antarctica.   (9, 12, 17, 25, 26)

ENGLISH COMPOSITION

a. Write a story about an animal that lives in the Arctic or Antarctica.   (1, 4, 6, 10, 11, 16, 19, 21, 22, 23, 26)

b. Write a poem about the Land of the Midnight Sun.   (2, 3, 4, 10, 22)

c. Pretend you are an Arctic or Antarctic explorer. Write a story about your journey and discoveries. What equipment do you need to take along? What hardships do you face?   (3, 4, 5, 6, 10, 12, 14, 17, 26, 27)

d. Pretend you are a travel agent. Write a brochure to convince people to book a trip to Antarctica, Lapland, Alaska, Greenland, or the Canadian Arctic with your agency. Use pictures if you like.   (3, 4, 5, 6, 8, 10, 11, 13, 14, 17, 19, 27)

e. Pretend you are an Inuit, Lapp, or member of another tribe that lives in the Arctic Circle. Write a diary covering a typical week in your life. Do you live in the traditional or modern way?   (1, 2, 5, 8, 10, 13, 20, 27)

f. In 1989, it was proposed that Antarctica be declared a wilderness reserve, the Antarctic World Park, instead of being developed or mined. Write a letter to an environmental group or government office stating your opinion on whether you support the idea of an Antarctic World Park.   (9, 12, 17, 25, 26)

g. Write an essay about one way in which industrialized nations exploit (or want to exploit) a polar land. Give your opinion on how you think the situation should be handled.   (1, 2, 9, 17, 19, 25, 26)

SCIENCE

a. Why is it so cold in the polar regions?   (3, 6, 9, 10, 12, 16)

b. What is a glacier? An ice sheet? An iceberg? How do they form? Do this experiment: Fill a tub with salt water. Place a large chunk of ice in it. Does it float or sink to the bottom? Why? Is most of the ice below or above the surface of the water? Is this an example of a glacier, ice sheet, or iceberg?   (4, 11, 12, 18, 24, 25)

c. During which months is it winter in the Arctic? When is summer? What is the position of the sun during these seasons? When are winter and summer in Antarctica?   (1, 4, 6, 9, 12, 21, 22)

d. What are lemmings? Explain their importance in the Arctic food chain. What are krill? Explain their importance in the Antarctic food chain.   (1, 4, 5, 6, 9, 10, 11, 12, 19, 21, 22, 23, 25, 26)

e. How could global warming affect the polar ice caps? How could that, in turn, affect the rest of the planet?   (4, 9, 25, 26)

f. How do polar animals adapt to the extremely cold climate? Choose one animal and tell how its body composition and migration patterns help it to survive.   (1, 5, 6, 11, 12, 17, 19, 23, 25)

g. Glaciologists, geologists, and other scientists conduct a great deal of research in the polar regions. Projects include weather and climate research and the study of the greenhouse effect, the ozone hole, the Earth's magnetic force, krill fishing, and the possibilities of drilling for oil or launching rockets into outer space from the poles. Choose one research topic from this list or make up one of your own. Write a report of your findings. (6, 9, 17, 25, 26)

HISTORY/SOCIOLOGY

a. The natives of Arctic Canada, Greenland, and Alaska do not like to be called "Eskimos." Why? What term do they prefer? Make a list of tribe names of these Arctic natives. What do their names mean? (9, 10, 12, 13, 20, 22, 25)

b. Draw up a timeline of the polar regions' explorers. For each explorer, note the method of transportation used, the date of the expedition, whether it was to the North or South Pole, and if it was successful. Include in your timeline Admiral Richard Byrd, Captain James Ross, Dr. Frederick Cook, Roald Amundsen, Ernest Shackleton, Captain Robert Scott, Admiral Robert Perry, Will Steger, and others. (3, 14, 20, 26)

c. Draw up a chart comparing the North American Inuit to the Lapps of Scandinavia. Compare their appearances, shelter, clothing, hunting methods, etc. How are the two races similar? How are they different? (1, 2, 5, 8, 15, 20, 27)

d. Some animals that live in the polar regions, such as the fur seal, snow goose, and baleen whales, have faced extinction. Trace the history of one such animal. Tell where it lives, why it was endangered, and any efforts that have been made to correct the problem. Is the animal still at risk? (1, 5, 9, 19, 25)

e. Who lives in Antarctica? What is the Antarctic Treaty? Who developed it and when? Why is it needed? What has succeeded it? (1, 4, 6, 9, 17, 25, 26)

f. The way of life of the Inuit people changed after the white man arrived. Make a chart that compares the old, traditional ways to the new, modern ways. Show differences in food, clothing, hunting methods, transportation, schooling, jobs, etc. (1, 2, 5, 9, 10, 13, 15, 19, 20, 25, 27)

g. Write a report of one scientist or adventurer who explored the Arctic or Antarctica. (6, 12, 13, 17, 26)

TOPICS FOR DISCUSSION

a. Why are people interested in the polar regions? What do you think is beautiful about these parts of the world? (3, 12, 14, 16, 21, 22)

b. About 18,000 years ago, there was about twice as much ice at the poles as there is now, which made the sea level in the world several feet lower than it is today. As a result, bodies of land (such as Alaska and Siberia) were connected. Look at a map and see what other land masses may have been connected. If half of the ice at the polar caps melted now, how do you think the world would look? (4, 9, 12)

c. What were some past threats to the environment of the Arctic and Antarctica? What are some present and future threats? (1, 6, 9, 10, 11, 12, 20, 21, 22, 23, 25, 26)

d. The polar regions are rich in oil and minerals. Should mining and drilling for oil be allowed there? Choose one side of this argument and give reasons for your decision. (1, 4, 9, 10, 12, 19, 20, 23, 25, 26)

e. What are the effects of overhunting and overfishing in the polar regions? How does this affect the rest of the world? What actions should be taken to correct this? (1, 9, 12, 17, 25, 26)

f. How has pollution in other parts of the world affected the Arctic and Antarctic? What has pollution done to the wildlife, atmosphere, and waters surrounding these areas? (1, 9, 10, 12, 17, 25, 26)

g. The white man's arrival in the Arctic has changed the Inuit people's traditional way of life. Are these changes good or bad? Take the position of an Inuit or a white man and discuss how you feel about this issue. The Lapps' traditional ways have also been modernized. Is this good or bad? How have the Lapps fared in comparison to the Inuit? (1, 2, 5, 8, 9, 10, 15, 19, 20, 25, 27)

SUGGESTED RESOURCES

(1) Aldis, Rodney. *Polar Lands* [Ecology Watch]. Dillon, 1992.
(2) Alexander, Bryan, and Alexander, Cherry. *Inuit* [Threatened Cultures]. Steck-Vaughn, 1993.
(3) Barrett, Norman. *Polar Lands* [Picture Library]. Watts, 1990.
(4) Byles, Monica. *Life in the Polar Lands* [Life in]. Watts, 1990.
(5) Hiscock, Bruce. *Tundra: The Arctic Land.* Atheneum, 1986.
(6) Hughes, Jill. *Arctic Lands* [A Closer Look At]. Gloucester, 1986.
(7) James, Alan. *Homes in Cold Places* [Houses and Homes]. Lerner, 1987.
(8) _____. *Lapps: Reindeer Herders of Lapland* [Original Peoples]. Rourke, 1989.
(9) James, Barbara. *Conserving the Polar Regions* [Conserving Our World]. Steck-Vaughn, 1991.
(10) Kalman, Bobbie. [The Arctic World] series. Crabtree, 1988.
(11) Khanduri, Kamini. *Polar Wildlife* [Usborne World Wildlife]. EDC, 1993.
(12) Lambert, David. *Polar Regions* [Our World]. Silver, 1988.
(13) Lepthien, Emilie U. *Greenland* [Enchantment of the World]. Childrens, 1989.
(14) Lye, Keith. *Take a Trip to Antarctica* [Take a Trip]. Watts, 1984.

(15) Osinski, Alice. *The Eskimo: The Inuit and Yupik People* [New True Books]. Childrens, 1985.

(16) Palmer, Joy. *Polar Lands* [First Series]. Steck-Vaughn, 1993.

(17) Pringle, Laurence. *Antarctica: The Last Unspoiled Continent*. Simon & Schuster, 1992.

(18) Simon, Seymour. *Icebergs and Glaciers*. Morrow, 1987.

(19) Siy, Alexandra. *Arctic National Wildlife Refuge* [Circle of Life]. Dillon, 1991.

(20) Smith, J.H. Greg. *Eskimos: The Inuit of the Arctic* [Original Peoples]. Rourke, 1987.

(21) Stone, Lynn M. *Antarctica* [New True Books]. Childrens, 1985.

(22) _____. *The Arctic* [New True Books]. Childrens, 1985.

(23) _____. *Arctic Tundra* [EcoZones]. Rourke, 1989.

(24) Walker, Sally M. *Glaciers: Ice on the Move* [Earth Watch]. Carolrhoda, 1990.

(25) Williams, Lawrence. *Polar Lands* [Last Frontiers for Mankind]. Cavendish, 1990.

(26) Winckler, Suzanne, and Rodgers, Mary M. *Antarctica* [Our Endangered Planet]. Lerner, 1992.

(27) Yue, Charlotte, and Yue, David. *The Igloo*. Houghton, 1988.

LIBRARY SKILLS RESOURCES

Kane, Joseph Nathan. *Famous First Facts*. H.W. Wilson, 1981.

Mattson, Mark. *Scholastic Environmental Atlas of the United States*. Scholastic, 1993.

The New Book of Popular Science. Grolier, 1994.

The Physical World [Using and Understanding Maps]. Chelsea, 1993.

The World Almanac and Book of Facts. World Almanac, 1994.

World Resources Institute. *The Information Please Almanac*. Houghton, 1993.

_____. *The Information Please Environmental Almanac*. Houghton, 1993.

ADDITIONAL READING—YOUNGER

Berger, Melvin. *Life in the Polar Regions*. Newbridge, 1994.

Bernhard, Emery. *Reindeer*. Holiday, 1994.

Cobb, Vicki. *This Place Is Cold* [Imagine Living Here]. Walker, 1989.

Cowcher, Helen. *Antarctica*. Farrar, 1990.

DeArmond, Dale. *The Seal Oil Lamp*. Sierra, 1988.

Dunphy, Madeline. *Here Is the Arctic Winter*. Hyperion, 1993.

George, Jean Craighead. *One Day in the Alpine Tundra*. Crowell, 1984.

Georges, D.V. *Glaciers* [New True Books]. Childrens, 1986.

Glimmerveen, Ulco. *A Tale of Antarctica*. Scholastic, 1989.

Harrison, Ted. *A Northern Alphabet: A Is for Arctic*. Tundra, 1987.

Humble, Richard. *The Expeditions of Amundsen* [Exploration Through the Ages]. Watts, 1992.

Kendall, Russ. *Eskimo Boy: Life in an Inupiaq Eskimo Village*. Scholastic, 1992.

Matthews, Rupert. *The Race to the South Pole* [Great Journies]. Bookwright, 1989.

Petersen, Palle. *Inunguaki: The Little Greenlander*. Lothrop, 1993.

Philip, Neil, editor. *Songs Are Thoughts: Poems of the Inuit*. Orchard, 1995.

Reynolds, Jan. *Far North* [Vanishing Cultures]. Harcourt, 1992.

_____. *Frozen Land* [Vanishing Cultures]. Harcourt, 1993.
Rosen, Mike. *The Journey to the North Pole* [Great Journies]. Bookwright, 1990.
Salisbury, Mike. *Arctic Expedition* [Young Explorers]. Stevens, 1989.
Selley, Lyndsey. *Oceans and Arctic* [Vanishing Animal Pop-Ups]. HarperCollins, 1993.
Sis, Peter. *A Small Tale from the Far North*. Knopf, 1993.
Steiner, Barbara. *Whale Brothers*. Walker, 1988.
Stille, Darlene R. *The Ice Age* [New True Books]. Childrens, 1990.

ADDITIONAL READING – OLDER

Beattie, Owen, and Geiger, John. *Buried in Ice: The Mystery of a Lost Arctic Expedition* [Time Quest]. Scholastic, 1992.
Bramwell, Martyn. *Glaciers and Ice Caps* [Earth Science Library]. Watts, 1994.
Bullen, Susan. *The Arctic and Its People* [People and Places]. Thomson, 1994.
Coleridge, Samuel Taylor. *The Rime of the Ancient Mariner*. Atheneum, 1992.
Davis, Deborah. *The Secret of the Seal*. Crown, 1989.
Feris, Jeri. *Arctic Explorer: The Story of Matthew Henson*. [Trailblazers]. Carolrhoda, 1989.
Gallant, Roy A. *The Ice Ages* [First Books]. Watts, 1985.
George, Jean Craighead. *Julie of the Wolves*. Harper, 1972.
_____. *Julie*. HarperCollins, 1994.
Hackwell, W. John. *Desert of Ice: Life and Work in Antarctica*. Scribner's, 1991.
Hallstead, William F. *Tundra*. Crown, 1984.
Hewitt, Garnet. *Ytek and the Arctic Orchid: An Inuit Legend*. Vanguard, 1981.
Johnson, Jinny. *Poles and Tundra Wildlife* [Close-Up]. Random, 1993.
L'Engle, Madeleine. *Troubling a Star*. Farrar, 1994.
Ley, Willey. *The Poles* [Life Nature Library]. Time, 1962.
O'Dell, Scott. *Black Star, Bright Dawn*. Houghton, 1988.
Paulson, Gary. *Dogsong*. Macmillan, 1985.
Sipiera, Paul P. *Roald Amundsen and Robert Scott* [The World's Great Explorers]. Childrens, 1990.
Stewart, Gail. *In the Polar Regions* [Living Spaces]. Rourke, 1989.
Swan, Robert. *Destination: Antarctica*. Scholastic, 1988.
Twist, Clint. *The Ice Caps and Glaciers: Projects with Geography*. Gloucester, 1993.
Vitebsky, Piers. *Saami of Lapland* [Threatened Cultures]. Thomson, 1994.

FOR MORE INFORMATION ABOUT THE POLAR REGIONS, WRITE TO:

Alaska Coalition
American Polar Society
The Antarctica Project
Arctic Institute of North America
Arctic Research Program

Environmental Defense Fund
Friends of the Earth
Greenpeace U.S.A.
National Geographic Society
Natural Resources Defense Council

III

Preserving Our Planet

URBAN
ENVIRONMENTS

Throughout history, cities have always been centers of commerce, cul-
ture, government, and opportunity. Today, many cities in the world have
grown to become sprawling metropolises. By the year 2000, it is esti-
mated that half of the world's people will live in urban areas. Many cities
are struggling to meet the needs of their vast populations. Careful city
planning and management of resources are necessary to insure the sur-
vival of urban environments.

LIBRARY SKILLS

a. Following is a list of things you may find in a city. Put them in
alphabetical order: parking lot, water treatment plant, gas station, newspaper,
college, office building, airport, movie theater, bus, hospital, factory, traffic
light, zoo, store, library.

b. Use *Rand McNally's Children's World Atlas* to make a list of some of
the capital cities in Asia and other continents.

c. In the *World Book Encyclopedia* or another encyclopedia, look up
City Government to answer the following questions: 1) What is a council-
manager form of government? How does it differ from a mayor-council form
of government? 2) What are a strong-mayor system and a weak-mayor system?

d. Look up Population of World's Largest Cities in *The World Almanac
and Book of Facts* to answer the following questions: 1) Which metropolitan
area currently has the largest population? 2) Which metro area has the highest
population density? 3) Which country has the largest number of metro areas
on the list? The second and third most? 4) How many cities have a population
density of over 100,000 per square mile? How many of these are in Asia?
5) Which city has the largest area in square miles? The smallest? 6) For many
decades, London was the most populous city in the world. Where does it rank
now? 7) Which cities are projected to have a decrease in population by the
year 2000? 8) Of the top 20 cities listed, how many are over 600 square miles?
9) Which three cities are expected to have the biggest population increases

by 2000? 10) In your opinion, which cities seem to be growing faster—ones in industrialized or non-industrialized nations?

   e. In *The Information Please Environmental Almanac*, look up Green Metro Areas to answer the following questions: 1) According to the Census Bureau, what constitutes a metropolitan area? 2) What is the largest United States metro area under this definition, and what does it include? 3) Which metro area has the greatest number of unhealthy air pollution days? 4) Which urban area has the most park land? 5) Which city's residents use the most water? 6) Which city has the highest recycling rate? 7) Which city obtains the highest percent of its electricity from coal? Gas? Nuclear power? 8) Which metro area releases the greatest amount of chemicals into the atmosphere? 9) Which metro area has the cheapest gasoline prices? 10) Overall, which metro area does the *Almanac* judge to have the best "Green" rating?

   f. Use *Fodor's . . . Europe's Great Cities* or another Fodor's travel guide to write an itinerary for a two week European tour. Plan to visit cities in one to four countries. Your schedule should include where you would stay and the places you would visit each day. Allow enough time for travel and sight-seeing, and make sure that the places you want to visit are open on the days you plan to be there.

   g. Use *Cities of the World* to answer the following questions: 1) What are the main cities of Indonesia? 2) To which schools do children of United States residents go in San José, Costa Rica? 3) Where do people go for entertainment in Helsinki? 4) Where is Tegucigalpa? What is the predominant architectural style there? 5) What type of clothing should you bring if you plan to vacation in Aukland? 6) According to legend, what famous play was set in Famagusta? 7) When can the midnight sun be seen in Tromsø? 8) What is the closest airport to Pretoria? 9) If you lived in Manila, what type of currency would you use? 10) If you lived in Rangoon, which two languages would you most likely speak?

ARTS AND CRAFTS

   a. There are many rules that people should follow to make living in a city safer. These include traffic rules, such as stoping at stop signs, and health rules, such as not smoking in public places. Draw a poster to illustrate a city safety rule. (13)

   b. Make a collage of modern city scenes.

   c. *Group project:* Create a mural or bulletin board of city plants and animals. Label each plant and animal pictured. (1, 3, 5, 11, 20)

   d. Draw a poster or make a collage that focuses on a problem of a modern city, such as pollution. Caption it with a slogan that calls attention to the problem or suggests a possible solution (for example, "Don't be a litterbug"). (1, 2, 5, 6, 12, 17, 18, 22)

e. Make a diagram or model of a city park, Your park may have a playground, pond, picnic area, trails, various trees and plants, a water fountain, statues, a baseball field or other sports area, public rest rooms, a refreshment stand, or whatever else you would like to include. Indicate the park entrances. Is your park in the center of the city, or near the outskirts? What is the name of your park? (1, 5, 11, 20)

f. Draw a picture, build a model, or create a collage of a city from the past. Your artwork can be of an ancient civilization, or a city anywhere in the world before 1940. Include appropriate buildings, methods of transportation, vegetation, etc. You may add figures of people dressed in clothes of the time. Note on your work the name of the city and the period in history. (4, 6, 15, 16, 24)

g. Design a model city of the future. Give your city a name and describe what special features it would have. Build a model or draw a picture of your futuristic city. (14, 15, 17, 22)

SPELLING/VOCABULARY

a. Complete a matching picture puzzle of types of transportation you may see in a city: monorail, subway, bus, trolley, motorcycle, helicopter, car, van, airplane, truck, bicycle, boat, train, rickshaw, taxi. (2, 13, 22, 24)

b. Complete a word search puzzle of types of buildings found in a city: apartment building, factory, skyscraper, stadium, store, restaurant, school, church, fire house, hospital, bank, theater, hotel, library, city hall, office, university, police station. (2, 5, 13, 22)

c. Complete a crossword puzzle of city terms: population, commute, civilization, traffic, goods, leisure, tourist, crowded, services, immigrant, trade, government, culture, highway, business. (2, 5, 6, 12, 13)

d. Complete a fill-in-the-blanks exercise of city government terms: taxation, municipal, city hall, mayor, election, laws, court, economy, board of aldermen, council, city manager, ordinance, legislature, school board, borough. (9, 12, 26)

e. Complete a crossword puzzle of terms that relate to ancient civilizations: hieroglyphics, theocracy, monarch, caste, aqueduct, citadel, shaman, subjugate, megalith, ziggurat, oracle, monotheism, gods, democracy, dynasty, sacrifice, empire, city-state, Great Bath, slaves. (4, 15, 16, 23)

f. The Greek word for "city" is *polis*. Latin words for "city" are *urbs* and *civilis* or *civis*. Make a list of English words that include these Greek and Latin roots. Define each of your words. (22)

g. Define these terms that relate to city planning: grid pattern, zoning, green belt, city wall, Utopia, developers, new towns, high-rise apartments, gentrification, pedestrian mall, suburb, downtown, community, allotment, inner city, eminent domain, master plan, residential area, commercial area, district. (9, 15, 21, 22)

GEOGRAPHY

a. Look up a map of your state. How are large cities and metropolitan areas shown? Compare this to the way smaller towns look. Locate some important cities. Where is the capital? How can you tell it is the capital?

b. On a map of the United states, locate the 50 capital cities and Washington, D.C. Is the capital always the largest city in the state?

c. On a map of the world, locate 50 major cities.

d. *Group project:* Divide the class into two teams. Play a game where you try to match a list of countries to their capital cities. (2, 6)

e. Make a list of major cities in your state. Look up the name of the mayor or town manager for each city. Also list the population figures and area in square miles for each city.

f. What is meant by the term "Third World Country"? Name and locate on a map some rapidly growing cities in Third World countries. (21, 22, 25)

g. On a map of the world, locate these ancient cities: Mesopotamia, Alexandria, Troy, Knossos, Anyang, Mohenjo-Dara, Sumaria, Babylon, Carthage, Tyre, Susa, Sparta, Nimrud, Ur, Byzantium, Loyang, Chan-Chan, Cuzco, Chichén Itzá, Tenochtitlan, Veracruz, Poverty Point, Teotihuacan, Pompeii, Mycenae, Harappa, Akhetaten. Approximately when did each of these cities exist? To which empires or cultures did they belong? In general, in what part of the globe are all these civilizations located? Why do you think that is so? (4, 8, 16, 23)

MATH

a. Following is a list of historical events that happened in cities. Arrange them in the order in which they occurred, from the furthest back in history to the most recent. 1) 1206: Delhi, India, is founded. 2) 1790: Washington, D.C., becomes the federal capital of the United States. 3) About 3000 BC: First known cities are built by Sumerians in what is now Iraq. 4) 1626: Dutch settlers build a fort in what is now New York City. 5) 632: The city of Mecca becomes the religious center of the world for Muslim people. 6) 1990: The Berlin Wall is torn down, re-joining East and West Germany. 7) 1421: Peking (now usually spelled Beijing) becomes the capital of China. 8) About 750 BC: The first Greek city-states are established. 9) 969: Cairo, Egypt, is founded. 10) 1906: Much of San Francisco is destroyed because of a major earthquake. (15)

   b. In 1985, there were about 5 billion people on Earth. About one-third of them lived in cities. How much is one third of a billion? By the year 2000, Earth's population could reach 6 billion. Half of these people may be living in cities. How many people would that be? Make a chart to illustrate these figures. (2)

   c. New York City, San Francisco, and Detroit are home to people from many racial and ethnic backgrounds. Following are percentage breakdowns of racial/ethnic groups for these cities. For each city, draw a bar chart to illustrate these figures. (*Note:* Figures may add up to more than 100 percent because many people are of mixed descent.) New York: 52% European-American, 29% African-American, 24% various Spanish-speaking ethnic groups, 7% Asian or Pacific Islander, 0.5% American Indian, 11.5% Other. San Francisco: 54% European-American, 29% Asian or Pacific Islander, 14% various Spanish-speaking ethnic groups, 11% African-American, 0.5% American Indian, 6% Other. Detroit: 75% African-American, 22% European-American, 1% Asian or Pacific Islander, 0.5% American Indian, 1.5% Other. (26)

   d. Most states require its citizens to pay a sales tax to help finance city services. 1) If one state has a sales tax of 5 percent (5 cents per every dollar), how much tax would be charged on items that cost $5, $12, $43, $290, and $687? 2) In addition, some large cities charge a city sales tax on top of the state sales tax. At a 2 percent rate, how much would the city tax be on the five amounts in question #1? 3) What would be the combined state and city sales taxes for each of the five amounts?

   e. Use the weather map in *USA Today* or another newspaper to chart the temperatures of United States cities over a two-week period. Choose ten cities from different parts of the country and record the temperatures each day. Draw a graph of your findings.

   f. The world's tallest buildings are located in cities. The tallest office buildings are the Sears Tower in Chicago (1,559 feet) and the World Trade Center in New York (1,353 feet). The Warsaw Radio mast is 2,120 feet, the Eiffel Tower in Paris is 984 feet, Central Plaza in Hong Kong is 1,028 feet, and Moscow State University is 994 feet. Convert these measurements to meters.

g. In 1950 London, England, was the most populated metropolitan area in the world with 8,700,000 people. Its estimated populations for the next decades were as follows: 1960, 8,222,000; 1970, 7,880,000; 1980, 6,970,000; 1990, 9,115,000. London's projected population for the year 2000 is 8,574,000. In 1990 Mexico City, Mexico, was the most populated metro area in the world with 20,899,000 people. Its estimated populations for other decades: 1950, 1,754,000; 1960, 4,967,000; 1970, 6,816,000; 1980, 13,994,000; 2000, 27,872,000. Sao Paulo, Brazil, is currently the world's fastest-growing metro area. Its estimated populations: 1950, 1,380,000; 1960, 3,417,200; 1970, 5,383,000; 1980, 7,198,000; 1990, 18,701,000; 2000, 25,354,000. 1) Make a graph to illustrate these comparisons. 2) What is the annual rate of population growth per decade for each city? Which decade had the largest rate of growth for each city? 3) Make a graph to illustrate the annual rate of population growth per decade for these cities. (Figures are from *World Almanac and Book of Facts*, various years.)

MUSIC AND THEATER ARTS

a. Think of some sounds you might hear in a city, such as a fire engine siren or the drilling of a jackhammer. Each person can imitate a different city sound. The rest of the class can try to guess what the sound is.

b. *Group project:* Act out a short scene showing a historical event that occurred in a city of your choice. (4, 6, 8, 10, 12, 15, 16, 23)

c. Many songs have been written about big cities. Listen to some of these, such as "New York, New York" or "I Left My Heart in San Francisco." How many more songs can you think of?

d. Many authors and poets, such as Carl Sandburg, wrote about cities. Choose one or more poems or part of a story about a city or city life to read aloud to the class. Your oral interpretation piece should be about three to five minutes long.

e. *Group project:* Act out a skit showing one reason why people move to cities, and how cities grow. (6, 10, 12, 15, 22)

f. Many famous plays are set in big cities. Read a scene or listen to music from a play, such as *Chicago* or *City of Angels*. Play a game where you try to match a scene or song from a play to the city in which it takes place.

g. *Class project:* Pretend all the students in the class are attending a city council meeting in which several issues of concern, such as taxes and school budget, are being discussed. Assign some students to role-play certain parts (the mayor, an irate taxpayer, etc.) Act out this meeting.

ENGLISH COMPOSITION

a. Write a poem about an American or foreign city. Tell something special about the city or why it interests you.   (2, 6, 10)

b. Many birds and other wildlife live in cities. Choose one animal and write a story about its life in a city. Where does it make its home? How does it find food? Is this animal beneficial to the city or is it a pest?   (1, 3, 5, 11, 19, 20)

c. Look at some old photographs or postcards of American cities in the past. Choose one picture and write a story based on what you see. Include some historical information about how people lived at the time.   (6, 12, 24, 26)

d. William Shakespeare once wrote, "The people are the city." Write an essay on this theme. Give some reasons that support this statement.   (6, 10, 17, 21, 22)

e. Write a fictional journal of a day in the life of a modern city dweller. Start from when he/she wakes up in the morning and end when he/she goes to bed in the evening. List everything this person does by time (ex: 7:00 AM — alarm clock goes off and Mary wakes up.) Give your person a name, family, occupation, etc. and have him/her experience a typical day.   (6, 7, 10, 21, 22, 25, 26)

f. Choose one city in the United States. Imagine that you are a politician who is running for mayor of that city. Write a campaign speech telling what you would do if you were elected.   (6, 9, 10, 21, 22, 26)

g. Choose one topic from the list the class compiles for the topics for discussion exercise (p. 181), item **g**. Write a report on how this factor affects city life.   (5, 6, 9, 12, 17, 18, 21, 22, 25, 26)

SCIENCE

a. What are some plants that grow wild in urban areas? Where do they grow?   (1, 5, 11, 20)

b. What are lichens? How can they be a way to measure air pollution in a city?   (1, 11, 18)

c. How does the climate of cities differ from that of the surrounding countryside? What causes these differences?   (1, 5, 6, 18).

d. Make a chart of wild animals and plants that live in each of these habitats: railroad embankments, cemeteries, garbage dumps, vacant lots, skyscrapers, parks, highway verges, zoos, reservoirs and gravel pits, back yards, sewage treatment plants, roofs and chimneys.   (1, 11, 19, 20)

e. If a city has poor sanitation, what problems may arise?   (12, 18, 21, 22)

f. How might advances in technology, especially electronics, affect cities of the future? Give some examples of how city life might change.   (14, 15, 22)

g. Cities use great quantities of water. Name some possible natural and artificial causes of a water shortage. What could happen to the inhabitants of a city that uses polluted water? Give some examples from past situations.   (9, 12, 17, 18, 21, 22)

HISTORY/SOCIOLOGY

a. How do people in American cities shop for food and other goods? How do city people in some other countries acquire goods?   (2, 6, 13)

b. Why do cities grow? What role does industry play in the growth of a city?   (5, 6, 12, 15, 17, 22)

c. Look up information on one ancient civilization. Where did the people build their city? Why was that spot chosen? Note some interesting facts about life there. Does the city exist today? If not, what happened to it?   (2, 4, 6, 10, 15, 16, 22, 26)

d. Many major cities from past civilizations were destroyed or otherwise lost. Look up some information on one lost city. Where was it located? When did it exist? Note some facts about the people who lived there and their way of life. Why does the city no longer exist?   (4, 8, 16, 23)

e. Trace the history of one major city which exists today. In what country is it located? When was the area settled and by whom? What changes has the city undergone over the years? Note some important events that happened there. How does the city's present compare to its past?   (6, 7, 10, 15, 16, 22, 23, 26)

f. Poverty, unemployment, and homelessness are major problems in today's cities, but they were also problems in cities of the past. Choose a period in history, either in America or another country. Compare poverty, unemployment, and homelessness of that era to these problems in a present-day American city.   (6, 12, 15, 17, 21, 22, 26)

g. Why has the population of cities around the world exploded in recent years? Give some examples of this population increase. How has this affected worldwide population overall? How has it affected the environment?   (5, 6, 9, 17, 21, 22, 25, 26)

TOPICS FOR DISCUSSION

a. What non-domestic animals live in cities? Why do they prefer an urban environment? Where in the city do they live? How do they survive? (1, 3, 5, 11, 19, 20)

b. Taxes collected from people and businesses in a city are used to run a city. Some services provided by the city include: fire department, parks, and schools. Name some other city services. (12, 13, 22)

c. Why do people choose to live in cities? What are some advantages and disadvantages of living in a city? (1, 2, 6, 7, 12, 15, 17, 22)

d. What are shanty towns? Who lives there? Why are shanty towns built? What can be done to solve this problem? (2, 12, 21, 22)

e. People from many different cultures and backgrounds may live together in a city. Sometimes, these differences or divisions between types of people cause conflicts. Name some of these divisions, such as rich versus poor, and the conflicts that may arise because of them. (7, 9, 21, 26)

f. What are some types of pollution suffered by modern city-dwellers? How serious is the problem in some cities? What are some causes of this pollution, and some possible solutions? (1, 6, 9, 12, 17, 18, 21, 22)

g. Make a list of some factors, such as waste disposal, public transportation, and crime, that affect the quality of life in a city. Choose one of these topics for a report in the English composition exercise, item **g**. (6, 9, 12, 17, 18, 21, 22, 26)

SUGGESTED RESOURCES

(1) Aldis, Rodney. *Towns and Cities* [Ecology Watch]. Dillon, 1992.
(2) Bailey, Donna. *Cities* [Facts About]. Steck-Vaughn, 1990.
(3) Bash, Barbara. *Urban Roosts: Where Birds Nest in the City.* Sierra Club, 1990.
(4) *Civilizations of the Americas* [History of the World]. Raintree, 1988. (Also other books in series.)
(5) Costa-Pau, Rosa. *The City* [The Junior Library of Ecology]. Chelsea, 1994.
(6) Davis, James E., and Hawke, Sherryl Davis. [World Cities] series. Raintree, 1990.
(7) [Downtown America] series. Dillon, 1988.
(8) Gallant, Roy A. *Lost Cities* [First Books]. Watts, 1985.
(9) Gay, Kathlyn. *Cities Under Stress* [Impact]. Watts, 1985.
(10) [Great Cities] series. Blackbirch, 1991.
(11) Hester, Nigel. *The Living Town* [Watching Nature]. Watts, 1992.
(12) Kalman, Bobbie. *Early City Life* [The Early Settler Life Series]. Crabtree, 1983.
(13) _____, and Hughs, Susan. *I Live in a City* [In My World]. Crabtree, 1986.
(14) Lambert, Mark. *Homes in the Future* [Houses and Homes]. Lerner, 1988.
(15) MacDonald, Fiona. *Cities, Citizens & Civilizations* [Timelines]. Watts, 1992.

(16) Oliphant, Margaret. *The Earliest Civilizations* [The Illustrated History of the World]. Facts on File, 1993. (Also other books in series.)
(17) Parker, Philip. *Global Cities* [Project Eco-City]. Thomson, 1995.
(18) _____. *Town Life* [Project Eco-City]. Thomson, 1995.
(19) _____. *Your Living Home* [Project Eco-City]. Thomson, 1994.
(20) _____. *Your Wild Neighborhood* [Project Eco-City]. Thomson, 1994.
(21) Reynolds, Tony. *Cities in Crisis* [World Issues]. Rourke, 1990.
(22) Royston, Robert. *Cities* [Your World 2000]. Facts on File, 1985.
(23) Unstead, R. J. *How They Lived in Cities Long Ago.* Arco, 1981.
(24) Von Tscharner, Renata, and Fleming, Ronald Lee. *New Providence: A Changing Cityscape.* Harcourt, 1992.
(25) Winckler, Suzanne, and Rodgers, Mary M. *Population Growth* [Our Endangered Planet]. Lerner, 1991.
(26) Wright, David. *A Multicultural Portrait of Life in the Cities* [Perspectives]. Cavendish, 1993.

LIBRARY SKILLS RESOURCES

Cities of the World. Gale, 1987.
Fodor's . . . Europe's Great Cities. Fodor Travel Publications, 1990. (Also other Fodor's travel guides.)
Rand McNally Children's World Atlas. Rand McNally, 1989.
The World Almanac and Book of Facts. World Almanac, 1994 and previous years.
World Book Encyclopedia. World Book, 1993.
World Resources Institute. *The Information Please Environmental Almanac.* Houghton, 1993.

ADDITIONAL READING – YOUNGER

Bunting, Eve. *Smoky Night.* Harcourt, 1994.
Cobb, Vicki. *This Place Is Crowded: Japan* [Imagine Living Here]. Walker, 1992.
Gibbons, Gail. *Up Goes the Skyscraper!* Four Winds, 1986.
Goodall, John S. *The Story of a Main Street.* Macmillan, 1987.
Higham, Charles. *The Earliest Farmers and the First Cities* [Cambridge Topic]. Lerner, 1977.
Kaufman, Curt, and Kaufman, Gita. *Hotel Boy.* Atheneum, 1987.
McHugh, Christopher. *Town and Country* [Discovering Art]. Thomson, 1993.
Maxwell, Roxie. *The Inside-Outside Book of London.* Dutton, 1989. (Also other books in series.)
Müller, Jorg. *The Changing City.* Macmillan, 1977.
_____. *The Changing Countryside.* Macmillan, 1977.
Provensen, Alice, and Provensen, Martin. *Shaker Lane.* Viking, 1987.
Steele, Philip. *City Through the Ages.* Troll, 1993.
Ventura, Piero. *Piero Ventura's Book of Cities.* Random, 1975.
Wheeler, Jill. *The City We Live In* [We Can Save the Earth]. Abdo, 1990.
_____. *The People We Live With* [We Can Save the Earth]. Abdo, 1991.
Whitlock, Ralph. *In the Town* [Use Your Eyes]. Wayland, 1986.

Williams, Vera B. *Scooter*. Greenwillow, 1993.
Wilson, Barbara Ker. *Acacia Terrace*. Scholastic, 1990.

ADDITIONAL READING – OLDER

Adoff, Arnold. *Street Music: City Poems*. HarperCollins, 1992.
Al-Salah, Khairat. *Fabled Cities, Princes & Jinn from Arab Myths & Legends*. Schocken, 1985.
Avi. *City of Light, City of Dark: A Comic-Book Novel*. Orchard, 1993.
Bruning, Nancy. *Cities Against Nature* [Saving Planet Earth]. Childrens, 1992.
Chicago (sound recording). Arista Records, 1975.
City of Angels (sound recording). Notable Music, 1989.
Danziger, Paula. *Remember Me to Harold Square*. Delacorte, 1987.
_____. *Thames Doesn't Rhyme with James*. Putnam, 1994.
Ebb, Fred, and Fosse, Bob. *Chicago: A Musical Vaudeville*. French, 1976.
Gelbart, Larry. *City of Angels*. Applause, 1991.
Hilton, Suzzanne. *A Capital Capital City 1790–1814*. Atheneum, 1992.
Huff, Barbara. *Greening the City Streets: The Story of Community Gardens*. Clarion, 1990.
James, Barbara. *Use of Land* [Young Geographer]. Thomson, 1993.
Krull, Kathleen. *City Within a City: How Kids Live in New York's China Town* [A World of My Own]. Lodestar, 1994.
_____. *The Other Side: How Kids Live in a California Latino Neighborhood* [A World of My own]. Lodestar, 1994.
Macaulay, David. *City: A Story of Roman Planning and Construction*. Houghton, 1974.
_____. *Underground*. Houghton, 1976.
Merriam, Eve. *The Inner City Mother Goose*. Simon & Schuster, 1994.
Millea, Nicholas. *Settlements* [Young Geographer]. Thomson, 1993.
Richardson, Wendy, and Richardson, Jack. *Cities: Through the Eyes of Artists* [The World of Art]. Childrens, 1991.
Shaffer, Carolyn, and Fielder, Erica. *City Safaris*. Sierra Club, 1987.
Stuart, Gene S. *America's Ancient Cities*. National Geographic, 1988.
Urban Wilds [The American Wilderness]. Time-Life, 1975.
Yepsen, Roger. *City Trains: Moving Through America's Cities by Rail*. Macmillan, 1993.

See also: books in ENVIRONMENTAL AWARENESS and WASTE AND RECY-
CLING units.

FOR MORE INFORMATION ABOUT URBAN ENVIRONMENTS, WRITE TO:

"Backyard Habitat Kit," National
  Wildlife Federation
Community Environment Council
Concerned Neighbors in Action
Environmental Action Coalition
Experimental Cities
Global ReLeaf Through Learning

Kids for Saving Earth
The National Institute for Urban
  Wildlife
Tree City U.S.A. Community Improve-
  ment Program
Trust for Public Land

FOOD AND FARMING

The foods we eat come from many different sources. Most of our meat, grains, fruits and vegetables are raised or grown on farms. In recent years, improvements in agricultural technology and the development of new breeds of animals and crops have greatly increased the modern farmers' food production. Yet all over the world, millions of people are starving and the environment is suffering. Farmers and governments must work together to insure a healthy diet for all people on Earth.

LIBRARY SKILLS

a. People who live in poor countries often live on a diet of simple basic foods, or staples. Following is a list of cereals and other foods that provide staple diets for many people. Put them in alphabetical order: rice, wheat, millet, potatoes, corn, sorghum, yams, barley, oats, fish, eggs, legumes.

b. Look up Cattle in *Pets and Farm Animals* to answer the following questions: 1) How do people in India regard cattle? 2) What was the aurochs, and when did it exist? 3) Name five types of beef cattle. 4) Name five types of dairy cattle. 5) Name five types of cattle that live in tropical and subtropical Africa, Asia, or South America.

c. Use *Atlas of World Issues* to answer the following questions: 1) According to Agricultural Systems, what are the four basic types of farming systems? What is alley cropping? 2) According to Farming & Plenty, what country is the main exporter of grain? Which countries import the most grain? In which countries do the majority of people not eat pork? Where do people not consume dairy products? 3) According to Food & Water, in what parts of the world are people hunter-gatherers?

d. Use *Lands and Peoples* to look up five countries in different parts of the world. For each one, list the main crops that are grown there and the livestock that is raised for food.

e. Use *Agriculture and Vegetation of the World* to find the answers to the following: 1) List the country that is the top producer in the world for each of these products: cacao, coffee, sugar, tobacco, tea, rubber, coconuts, sheep, wheat, potatoes, olives, oats, barley, cotton, wood. 2) Which three countries rely the most on irrigation for raising crops? 3) Which countries employ 75 percent or more of the work force in agriculture? 4) Which three countries use the most fertilizer per acre? 5) Which countries are the main donors of food aid? Which are the main recipients of food aid?

f. Use the Planting Table in *The Old Farmer's Almanac* to answer the following questions: 1) In your weather region, when would be the best day to plant an early crop of broccoli? Radishes? Peas? Eggplant? 2) What is the earliest date recommended for planting a late crop of beets? Celery? Carrots? Sweet corn? Use the Gestation and Mating Table to answer these questions: 1) At least how old should a ewe be when it is mated for the first time? How much should a Jersey cow weigh by its first mating? 2) What is the incubation period for a chicken? A goose? 3) What is the maximum life span of a domestic horse? A pig?

g. In *The New Book of Popular Science*, look up Agriculture: Using Genetics for Food Production to answer the following: 1) Name some qualities that scientists are trying to breed in tomatoes. 2) List some advantages and disadvantages of Green Revolution crops. 3) What vegetable did Gregor Mendel use in his genetics experiments? 4) Why are legumes important to farmers? 5) What are some other areas for plant improvement?

ARTS AND CRAFTS

a. There are many things you can do to be sure your food is safe to eat. Design a poster that shows one of these safety hints. (13, 25, 26)

b. Make a collage of pictures of farm products. (2, 6, 14, 29)

c. Glue dried seeds, beans, and macaroni onto paperboard to make mosaic designs.

d. *Group project:* Use discarded clothing and straw to make a life-size scarecrow.

e. Use corn husks to make corn dollies. (29)

f. The worldwide increase of ranching and agriculture has caused the destruction of many wildlife habitats. Make a collage, poster, or mural that draws attention to this tragedy. You can focus on a specific habitat or animal, or choose several examples to illustrate. (13, 16, 17, 18, 20, 25, 29)

g. Make a model or a picture of a farm of the future. Things to consider: energy sources, use of chemicals versus organic farming, crops grown and where they would be planted, harvesting techniques, new technology and machinery, and the possibility of controlling variables such as weather and product demand. (5, 17, 18, 21)

SPELLING/VOCABULARY

a. Complete a word search puzzle of farming tools and machines: baler, plow, combine, sickle, thresher, harrow, reaper, drill, tractor, crawler, cultivator, hoe, flail, mower, seeder, hopper, fieldchopper, windrower, highboy, auger. (3, 4, 6, 9, 15, 17)

b. Complete a crossword puzzle of terms relating to farm animals: shear, stable, ewe, calf, foal, barn, cud, fleece, sow, fowl, graze, hoof, milking, feed, heifer, kennel, egg, kid, cattle, udder. (2, 8, 12, 14, 19, 22, 23)

c. Complete a fill-in-the-blanks exercise of agricultural terms: bale, harvest, plow, winnow, disk, till, furrow, silage, weeds, chaff, acre, sow, fertile, cultivate, maize, thresh, straw, stalk, shuck, field. (4, 6, 7, 12, 15, 17)

d. Complete a matching puzzle of dietary terms: protein, fruit, calcium, vitamins, carbohydrates, iron, nutrients, minerals, starches, sugars, fiber, fats, energy, nourishment, balanced diet, cereals, staple diet, vegetables, dairy products, legumes. (2, 10, 13, 23, 25, 26, 27, 29)

e. Complete a crossword puzzle of terms that relate to raising farm animals for food: livestock, poultry, ranching, breed, vaccinate, intensive farms, paddock, hormones, salmonella, cattle, fodder, antibiotics, slurry, domesticate, free-range, aquaculture, feed lots, lean meat, pastureland, battery cage. (1, 7, 8, 13, 16, 17, 20, 25, 27, 29)

f. Define these agricultural terms: organic farming, bumper crop, luxury crop, selective breeding, fertilizer, Green Revolution, yield, pesticide, irrigate, herbicide, modernizing, hydroponics, superwheat, cover crops, crop rotation, fallow land, contour plowing, silviculture, hybrid, sustainable agriculture. (1, 4, 7, 9, 13, 16, 17, 18, 20, 21, 24, 25, 27, 29)

g. Complete a matching puzzle of terms that relate to the business of farming and types of farms: collective farm, farm cooperative, corporate farm, commercial farming, subsistence farming, kibbutz, mixed farming, intensive farming, extensive farming, specialized farm, dairy farm, cash crop, grain farm, livestock ranching, nomadic herding, factory farm, fish farm, poultry farm, family farm, farm management. (1, 2, 13, 26, 25, 29)

GEOGRAPHY

a. In what parts of the world are sheep raised for food? Goats? Chickens? Pigs? Beef cattle? Dairy cattle? What animals are herded in the Arctic regions? (8, 25, 29)

b. In the 1930s, there was a major drought in the United States. An area of the country became known as the Dust Bowl. On a map of the United States, color in this area and name the states that were affected. What caused the Dust Bowl? How did it affect the American farmer and food prices? Could it ever happen again? (16, 20, 28, 29)

c. Name some places where the following foods are grown commercially: cassavas, olives, rice, oranges, potatoes, tea, yams, wheat, corn, millet, peppers, bananas, apples, cacao, sugarcane, coffee beans. (2, 4, 13, 25, 29)

d. More than half of the world's people rely on rice as their most important staple food. On a map of the world, locate these countries: Bangladesh, Burma, China, Hong Kong, India, Indonesia, Japan, North Korea, South Korea, Laos, Malaysia, Nepal, Philippines, Singapore, Sri Lanka, Thailand, Vietnam, the Gambia, Guinea, Ivory Coast, Liberia, Madagascar, Mauritius, Sierra Leone, Brazil, Columbia, Dominican Republic, Guyana, Panama, and Suriname. In which of these countries are many of the people poor and undernourished? (10, 11, 13, 25, 28)

e. For each of the following agricultural conditions, tell what crops can be grown there: flooded fields in China; prairies in the United States; warm, moist hillsides in Sri Lanka; high in the Andes mountains; a tropical rainforest in South America; dry, poor soils in Africa; sunny areas in the Mediterranean; bogs in the northeast United States; hot, dry climates in the Middle East; cool climates of northern Europe. (2, 13, 25, 29)

f. Many parts of the world have suffered famines, drought, flooding, or plagues in recent years. Name some countries that have experienced these natural disasters. Tell where and when each disaster occurred, and how it affected the farming industry there. (10, 11, 13, 16, 24, 25, 27, 28, 29)

g. Write a report about farming today in another country. How does climate, the type of soil and other challenges of nature, as well as political concerns, affect the life of the farmer, the crops and livestock grown, and the business of farming? (2, 10, 13, 16, 25, 27, 29)

MATH

a. A mother pig, or sow, usually has between 10 and 14 piglets in a litter. 1) If a sow has 12 piglets in each of six litters, how many piglets would that be? 2) If a sow has 10 piglets in her first litter, 13 in the second, 14 in the third, 11 in the fourth, and 12 in the fifth, how many piglets would that be? 3) If sow A has 14 piglets in each of five litters, and sow B has 10 piglets in each of six litters, which sow has the most piglets?

b. In the United States, about 3 percent of the work force are farmers. Following is a list of other countries and the approximate percent of workers who are employed in agriculture. Draw a chart to compare these numbers: Kenya 80%; Indonesia 50%; Ireland 13%; Albania 55%; Iran 30%; Philippines 45%; Greece 25%; Switzerland 30%; Rwanda 80%; Saudi Arabia 40%; Laos 70%; Poland 30%; Western Samoa 70%; Israel 3%; Papua New Guinea 70%. Why do you think so few Americans are farmers, considering the great amount of food that is produced here? (*Agriculture and Vegetation of the World*)

c. Answer the following problems: 1) If a bale of hay weighs 1,000 pounds and a farm produces 60 bales of hay in one day, how many pounds of hay is that? How many tons? 2) If a bale of hay weighs 1,500 pounds and a farm produces 50 bales in a day, how many pounds is that? How many tons?

d. A dairy cow usually gives about 12 gallons of milk per day. 1) How many gallons is that in a year? 2) If a farmer has 25 dairy cows, how much milk can he expect to get in one day? In a week? In a year? 3) How many gallons of milk in a day, week, and year can a farmer get from 200 cows? 1,000 cows?

e. Beef cattle need to consume 10 pounds of feed to produce 1 pound of beef. Chickens need to eat 2.5 pounds of feed to produce 1 pound of meat. Fish need only 1.5 pounds of feed for every pound of food produced. Make a chart that shows how much feed a beef steer, a chicken, and a fish would need to consume in order to produce 5, 10, 15, 20, and 25 pounds of food each.

f. According to 1980 figures by the United Nations' Food and Agriculture Organization, about 500 million people in the world are seriously malnourished, mostly in Third World countries. Following is a partial list of countries and the number of starving people (in millions) who live there: Indonesia, 33; Bangladesh, 27; Nigeria, 14; India, 201; Afghanistan, 6; Brazil, 12; Ethiopia, 12; Pakistan, 12; Philippines, 10; Burma, 5; Colombia, 5; Thailand, 5; Chad, 2; Haiti, 2. Make a chart that shows what percent of the world's 500 million starving people live in each of these countries. (*Note:* Chart will not add up to 100%. Label the leftover amount "Other Countries.") (10)

g. United States farms in the 1930s produced 25 bushels of corn per acre. With the development of hybrid corn and mechanized farming methods, United States farmers in 1990 produced 120 bushels of corn per acre. 1) Make a graph to show how many bushels of corn could be grown in the 1930s and in 1990 on 80, 100, 120, and 140 acres. 2) In 1930, an average farm was about 120 acres. In 1990, an average farm may be 1,000 acres. How many bushels of corn could be grown on an average farm in the 1930s, and in 1990? What percent of the 1990 yield was the 1930s yield? 3) Two-thirds of all corn grown in the United States is used to feed livestock. How many bushels of corn grown on an average size farm in 1990 would be fed to livestock?

MUSIC AND THEATER ARTS

a. Perform a puppet show to farm folk songs, such as "The Farmer in the Dell," or stories, such as "The Little Red Hen."

b. Pretend you are a chef on a television cooking show. Tell how to prepare an exotic new dish you invented, using pretend food. Inform your audience of the food's nutritional value and any other important information.

c. Barn dances, or square dancing, gained popularity in the United States during the 1800s. Learn some of these dances.

d. The musical play *Oklahoma!* is about American farmers and ranchers. Sing songs and act out scenes from this play.

e. *Group project:* Many cultures celebrate festivals for planting or harvesting crops. Pick one celebration from the past or present to act out.   (2, 7, 29)

f. *Class project:* Some musicians have staged an annual Farm Aid concert for the past several years to help struggling American farmers. Stage your own Farm Aid concert. Play records by some of the artists that have performed at these concerts. Give speeches to make people aware of the farmers' plight.

g. *Class project:* Have a mock county fair. Include such entertainments as a mock rodeo, square dancing, awarding prizes for show animals and vegetables, etc. (12, 29)

ENGLISH COMPOSITION

a. Write a story about your favorite food.

b. Write a factual story about a farm animal.   (3, 14, 19, 22)

c. Write and illustrate a picture book about a year on a farm. Tell what happens in each season. Your story can take place on any kind of farm, in the United States or another country, past or present.   (3, 6, 7, 15, 25, 29)

d. *Group project:* Compile a cookbook of recipes using corn, wheat, barley, or other grains.

e. Write a description of a corn or wheat harvest, past or present. Tell how the crop looks when it is ready to harvest and the tools or machines that are used. What happens to the harvested grain?   (1, 4, 12, 17)

f. Write a story, poem, or essay on the theme "Farmers are the caretakers of the land."   (1, 5, 16, 20, 21, 25, 29)

g. Farming as a way of life is dying out in many Third World countries.

Increasing numbers of people are leaving the farms and moving to the cities in hopes of a better way of life. Pretend you are a young man or woman who grew up on a family farm. Now you must decide whether to stay or try your luck in a city. Write an essay about your decision and your reasons for choosing it.   (10, 18, 25, 29)

SCIENCE

a. Where does the milk we drink come from? Name some dairy products that are made from milk. What are other foods that come from cattle, pigs, sheep, and hens?   (2, 8, 13, 19, 22, 23)

b. What are the different food groups? List some of the foods in each group. Tell how these foods are good for your health. What are some ways food is processed?   (2, 8, 13, 23, 25, 26, 29)

c. Why might food become spoiled or diseased? What precautions should you take to avoid food poisoning?   (8, 16, 18, 23, 25, 26, 28)

d. Why are herbicides and pesticides used? What are some undesirable effects of their use?   (5, 10, 13, 16, 17, 18, 20, 24, 25, 27, 28, 29)

e. How do modern industrial farming methods cause water pollution? What happens to groundwater and streams? How does this affect the ecology of ponds and lakes?   (5, 16, 17, 18, 20, 27)

f. What are some advances in technology that have made farming easier and more productive? How has selective breeding changed the types of crops that are grown? What does this mean for the modern industrialized farmer? (13, 16, 17, 18, 21, 25, 27, 29)

g. Many modern farmers make use of chemical fertilizers, pesticides, and herbicides to grow crops. Other farmers prefer to use organic methods, such as composting, integrated pest management, and double cropping. What are some advantages and disadvantages of using chemicals versus organic farming?   (1, 3, 7, 13, 16, 17, 18, 20, 21, 24, 25, 27, 28, 29)

HISTORY/SOCIOLOGY

a. Finding a water supply has always been important for successful farming. How did some past civilizations obtain water? Where were some of the first irrigations systems built?   (7, 9, 15, 25, 29)

b. How did people plow their fields and harvest their crops before the invention of modern machinery? How were cows milked before milking machines were invented?   (3, 7, 9, 12, 15, 17, 29)

c. What are some tools that were used by farmers throughout history? For each tool, name a civilization that used it, at what time in history, and the tool's purpose.   (7, 9, 15, 17, 21, 29)

d. How did the invention of farming eventually lead to the settlement of cities and the beginning of commerce?   (7, 9, 18, 24, 29)

e. Farming was an important aspect of many past civilizations. Choose one nation and period in history and write a report about farming at that time. Who worked the farms and how? What crops or animals were raised? What happened to the food that was produced? ·What was the life of a farmer like?   (7, 15, 21, 27, 29)

f. In many cultures and civilizations throughout history, farms were worked by slave or forced labor. Choose two examples of this from any time or place and compare them. For whom did the farmers work? What did they receive in return for their labors? How were they treated?   (7, 10, 11, 29)

g. How does farming in the United States today compare to farming here in the past? How have crops, livestock, and farming methods changed? How has this affected the lives of farmers and the farming community in general?   (1, 5, 7, 12, 17, 25, 29)

TOPICS FOR DISCUSSION

a. What are the differences among crop farming, dairy farming, poultry farming, and ranching? How do farmers decide what crops to grow or what animals to raise on their land?   (9, 22, 25, 29)

b. What are some differences between the livelihoods of hunter-gatherers and farmers? Which way of life produces a more reliable source of food? What are some problems with each of these methods of obtaining food?   (7, 8, 9, 16, 29)

c. How might farming and ranching cause soil erosion? What effect can this have on the environment? What can be done to prevent soil erosion?   (5, 13, 16, 18, 20, 21, 24, 25, 27, 28)

d. All farms need water in order to thrive. What are some advantages and disadvantages of dams and other methods of irrigation? How do farms sometimes endanger the water supply or water habitats? What are some environmentally safe methods of irrigation?   (13, 16, 17, 20, 21, 24, 27)

e. What is a famine? What are some conditions that may cause famines to occur? What can be done to prevent or lessen the effects of a famine?   (10, 11, 13, 16, 25, 27, 28, 29)

f. In some farms, livestock is raised intensively. Do you think this is a better way to raise food animals than free-range farming? Why or why not? What are some advantages and disadvantages of each method? Which is more cost-efficient? Which is better for the environment?   (7, 10, 13, 16, 17, 25, 27)

g. Because of advanced technology, farmers are able to produce more food than ever before. Yet, while surplus foods rot away in storage, two-thirds of the world's population are undernourished or starving. Why does this happen? What are some proposed solutions to this dilemma?   (10, 11, 13, 16, 17, 18, 24, 25, 27, 28, 29)

SUGGESTED RESOURCES

(1) Ancona, George, and Anderson, Joan. *The American Family Farm*. Harcourt, 1989.
(2) Bailey, Donna. *Farmers* [Facts About]. Raintree, 1990.
(3) Bellville, Cheryl Walsh. *Farming Today Yesterday's Way* [Photo Books]. Carolrhoda, 1984.
(4) Bial, Raymond. *Corn Belt Harvest*. Houghton, 1991.
(5) Billings, Charlene W. *Pesticides: Necessary Risk* [Issues in Focus]. Enslow, 1993.
(6) Bushey, Jerry. *Farming the Land: Modern Farmers and Their Machines* [Photo Books]. Carolrhoda, 1987.
(7) Chrisp, Peter. *The Farmer Through History* [Journey Through History]. Thomson, 1993.
(8) Clark, Elizabeth. *Meat* [Foods We Eat]. Carolrhoda, 1990. (Also other books in series.)
(9) Fradin, Dennis. *Farming* [New True Books]. Childrens, 1983.
(10) Fyson, Nance Lui. *Feeding the World* [Today's World]. Batsford, 1984.
(11) Gibb, Christopher. *Food or Famine?* [World Issues]. Rourke, 1987.
(12) Gunby, Lise. *Early Farm Life* [The Early Settler Life Series]. Crabtree, 1983.
(13) Hawkes, Nigel. *Food and Farming* [Energy]. Watts, 1982.
(14) Jacobsen, Karen. *Farm Animals* [New True Books]. Childrens, 1981.
(15) Kerr, Jim. *Egyptian Farmers* [Beginning History]. Bookwright, 1990.
(16) Lambert, Mark. *Farming and the Environment* [Conserving Our World]. Steck-Vaughn, 1991.
(17) _____. *Farming Technology* [Technology in Action]. Watts, 1990.
(18) Leggett, Dennis, and Leggett, Jeremy. *People Trap* [Operation Earth]. Cavendish, 1991.
(19) McFarland, Cynthia. *Cows in the Parlour: A Visit to a Dairy Farm*. Atheneum, 1990.
(20) Manci, William E. *Farming and the Environment* [Environment Alert!]. Stevens, 1993.
(21) Murphy, Wendy. *The Future World of Agriculture* [Walt Disney World Epcot Center Book]. Grolier, 1984.
(22) Patent, Dorothy Hinshaw. *Farm Animals*. Holiday, 1984.
(23) _____. *Where Food Comes From*. Holiday, 1991.
(24) Peckham, Alexander. *Changing Landscapes* [Green Issues]. Gloucester, 1991.
(25) Reed-King, Susan. *Food and Farming* [Young Geographer]. Thomson, 1993.

(26) Smith, David. *The Food Cycle* [Nature Cycles]. Thomson, 1993.

(27) Tesar, Jenny. *Food and Water: Threats, Shortages and Solutions* [Our Fragile Earth]. Facts on File, 1992.

(28) Walker, Jane. *Famine, Drought and Plagues* [Natural Disasters]. Gloucester, 1992.

(29) Williams, Brian. *Farming* [Ways of Life]. Steck-Vaughn, 1993.

LIBRARY SKILLS RESOURCES

Agriculture and Vegetation of the World [Using and Understanding Maps]. Chelsea, 1993.

Lands and Peoples. Grolier, 1993.

Middleton, Nick. *Atlas of World Issues* [Issues Atlases]. Facts on File, 1989.

The New Book of Popular Science. Grolier, 1994.

Pets and Farm Animals [Encyclopedia of the Animal World]. Facts on File, 1990.

Thomas, Robert B. *The Old Farmer's Almanac.* Yankee, 1994.

ADDITIONAL READING—YOUNGER

Amos, Janine. *Feeding the World* [First Starts]. Raintree, 1993.

Bial, Raymond. *County Fair.* Houghton Mifflin, 1992.

Cook, Brenda. *All About Farm Animals.* Doubleday, 1989.

Cooper, Jason. *Farms* [Great Places to Visit]. Rourke, 1992.

[Food Facts] series. Carolrhoda.

Gibbons, Gail. *Farming.* Holiday, 1988.

Gross, Ruth Belov. *What's on My Plate?* Macmillan, 1990.

Hausherr, Rosmarie. *What Food Is This?* Scholastic, 1994.

Lynn, Sara, and James, Diane. *What We Eat* [Play & Discover]. Thomson, 1994.

Miller, Jane. *Seasons on the Farm.* Prentice-Hall, 1986.

Mitgutsch, Ali. *From Grain to Bread* [Start to Finish]. Carolrhoda, 1981.

———. *From Grass to Butter* [Start to Finish]. Carolrhoda, 1981.

Provensen, Alice, and Provensen, Martin. *The Year at Maple Hill Farm.* Atheneum, 1978.

Sabin, Louis. *Agriculture.* Troll, 1985.

Stephen, R. J. *Farm Machinery* [Picture Library]. Watts, 1986.

Stone, Lynn M. *Dairy Country* [Back Roads]. Rourke, 1993.

———. [Farm Animals Discovery Library]. Rourke, 1990.

Turner, Ann. *Dust for Dinner* [I Can Read Book]. HarperCollins, 1995.

Versfield, Ruth. *Why Are People Hungry?* [Let's Talk About]. Gloucester, 1988.

Wheeler, Jill. *The Food We Eat* [We Can Save the Earth]. Abdo, 1991.

White, E. B. *Charlotte's Web.* Harper, 1952.

Whitlock, Ralph. *On the Farm* [Use Your Eyes]. Wayland, 1986.

ADDITIONAL READING—OLDER

Altman, Linda Jacobs. *Migrant Farm Workers* [Impact]. Watts, 1994.

Ashabranner, Brent. *Born to the Land: An American Portrait.* Putnam, 1989.

Becklake, John, and Becklake, Sue. *Food and Farming* [Green Issues]. Gloucester, 1991.

Burke, Deidre. *Food and Fasting* [Comparing Religions]. Thomson, 1993.

Carson, Rachel. *Silent Spring.* Houghton, 1962.

Facklam, Margery. *Corn-Husk Crafts.* Sterling, 1973.

Graff, Nancy Price. *The Strength in the Hills: A Portrait of a Family Farm.* Little, 1989.

Johnson, Sylvia A. *Rice* [Natural Science]. Lerner, 1985.

_____. *Wheat* [Natural Science]. Lerner, 1990.

Kerrod, Robin. *Food Resources* [World's Resources]. Thomson, 1994.

Knapp, Brian. *Drought* [World Disasters!]. Steck-Vaughn, 1990.

Leonard, Jonathan Norton. *The First Farmers* [The Emergence of Man]. Time-Life, 1973.

Lobstein, Tim. *Poisoned Food?* [Issues]. Watts, 1990.

McCay, J.J. *How Safe Is Our Food Supply?* [Impact]. Watts, 1990.

McHugh, Christopher. *Food* [Discovering Art]. Thomson, 1993.

Oklahoma! (sound recording). CBS, 1964.

Paladino, Catherine. *Our Vanishing Farm Animals* [Saving America's Rare Breeds]. Little, 1991.

Rodgers, Richard, and Hammerstein, Oscar. *Oklahoma!: A Musical Play.* Williamson, 1954.

Sproule, Anna. *Food for the World* [Discovering Science]. Facts on File, 1987.

Swallow, Su. *Food for the World* [Facing the Future]. Raintree, 1991.

Taylor, Ron. *Facts on Pesticides and Fertilizers in Farming* [Facts on]. Watts, 1990.

Timberlake, Lloyd. *Famine in Africa* [Issues]. Watts, 1986.

Wilder, Laura Ingalls. *Farmer Boy.* Harper, 1961.

See also: books in GRASSLANDS unit.

FOR MORE INFORMATION ABOUT FOOD AND FARMING, WRITE TO:

4-H Program and Youth Development

American Minor Breeds Conservancy

End Hunger Network

Farm Aid

Farm Animal Reform Movement

Farm Committee for Sustainable Agriculture

The Humane Farming Association

National FFA Organization (formerly, Future Farmers of America)

National Grange

Organic Foods Production Association of North America

Oxfam America

WASTE AND RECYCLING

Americans discard 160 million tons of garbage each year. This waste is deposited in landfills, burned in incinerators, and dumped into the sea, polluting Earth's land, air and water. But much of this waste — including about four-fifths of our household trash — need not become garbage. We must all learn to reduce the amount of waste we generate, reuse what we can, and recycle what we no longer need, in order to conserve Earth's resources and clean up the environment.

LIBRARY SKILLS

a. Use the *Scholastic Environmental Atlas of the United States* to answer to following questions: 1) What states have recycling laws? 2) What percent of our trash goes to landfills? Is incinerated? Is recycled? 3) How many landfills are there in your state?

b. Use a book of synonyms or a thesaurus to find some other words for "trash." List all the words you find.

c. Use *The Information Please Kids Almanac* to answer these questions: How is glass recycled? How much glass is recycled in the United States? Is that a lot compared to other countries?

d. In the Yellow Pages of your local telephone directory, look up Recycling Centers, and Recycling Equipment and Services. How many companies are listed? What services do they offer? What do they recycle?

e. Aluminum cans are made from an ore called bauxite. Use an encyclopedia to make a list of countries where bauxite is mined. In what part of the world are the richest deposits of bauxite located? What are the leading bauxite-mining countries, and how many tons are mined in a year?

f. Use *Environmental Literacy: Everything You Need to Know About Saving Our Planet* to write a short explanation of each of the following subjects: Canadian Green Plan, Superfund, cruise-ship pollution, aseptic containers, Waste Isolation Pilot, green marketing, PET, Resource Conservation and Recovery Act of 1976, NIMBY, junk mail, jimsonweed, methane digester, Garbage Magazine.

g. Use *The Information Please Environmental Almanac* to compare Waste Data of the Fifty States. Choose one of the following categories: total amount of solid waste that is generated annually, number of municipal landfills, number of curbside recycling programs, number of hazardous waste sites, or number of incinerators. Graph the data in your chosen category for all 50 states. How does your state compare to the rest of the country in that category?

ARTS AND CRAFTS

a. Color in pictures of the "chasing arrow" recycling symbols. Which is for materials that can be recycled? Which is for materials that have been recycled? How are the two symbols different? (12, 13)

b. Create a poster to encourage people to reduce, reuse, recycle, or buy recycled goods. (1, 4, 8, 12, 13, 14, 16, 18, 20, 25)

c. Draw diagrams of an open dump and a sanitary landfill to show the differences between them. Label what happens to the garbage in each picture. Which is safer for the environment? Why? (14, 20, 24, 25)

d. Glue pictures cut from recycled gift wrap and greeting cards into the centers of old foil pie tins to make holiday or party decorations. Cover washed-out tin cans with old gift wrap and wallpaper scraps to make pencil holders. Trim them with scraps of ribbon or yarn. What other gift items can you make from recycled materials? (12, 20)

e. Use discarded egg cartons, milk cartons, yarn scraps, toilet paper tubes, plastic bottles, and other clean waste materials to create a work of art. You can make a model space ship, robot, hat, sculpture, mobile, jewelry, or anything else you can think of. (5, 13, 20)

f. Make a poster, collage, or diorama on the theme of "The High Cost of Waste." You may show how waste has contributed to pollution, disease, the destruction of natural habitats, high clean-up costs, or another problem. Include at least one related statistic about waste. You can use (clean) waste materials, such as excess packaging, in your project. (3, 6, 7, 11, 14, 15, 17, 19, 22, 23, 24)

g. Some waste materials can be turned into sources of energy. Create a diagram for a machine that runs on, or a building that is heated by, recycled waste. Label the parts of your invention and explain how it would work. (3, 4, 8, 9, 10, 19, 20, 24)

SPELLING/VOCABULARY

a. Complete a word search puzzle of words related to waste problems: disposable, disease, germs, litter, eyesore, packaging, styrofoam, drink box, pollution, wrappers, contaminate, poison, sewage, junk mail, slurry. (1, 2, 9, 12, 16, 20, 25)

b. Complete a matching puzzle of recycling terms: curbside, drop-off center, biodegradable, pulp, reduce, resources, organic, recycling drive, treatment center, compost, RDF, mulch, deposit, sterilize, glassphalt, hand-me-downs, cullet, reusable, foundry, source separation. (1, 6, 12, 13, 14, 16, 20, 21, 25)

c. Complete a crossword puzzle of trash disposal terms: ash, methane, landfill, solid waste, garbage truck, sea dumping, contaminant, salvage, leachate, toxic gas, scrap, compactor, dumpster, groundwater, decompose, mass burn, incinerator, open dump, transfer station. (1, 2, 6, 12, 15, 20, 25, 26)

d. What is a natural resource? Define these related terms: nonrenewable resource, processed, petroleum, conservation. What is meant by "a consumer society"? Define these related terms: industrialized society, convenience items, synthetic, polystyrene foam. (3, 7, 11, 13, 14, 20)

e. Create a word search puzzle of 15 or more things that can be recycled. (1, 3, 4, 5, 6, 8, 12, 13, 14, 16, 18, 19, 20, 21, 22)

f. What is hazardous waste? Match the following terms to their warning symbols. Then define each term and give examples: corrosive, flammable (or ignitable or combustible), reactive, nuclear, toxic (or poisonous). Also define and give examples: radioactive, infectious, carcinogenic, halogenated hydrocarbons, industrial waste, agricultural waste, vehicle exhaust, organic waste, sewage, litter, medical waste, nuclear waste, municipal waste. (9, 11, 13, 15, 17, 20, 23, 24)

g. Match these toxic waste terms to their meanings: halogens, PCBs, slag, "heavy metals," dioxin, DDT, pesticides, methane, bottom ash, fly ash, acid rain, benzene, latex, battery acid, pesticide, polystyrene foam, aerosols, solvents, asbestos, HHCs. (6, 9, 11, 13, 15, 17, 20, 23, 24)

GEOGRAPHY

a. How is trash handled in your school? Look around your classroom, cafeteria, schoolyard, etc. to see where the trash goes. Draw a map of the school and indicate all the trash containers on the premises. Are any of these recycling bins? Where in your school would you put recycling bins? Note these suggestions on your map. Post your map where everyone can see it and convince your classmates and teachers to recycle! (5, 7)

b. Look around your community to find examples of litter, such as trash and cigarette butts thrown into the street or overflowing trash cans. Make a list of where you find litter, and take a photograph of it if you can. Where are the messiest places in your community? Note these areas on a local map. Send your list and photos to a local official and suggest having a community clean-up day. (7)

c. Some industrialized countries dump their toxic wastes (legally or illegally) in other countries. Make a list of some industrialized countries and where they send their waste. Locate these places on a world map. Draw lines connecting the "to" and "from" nations. (3, 9, 11, 15, 20, 24, 26)

d. How does your community dispose of garbage? Is it sent to an open dump, an incinerator, or a landfill? Is it dumped in your community or hauled off somewhere else? Does it pass through a transfer station? Do you have a recycling center in your community? Where is hazardous waste sent? On a local or state map, indicate where these facilities are located. (3, 7, 20, 26)

e. States vary widely in the amounts of solid waste they produce annually. On a map of the United States, color in green these states that produce between .50 and .75 ton per capita of solid waste: Colorado, Georgia, Mississippi, Montana, North Dakota, Utah, Vermont, Wisconsin, Wyoming. Color in blue these states with between .76 and 1.00 tons: Alaska, Arizona, Arkansas, Connecticut, Idaho, Iowa, Kansas, Kentucky, Louisiana, Maine, Nebraska, Nevada, New Hampshire, New Jersey, New Mexico, North Carolina, Oklahoma, Pennsylvania, West Virginia. Color in red these states with 1.01 to 1.25 tons: Alabama, Delaware, Hawaii, Indiana, Maryland, Massachusetts, Minnesota, New York, Oregon, Rhode Island, South Carolina, South Dakota, Tennessee, Texas, Washington. The states that are left produce more than 1.25 tons of solid waste per capita each year. Label them on your map and color them black. (*The Information Please Environmental Almanac*)

f. Dumping at sea is a major environmental problem. Make a list of countries and the rivers and seas in which they dump their waste. What do they dump? Locate these water-dumps and countries on a world map. (9, 15, 24, 26)

g. Research how trash is handled in other countries. Which countries have recycling laws? How do they handle hazardous waste? Do they dump or burn their garbage? What restrictions are there? Are permits needed to dispose of garbage? Are their habits safe or unsafe for the environment? Make a list of the five best and five worst countries, according to their waste disposal policies. Locate these countries on a world map. (3, 10, 11, 15, 20, 24, 26)

MATH

a. On a map of a recycling center, there are several numbered areas. Figure out what items can be recycled in which areas by answering the following questions: 1) Newspapers are recycled in the area that equals the number of sides in a hexagon. 2) Cardboard goes in the area that equals one dozen. 3) Office paper is deposited in the area that equals the number of feet in a yard. 4) Clear glass is dropped into the area that equals the number of nickels in 45 cents. 5) Brown glass is left in the area that equals the number of ounces in a cup. 6) Green glass belongs in the area that equals the number of quarts in a gallon. 7) Aluminum cans are tossed into the area that equals the number of years in a decade. 8) Plastic is brought to the area that equals the number that is used to divide things in half. 9) Yard waste is dumped into the area that equals the number of hours in a day. 10) Tires are piled up in the area that equals the number of quarters in $1.25.

b. About 40% of the trash generated by a typical American family consists of paper and cardboard, 18% is garden waste, 7% is glass, 7½% is food, 8½% is metal, 8% is plastic, 2½% is rubber, 3½% is wood, 2% is cloth, and 3% is other types of waste. Make a chart to illustrate these figures. (*Scholastic Environmental Atlas of the United States*)

c. Many states return a 5 cent deposit on every soda can or bottle that is returned to the store to be recycled. At that rate, how much money will you receive for recycling 15 cans? 89 cans? 247 cans? How many cans must you return in order to earn 50 cents? $3.45? $16.50?

d. Americans recycle only 10% of all recyclable materials. At that rate, how much is recycled out of 20 tons of glass? 140 tons? 320 tons? If we recycled all our paper, aluminum cans and glass, we could reduce the amount of garbage sent to landfills by 25%. At that rate, how much waste would we recycle out of 20 tons? 140 tons? 320 tons?

e. Every day, each person in the United States throws away about 4½ pounds of solid waste. If there are 250 million people in the United States, how many pounds of trash do we throw away each day? In a week? In a year? Using these figures, about how much trash have you thrown out in your lifetime?

f. Some decomposing garbage turns into methane, or natural gas, which can be used as heating fuel. About 2,970,000 tons of trash can produce enough methane to heat 18,000 homes for 15 years. At that rate, how many tons of trash will produce enough methane to heat one home for 15 years? One home for one year? 50 homes for one year? 50 homes for 5 years? 25 homes for 10 years?

g. One day in 1989, volunteers in Connecticut picked up 3 tons of trash from the state's 58 miles of beach. 1) Of this amount, 62% was plastic. How many pounds of plastic is that? 2) Included in this waste were 3,982 plastic eating utensils; 1,343 plastic lids; 1,202 plastic bags; 979 plastic bottles; 1,574 polystyrene cups; 2,430 pieces of plastic foam; 2,444 other plastic pieces; 3,300 glass pieces; 2,118 cigarette butts; 1,977 pieces of paper; 1,350 metal beverage cans; 799 metal bottle caps; 6 syringes; 24 tires; and other miscellaneous waste. Make a chart that compares these quantities of beach litter. 3) Choose another coastal state and find out how many miles of beach it has. If Connecticut generated 3 tons of garbage along a 58-mile stretch, how much garbage might be collected from your chosen state's beaches?   (24)

MUSIC AND THEATER ARTS

a. Make musical instruments from recycled materials. Place elastic bands around an old tissue box or plastic container. Adjust the elastic "strings" so that they will make different sounds when you pluck them. What other recycled musical instruments can you make?

b. What kind of song is a Round? Make up a simple song about recycling to sing as a round. Why is a round an appropriate type of music for a song about recycling?

c. Make a robot or monster costume out of recycled paper bags, cardboard boxes, jar lids, plastic containers, string, buttons, etc. Have a Monster Mash dance!

d. Act out short skits on these topics: 1) Two people are in a public park. One person throws litter on the ground. The second person tells the litterbug to clean up. 2) A child tries to convince his or her parents to reduce waste when preparing school lunches. 3) Some children discover that a local manufacturer is illegally dumping hazardous waste in a river. They discuss what they should do about it.   (2, 13, 14, 20)

e. Write lyrics for a song called "Where Has All the Garbage Gone?" to be sung to the tune of the folk song "Where Have All the Flowers Gone?" Your lyrics should illustrate the fact that we can never completely dispose of waste. For example, you can tell how poisonous waste materials can leak into the ground, air, or water and eventually return to harm the environment, animals, and humans. Or you can tell how improperly disposed trash, such as plastic six-pack rings thrown into the ocean, can kill wildlife.   (3, 7, 11, 14, 15, 17, 19, 20, 23, 24, 26)

f. Act out short skits in which the pros and cons of using the following items are discussed: 1) Two mothers trying to decide whether to use plastic disposable diapers or cloth diapers. 2) The owner of a fast food restaurant that puts food in polystyrene foam boxes defending their use to a customer who wants to ban them. 3) Two campers debating the use of drink boxes. (3, 14, 20, 22, 24)

g. Look through your house for old clothes that you and your family no longer wear. Bring to school any clothes you think can be used as a costume in a play. Wear your recycled-clothes costume and act out a short scene (either from a published play or your own script) in the character of someone who would dress like that. Donate any interesting clothes to your school drama club or a local theater company.

ENGLISH COMPOSITION

a. Think of five ways that you can recycle waste materials. Then write a picture book that shows your ideas. (1, 5, 8, 12, 14, 16, 25)

b. *Group project:* Make a list of store-bought items that are overpackaged, and the names and addresses of the companies that make them. Each student in the class should write a letter to a different manufacturer stating what is wrong with the packaging of the product in question. Refuse to buy the product until the packaging is changed. You can collect signatures from other people in your class and in the school. Then mail the letters to the manufacturers. (4, 5, 7, 13, 20)

c. Write an essay on the theme "We live in a throwaway society." (2, 3, 5, 7, 8, 9, 11, 13, 14, 18, 20, 21, 25)

d. Keep a personal waste diary for two weeks. Each time you throw something away, write down what it is and how you disposed of it. Include everything: food leftovers, packaging, broken toys, worn out clothing, paper cups/plates/napkins/straws, soda cans, tin cans and their labels, etc. Place an asterisk (*) next to anything you recycled. Review your diary every day. Try to waste less and reduce/reuse/recycle more. At the end of two weeks, have you begun to generate less waste? (3, 5, 7, 11, 13, 20)

e. *Group project:* Create a Healthy Planet Recipe Book. Include "recipes" for making a compost pile, making paper out of recycled paper, organizing a used goods sale, reusing old tires, making household cleaners out of safe materials, etc. (3, 5, 12, 13, 14, 20, 23, 26)

f. Write a recycling story that starts with a tree that is cut down, or a metallic ore that is mined. Tell how the wood or metal is made into a product. When the usefulness of this product is over, tell how it can be recycled into a second product. Recycle it for a third and fourth time, in different forms, before it is finally discarded. Or, you may write a story of how plastic is recycled four times. (3, 7, 15, 17, 18, 22, 24)

g. *Group project:* As a class, create a superhero character whose mission is to save Planet Earth by battling Waste. Give your superhero a name, costume, superpowers, etc. Then, each student should write an adventure in which the superhero reduces, reuses, or recycles waste. Put together a book of your stories.

SCIENCE

a. What are some problems with trying to recycle plastic? What happens to plastic in a landfill? In an incinerator? In the ocean? (6, 7, 8, 17, 20)

b. What are some things that can be made from recycled paper? Aluminum? Plastic? Glass? Tires? Food scraps? Yard waste? What can be done with used motor oil? (6, 12, 13, 14, 20, 21)

c. How can trash produce energy? (1, 3, 4, 8, 9, 10, 20, 21, 24, 25)

d. What is compost? How can you make compost? What can you use it for? How does composting help the environment? (3, 5, 6, 7, 11, 14, 20, 21, 24)

e. What happens to garbage in a landfill or open dump when it decomposes? Why can dumps and landfills be dangerous to the environment? What are reclaimed landfills? Are they safe? (3, 4, 6, 9, 11, 14, 15, 17, 19, 20, 23, 24)

f. What is hazardous waste? How do we generate it? What happens when hazardous waste is disposed of improperly? How should we dispose of household hazardous waste? Make a list of household products that should never be poured down the drain or go out with the garbage. (7, 9, 14, 17, 20, 23, 24, 26)

g. What are CFCs? Where are they found? Are they considered to be hazardous waste? Why are they harmful to Earth's environment? (3, 5, 6, 7, 9, 22, 24)

HISTORY/SOCIOLOGY

a. Waste from ancient times tells us a lot about the people and animals that lived on Earth before us. Some of this waste is considered valuable to historians, scientists, and archaeologists, and is displayed in museums. Some examples are dinosaur bones and tools from various cultures. Name some other types of historical waste found in museums. What do you think future generations will think of our waste? (5, 19)

b. Discuss the history of garbage collection. How and why did it come about? How was it collected in the past? How is garbage collected today? Where does it go? (14, 19, 20, 25)

c. How was trash handled 200 years ago in America? What happened about 150 years ago that changed most Americans' way of life and attitude toward trash? (13, 14, 19)

d. There have been several instances of barges hauling garbage from place to place looking for a location to dump their cargo. Find out about one such incident. Where was the garbage from? To where did it travel? Where was it eventually dumped? (3, 9, 11, 15, 17, 22, 23, 24)

e. Many materials were recycled during World War II. Tell what was recycled, how it was collected, and what was made from these materials. Why did people stop recycling after the war ended? (3, 11, 17, 22)

f. What are some state, national, and international laws about waste disposal, recycling, and pollution control? Research one law. What issue does it address? What are the terms of the law? What area does it affect? Has the law been enacted yet? If so, has it been successful? (3, 4, 9, 11, 15, 17, 18, 22, 23, 24)

g. There have been several disasters involving toxic or nuclear waste. Write a report on one such incident. Tell where and when it happened, the cause, and who was responsible. What was the result of this disaster? Has the responsible party attempted to rectify the situation? How? (9, 11, 15, 17, 19, 22, 23, 24, 26)

TOPICS FOR DISCUSSION

a. Make a list of different types of packaging. What products could use less or no packaging? How would you package them so there would be less waste? (1, 2, 5, 11, 12, 13, 20)

b. What are some dangers of waste that has been disposed of carelessly? (1, 2, 4, 12, 18, 19, 20, 21, 25)

c. How does recycling save energy, resources, space and money? How does it protect the environment? (2, 4, 5, 6, 7, 8, 9, 11, 13, 15, 16, 18, 20, 21)

d. Suppose your community is proposing to build an energy-from-waste (waste-to-energy) incinerator. Discuss some concerns you might have about this facility. Is it preferable to having a landfill site? What would be the advantages and disadvantages of having the incinerator in your community? (3, 10, 11, 14, 15, 17, 19, 20, 22, 24)

e. What are some ways of reducing the amount of garbage we create?

How can you reuse trash? What does it mean to be a careful consumer?   (3, 4, 5, 7, 11, 13, 14, 15, 17, 20, 22, 23, 24)

f. Not everything is recyclable. Why? Make a list of some non-recyclable items you use. Then think of recyclable or reusable things that can take the place of these throwaway items.   (3, 4, 7, 13, 22, 23, 24)

g. Is there a safe way to dispose of radioactive waste? Of other types of hazardous waste? What are some methods of disposal in use now? What are some proposed methods? What are some companies doing to reduce the amount of hazardous waste they generate?   (9, 11, 15, 23, 24, 26)

SUGGESTED RESOURCES

(1) Amos, Janine. *Waste and Recycling* [First Starts]. Raintree, 1993.
(2) Asimov, Isaac. *Why Does Litter Cause Problems?* [Ask Isaac Asimov]. Stevens, 1992.
(3) Blashfield, Jean F., and Black, Wallace B. *Recycling* [Saving Planet Earth]. Childrens, 1991.
(4) Condon, Judith. *Recycling Paper* [Waste Control]. Watts, 1991.
(5) The EarthWorks Group. *50 Simple Things Kids Can Do to Save the Earth*. Scholastic, 1990.
(6) _____. *The Recycler's Handbook*. EarthWorks, 1990.
(7) Elkington, John, et al. *Going Green: A Kid's Handbook to Saving the Planet*. Puffin, 1990.
(8) Hare, Tony. *Recycling* [World About Us]. Gloucester, 1991.
(9) Hawkes, Nigel. *Toxic Waste and Recycling* [Issues Update]. Gloucester, 1991.
(10) Houghton, Graham. *Bioenergy* [Alternative Energy]. Stevens, 1991.
(11) James, Barbara. *Waste and Recycling* [Conserving Our World]. Steck-Vaughn 1989.
(12) Kalbacken, Joan, and Lepthien, Emilie U. *Recycling* [New True Books]. Childrens, 1991.
(13) Kalman, Bobbie. *Reducing, Reusing, Recycling* [The Crabtree Environment Series]. Crabtree, 1991.
(14) _____, and Schaub, Janine. *Buried in Garbage* [The Crabtree Environment Series]. Crabtree, 1991.
(15) Leggett, Jeremy. *Waste War* [Operation Earth]. Cavendish, 1991.
(16) Lowery, Linda, and Lorbiecki, Marybeth. *Earthwise at Home* [Earthwise]. Carolrhoda, 1993.
(17) O'Connor, Karen. *Garbage* [Overview Series: Our Endangered Planet]. Lucent, 1989.
(18) Palmer, Joy. *Recycling Metal* [Waste Control]. Watts, 1990.
(19) Pringle, Laurence. *Throwing Things Away: From Middens to Resource Recovery*. Crowell, 1986.
(20) Savage, Candice. *Trash Attack* [Earth Care]. Douglas-McIntyre, 1990.
(21) Skidmore, Steve. *What a Load of Trash!* [A Lighter Look]. Millbrook, 1991.
(22) Stefoff, Rebecca. *Recycling* [Earth at Risk]. Chelsea House, 1991.

(23) Stenstrup, Allen. *Hazardous Waste* [Saving Planet Earth]. Childrens, 1991.
(24) Tesar, Jenny. *The Waste Crisis* [Our Fragile Planet]. Facts on File, 1991.
(25) Wilcox, Charlotte. *Trash!* [Photo Books]. Carolrhoda, 1988.
(26) Woodburn, Judith. *The Toxic Waste Time Bomb* [Environment Alert!] Stevens, 1991.

LIBRARY SKILLS RESOURCES

Dashefsky, H. Steven. *Environmental Literacy: Everything You Need to Know About Saving the Planet.* Random, 1993.
Mattson, Mark. *Scholastic Environmental Atlas of the United States.* Scholastic, 1993.
Siegal, Alice, and Basta, Margo McLoone. *The Information Please Kids Almanac.* Houghton, 1992.
World Resources Institute. *The Information Please Environmental Almanac.* Houghton, 1993.

ADDITIONAL READING – YOUNGER

Allison, John P., and Allison, Lee A. *David the Trash Cop: A Child's Guide to Recycling.* R.M.C., 1992.
Asimov, Isaac. *Where Does Garbage Go?* [Ask Isaac Asimov]. Stevens, 1992.
Bailey, Donna. *What We Can Do About Litter* [What We Can Do About]. Watts, 1991.
_____. *What We Can Do About Recycling Garbage* [What We Can Do About]. Watts, 1991.
Brown, Laurie Krasney, and Brown, Marc. *Dinosaurs to the Rescue: A Guide to Protecting Our Planet.* Little, 1992.
Cobb, Vicki. *Lots of Rot.* Lippincott, 1981.
Daniel, Jamie, and Bonar, Veronica. [Trash Busters] series. Stevens.
Fiarotta, Phyllis, and Fiarotta, Noel. *Cups & Cans & Paper Fans: Craft Projects from Recycled Materials.* Sterling, 1993.
Gardiner, Brian. *Nuclear Waste* [World About Us]. Watts, 1992.
Gibbons, Gail. *Recycle! A Handbook for Kids.* Little, 1992.
Gilman, Phoebe. *Something from Nothing.* Scholastic, 1993.
Johnson, Jean. *Sanitation Workers A to Z* [Community Helpers]. Walker, 1988.
Lord, Suzanne. *Garbage! The Trashiest Book You'll Ever Read.* Scholastic, 1993.
Seltzer, Meyer. *Here Comes the Recycling Truck!* Whitman, 1992.
Showers, Paul. *Where Does the Garbage Go?* [Let's-Read-and-Find-Out Science]. HarperCollins, 1994.
Spence, Margaret. *Toxic Waste* [World About Us]. Watts, 1992.
Walter, F. Virginia. *Great Newspaper Crafts.* Sterling/Hyperion, 1991.
Wheeler, Jill. *Recycle It! Once Is Not Enough!* [We Can Save the Earth]. Abdo, 1990.
_____. *Throwaway Generation* [We Can Save the Earth]. Abdo, 1991.
[Why Throw It Away?] series. Gloucester, 1992.

ADDITIONAL READING – OLDER

Becklake, Sue. *Waste Disposal and Recycling* [Green Issues]. Gloucester, 1991.

Donnelly, Judy, and Kramer, Sydelle. *Space Junk: Pollution Beyond the Earth*. Morrow, 1990.

Foster, Joanna. *Cartons, Cans & Orange Peels: Where Does Your Garbage Go?* Clarion, 1991.

Goodman, Billy. *A Kid's Guide to How to Save the Planet*. Avon, 1990.

Hadingham, Evan, and Hadingham, Janet. *Garbage! Where It Comes from, Where It Goes* [Nova Books]. Simon & Schuster, 1990.

Handelman, Judith F. *Gardens from Garbage: How to Grow Plants from Recycled Kitchen Scraps*. Millbrook, 1993.

Hare, Tony. *Nuclear Waste Disposal* [Save Our Earth]. Watts, 1991.

―――――. *Toxic Waste* [Save Our Earth]. Watts, 1991. (Also other books in series.)

Johnstone, Hugh. *Facts on Domestic Waste and Industrial Pollutants* [Facts on]. Watts, 1990.

Kimball, Debi. *Recycling in America* [Contemporary World Issues]. ABC-Clio, 1992.

Lavies, Bianca. *Compost Critters*. Dutton, 1993.

Lee, Sally. *The Throwaway Society* [Impact]. Watts, 1990.

Miles, Betty. *Save the Earth*. Knopf, 1991.

Porritt, Jonathan, and Nadler, Ellis. *Captain Eco and the Fate of the Earth*. Kindersley, 1991.

Rott, Joanna R., and Groves, Seli. *How on Earth Do We Recycle Glass?* Millbrook, 1992.

Rybolt, Thomas R., and Mebane, Robert C. *Environmental Experiments About Land* [Science Experiments for Young People]. Enslow, 1993.

Schwartz, Linda. *Earth Book for Kids: Activities to Heal the Environment*. Learning Works, 1990.

Silverstein, Alvin, et al. *Recycling: Meeting the Challenge of the Trash Crisis*. Putnam, 1992.

Simons, Robin. *Recyclopedia: Games, Science Equipment, and Crafts from Recycled Materials*. Houghton-Mifflin, 1976.

Szumski, Bonnie, and Buggey, JoAnne. *Toxic Wastes: Examining Cause and Effect Relationships* [Opposing Viewpoints]. Greenhaven, 1989.

See also: books in ENVIRONMENTAL AWARENESS unit.

FOR MORE INFORMATION ABOUT WASTE AND RECYCLING, WRITE TO:

Air and Waste Management Association

Aluminum Recycling Association

Citizens Clearinghouse for Hazardous Wastes

Coalition for Responsible Waste Incineration

Coalition on Resource Recovery and the Environment

Council on Packaging in the Environment

Environmental Action Coalition

Household Hazardous Waste Project

Institute of Scrap Recycling Industries

Mail Preference Services, Direct Marketing Association (To stop receiving junk mail)

National Environmental Development Association / Resource Conservation and Recovery Act Project

National Recycling Coalition

Plastics Recycling Foundation

Super Kids Recycling Program

ENDANGERED SPECIES AND HABITATS

Earth is home to a wonderful variety of life. Each species is specially adapted to survive in its own unique habitat. Over millions of years, the forces of nature may cause species to become extinct. However, during the past few hundred years, humans have accelerated the extinction of Earth's wildlife dramatically. Today, many plants, animals and their habitats are being destroyed at alarming rates. All people must realize that we are endangering our own survival each time we upset another habitat or kill another species.

LIBRARY SKILLS

a. Choose five animals from *Children's Guide to Endangered Animals.* Write a sentence for each, telling why it is endangered.

b. Use *The Endangered World* to answer the following questions: 1) What is happening to much of the rainforest of South America? 2) How does acid rain endanger habitats and wildlife? 3) What is the world's largest butterfly? Where does it live? 4) What is a kagu? Where does it live and why is it endangered? 5) What type of habitat destruction is occurring in Northern Africa?

c. There are many reasons for the destruction of the Earth's natural habitats. The loss of natural habitats causes the plants and animals that live there to become endangered. In *Atlas of Environmental Issues,* read the unit on Threatened Species. Then choose one of the other units, such as Deforestation, that discusses the destruction of a habitat. Answer the following questions as they relate to that unit: 1) What type of habitat is threatened? 2) How is it threatened? 3) What effect has this had on the local ecosystem?

d. In *The Atlas of Endangered Animals,* what do the designations E, V, and R mean? Divide a sheet of paper into three columns. Label them E, V and R. In each column, list some forest and scrub animals that have been given these designations.

   e. Use *The Atlas of Endangered Species* to answer the following: 1) What are some threats to mountain habitats in the Palearctic Region? 2) Name three endangered plants in the Nearctic Region. 3) Why are mangroves valuable? Why are they endangered? 4) Name some human activities that harm coral reef communities. 5) Name five endangered birds in the Australasian Region.

   f. Following is a list of extinct, rare, endangered or vulnerable animals. Use *The Grolier World Encyclopedia of Endangered Species* to find out to which category each of these animals belongs: Chinese egret, central hare-wallaby, gorilla, Galápagos marine iguana, brown lemur, Javan tiger, ocelot, Utah prairie dog, Barbary hyena, Caribbean monk seal, gila monster, giant panda, Nile crocodile, humpback whale, Mexican grizzly bear, giant armadillo, wild yak, pygmy hippopotamus, wild Asiatic water buffalo, southern bald eagle, loggerhead turtle, takahe, dugong, Amazon manatee, Gevy's zebra.

   g. Use *Endangered Wildlife of the World* to make a list of 15 threatened animals. Tell where each one lives and why it is threatened. Then find five animals that survive only in captivity. Where did they originally live and why are they endangered?

ARTS AND CRAFTS

   a. Draw a picture or make a model of an endangered animal or plant.

   b. Draw a poster to encourage people to save an endangered animal or habitat.

   c. Bluebirds became rare in North America because their nesting places were disappearing. You can help to save these birds by building a birdhouse or feeder. (13, 15, 21)

   d. Make a diorama of a healthy wildlife habitat. Include figures of animals that live there.

   e. There are several things people can do to save endangered species. Create a board or card game where the object is to save an animal, plant, or habitat. Points can be awarded for landing on a space, making a choice, choosing a card, etc. that helps the player reach this goal. Points can be lost for polluting, poaching, and doing other things that harm endangered species and habitats. (2, 3, 9, 12, 14, 15, 21, 25, 26)

   f. *Group project:* Make a mural or bulletin board of endangered species.

For each plant and animal, post a fact card that includes information about it, such as its name, habitat, and where it lives.

g. Some animals, such as the black-footed ferret, are endangered because their food supply is disappearing or becoming contaminated. Draw the food chain of an endangered animal in this situation. (1, 3, 5, 9, 12, 16, 24, 25)

SPELLING/VOCABULARY

a. Complete a matching picture puzzle of endangered animals: tiger, bison, whale, aye-aye, leopard, crocodile, ferret, eagle, condor, polar bear, lemur, ocelot, elephant, pupfish, kangaroo, gorilla, ostrich, panda, addax, vicuña. (1, 4, 5, 9, 10, 14, 17, 18, 23, 24, 25)

b. Complete a word search puzzle of extinct animals: dodo, passenger pigeon, Cape lion, mammoth, moa, auk, rail, quagga, musk-shrew, aurochs, huia, caracara, sea mink, atlas bear, mamo, thylacine, tarpan, giant sloth, dwarf emu, dusky sparrow. (2, 4, 5, 7, 8, 10, 12, 14, 15, 20, 21, 23)

c. Complete a crossword puzzle of types of habitats: pampas, rainforest, wetland, mountain, ocean, polar, island, prairie, lake, coniferous, savannah, tundra, deciduous, steppe, swamp, temperate, marsh, river, grassland, pond. (2, 7, 11, 15, 16, 18, 22, 23)

d. What is biology? Define these related terms: vertebrates, invertebrates, adapt, genetics, speciation, keystone species, biodiversity, evolution, ecology, mutation, habitat. (12, 14, 19, 21, 25)

e. Complete a fill-in-the-blanks exercise of terms that relate to vanishing species: endangered, extinct, threatened, rare, vulnerable, feral animals, poaching, hunting, overfishing, ivory, disease, fur trade, pesticides, ranching, evolution, smuggling, alien species, food loss, habitat destruction, commercial pet trade. (2, 3, 4, 6, 7, 8, 12, 15, 17, 18, 21, 23, 24)

f. Complete a matching exercise of habitat destruction terms: herbicides, logging, pollution, irrigation, dumping, industry, damming, development, overpopulation, climate change, acid rain, fertilizer, oil spills, desertification, mining, tourism, deforestation, drainage, agriculture, global warming. (2, 4, 7, 10, 11, 12, 15, 18, 19, 22, 24, 25)

g. Complete a fill-in-the-blanks exercise of terms that relate to saving endangered habitats and species: conservation, captive breeding, environmentalist, preservation, wildlife refuge, reintroduction, indigenous species, nature reserves, ecosystem, tagging, regulation, cross-breeding, national park, protective laws, radio tracking, research projects, ecological restoration, sanctuary, education. (4, 6, 12, 14, 17, 18, 21, 22)

GEOGRAPHY

a. What wildlife habitats are in your state? List any that apply: prairie, marsh, swamp, river, lake, mountain, desert, temperate forest, polar, rainforest. Indicate where these habitats are on a state map.

b. Find out if there are any threatened habitats in your state. Locate these areas on a state map. Are there any endangered plants or animals in your state? (15)

c. Earth has many habitats, each with its own climate. Choose one habitat from the spelling/vocabulary exercise, item **c.** On a map of the world, color in the areas of that habitat. Then describe the typical climate there. (2, 3, 7, 11, 18, 21, 22, 23, 24, 26)

d. Divide a sheet of paper into seven columns and label them: ocean, wetland, desert, grassland, forest, polar lands, and rainforest. List some endangered plants and animals that belong to each of these natural habitats. (1, 2, 3, 4, 5, 7, 11, 15, 17, 21, 22, 23, 24, 25)

e. Following is a list of extinct animals. Name the area in which it once lived, and locate it on a map of the world: Cuban red macaw, dodo, quagga, great auk, Indian pink-headed duck, dusky seaside sparrow, Steller's sea cow, spectacled cormorant, blaauwbok (or blaubok), Christmas Island musk-shrew, passenger pigeon, aurochs, huia, Guadaloupe caracara, red-shafted flicker, thylacine, giant sloth, tarpan, Cape lion, atlas bear. (2, 4, 5, 7, 8, 12, 20)

f. Following is a list of endangered animals and plants. For each one, name the area where it lives: aye-aye, egret, cheetah, peregrine falcon, Arabian oryx, chimpanzee, nene, snow leopard, alligator, Przewalski's horse, Raven's manzanita, rafflesia, leek orchid, pitcher plant, rosy periwinkle, bamboo, edelweiss, puzzle sunflower, adder's tongue spearwort, wild African violet. (1, 2, 4, 5, 6, 7, 8, 9, 10, 12, 13, 15, 17, 18, 21, 22, 23, 24)

g. There are many national parks, wildlife refuges, preserves, zoos, and sanctuaries that are dedicated to saving natural habitats and endangered wildlife. Make a list of 20 or more of these, inside or outside of the United States. Give the location of each one, tell what type of habitat it is, and name some of the wildlife there. (3, 5, 9, 14, 18, 21, also *Endangered Wildlife of the World*)

MATH

a. Following is a list of animals and the approximate years they became extinct. Place them in chronological order: Indian pink-headed duck, 1935; Steller's sea cow, 1768; great auk, 1844; red-billed rail, 1938; dodo, 1680; dusky seaside sparrow, 1989; thylacine, 1930; quagga, 1883; passenger pigeon, 1914; aurochs, 1627; huia bird, 1907; red-shafted flicker, 1906. (10, 20)

b. Between 1981 and 1989, many African elephants were killed. Following is a list of countries and the percent of its total elephant population that was destroyed: Kenya 70%, Nigeria 40%, Somalia 90%, Sudan 80%, Zaire 70%. Make a chart to illustrate this fact. (*The Endangered World*)

c. Following are the largest possible lengths of some endangered reptiles. Make a chart or graph to compare their sizes: Fijian banded iguana, 35 inches; spotted salamander, 10 inches; West African dwarf crocodile, 5 feet; broad-headed snake, 24 inches; olm 12 inches; tuatara, 26 inches; Komodo dragon, 10 feet; pancake tortoise, 7 inches; American alligator, 19 feet; rhinoceros iguana, 4 feet; spectacled caiman, 8 feet; chaco tortoise, 14 inches. (*Children's Guide to Endangered Animals*)

d. Answer the following problems about endangered animals. If the result is a fraction, round it up to the next whole number: 1) In 1980, there were 1,300,000 African elephants. In ten years half of them had been killed. How many were left? What is the average number of elephants killed per year? 2) There were about 60,000,000 bison in North America in 1800. Pioneers killed so many that by 1900, there were only 50 left in the wild. On the average, how many bison were killed each year? 3) In Kenya in 1970, there were 20,000 black rhinoceros. In 1985, there were only 425. What was the average number of rhinos killed per year during that time? 4) In 1900, India had 40,000 tigers. In 1970, approximately 18,000 were left. How many tigers had died each year? (3, 10, 21)

e. Because of captive breeding and various preservation programs, some endangered animals are increasing their numbers. Following is a list of animals, their populations at their lowest point, and their approximate populations in 1990: Nene 30/2500; whooping crane 16/200; black-footed ferret 18/300; pronghorn 20,000/500,000; grey whale 200/21,000; Rodrigues flying fox 80/400; Mauritius kestrel 6/200; Siberian tiger 30/200; trumpeter swan 100/10,000; vicuña 8,000/100,000; Przewalski's horse 13/600. Reduce these numbers to the smallest possible fraction. Example: nene = 30/2500 = 3/250. (4, 9, 21, also *Children's Guide to Endangered Animals*)

f. Compute the answers to the following problems. Then make graphs to illustrate your answers: 1) By the end of the 1980s, Earth's plant and animal species were becoming extinct at an average rate of one per day. At that rate, how many species were lost in 1, 2, 3, 4, and 5 years? 2) One source estimates that in the 1990s, a plant or animal becomes extinct at the rate of one per hour. How many species would become extinct in 1, 2, 3, 4, and 5 years? 3) It is predicted that by the year 2000, this rate may increase to 100 species per day. How many species is that in 1, 2, 3, 4, and 5 years? 4) Scientists estimate there may be 5,000,000 species in the world, although only a fraction of them have been identified. During the next century, it is possible that one-third of these could be destroyed. How many species may vanish every ten years over the next 100 years? (3, 10)

g. Choose ten endangered animals. For each one, note: 1) The number of its greatest population; 2) Its numbers when it was deemed to be at risk; and 3) Its approximate population now. Then calculate 4) The percentage of animals that exist now in comparison to its greatest population. (3, 4, 9, 10, 17, 18, 21, also see LIBRARY SKILLS RESOURCES)

MUSIC AND THEATER ARTS

a. The dinosaurs became extinct many millions of years ago. Perform a puppet show of dinosaurs to demonstrate how they lived. Why do you think they died out?

b. Listen to selections from "The Carnival of the Animals" by Camile Saint-Saëns, or other musical pieces with animal themes. How does the music help to describe the animals?

c. *Group project:* Each student should choose a different endangered animal. Then pretend you are all delegates to the Worldwide Association to Save Endangered Animals. Take turns telling your fellow conference members how important your animal is to the world. Give a progress report on your efforts to save it from extinction.

d. Read aloud some poetry written about animals that are now endangered, such as "Tiger, Tiger" by William Blake.

e. Animals are popular characters in folklore of all nations. Choose one story whose main character is an endangered animal. Perform the story as a play or puppet show.

f. Captive breeding programs and zoos play an important role in saving endangered animals. Perform a skit that shows what happens in one of these programs, as it regards to one specific animal. (2, 3, 6, 9, 15, 17, 21)

g. Many animals have become endangered or extinct due to human greed, selfishness, or superstition. Act out a scene which shows this. For example: A poacher kills a rhinoceros because people in the Far East believe the rhino horn has medicinal powers. Or, the egret is hunted because its feathers are fashionable in women's hats, etc. (2, 3, 6, 8, 9, 14, 18, 24, 25)

ENGLISH COMPOSITION

a. Write a letter to one of the organizations listed on page 218. Ask for information on how you can help save an endangered animal. Or, write to your local government about saving an endangered habitat in your state.

b. Write the name of an endangered animal vertically on the left-hand side of a sheet of paper, so that each letter starts a new line. Then write a poem or a description of that animal, using the letters in its name to begin the first word on each line.

c. Write a story about an endangered animal. Include some facts about its appearance, food, home, habitat, natural enemies, etc.   (2, 3, 4, 5, 6, 7, 8, 9, 10, 13, 15, 17, 18, 22, 23, 24)

d. Many people like to observe animals in their natural habitats. Pretend you work for a national park, zoo, or other place where animals are kept in natural settings. Write a page of instructions for visitors to follow so they will not disturb the animals or upset the habitat. Example: Walk only on the paths that are provided.   (5, 6, 14, 16, 22)

e. Look up some information on an endangered plant or animal. Then write an essay telling why you think this species should be saved. Include some suggestions on how the species could be protected.   (2, 3, 4, 5, 6, 7, 8, 9, 10, 13, 15, 17, 18, 22, 23, 24)

f. Choose one animal that has become extinct. Write a story about how it might live if it were still alive today. Include some factual information about the animal in your story. Would it be able to adapt to a modern environment? How?   (2, 3, 4, 7, 10, 20)

g. The Endangered Species Act, which the United States Congress passed in 1973, protects animals that are close to extinction. Although this is a good law, many conservationists think it does not go far enough. Write an amendment to the Endangered Species Act that would expand the law and make it more effective. You may want to read about other laws and treaties, such as CITES, for ideas.   (2, 3, 4, 9, 10, 12, 25)

SCIENCE

a. What is a habitat? Name some types of habitats.   (5, 7, 11, 14, 15, 16, 18, 22, 24)

b. Divide a sheet of paper into four columns and label them: plants, birds, mammals, reptiles. List at least five endangered species in each column.   (1, 2, 4, 5, 6, 7, 8, 9, 11, 13, 14, 17, 18, 22, 23, 25, 26)

c. How does pollution endanger plants and animals? Give at least three examples.   (1, 2, 3, 5, 7, 9, 10, 12, 13, 14, 15, 16, 18, 21, 22, 24, 25, 26)

d. Nobody knows for sure why the dinosaurs became extinct. What are some theories people have? Could some of these reasons cause animals to become extinct today?   (2, 10, 19)

e. What are some natural causes of species extinction? Name some plants and animals that died out of natural causes.   (2, 4, 5, 10, 12, 14, 21, 25, 26)

f. All species on Earth must evolve or adapt to its environment in order to survive. Explain the concept of natural selection. Give two examples of how a plant or animal evolved in order to survive.   (6, 8, 10, 19, 25, 26)

g. What is habitat destruction? Give specific examples of two different habitats and how their destruction affected the plants and animals that had originally lived there.   (2, 3, 4, 5, 6, 8, 9, 10, 12, 15, 18, 19, 22, 24, 25)

HISTORY/SOCIOLOGY

a. Many species have become extinct or endangered because of people. Name some things people have done in the past and present that have endangered plants and animals.   (1, 2, 4, 5, 6, 7, 8, 10, 11, 15, 17, 18, 20, 21, 23, 24)

b. In the mid–1900s, a chemical called DDT was widely used to kill insect pests. Unfortunately, it also endangered birds and other animals. Give some examples of how animal populations fell because of DDT and other pesticides. (1, 3, 5, 7, 12, 15, 21, 22, 24)

c. Give one example of how humans destroyed an animal population. Were the animals eventually saved or not?   (2, 3, 4, 6, 9, 10, 12, 15, 17, 18, 21, 24, 25)

d. Conservationists and wildlife experts are trying to save endangered animals. Give two examples of how people have succeeded in saving an endangered animal from extinction.   (2, 3, 4, 5, 6, 8, 9, 10, 12, 15, 17, 18, 21, 25)

e. Explain how some people's superstitions or cultural traditions have caused an animal to become endangered or extinct.   (2, 3, 8, 9, 12, 15, 18, 21, 25)

f. What are some organizations that are dedicated to preserving wildlife? Write a summary of one organization's goals, activities, structure, and specific area(s) of interest. Give at least one example of its work or special projects.   (2, 3, 4, 5, 9, 12, 14, 15, 17, 18, 19, 21, 22, 25)

g. Look up information about a person who worked to save an endangered species or habitat, such as Jim Corbett or Jane Goodall. Write a short biography of this person and his/her work.   (3, 10, 14, 21, 25)

TOPICS FOR DISCUSSION

a. Some endangered animals, such as tigers, have been known to kill people and farm animals. Do you think people should try to save tigers and other dangerous animals? How about bats and other "un-cuddly" animals? Give reasons for your answer. (1, 4, 5, 8, 21, 24)

b. What are some things people are doing to save endangered animals? (2, 3, 4, 5, 6, 7, 8, 9, 12, 15, 16, 17, 18, 21, 23, 24, 26)

c. What is poaching? How does poaching endanger animals? Name some animals that are targets of poachers. (2, 3, 4, 9, 10, 12, 14, 17, 18, 20, 21)

d. Humans have introduced many animals, such as rats, goats, or starlings, to lands where they had not lived before. How do these alien species contribute to the destruction of native plant or animal populations? (2, 4, 5, 6, 9, 10, 12, 17, 21, 22, 23, 25)

e. What are some things you can do to help save endangered species and habitats? (3, 9, 12, 14, 15, 16, 18, 21, 24, 25, 26)

f. Why is it to our advantage to prevent plants and animals from becoming extinct? What can humans gain by preserving as many natural species as possible? (2, 3, 7, 9, 12, 13, 14, 15, 19, 21, 22, 25, 26)

g. How do some collectors, museums, and countries purposely or inadvertently encourage the killing of endangered wildlife? Why do some countries allow the destruction of natural habitats? (3, 5, 8, 10, 12, 14, 19, 20, 25)

SUGGESTED RESOURCES

(1) [Animals in Danger] series. Rourke, 1982.

(2) Banks, Martin. *Endangered Wildlife* [World Issues]. Rourke, 1988.

(3) Bloyd, Sunni. *Endangered Species* [Overview Series: Our Endangered Planet]. Lucent, 1989.

(4) Burton, John. *Close to Extinction* [Survival]. Gloucester, 1988. (Also other books in series.)

(5) Burton, Robert. *Wildlife in Danger* [The Silver Burdett Color Library]. Silver, 1983.

(6) Cook, David. *Birds* [Our Endangered Planet]. Crown, 1983.

(7) _____. *Environment* [Our Endangered Planet]. Crown, 1983.

(8) _____. *Land Animals* [Our Endangered Planet]. Crown, 1983.

(9) *Endangered Animals* [Ranger Rick Books]. National Wildlife, 1989.

(10) Facklam, Margery. *And Then There Was One: The Mysteries of Extinction*. Sierra Club, 1990.

(11) Hare, Tony. *Vanishing Habitats* [World About Us]. Gloucester, 1991.

(12) Hoff, Mary, and Rodgers, Mary M. *Life on Land* [Our Endangered Planet]. Lerner, 1992.

(13) Landau, Elaine. *Endangered Plants* [First Books – Our Environment]. Watts, 1992.

(14) Lazo, Caroline Evensen. *Endangered Species* [Earth Alert]. Crestwood, 1990.
(15) Love, Ann, and Drake, Jane. *Take Action: An Environmental Book for Kids* [World Wildlife Fund]. Tambourine, 1992.
(16) Lowery, Linda, and Lorbiecki, Marybeth. *Earthwise at Play* [Earthwise]. Carolrhoda, 1993.
(17) Maynard, Thane. *Saving Endangered Mammals: A Field Guide to Some of Earth's Rarest Animals* [Cincinnati Zoo Books]. Watts, 1992.
(18) Penny, Malcolm. *Protecting Wildlife* [Conserving Our World]. Steck-Vaughn, 1989.
(19) Pringle, Laurence. *Living Treasure: Saving Earth's Threatened Biodiversity*. Morrow, 1991.
(20) Rice, Paul, and Mayle, Peter. *As Dead as a Dodo*. Godine, 1981.
(21) Rinard, Judith E. *Wildlife: Making a Comeback* [Books for World Explorers]. National Geographic, 1987.
(22) Simon, Noel. *Vanishing Habitats* [Survival]. Gloucester, 1987.
(23) Stone, Lynn M. *Endangered Animals* [New True Books]. Childrens, 1984.
(24) Taylor, Dave. [Endangered Animals] series. Crabtree, 1992.
(25) Tesar, Jenny. *Endangered Habitats* [Our Fragile Planet]. Facts on File, 1992.
(26) Whitfield, Philip. *Can the Whales Be Saved?* Viking, 1989.

LIBRARY SKILLS RESOURCES

Burton, John, editor. *The Atlas of Endangered Species*. Macmillan, 1991.
Endangered Wildlife of the World. Marshall Cavendish, 1993.
The Endangered World [Using and Understanding Maps]. Chelsea, 1993.
Few, Roger. *Children's Guide to Endangered Animals*. Macmillan, 1993.
The Grolier World Encyclopedia of Endangered Species. Grolier, 1993.
Middleton, Nick. *Atlas of Environmental Issues* [Issues Atlases]. Facts on File, 1989.
Pollock, Steve. *The Atlas of Endangered Animals* [Environmental Atlases]. Facts on File, 1993.

ADDITIONAL READING—YOUNGER

Allen, Judy. *Tiger*. Candlewick, 1992. (Also other titles by author.)
Amos, Janine. *Animals in Danger* [First Starts]. Raintree, 1993.
Ancona, George. *Turtle Watch*. Macmillan, 1987.
Arnold, Caroline. *On the Brink of Extinction: The California Condor*. Harcourt, 1993.
_____. *Saving the Peregrine Falcon* [Nature Watch]. Carolrhoda, 1985.
Asimov, Isaac. *Why Are Animals Endangered?* [Ask Isaac Asimov]. Stevens, 1993.
Burningham, John. *Hey! Get Off Our Train*. Crown, 1989.
Cajacob, Thomas. *Close to the Wild: Siberian Tigers in a Zoo*. [Nature Watch]. Carolrhoda, 1986.
Dewey, Jennifer Owings. *Wildlife Rescue: The Work of Dr. Kathleen Ramsay*. Boyds Mills, 1994.
Geraghty, Paul. *The Hunter*. Crown, 1994.
Greene, Carol. [Friends in Danger] series. Enslow, 1993.
Havill, Juanita. *Sato and the Elephants*. Lothrop, 1993.

Lepthien, Emilie U. *Manatees* [New True Books]. Childrens, 1991.
London, Jonathan. *Voices of the Wild.* Crown, 1993.
McGrath, Susan. *Saving Our Animal Friends* [Books for Young Explorers]. National Geographic, 1986.
Pallotta, Jerry. *The Extinct Alphabet Book.* Charlesbridge, 1993.
Peet, Bill. *Farewell to Shady Glade.* Houghton Mifflin, 1966.
[Project Wildlife] series. Gloucester.
Steele, Philip. [Extinct] series. Watts.
[Where Animals Live] series. Stevens.
[Wildlife at Risk] series. Bookwright.
[Wildlife in Danger] series. Rourke.
Wright, Alexandra. *Will We Miss Them? Endangered Species.* Charlesbridge, 1992.

ADDITIONAL READING—OLDER

Barton, Miles. *Vanishing Species* [Green Issues]. Gloucester, 1991.
Behm, Barbara J., and Balouet, Jean-Christophe. [In Peril] series. Stevens, 1994.
Cutchins, Judy. *The Crocodile and the Crane: Surviving in a Crowded World.* Morrow, 1986.
Facklam, Howard, and Facklam, Margery. *Plants: Extinction or Survival?* Enslow, 1990.
Friedman, Judi. *Operation Siberian Crane: The Story Behind the International Effort to Save an Amazing Bird.* Dillon, 1992.
[Gone Forever] series. Crestwood.
Habitats and Environments [More Science in Action]. Cavendish, 1990.
Hacker, Randi, and Kaufman, Jackie. *Habitats: Where the Wild Things Live.* Muir, 1992.
Halpern, Robert R. *Green Planet Rescue: Saving the Earth's Endangered Plants* [Cincinnati Zoo Books]. Watts, 1993. (Also other books in series).
Hickman, Pamela M. *Habitats: Making Homes for Animals and Plants.* Addison-Wesley, 1993.
Hoyt, Erich. *Extinction A–Z* [Environment Reference]. Enslow, 1991.
Irvine, Georgeanne. *Protecting Endangered Species at the San Diego Zoo.* Simon & Schuster, 1990.
Liptak, Karen. *Saving Our Wetlands and Their Wildlife* [First Books—Our Environment]. Watts, 1991.
McClung, Robert M. *America's Endangered Birds.* Morrow, 1979.
_____. *Lost Wild America: The Story of Our Extinct and Vanishing Wildlife.* Shoe String, 1993.
McMillan, Bruce. *A Beach for the Birds.* Houghton, 1993.
Nardo, Don. *The Extinction of the Dinosaurs* [Exploring the Unknown]. Lucent, 1994.
Patent, Dorothy Hinshaw. *Gray Wolf, Red Wolf.* Clarion, 1990.
_____. *Habitats: Saving Wild Places* [Better Earth]. Enslow, 1993.
[Save Our Species] series. Steck-Vaughn.
Secrets of Animal Survival [Books for World Explorers]. National Geographic, 1993.
Silver, Donald M. *Extinction Is Forever.* Simon & Schuster, 1995.
Stefoff, Rebecca. *Extinction* [Earth at Risk]. Chelsea, 1992.

See also: books in ENVIRONMENTAL AWARENESS and various habitats units.

FOR MORE INFORMATION ABOUT ENDANGERED SPECIES AND HABI-
TATS, WRITE TO:

African Wildlife Foundation
American Minor Breeds Conservancy
The Center for Plant Conservation
Conservation International
Defenders of Wildlife
Endangered Species Coalition
National Audubon Society
National Geographic Society
National Parks and Conservation
  Association

The Nature Conservancy
Ranger Rick's Nature Club, National
  Wildlife Federation
Sierra Club
Society for the Preservation of
  Birds of Prey
Wildlife Preservation Trust Interna-
  tional
World Wildlife Fund

ENVIRONMENTAL
AWARENESS

Every living thing on Earth is affected by its environment. And, although plants and animals do have an impact on their surroundings, only humans have the power to vastly alter Earth's climate, resources, habitats, and wildlife. Some of these changes have damaged the environment. Pollution, habitat destruction, species extinction, global warming, overpopulation and other problems lessen the quality of life on Earth. All people must become aware of these environmental concerns, and work together to save our planet.

LIBRARY SKILLS

a. Pick one subject from *Atlas of Environmental Issues*. Read the two pages of information on this subject. Then, in your own words, write a short summary of the issue.

b. Choose one map or chart from the *Scholastic Environmental Atlas of the United States*. Make a copy of this chart or map (Note: If there are two maps that go together, copy both of them.) Then explain what the chart or map(s) says about the environment.

c. In *Young Scientist, Volume 8*, choose one of the following sections under Conservation: Disappearing life, Tropical rain forests, The ozone layer, Living in a greenhouse, Farming the land, Spreading deserts, Fresh air?, Acid rain, Poisoned rivers, The dirty oceans, or Nuclear dump. Then, for the section you chose: 1) Give a brief explanation of the problem. 2) Define five related terms. 3) Tell how this problem can harm people, wildlife, and/or the environment.

d. Use *Population of the World* to complete the following activities: 1) List five countries where people have a life expectancy of less than 50 years. 2) About how many human babies are born each year? 3) What fraction of all the people in the world now live in urban areas? 4) Which two countries have the highest birth rates? The lowest? 5) Which two countries have the highest rate of child deaths? The lowest? 6) Name three countries that have an extremely high population density. 7) What parts of the United States have a high population density? What part of the United States is uninhabited? 8) How many cities in Asia have over 5 million people?

e. Use *The Environmental Career Guide* to complete the following activities: 1) Make a list of ten environmental careers. Write a one-sentence description of each. 2) List ten environmental laws and the years they were enacted. 3) List three major industrial accidents that damaged the environment and the years in which they occurred. 4) Write the full names of these anagrams: OSHA, EPA, NIMBY, RCRA, NRC, CAA, TSCA, OPEC, SDWA, BLM. 5) List five nonprofit organizations that offer environmental occupations.

f. Use *The 1993 Information Please Environmental Almanac* to answer the following: 1) What is the telephone number of the EPA's Safe Drinking Water Hotline? 2) Use the State Profiles to look up the following information for any five states: renewables as source of total energy, number of curbside recycling programs, and per capita budget spent on environmental and natural resources. Draw three charts to compare your findings. 3) List the major environmental problems of these countries: Rwanda, Uganda, Iceland, Kuwait, Bangladesh, Singapore, the Gambia, Armenia, Belize, El Salvador, New Zealand, Suriname. 4) List the top two states for greenhouse gas emissions and the state with the highest per capita water use. 5) What are the top five endangered rivers in the United States? 6) What was the Pittman-Robertson Act of 1937? 7) Approximately what percent of the ozone layer is depleted over Antarctica? 8) List five alternate energy sources the United States could tap in order to decrease its dependency on fossil fuels.

g. Use the *1993 Earth Journal* to write short answers for the following: 1) List five ecology-related organizations that need volunteers, and tell what they do. 2) Write the titles and brief summaries of five ecology-related films, sound recordings, or computer games. 3) List the five countries with the most wilderness. 4) Read the summaries of Worst Environmental Disasters of 1992 and Best Environmental Success Stories of 1992. Choose one from each list and tell why you think it was the worst/best environmental story of the year. 5) Write an outline or short summary of one article from either Earth Issues or Regional Reports. 6) List the titles and publishers of five ecology-related magazines or books. 7) List five airlines that have refused to transport wild-caught birds. 8) List five companies that offer Eco-Travel Adventures. 9) Quote one trivia-fact footnote from the book. 10) Name five other types of information you can find out from this book.

ARTS AND CRAFTS

a. Design a poster that suggests one thing kids can do to help the environment.   (4, 5, 8, 9, 11, 13, 15, 17, 18, 19, 20, 22, 23, 25, 27)

b. Choose one type of habitat. Make a collage using pictures of plants and animals from this habitat. (7, 18, 19, 23, 26)

c. Use recyclable materials, such as milk cartons, plastic jugs, and aluminum cans to make a toy, musical instrument, bird house, costume, etc. (4, 8, 17, 23)

d. Make an alphabet book of environmental terms. Illustrate your book with original drawings or pictures cut from recycled materials. (4, 5, 8, 9, 13, 14, 15, 17, 23, 25)

e. Look through newspapers and magazines for news about the environment. Clip these articles and pictures and include them in a scrap book. Your scrap book may be on a single theme, such as water pollution, or divided into sections for various concerns. Include both good and bad news about the environment.

f. Create a board or card game about environmental awareness. Award points for landing on a space or choosing a card that helps the environment. Give penalties for actions that harm the environment. (23)

g. Create a diagram or a diorama of a building or a city that works in harmony with the environment. Include systems that eliminate pollution, reduce and recycle waste, and do not destroy habitats. You can use technology that already exists or invent what you need. Write a description of your project that explains its features and how it would work.

SPELLING/VOCABULARY

a. Complete a word search puzzle of things that can be recycled: wood, paper, plastic, toys, clothes, glass, metal, aluminum, tires, newspapers, motor oil, cardboard, food scraps, yard waste, batteries, chemicals, grocery bags, books. (4, 5, 8, 9, 13, 14, 15, 17, 23, 25)

b. Complete a matching exercise of types of habitats: desert, rainforest, mountain, island, swamp, lake, ocean, temperate forest, tundra, grassland, marsh, river, coniferous forest, polar region, savannah, prairie, seashore, pond. (7, 14, 23, 26)

c. What is a renewable resource? What is a nonrenewable resource? Choose either renewable or nonrenewable resources and think of ten or more items of that category. Create a word search puzzle with these terms. (9, 14, 15, 19, 21, 23)

d. Complete a crossword puzzle of environmental terms: climate, ecology, biome, population, ecosystem, community, conservation, interdependence, habitat, niche, balance, cycle, biodegradable, resource, succession, sustainable, biosphere, zone, nature, food chain. (6, 7, 11, 13, 15, 20, 21, 22, 25, 26)

e. Complete a fill-in-the-blanks exercise of environmental hazards: pollution, desertification, deforestation, ozone hole, drought, logging, global warming, acid rain, habitat destruction, greenhouse effect, overpopulation, erosion, waste disposal, pesticides, oil spills, overhunting, extinction, mining, water shortage, overfishing.   (3, 8, 9, 11, 12, 16, 19, 20, 21, 22, 23, 25, 28)

f. Complete a fill-in-the-blanks exercise of population terms: density, life expectancy, population crash, birth rate, census, population explosion, pyramid, death rate, demographics, birth potential, growth rate, family planning, infant mortality rate, zero population growth, industrialized nations, Third-World countries, standard of living, birth control.   (16, 28, *Population of the World*)

g. Complete a crossword puzzle of environmental pollutants: toxic waste, nitrates, radiation, asbestos, smoke, radon, carcinogens, particulates, chemicals, carbon monoxide, PCBs, pesticides, lead, mercury, fertilizer, phosphates, dioxin, sewage, CFCs, sulfur dioxide, gasoline.   (1, 3, 11, 12, 14, 16, 17, 19, 20, 21, 22, 25)

GEOGRAPHY

a. What wildlife habitats exist in your state? Name some plants and animals that live in one of these habitats. How does the climate effect the habitat?   (6, 7, 13, 18, 23, 25, 26)

b. *Class project:* Look around your neighborhood or town. Take a survey of places you consider to be environmental problems, such as a vacant lot where garbage is dumped, or a factory that pollutes the air. Note these areas on a map of your town. What types of problems are common where you live? Are some areas worse than others?   (9, 18, 19, 20, 22, 23)

c. Divide a sheet of paper into columns and label them: Polar Regions, Temperate/Coniferous Forest, Seashore, Grassland, Desert, Mountain, and Rainforest. In each column, list some plants and animals that live in that habitat.   (6, 7, 23, 26)

d. The following states have 100 or more curbside recycling programs. Locate them on a United States map and color them green: California, Connecticut, Florida, Illinois, Michigan, Minnesota, New Jersey, New York, Ohio, Oregon, Pennsylvania, Wisconsin. The following states have one to ten recycling programs. Color them red: Alabama, Arkansas, Hawaii, Idaho, Kansas, Kentucky, Montana, Nebraska, Nevada, New Mexico, North Dakota, South Carolina, South Dakota, Tennessee, Texas, Utah. These states have no recycling programs. Color them black: Alaska, Delaware, Wyoming.   (*The 1993 Information Please Environmental Atlas*)

e. For many years, the wealthy, industrialized countries of the world have exploited the resources of the poor, developing nations. List some industrialized countries and some developing ones. On a map of the world, color the first group in red and the second group blue. In general, what part(s) of the world have more poor countries? (14, 16, 28)

f. Choose one of the following habitats. Then list several natural resources that may be found there and some of their uses: lake, ocean, rainforest, old growth forest, desert, prairie, mountain. (For example, a river may contain fish that can be used as food, energy in the form of hydroelectricity, and silt which could provide fertile topsoil when it is deposited downstream.) (7, 14, 21, 23)

g. There have been many environmental disasters. Make a list of 20 or more oil spills, nuclear energy leaks, industrial accidents and other environmentally harmful events. On a map of the world, mark where each of these happened. (4, 12, 20, 24)

MATH

a. *Class project:* Each student should take a survey of his/her home. 1) Count the number of light bulbs that are in use. 2) Count the number of electrical appliances that are plugged into electrical outlets. 3) Of all the appliances counted in #2, count how many are always on, such as refrigerators and clocks. The class can use this information to make three charts that show how much we rely on energy. (17)

b. Most toilets use six gallons of water for each flush. For one day, keep a record of how many times you flush a toilet. How many gallons of water did you use? Then keep track of how many times you flushed in one week. How many gallons was that? Add up the number of gallons used per week by each person in the class. What is the total? Do you think this is a lot of water? (23)

c. Use a calculator to answer these questions about habitat destruction: 1) An average of about 100 acres of tropical rainforest are destroyed every minute of every day. How many acres are lost in one day? In a year? 2) In the past 200 years, the lower 48 states of the United States have lost over half of their wetlands. There are now 104,000,000 acres of wetlands. If the United States continues at its present rate of destroying 300,000 acres of wetlands each year, how long will it be before all the wetlands are gone? 3) Of the 25,000,000 acres of old growth forest that once grew in the Pacific Northwest, only 4,000,000 acres remain. In 1988, loggers cut down 100,000 acres of trees. At this rate, how many years will it be before all the trees are gone? (11, *The Information Please Environmental Almanac*)

d. There are about 500,000,000 cars on Earth. 1) If each car uses an average of two gallons of gasoline per day, how many gallons of gas are consumed in one day? In a week? 2) Each gallon of gasoline pours 20 pounds of carbon dioxide into the air as it is used. How many pounds of carbon dioxide enter the air from cars in one day? In a week? 3) Ask a parent or friend to estimate how many gallons of gasoline he/she uses in one week. Then figure out how many pounds of carbon dioxide he/she puts into the atmosphere during that time. (11)

e. About 500,000 trees are cut down each week to supply paper for America's Sunday newspapers. 1) How many trees are killed in a year for Sunday's newspapers? 2) For every ton of recycled newspapers, 17 trees are saved. About how many tons of recycled newspapers would be needed so that no new trees would have to be cut down for one week's worth of Sunday newspapers? For one year's worth of Sunday newspapers? (Round off your answers to the nearest whole number.) 3) About 80 percent of all newspapers are never recycled. If 5 tons of newspapers are recycled, how many tons are not? If one ton equals 17 trees, how many trees are recycled and how many are not in this example? (19, 23)

f. Each day, a person living in the United States makes about 4½ pounds of garbage. The average amounts of daily garbage created per one person in a few other countries are as follows: Canada, 3¾ pounds; Philippines, 1 pound; Sweden, 2 pounds; Ghana, ½ pound. About how many pounds of garbage are created per person in each of these countries after 10 days? 20 days? 30 days? 40 days? 50 days? 60 days? 70 days? 80 days? 90 days? Make a graph to illustrate your answer. (17)

g. Compile a list of 10 or more statistics about what Americans waste each year. Then match each of these with a statistic telling how recycling and conservation can save resources and cut down on pollution. For example: About 500,000 trees are cut down each week to supply paper for America's Sunday newspapers. For every ton of recycled newspapers, 17 trees are saved. (19)

MUSIC AND THEATER ARTS

a. Make puppets from recycled materials, such as paper bags or old socks stuffed with newspapers or torn tights. Produce a puppet show with these creations. (23)

b. Listen to selections from *The Pretty Planet Songs for Earth* (Peter and Mary Alice Amidon, 1990). Sing along to some of these songs.

c. There are many folktales and other children's stories about the environment. Some stories tell us how we should care for our Earth, while others warn us what might happen if we continue to abuse our planet. Choose one environmental story. Perform a puppet show, skit, or dramatic reading based on the story.

d. *Class project:* Have an Earth Day celebration. Students can present skits and songs they wrote about how to help the environment. Present the results of the science projects done for the science exercise, item **d.**

e. Many companies, such as Nature Recordings, Soundings of the Planet, Living Music Records, and The Nature Company, produce recordings of nature sounds from a variety of environments. Listen to some of these and discuss what you hear. (*1993 Earth Journal*)

f. Many popular singers and groups, such as Peter Gabriel, Sting, Midnight Oil, and the B-52s, have recorded songs with environmental themes. Listen to some of these songs. What do you think is the message that the singer/songwriter is trying to get across? (*1993 Earth Journal*)

g. Bring in an item that would ordinarily be thrown away after one use, such as an egg carton, paper towel tube, light bulb, or soda bottle. Then do a short presentation for the class where you mime different uses for the object. Example: A paper towel tube could be a telescope, a trombone, a straw, a hose, etc. Try to create unusual uses for your object.

ENGLISH COMPOSITION

a. Write a poem or story about taking care of our Earth. (4, 5, 8, 10, 13, 17, 19, 22, 23, 25)

b. Think of some environmental problems, such as pollution and habitat destruction, that can harm wildlife. Then write a story from one animal's point of view. Write how the animal is affected by one of these problems. (7, 8, 23, 24)

c. Think of some everyday things people can do to conserve resources or protect the environment. Then write an environmental survey of 10 to 20 questions you could ask people to find out if they are environmentally aware. Your questions should be simple enough to answer with either a yes/no or an always/sometimes/never response. Your survey may concentrate on a particular issue, such as water conservation, or have a broader range of questions. (4, 5, 8, 9, 10, 11, 13, 15, 17, 19, 20, 23, 25)

d. For one week, keep a diary of your daily water use and the amount of trash you throw out. At the end of the week, write a summary of your findings. Do you think your habits are wasteful or not? How can you conserve resources? (9, 13, 20, 23)

e. Think about what our planet may be like when you are 50 years older.

Have humans learned how to live in harmony with the environment or not? Write a science fiction story that tells how Earth will have changed, for the better or worse, 50 years in the future.   (12, 16, 19, 21, 25, 28)

f. *Class project:* Publish a newspaper to make your school aware of environmental matters. You can include news articles on various subjects of local or global concern, editorial cartoons, ads for environmentally safe products, etc. Distribute the newspaper to other people in your school.   (13, 23)

g. Think of an environmental issue you care about, such as rainforest destruction, toxic waste, or recycling. Write an essay explaining the problem and suggesting a solution to it.

SCIENCE

a. *Class project:* Create a small wildlife habitat, such as an ant farm or fresh water pond, to observe in the classroom. Watch the habitat every day and record any changes.   (6, 24)

b. Earth is home to many tiny organisms. Use a magnifying glass or microscope to observe life in a drop of water, a shovelful of dirt, a plant leaf, etc.   (6, 13, 26, 27)

c. *Class project:* What is a naturalist? Go on a nature walk and record what you see, such as types of plants, birds, and animal tracks. What type of habitat are you exploring? Is the area clean or polluted? What can you do to protect this habitat? (6, 7, 8, 11, 13, 18, 23, 26)

d. Name some environmental problems, such as acid rain. Choose one of these problems and list some things that cause it. Then do an experiment that shows how the problem affects the environment.   (3, 8, 9, 11, 16, 17, 19, 20, 23, 25, 27, 28)

e. Do one of the following: 1) Draw a picture of one type of nature cycle, such as the water cycle or nitrogen cycle. Label all parts and include an explanation of what happens. 2) Draw a food web that includes at least five stages of plants and animals.   (3, 6, 7, 11, 16, 23, 25)

f. Do one of the activities in the science exercise, item **e**. Then research a specific environmental problem and show how it affects a habitat or animal. Example: After drawing a picture of the water cycle, show how factory smoke can turn water into acid rain, and how acid rain harms a lake.   (1, 3, 6, 7, 11, 16, 23, 24, 25, 28)

g. *Class project:* Hold an Environmental Awareness Science Fair. Each student can either: 1) Design an invention that makes use of recyclable materials; 2) Conduct an experiment about one aspect of the environment; or 3) Prove how a bad environmental practice is harmful.   (6, 8, 13, 19, 20, 23)

HISTORY/SOCIOLOGY

a. How have humans changed Earth's forests, seas, and other habitats? How have we changed the air? (3, 5, 7, 10, 11, 13, 14, 17, 18, 19, 20, 21, 22, 23, 25)

b. How have humans caused some animals to become extinct or endangered? (7, 8, 9, 10, 13, 14, 15, 18, 19, 20, 21, 23)

c. When there is a war, people are often killed. But wars can also harm the environment in many ways. Give some examples of how plants, animals, and habitats have been destroyed because of wars. How have some wars polluted the Earth? (19, 24)

d. Many people today and in the past have been concerned about Earth's environment. Research the life of a naturalist, conservationist, or environmentalist. Write a brief biography about this person and his/her work. (6, 12, 20, 23, 28)

e. There have been many environmental disasters, such as the *Exxon Valdez* oil spill and the nuclear power plant failure at Chernobyl. Write a paper about one such disaster. Tell how it happened, how it affected the environment, and what was done about it. (2, 12, 20, 24)

f. Compare the lifestyles of people who live in wealthy, industrialized countries to that of people in poor, developing nations. Who has a better standard of living? Compare their use of resources. Who supplies whom with resources such as oil and minerals? Who uses the most resources? Who wastes the most? Who is better at conservation? (16, 21, 28)

g. How did the development of agriculture affect human populations? How, in turn, has this affected Earth's environments, resources, and wildlife populations? (7, 9, 11, 12, 14, 16, 21, 25, 28)

TOPICS FOR DISCUSSION

a. What are some ways that people waste water? How do we waste energy? (3, 4, 5, 8, 9, 13, 15, 17, 19, 20, 21, 23, 25)

b. What are some things kids can do to save natural resources? What can your class do to help the environment? (3, 4, 5, 8, 9, 10, 11, 13, 15, 16, 17, 18, 19, 20, 23, 25, 27)

c. Before class, ask ten or more people the survey questions you wrote for the English composition exercise, item c. In class, discuss the results of your survey. Are the people you know doing all they can to protect the environment?

d. Why should we try to conserve Earth's natural habitats and wildlife? Why should Americans care about what happens to plant and animal life in other parts of the world? (7, 8, 9, 10, 11, 13, 14, 15, 19, 20, 23, 26)

e. Trash disposal, especially of toxic, radioactive, and non-biodegradable materials, is a major problem. If money were not a consideration and advanced technology were available, how would you propose to solve Earth's trash disposal problems? (3, 11, 12, 15, 16, 19, 20, 21, 23)

f. Many companies are discovering that recycling items, such as paper or wooden pallets, can save them money. Give some examples of how recycling waste is cost-efficient. (12, 13, 15, 19)

g. How does our rapidly-increasing consumption of energy and other natural resources endanger our environment? How does this ultimately affect our health? (9, 12, 14, 16, 20, 21, 28)

SUGGESTED RESOURCES

(1) Anderson, Madelyn Klein. *Environmental Diseases* [First Books—Medicine & Disease]. Watts, 1987.
(2) Baines, John. *Environmental Disasters* [The World's Disasters]. Thomson. 1993.
(3) Bennett, Paul. *Earth: The Incredible Recycling Machine.* Thomson, 1993.
(4) Berry, Joy. *Every Kid's Guide to Saving the Earth.* Forest, 1993.
(5) Brown, Laurie Krasny, and Brown, Marc. *Dinosaurs to the Rescue: A Guide to Protecting Our Planet.* Little, 1992.
(6) Burnie, David. *How Nature Works.* Reader's Digest, 1991.
(7) Cook, David. *Environment* [Our Endangered Earth]. Crown, 1983.
(8) The EarthWorks Group. *50 Simple Things Kids Can Do to Save the Earth.* Scholastic, 1990.
(9) Elkington, John, et al. *Going Green: A Kid's Handbook to Saving the Planet.* Viking, 1990.
(10) Gates, Richard. *Conservation* [New True Books]. Childrens, 1982.
(11) Goodman, Billy. *A Kid's Guide to How to Save the Planet.* Avon, 1990.
(12) Herda, D. J. *Environmental America: The Northeastern States* [American Scene]. Millbrook, 1991. (Also other books in series.)
(13) Holmes, Anita. *I Can Save the Earth: A Kid's Handbook for Keeping the Earth Healthy and Green.* Messner, 1993.
(14) Lambert, David. *Planet Earth* [Your World 2000]. Facts on File, 1985.
(15) Lefkowitz, R. J. *Save It! Keep It! Use It Again!: A Book About Conservation and Recycling* [Finding-Out Books]. Parents, 1977.
(16) Leggett, Dennis, and Leggett, Jeremy. *People Trap* [Operation Earth]. Cavendish, 1991.
(17) Lowery, Linda, and Lorbiecki, Marybeth. *Earthwise at Home* [Earthwise]. Carolrhoda, 1993.
(18) _____. *Earthwise at Play* [Earthwise]. Carolrhoda, 1993.
(19) _____. *Earthwise at School* [Earthwise. Carolrhoda, 1993.

(20) Miles, Betty. *Save the Earth.* Knopf, 1991.
(21) Peckham, Alexander. *Resources Control* [Green Issues]. Gloucester, 1990.
(22) Santrey, Laurence. *Conservation and Pollution.* Troll, 1985.
(23) Schwartz, Linda. *Earth Book for Kids: Activities to Heal the Environment.* Learning Works, 1990.
(24) Sirimarco, Elizabeth. *War and the Environment* [Environmental Alert!]. Stevens, 1991.
(25) Stidworthy, John. *Environmentalist* [Be an Expert]. Gloucester, 1992.
(26) _____. *Naturalist* [Be an Expert]. Gloucester, 1991.
(27) Wilkes, Angela. *My First Green Book.* Knopf, 1991.
(28) Winckler, Suzanne, and Rodgers, Mary M. *Population Growth* [Our Endangered Planet]. Lerner, 1991.

LIBRARY SKILLS RESOURCES

Basta, Nicholas. *The Environmental Career Guide: Job Opportunities with the Earth in Mind.* Wiley, 1991.
Buzzworm Magazine editors. *1993 Earth Journal: Environmental Almanac and Resource Directory.* Buzzworm, 1992.
Mattson, Mark. *Scholastic Environmental Atlas of the United States.* Scholastic, 1993.
Middleton, Nick. *Atlas of Environmental Issues* [Issues Atlases]. Facts on File, 1989.
Population of the World [Using and Understanding Maps]. Chelsea, 1993.
World Resources Institute. *The 1993 Information Please Environmental Almanac.* Houghton Mifflin, 1993.
Young Scientist, Volume 8: Energy, Conservation. World Book, 1991.

ADDITIONAL READING – YOUNGER

Amos, Janine. *Pollution* [First Starts]. Raintree, 1993. (Also other books in series.)
Bailey, Donna. *What We Can Do About Protecting Nature* [What We Can Do About]. Watts, 1992.
Boyle, Doe. *Earth Day Every Day* [Adventures of Ranger Rick]. National Wildlife, 1993.
Brennan, Matthew J. *The How and Why Wonder Book of the Environment and You* [How and Why Wonder]. Grosset, 1972.
Brenner, Barbara, editor. *The Earth Is Painted Green: A Garden of Poems About Our Planet.* Scholastic, 1994.
Brooks, F. *Protecting Our World* [Conservation Guides]. Usborne, 1992.
Docekal, Eileen M. *Nature Detective: How to Solve Outdoor Mysteries.* Sterling, 1991.
Gove, Doris. *One Rainy Night.* Atheneum, 1994.
Greene, Carol. [Caring for Our Earth] series. Enslow, 1991.
Hallinan, P. K. *For the Love of Our Earth.* Forest, 1992.
Keller, Holly. *Grandfather's Dream.* Greenwillow, 1994.
Livingston, Myra Cohen. *Earth Songs.* Holiday, 1986.
Lopez, Barry. *Crow and Weasel.* North Point, 1990.
Lowery, Linda. *Earth Day* [On My Own]. Carolrhoda, 1991.
Peppin, Anthea. *Nature in Art* [Millbrook Arts Library]. Millbrook, 1992.

[Target Earth] series. Abdo.
Van Allsburg, Chris. *Just a Dream*. Houghton, 1990.
[We Can Save the Earth] series. Abdo, 1990.

ADDITIONAL READING—OLDER

Baines, John. *Exploring Humans and the Environment* [Exploring Science]. Steck-Vaughn, 1993.
[Better Earth] series. Enslow.
The Big Book for Our Planet. Dutton, 1993.
The Curious Naturalist. National Geographic, 1991.
Dashefsky, H. Steven. *Environmental Literacy: The A-to-Z Guide*. Random, 1993.
The Dictionary of Nature. Kindersley, 1994.
[Earth Keepers] series. Twenty-First Century.
[Environmental Issues] series. Enslow.
Habitats and Environments [More Science in Action]. Cavendish, 1990.
Hare, Tony. [Save Our Earth] series. Watts.
Harris, Colin. *Protecting the Planet* [Young Geographer]. Thomson, 1993.
Herda, D. J., and Madden, Margaret L. *Land Use and Abuse* [Science, Technology & Society]. Watts, 1990.
Kerrod, Robin. *The Environment* [Let's Investigate Science]. Cavendish, 1994.
Lambert, David. *The World's Population* [Young Geographer]. Thomson, 1993.
Leinwand, Gerald. *The Environment* [American Issues]. Facts on File, 1990.
Markham, Adam. *The Environment* [World Issues]. Rourke, 1989.
Penny, Malcolm. *Pollution and Conservation* [Our World]. Silver, 1988.
Porritt, Jonathan, and Nadler, Ellis. *Captain Eco and the Fate of the Earth*. Kindersley, 1991.
Pringle, Laurence. *Restoring Our Earth*. Enslow, 1987.
[Project Ecology] series. Bookwright, 1987.
Roth, Charles E. *The Amateur Naturalist: Explorations and Investigations* [Amateur Science]. Watts, 1993.
Seidenberg, Steven. *Ecology and Conservation* [Gareth Stevens Information Library]. Stevens, 1989.
Wallace, Aubrey. *Eco-Heroes: Twelve Tales of Environmental Victory*. Mercury, 1993.
Young, Donald, and Bix, Cynthia Overbeck. *The Sierra Club Book of Our National Parks*. Sierra Club, 1990.

See also: books in all other units.

FOR MORE INFORMATION ABOUT ENVIRONMENTAL AWARENESS, WRITE TO:

Citizens for a Better Environ-
    ment
Conservation International
Earth Day U.S.A.
Environmental Action Coalition

Environmental Defense Fund
Friends of the Earth
Keep America Beautiful
The Kids' EarthWorks Group
Kids for Saving Earth

National Coalition Against the Misuse of Pesticides

Renew America

Renewable Natural Resources Foundation

Student Environmental Action Coalition

Worldwatch Institute

Zero Population Growth

ADDRESSES OF ORGANIZATIONS AND MUSIC COMPANIES

The Acid Rain Foundation, 1410 Varsity Drive, Raleigh, NC 27606-2010

African Wildlife Foundation, 1717 Massachusetts Avenue NW, Washington, DC 20036

Air and Waste Management Association, P.O. Box 2861, Pittsburgh, PA 15230

Alaska Coalition, 408 C Street NE, Washington, DC 20002

Alliance for Responsible CFC Policy, 2111 Wilson Blvd., Suite 850, Arlington, VA 22201

Alliance for the Wild Rockies, 415 N. Higgins Avenue, Missoula, MO 59802

Alliance to Save Energy, 1725 K Street NW, Suite 509, Washington, DC 20006-1401

Alternative Energy Resources Organization, 44 N. Last Chance Gulch, Helena, MT 59601

Aluminum Recycling Association, 1000 16th Street NW, Suite 400, Washington, DC 20036

American Cave Conservation Association, 131 Main and Cave Streets, P.O. Box 409, Horse Cave, KY 42749

American Council for an Energy-Efficient Economy, 1001 Connecticut Avenue NW, Suite 801, Washington, DC 20036

American Forestry Association, 1516 P Street NW, Washington, DC 20005

American Friends of the Wildfowl and Wetlands Trust, 69063 Wallowa Road, White Pigeon, MI 49099-9745

American Minor Breeds Conservancy, Box 477, Pittsboro, NC 27312

American Petroleum Institute, 1220 L Street NW, Washington, DC 20005

American Polar Society, 108 Scott Hall, Columbus, OH 43210

American Rivers, 801 Pennsylvania Avenue SE, Suite 400, Washington, DC 20003

American Shore and Beach Preservation Association, P.O. Box 279, Middletown, CA 95461

American Solar Energy Society, 2400 Central Avenue, G-1, Boulder, CO 80301

American Water Resources Association, 5410 Grosvenor Lane, Suite 220, Bethesda, MD 20814-2192

American Water Works Association, 6666 W. Quincy Avenue, Denver, CO 80235

American Wildlands, 3609 S. Wadsworth Blvd., Suite 123, Lakewood, CO 80235

American Wind Energy Association, 777 N. Capitol Street NE, Suite 805, Washington, DC 20002

The Antarctica Project, P.O. Box 76920, Washington, DC 20013

Arctic Institute of North America,

University of Calgary, 2500 University Drive NW, Calgary, AB, Canada T2N 1N4

Association of National Grasslands, Box 1028, Hettinger, ND 58639

"*Backyard Habitat Kit*," c/o National Wildlife Federation, 1400 16th Street NW, Washington, DC 20036-2266

Big Island Rainforest Action Group, P.O. Box 341, Kurtistown, HI 96760

Biomass Energy Research Association, 1825 K Street NW, Suite 503, Washington, DC 20006

CAPE (Children's Alliance for Protection of the Environment), P.O. Box 307, Austin, TX 78767

Center for Coastal Studies, 59 Commercial Street, P.O. Box 1036, Provincetown, MA 02657

Center for Marine Conservation, 1725 DeSales Street NW, Suite 500, Washington, DC 20036

The Center for Plant Conservation, Botanical Gardens, P.O. Box 299, St. Louis, MO 63166

Charles Darwin Foundation for the Galápagos Isles, National Zoological Park, Washington, DC 20008

Chihuahuan Desert Research Institute, Box 1334, Alpine, TX 79831

Children of the Green Earth, Box 95219, Seattle, WA 98145

The Children's Rainforest, P.O. Box 936, Lewiston, ME 04240

Citizens Clearinghouse for Hazardous Wastes, P.O. Box 6806, Falls Church, VA 22040

Citizens for a Better Environment, 407 S. Dearborn, Suite 1775, Chicago, IL 60605

Clean Water Action, 1320 18th NW, Suite 300, Washington, DC 20036

Coalition for Responsible Waste Incineration, 1330 Connecticut Avenue NW, Suite 300, Washington, DC 20036

Coalition on Resource Recovery and the Environment, Solid Waste Association of North America, 8750 Georgia Avenue, Suite 140, Silver Spring, MD 20910

Coastal Conservation Association, 4801 Woodway, Suite 22 W, Houston, TX 77056

Coastal States Organization, Hall of States, 444 N. Capitol Street NW, Suite 322, Washington, DC 20001

Community Environment Council, 930 Miramonte Drive, Santa Barbara, CA 93109

Concerned Neighbors in Action, P.O. Box 3847, Riverside, CA 92519

Conservation International, 1015 18th Street NW, Suite 1000, Washington, DC 20036

Council of the Alleghanies, Route 2 Box 250, Frostburg, MD 21532

Council on Ocean Law, 1709 New York Avenue NW, 7th Floor, Washington, DC 20006

Council on Packaging in the Environment, 1001 Connecticut Avenue NW, Suite 401, Washington, DC 20036

The Cousteau Society, 870 Greenbriar Circle, Suite 402, Chesapeake, VA 23320

Defenders of Wildlife, 1244 19th Street NW, Washington, DC 20036

Desert Fishes Council, P.O. Box 337, Bishop, CA 93515

Desert Protective Council, P.O. Box 2312, Valley Center, CA 92082-2312

Earth Day U.S.A., 2 Elm Street, Box 470, Peterborough, NH 03458

Earthwatch, 680 Mt. Auburn Street, Box 403, Watertown, MA 02274

Electric Power Research Institute, 3412 Hillview Avenue, Palo Alto, CA 94104

Elektra Nonesuch, Elektra Entertainment, 590 5th Avenue, New York, NY 10036

End Hunger Network, 365 Sycamore Road, Santa Monica, CA 90402

Endangered Species Coalition, 666 Pennsylvania Avenue SE, Washington, DC 20003

Environmental Action Coalition, 625

Broadway, 2nd Floor, New York, NY 10012

Environmental Defense Fund, 257 Park Avenue S., New York, NY 10010

Experimental Cities, P.O. Box 731, Pacific Palisades, CA 90272-0731

Farm Aid, 334 Broadway, Suite 5, Cambridge, MA 02139

Farm Animal Reform Movement, P.O. Box 30654, Bethesda, MD 20824

Farm Committee for Sustainable Agriculture, P.O. Box 1300, Colfax, CA 95713

Forest Ecosystem Rescue Network, P.O. Box 672, Dahconega, GA 30533-0672

4-H Program and Youth Development, U.S. Dept. of Agriculture, Extension Service, Washington, D.C. 20250

The Freshwater Foundation, 725 County Road 6, Wayzata, MN 55391

Friends of the Earth, 218 D Street SE, Washington, DC 20003

Friends of the Everglades, 101 Westward Drive No. 2, Miami Springs, FL 33166

Friends of the River Foundation, 909 12th Street, No. 207, Sacramento, CA 95814

Gas Research Institute, 8600 W. Bryn Mawr Avenue, Chicago, IL 60631

Geothermal Education Office, Geothermal Resources Council, P.O. Box 1350, Davis, CA 95617

Global Coral Reef Alliance, 324 N. Bedford Road, New York, NY 10514

Global ReLeaf Through Learning, P.O. Box 2000, Washington, DC 20013

Grassland Heritage Foundation, 5450 Buena Vista, Shawnee Mission, KS 66205

Great Lakes United, State College University at Buffalo, Cassety Hall, 1300 Elmwood Avenue, Buffalo, NY 14222

Great Plains Agricultural Council, Colorado State University, Dept. of Agricultural and Resource Economics, Fort Collins, CO 80523-0002

Greenhouse Crisis Foundation, 1130 17th Street NW, Suite 630, Washington, DC 20036

Greenpeace U.S.A., 1436 U Street NW, Washington, DC 20009

Hawaii Volcanoes National Park, Hawaii Island, HI 96718

Household Hazardous Waste Project, 1031 E. Battlefield, Suite 214, Springfield, MO 65807

The Humane Farming Association, 1550 California Street, Suite 6, San Francisco, CA 94109

Institute of Andean Studies, P.O. Box 9307, Berkeley, CA 94709

Institute of Scrap Recycling Industries, 1325 G Street NW, Suite 1000, Washington, DC 20005

International Erosion Control Association, Box 4904, Steamboat Springs, CO 80477

International Mountain Society, P.O. Box 1978, Davis, CA 95617-1978

International Water Resources Association, University of Illinois, 205 N. Mathews Avenue, Urbana, IL 61801

The Izaak Walton League of America, 1401 Wilson Blvd., Level B, Arlington, VA 22209

Keep America Beautiful, Mill River Plaza, 9 W. Broad Street, Stamford, CT 06902

The Kids' EarthWorks Group, 1400 Shattuck Avenue #25, Berkeley, CA 94709

Kids for Saving Earth, P.O. Box 47247, Plymouth, MN 55447-0247

The Land Institute, 2440 E. Water Well Road, Salina, KS 67401

Living Music Records, Box 68, Litchfield, CT 06759

Mail Preference Services, Direct Marketing Association, 11 W. 42nd Street, New York, NY 10036-8096

Mountaineers, 300 Third Avenue W, Seattle, WA 98119

National Arbor Day Foundation, 100 Arbor Avenue, Nebraska City, NE 68410

National Audubon Society, 950 3rd Avenue, New York, NY 10022

National Coalition Against the Misuse of

Pesticides, 701 E Street SE, Suite 200, Washington, DC 20003

National Coalition for Marine Conservation, 5105 Paulsen Street, Suite 243, Savannah, GA 31405

National Environmental Development Association/Resource Conservation and Recovery Act Project, 1440 New York Avenue NW, Suite 300, Washington, DC 20005

National FFA Organization, National FFA Center, Box 15160, 5632 Mt. Vernon Memorial Highway, Alexandria, VA 22309-0160

National Geographic Society, 17th & M Streets NW, Washington, DC 20036

National Grange, 1616 H Street NW, Washington, DC 20006

The National Institute for Urban Wildlife, 10921 Trotting Ridge Way, Columbia, MD 21044

National Parks and Conservation Association, 1776 Massachusetts Avenue NW, Suite 200, Washington, DC 20036

National Recycling Coalition, 1101 30th Street NW, Suite 305, Washington, DC 20007

National Speleological Society, 2813 Cave Avenue, Huntsville, AL 35810-4431

National Wildlife Federation, 1400 16th Street NW, Washington, DC 20036-2266

Natural Resources Defense Council, 40 W. 20th Street, New York, NY 10011

The Nature Company Catalog, P.O Box 188, Florence, KY 41022

The Nature Conservancy, 1815 N. Lynn Street, Arlington, VA 22209

Nature Recordings, World Disc Productions, Inc., 915 Spring Street, Friday Harbor, WA 98250

Nuclear Energy Information Service, P.O. Box 1637, Evanston, IL 60204

The Oceanic Society, 218 D Street SE, Washington, DC 20003

Organic Foods Production Association of North America, P.O. Box 1078, Greenfield, MA 01301

Oxfam America, 26 West Street, Boston, MA 02111-1206

Ozark Society, P.O. Box 2914, Little Rock, AR 72203

Pacific Whale Foundation, Kealia Beach Plaza, Suite 25, 101 N. Kihei Road, Kihei, HI 96753

Plastics Recycling Foundation, 1275 K. Street NW, Suite 400, Washington, DC 20005

Rainforest Action Network, 450 Sansome Street, Suite 700, San Francisco, CA 94111

Rainforest Alliance, 270 Lafayette Street, Suite 512, New York, NY 10012

Ranger Rick's Nature Club, National Wildlife Federation, 8925 Leasburg Pike, Vienna, VA 22184-0001

Renew America, 1400 16th Avenue NW, Suite 710, Washington DC 20036

Renewable Natural Resources Foundation, 5430 Grosvenor Lane, Bethesda, MD 20814

Rykodisc, 530 North 3rd Street, Minneapolis, MN 55401

Save Our Streams, The Izaak Walton League of America, 1401 Wilson Blvd., Level B, Arlington, VA 22209

Save-the-Redwoods League, 114 Sansome Street, Room 605, San Francisco, CA 94104

Sierra Club, 730 Polk Street, San Francisco, CA 94109

Smithsonian/Folkways Recordings, 955 L'Enfant Plaza, Suite 2600, Smithsonian Institution, Washington, DC 20560

Society for the Preservation of Birds of Prey, P.O. Box 66070, Los Angeles, CA 90066

Soil and Water Conservation Society, 7515 NE Ankeny Road, Ankeny, IA 50021

Soundings of the Planet, P.O. Box 43512, Tucson, AZ 85733

Student Environmental Action Coalition, P.O. Box 1168, Chapel Hill, NC 27514-1168

Sukay, 3315 Sacramento Street, Suite 523, San Fransisco, CA 94118

Super Kids Recycling Program, P.O. Box 242, Iselin, NJ 08830

Tree Amigos Project, Center for Environmental Study, 143 Bostwick NE, Grand Rapids, MI 49503

Tree City U.S.A. Community Improvement Program, National Arbor Day Foundation, 100 Arbor Avenue, Nebraska City, NE 68410

Trust for Public Land, 116 New Montgomery Street, 4th Floor, San Francisco, CA 94105

United Citizens Coastal Protection League, P.O. Box 46, Cardiff by the Sea, CA 92007

Upper Mississippi River Conservation Committee, 4469 48th Avenue Ct., Rock Island, IL 61201

Walden Forever Wild, P.O. Box 275, Concord, MA 01742

Wetlands Watch, The Izaak Walton League of America, 1401 Wilson Blvd., Level B, Arlington, VA 22209

Wildlife Preservation Trust International, 3400 W. Girard Avenue, Philadelphia, PA 19104

World Aquaculture Society, Louisiana State University, 143 J. M. Parker Coliseum, LSU, Baton Rouge, LA 70803

World Nature Association, P.O. Box 673, Silver Spring, MO 20901

World Wildlife Fund, 1250 24th Street NW, Washington, DC 20037

Worldwatch Institute, 1776 Massachusetts Avenue NW, Washington, DC 20036

Zero Population Growth, 1400 16th Street NW, Suite 320, Washington, DC 20036

INDEX

Aardema, Verna 159
Abbott, R. Tucker 83
Abels, Harriette 16
About Life in the Sea [Do You Know...?] 63
Abrams, Kathleen 124
Abrams, Lawrence 124
Acacia Terrace 183
Aces, Heroes, and Daredevils of the Air 28
Acid Rain [Save Our Earth] 27, 37
Acid Rain [Saving Planet Earth] 27, 37, 49
Acid Rain: A Sourcebook for Young People 28
Acid Rain Foundation, The 29, 39, 233
Action Science (series) 84
Adams, Jeanie 74
Adams, Peter D. 124
Addie Across the Prairie 150
Adler, David A. 27
Adoff, Arnold 183
Adventure in the Amazon, An 104
Adventures of Hucklberry Finn, The 106
Adventures of Ranger Rick (series) 229
Africa: Desert Solitude at Bushman Fountain 155
African Animals [New True Books] 149
African Wildlife Foundation 150, 218, 233
Agriculture 193
Agriculture and Vegetation of the World [Using and Understanding Maps] 193
Ahrens, Lynn 75
Air [Science Through Art] 28
Air, Air All Around [First Facts] 27

Air, Air, Everywhere [Science in Action] 27
Air and Waste Management Association 29, 206, 233
Air Crafts 28
Air Disasters [The World's Disasters] 27
Air in Action [Secrets of Science] 27
Air Pollution [New True Books] 27
Air Scare [Operation Earth] 27
Air Travel [The World on the Move] 27
Air, Water and Weather [Discovering Science] 27, 37
Air We Breathe, The [We Can Save the Earth] 28
Aircraft Technology [Technology in Action] 28
Al-Salah, Khairat 183
Alaska Coalition 170, 233
Albert, Richard E. 159
Albyn, Carole Lisa 75
Aldis, Rodney 114, 181, 168
Alejandra's Gift 159
Alexander, Bryan 168
Alexander, Cherry 168
Aliki 15
All About Farm Animals 193
All About Islands [Question and Answer Book] 73
All About Niagara Falls 104
All About Ponds [Question and Answer Book] 96
All Eyes on the Pond 95
Allen, Judy 216
Allen, Linda B. 138
Alliance for Responsible CFC Policy 29, 233
Alliance for the Wild Rockies 139, 233
Alliance to Save Energy 51, 233
Alligators to Zooplankton: A Dictionary

of Water Babies [New England
Aquarium Books] 39
Allison, John P. 205
Allison, Lee A. 205
Alps and Their People, The [People
and Places] 138
Alternative Energy (series) 27, 37,
49, 204
Alternative Energy Sources Organi-
zation 51, 233
Altman, Linda Jacobs 193
Aluminum Recycling Association
206, 233
Amateur Geologist: Explorations and
Investigations, The [Amateur Sci-
ence] 17
Amateur Naturalist: Explorations and
Investigations, The [Amateur Sci-
ence] 230
Amateur Science (series) 17, 230
Amato, Carol J. 15
Amazing Grace: Smith Island and the
Chesapeake Watermen 75
Amazon [Vanishing Cultures] 115
Amazon: A Young Reader's Look at
the Last Frontier 116
Amazon Adventure [Young Explor-
ers] 115
Amazon Rain Forest and Its People,
The [People and Places] 116
America the Beautiful (series) 74
American Cave Conservation Asso-
ciation 18, 233
American Council for an Energy-
Efficient Economy 51, 233
American Family Farm, The 192
American Forestry Association 126,
233
American Friends of the Wildfowl
and Wetlands Trust 96, 233
American Issues (series) 230
American Minor Breeds Conservancy
194, 218, 233
American Petroleum Institute 51, 233
American Pioneer Family, An [How
They Lived] 149
American Polar Society 170, 233
American Rivers 106, 233
American Scene (series) 228
American Shore and Beach Preserva-
tion Association 85, 233

American Solar Energy Society 51,
233
American Water Resources Associa-
tion 39, 233
American Water Works Association
39, 106, 233
American Wilderness, The (series)
95, 96, 183
American Wildlands 96, 106, 126,
233
American Wind Energy Association
29, 51, 233
Americans on the Move (series) 106
America's Ancient Cities 183
America's Early Canals [Americans
on the Move] 106
America's Endangered Birds 217
Ames, Lee J. 28
Amos, Janine 193, 204, 216, 229
Amos, William H. 84
Amphibians: Creatures of the Land
and Water [Cincinnati Zoo Books]
96
Amsel, Sheri 95, 115, 137, 148, 159
Ancient Egypt [Cultural Atlas for
Young People] 94
Ancient Forest, An [Let's Take a
Trip] 126
Ancient Forests [Circle of Life] 125
Ancona, George 105, 192, 216
And Then There Was One: The Mys-
teries of Extinction 215
Anderson, Henry M. 75
Anderson, Joan 192
Anderson, Madelyn Klein 228
Anderson, Tim 138
Andryszewski, Tricia 160
Animal Homes: Forests [Oxford
Scientific Films] 125
Animal Odysseys (series) 150
Animal Tracks and Traces 126
Animals and Their Ecosystems
(series) 149
Animals and Their Homes (series)
94, 124, 138
Animals in Danger [First Starts] 216
Animals in Danger (series) 215
Animals in Rivers and Ponds [Ani-
mals and Their Homes] 94
Animals in the Forest [Animals and
Their Homes] 124

Animals in the Mountains [Animals and Their Homes] 138
Animals of the African Plains [Nature's Hidden World] 148
Animals of the High Mountains [Books for Young Explorers] 139
Animals of the Islands [In Peril] 75
Animals of the Seashore [Nature Close-Ups] 83
Animals That Live in Trees [Books for Young Explorers] 126
Antarctica 169
Antarctica [New True Books] 169
Antarctica [Our Endangered Planet] 169
Antarctica: The Last Unspoiled Continent 169
Antarctica Project, The 170, 233
Antarctica Vangelis 165
Antonio's Rain Forest [Photo Books] 115
Appalachia: The Voices of Sleeping Birds 138
Applebaum, Diana 126
Arbor Day [On My Own] 125
Arctic, The [New True Books] 169
Arctic and Its People, The [People and Places] 170
Arctic Expedition [Young Explorers] 170
Arctic Explorer: The Story of Matthew Henson [Trailblazers] 170
Arctic Institute of North America 170, 233
Arctic Lands [A Closer Look At] 168
Arctic National Wildlife Refuge [Circle of Life] 169
Arctic Research Program 170
Arctic Tundra [EcoZones] 169
Arctic World, The (series) 168
Ardley, Neil 26, 49
Arnold, Caroline 16, 62, 216
Arnold, Guy 50
Arnosky, Jim 74, 84, 124, 125
Aron, Jon 28
Arthur's New Power 50
Artists of the World (series) 39
As Dead as a Dodo 216
As Old as the Hills [Discovering Science] 138
Ashabranner, Brent 193

Asia — Misty Isle 69
Asimov, Isaac 27, 28, 38, 50, 83, 115, 204, 205, 216
Ask Isaac Asimov (series) 28, 38, 83, 115, 204, 205, 216
Assateague: Island of the Wild Ponies 74
Association of National Grasslands 150, 234
Astronauts [New True Books] 28
At Risk (series) 126
At the Edge of the Pond 95
Atlantic Ocean, The [New True Books] 63
Atlas of Animal Migration 149
Atlas of Endangered Animals, The [Environmental Atlas] 216
Atlas of Endangered Species, The 94, 216
Atlas of Environmental Issues [Issues Atlases] 95, 115, 216, 229
Atlas of World Issues [Issues Atlases] 159, 193
Atlas of World Issues [World Contemporary Issues] 49
Atmosphere: Projects with Geography, The [Hands on Science] 28
Atmosphere in Danger, The [Man-Made Disasters] 29
Australian Aborigines [Threatened Cultures] 159
Autumn of the Elk [Animal Odysseys] 150
Avalanche! [Nature's Disasters] 137
Avi 183
Ayer, Elanor 105
Aylesworth, Thomas G. 15, 137

Babbitt, Natalie 38
Back Roads (series) 126, 193
"Backyard Habitat Kit" 183, 234
Bailey, Donna 27, 38, 49, 104, 124, 137, 158, 159, 181, 192, 205, 229
Bain, Iain 137, 138
Baines, John 27, 37, 62, 83, 228, 230
Baker, Jeannie 115
Baker, Lucy 62, 114, 158
Baker, Susan 48, 104, 138
Ballard, Robert D. 73
Balouet, Jean-Christophe 75, 217

Banks, Martin 114, 215
Bannan, Jan Gumprecht 83
Bannatyne-Cugnet, Jo 149
Barge Book, The 105
Barkan, Joanne 27
Barkin, Carol 125
Barnes-Svarney, Patricia L. 17, 138
Barrett, Norman 74, 137, 168
Barss, Karen J. 38
Barton, Miles 217
Base, Graeme 63
Bash, Barbara 148, 158, 181
Basta, Margo McLoone 205
Basta, Nicholas 229
Bat-Ami, Miriam 84
Baylor, Byrd 159
Be an Expert (series) 229
Beach [Land Shapes] 83
Beach for the Birds, A 85, 217 .
Beattie, Owen 170
Beaver at Long Pond 95
Becklake, John 194
Becklake, Sue 194, 206
Bedouin [Threatened Cultures] 159
Beginning History (series) 192
Behm, Barbara J. 75, 83, 104, 125,
　137, 158, 217
Beiser, Arthur 17
Bellamy, David 83, 105, 125
Bellville, Cheryl Walsh 192
Bender, Lionel 15, 73, 74, 104, 137,
　158
*Beneath the Waves: Exploring the
　Hidden World of the Kelp Forest*
　64
Bennett, Paul 15, 28, 37, 228
Berger, Melvin 50, 84, 138, 169
Bernard, Alan 160
Bernhard, Emery 169
Berry, Joy 228
Berry, Louise A. 28, 84, 114
Better Earth (series) 217, 230
Between Cattails 95
Bial, Raymond 192, 193
Biesty, Stephen 63
Big Book for Our Planet, The 230
Big Island Rainforest Action Group
　75, 116, 234
Big River (sound recording) 106
*Big River: The Adventures of
　Huckleberry Finn* 106

Bigfoot [The Mystery of. . .] 138
Billings, Charlene W. 192
Bioenergy [Alternative Energy] 49,
　204
Biomass Energy Research Associa-
　tion 51, 234
Birds [Our Endangered Planet] 215
Bison and the Great Plains, The [Ani-
　mals and Their Ecosystems] 149
Bix, Cynthia Overbeck 38, 230
Black, Wallace B. 37, 48, 62, 204
Black Jack: Last of the Big Alligators
　96
Black Star, Bright Dawn 170
Blackman, Steve 28
Blashfield, Jean F. 37, 48, 62, 204
Bloch, Marie Halun 95
Bloyd, Sunni 215
*Blue Ridge Range: The Gentle Moun-
　tains* 138
Bolt, Stephen 63
Boltz, C. L. 48
Bonar, Veronica 83, 104, 125, 137,
　158, 205
Books for World Explorers (series)
　16, 84, 95, 105, 125, 126, 139,
　216, 217
Booth, Basil 126
*Born of Fire: Volcanoes and Igneous
　Rocks* [Earth Processes] 139
*Born of Heat and Pressure: Mountains
　and Metamorphic Rocks* [Earth
　Processes] 138
*Born to the Land: An American Por-
　trait* 193
Bosse, Malcolm 115
Boyer, Edward 104
Boyle, Doe 229
Boyne, Walter J. 27
Bradley, Catherine 137
Bramwell, Martyn 28, 63, 106, 137,
　170
Brandenberg, Jim 159
Brandt, Keith 38, 137
Brandt, Sue R. 125
Branston, Brian 75
Brazilian Rain Forest, The [Circle of
　Life] 116
Breakthroughs in Science (series) 15
Breiter, Herta 48
Brennan, Matthew J. 229

Brenner, Barbara 229
Bridges [New True Books] 104
Bright, Michael 115
Bringing the Rain to Kapiti Plain: A Nandi Tale 159
Broekel, Ray 28, 37
Brooks, F. 125, 229
Brown, Laurie Krasney 205, 228
Brown, Marc 205, 228
Brown, Mary Barrett 95
Browne, Tom 104
Bruchac, Joseph 95
Bruning, Nancy 183
Brusca, Maria Cristina 149
Buffalo Hunt 148
Buggey, JoAnne 206
Bulla, Clyde Robert 95
Bullen, Susan 138, 170
Bunting, Eve 182
Buried in Garbage [The Crabtree Environment Series] 204
Buried in Ice: The Mystery of a Lost Arctic Expedition [Time Quest] 170
Burke, Deidre 194
Burnie, David 228
Burningham, John 216
Burns, Diane L. 125
Burton, John 94, 215, 216
Burton, Robert 215
Bushey, Jerry 105, 192
Bushman of the Kalahari, The [Original Peoples] 159
Butler, Daphne 16, 125
Buzzworm Magazine editors 229
By the River [Use Your Eyes] 106
Byles, Monica 168

Cacti and Other Succulents [Green World] 160
Caduto, Michael J. 95
Caitlin, Stephen 94
Cajacob, Thomas 216
Cambridge Topic (series) 182
Campbell, Andrew 75, 83
Can the Whales Be Saved? 216
Canada's Incredible Coasts 84
Cannonball River Tales 106
CAPE (Children's Alliance for Protection of the Environment) 85, 234

Capital Capital City 1790-1814, A 183
Captain Eco and the Fate of the Earth 206, 230
Carey, Helen H. 16, 63, 115
Caribbean, The [Looking at Islands] 74
Caring for Environments (series) 114, 148
Caring for Our Earth (series) 38, 229
Caring for Our Water [Caring for Our Earth] 38
Carle, Eric 84
Carlisle, Madelyn 104
Carlisle, Norman 104
Carlsbad Caverns [National Parks] 17
Carr, Archie 95
Carrick, Carol 95
Carson, Rachel 85, 158, 194
Carter, Alden R. 106, 160
Carter, Katherine Jones 62
Cartons, Cans & Orange Peels: Where Does Your Garbage Go? 206
Catch the Wind! 28
Catchpole, Clive 114, 138, 148, 158
Catherall, Ed 15, 50
Caught on a Cliff Face 138
Cave [The Story of the Earth] 15
Cave Life [Look Closer] 16
Caves 17
Caves [Science Adventure] 16
Caves: An Underground Wonderland [Wonderworks of Nature] 16
Celia's Island Journal 74
Center for Coastal Studies 85, 234
Center for Marine Conservation 64, 75, 234
Center for Plant Conservation, The 218, 234
Challand, Helen J. 95, 125
Challenge of Clean Air, The [Environmental Issues] 28
Challenge of Supplying Energy, The [Environmental Issues] 50
Changing City, The 182
Changing Countryside, The 182
Changing Desert, The 160
Changing Earth, The [Young Geographer] 17, 85
Changing Landscapes [Green Issues] 16, 192
Charles Darwin Foundation for the Galápagos Isles 75, 234

Charlie's House 95
Charlotte's Web 193
Charman, Andrew 50
Cheripko, Jan 106
Chernobyl Catastrophe, The [Great Disasters] 50
Cherry, Lynne 105, 115
Chicago (sound recording) 183
Chicago: A Musical Vaudeville 183
Chico Mendes: Fight for the Forest [Earth Keepers] 115
Chiefari, Janet 125
Chihuahuan Desert Research Institute 160, 234
Children of the Dust Bowl: The True Story of the School at Weedpatch Camp 160
Children of the Green Earth 160, 234
Children of the World (series) 74
Children's Animal Atlas, The 94
Children's Atlas of People & Places, The 74, 84, 115, 159
Children's Guide to Endangered Animals 105, 115, 149, 216
Children's Rainforest, The 116, 234
Chinery, Michael 148
CHP Technology Series (series) 62
Chrisp, Peter 192
Christian, Mary Blount 138
Churchill, E. Richard 28
Cincinnati Zoo Books (series) 96, 216, 217
Circle of Life (series) 116, 125, 149, 169
Cities [Facts About] 181
Cities [Your World 2000] 182
Cities: Through the Eyes of Artists [The World of Art] 183
Cities Against Nature [Saving Planet Earth] 183
Cities, Citizens & Civilizations [Timelines] 181
Cities in Crisis [World Issues] 182
Cities of the World 182
Cities Under Stress [Impact] 181
Citizens Clearinghouse for Hazardous Wastes 206, 234
Citizens for a Better Environment 230, 234
City, The [The Junior Library of Ecology] 181
City: A Story of Roman Planning and Construction 183
City of Angels 183
City of Angels (sound recording) 183
City of Light, City of Dark: A Comic-Book Novel 183
City Safaris 183
City Through the Ages 182
City Trains: Moving Through America's Cities by Rail 183
City We Live In, The [We Can Save the Earth] 182
City Within a City: How Kids Live in New York's China Town [A World of My Own] 183
Civilizations of the Americas [History of the World] 181
Civilizations of the Middle East [History of the World] 158
Clark, Elizabeth 192
Clark, Eugene 74
Clark, John 28
Clean Water [Earth at Risk] 38
Clean Water Action 96, 234
Clocks on the Rocks: Learning About Earth's Past [Earth Processes] 17
Close to Extinction [Survival] 215
Close to the Wild: Siberian Tigers in a Zoo [Nature Watch] 216
Close-Up (series) 170
Closer Look (series) 159
Closer Look at, A (series) 114, 168
Closer Look at Deserts, A [Closer Look] 159
Clouds of Terror 150
Coalition for Responsible Waste Incineration 206, 234
Coalition on Resource Recovery and the Environment 206, 234
Coastal Conservation Association 85, 234
Coastal Rescue: Preserving Our Seashores 84
Coastal States Organization 85, 234
Coastlines [Planet Earth] 84
Coasts [Our World] 83
Cobb, Vicki 38, 49, 50, 115, 138, 159, 169, 182, 205
Coburn, Doris K. 83
Cochrane, Jennifer 114
Cohen, Peter Zachary 106

Coldrey, Jennifer 84
Cole, Joanna 16, 38, 63
Cole, Sheila 84
Coleridge, Samuel Taylor 170
Collier, James Lincoln 106
Collinson, Alan 137, 148
Community Environment Council 183, 234
Community Helpers (series) 205
Comparing Religions (series) 194
Complete Pogo, Vols. 1 & 2 95
Compost Critters 206
Concerned Neighbors in Action 183, 234
Condon, Judith 204
Connor, Judith 85
Conrad, Pam 148, 150
Conservation [New True Books] 228
Conservation and Pollution 229
Conservation Guides (series) 125, 229
Conservation International 116, 218, 230, 234
Conservation of the Sea [Junior Library of Ecology] 62
Conserving Our Rain Forests [Conserving Our World] 114
Conserving Our World (series) 27, 62, 83, 114, 159, 168, 192, 204, 216
Conserving the Atmosphere [Conserving Our World] 27
Conserving the Polar Regions [Conserving Our World] 168
Contemporary World Issues (series) 206
Continents [Earth in Action] 16, 62, 137
Cook, Brenda 193
Cook, David 215, 228
Cook, Kevin J. 148
Cooney, Barbara 74
Cooper, Jason 193
Cooper, Susan 138
Coote, Roger 27, 37, 62
Coral Reef [Look Closer] 75
Coral Reef [Picture Library-Science] 74
Coral Reefs [Natural Science] 73, 83
Coral Reefs: Hidden Colonies of the Sea [Wonderworks of Nature] 63, 74, 84
Coral Reefs in Danger 75

Corn Belt Harvest 192
Corn-Husk Crafts 194
Cornerstones of Freedom (series) 106, 149
Cortesi, Wendy W. 95
Corwin, Judith Hoffman 74
Cossi, Olga 38
Costa-Pau, Rosa 27, 62, 104, 125, 181
Coucher, Helen 115
Couffer, Jack 95
Couffer, Mike 95
Council of the Alleghanies 139, 234
Council on Ocean Law 64, 234
Council on Packaging in the Environment 206, 234
Countries of the World (series) 74
County Fair 193
Cousteau Society, The 64, 104, 106, 234
Cowcher, Helen 169
Cowing, Sheila 94
Cows in the Parlour: A Visit to a Dairy Farm 192
Cox, Shirley 17
Crabtree Environment Series, The (series) 204
Crafts Around the World (series) 74
Creatures of the Woods [Books for Young Explorers] 125
Crespo, George 74
Crinklefoot's Book of Animal Tracks and Wildlife Signs 125
Crinklefoot's Guide to Knowing Trees 124
Crocodile and the Crane: Surviving in a Crowded World, The 217
Cronyn, Hume 138
Cross-Sections Man-of-War 63
Crow and Weasel 229
Cruise of the Atlantic Star, The 85
Crump, Donald J. 85
Cuisin, Michel 148
Cultural Atlas for Young People (series) 94
Cultural Geography (series) 75
Cultures of the World (series) 75
Cumbre 134
Cumming, David 106
Cups & Cans & Paper Fans: Craft Projects from Recycling Materials 205

Curious Naturalist, The 230
Cutchins, Judy 95, 217

Dahlstedt, Marden 38
Dailey, Robert 17
Dairy Country [Back Roads] 193
Dakota Dugout 150
Daniel, Jamie 205
Danziger, Paula 183
Dark and Full of Secrets 95
Darwin and the Enchanted Isles 75
Darwin & the Voyage of the Beagle
   75
Dashefsky, H. Steven 205, 230
David, Andrew 106
David the Trash Cop: A Child's
   Guide to Recycling 205
Davies, Eryl 37, 62
Davis, Deborah 170
Davis, James E. 181
Davis, Kenneth S. 39, 106
Davol, Marguerite W. 125
Dawn to Dusk in the Galápagos 73
Day in the Life of a Marine Biologist,
   A 63
DeArmond, Dale 169
Death Valley: A(lluvial) Fans-to-
   Z(abriske) Quartzite 160
Deep Dream of the Rain Forest 115
Deep Sea Vents: Living Worlds With-
   out Sun 64
Deep Wizardry 63
DeFelice, Cynthia 95
Defenders of Wildlife 150, 218, 234
de Larramendi, Alberto Ruiz 115
Desert [The Story of the Earth] 158
Desert Beneath the Sea, The 74
Desert Fishes Council 160, 234
Desert Giant: The World of the Sa-
   guaro Cactus [Tree Tales] 158
Desert Is Theirs, The 159
Desert Life [Look Closer] 159
Desert Moon Song 155
Desert of Ice: Life and Work in Ant-
   arctica 170
Desert Plants [Plant Life] 160
Desert Protective Council 160, 234
Desert Trek [Young Explorers] 160
Desert Voices 159
Desert Year, A 159

Deserts 159
Deserts [Earth in Action] 159
Deserts [Ecology Watch] 159
Deserts [EcoZones] 159
Deserts [Exploring Our World] 159
Deserts [Facts About] 158
Deserts [First Starts] 160
Deserts [Habitats of the World] 159
Deserts [Last Frontiers for Mankind]
   159
Deserts [The Living World] 158
Deserts [New True Books] 160
Deserts [Our World] 159
Deserts and People [Nature's Land-
   scapes] 158
Deserts and Wastelands [Franklin
   Watts Picture Atlas] 159
DeStefano, Susan 115
Destination: Antarctica 170
Devonshire, Hilary 28, 38
Dewey, Jennifer Owings 95, 158, 216
Diagram Group, The 17, 106, 139
Dictionary of Nature, The 230
Digging Deeper: Investigations into
   Rocks, Shocks, Quakes, and Other
   Earthly Matters 16, 137
Dinosaurs to the Rescue: A Guide to
   Protecting Our Planet 205, 228
Dinosaurs Walked Here and Other
   Tales Fossils Tell 16
Disappearing Grasslands [Environ-
   ment Alert!] 148
Disappearing Wetlands [Saving Planet
   Earth] 95
Disaster! (series) 64
Discovering Art (series) 38, 182, 194
Discovering Nature (series) 94
Discovering Pond Life [Discovering
   Nature] 94
Discovering Science (series) 27, 37,
   50, 138, 194
Discovering Seashells 84
Discovery! (series) 27, 73, 114
Discovery Library (series) 193
Dive to the Coral Reefs [New En-
   gland Aquarium Books] 74
Dixon, Dougal 16, 17, 85, 114, 125,
   137, 159
Do You Know...? (series) 63
Docekal, Eileen M. 229
Dogsong 170

Dolan, Edward F. 28
Donnelly, Judy 206
Dorris, Michael 75
Dorros, Arthur 38, 114
Downer, Ann 94
Downriver 106
Downtown America (series) 181
Downwind 50
Dragonwings 29
Drake, Jane 216
Draw 50 Airplanes, Aircraft, and Spacecraft 28
Drip Drop: Water's Journey 39
Drought [World Disasters!] 37, 160, 194
Duane, Diane 63
Duffy, Trent 95
Dune [Land Shapes] 159
Dunphy, Madeline 169
Dust Bowl, The [World Disasters] 160
Dust Bowl: Disaster on the Plains, The [Spotlight on American History] 160
Dust for Dinner [I Can Read Book] 193
Dvorak, David 149
Dying Forests [Operation Earth] 125

Earliest Civilizations, The [The Illustrated History of the World] 182
Earliest Farmers and the First Cities, The [Cambridge Topic] 182
Early City Life [The Early Settler Life Series] 181
Early Farm Life [Early Settler Life] 192
Early Loggers and the Sawmill [The Early Settler Life Series] 124
Early River Travel [Americans on the Move] 106
Early Settler Life Series, The (series) 124, 181, 192
Earth [First Books—Planets] 17
Earth: A Day in the Life of a Planet 12
Earth: Our Planet in Space 17
Earth: The Ever-Changing Planet [Random House Library of Knowledge] 16, 137

Earth: The Incredible Recycling Machine 15, 28, 37, 228
Earth, The [Breakthroughs in Science] 15
Earth, The [Exploring Our World] 15
Earth, The [Life Nature Library] 17
Earth, The [Science Project Book] 17
Earth, The [Young Readers' Nature Library] 17
Earth Alert (series) 64, 216
Earth at Risk (series) 38, 204, 217
Earth Book for Kids: Activities to Heal the Environment 206, 229
Earth Calendar 17
Earth Care (series) 38, 204
Earth Day [On My Own] 229
Earth Day, Every Day [Adventures of Ranger Rick] 229
Earth Day U.S.A. 18, 230, 234
Earth in Action (series) 16, 62, 105, 137, 159
Earth Is Painted Green: A Garden of Poems About Our Planet, The 229
Earth Keepers (series) 115, 230
Earth Moves: Get There with Energy to Spare [We Can Save the Earth] 50
Earth Processes (series) 15, 16, 17, 64, 137, 138, 139
Earth Science [Science Fair] 17
Earth Science Library (series) 28, 63, 106, 137, 170
Earth, Sea & Sky 12
Earth Songs 229
Earth Watch (series) 37, 49, 83, 126, 169
Earthquake [World Disasters] 15
Earthquakes 16
Earthquakes: Looking for Answers [Earth Processes] 16
Earth's Vanishing Forests 114, 125
Earthwatch 18, 234
Earthwise (series) 50, 204, 216, 228
Earthwise: Earth's Energy [Earthwise] 50
Earthwise at Home [Earthwise] 204, 228
Earthwise at Play [Earthwise] 216, 228
Earthwise at School [Earthwise] 228
EarthWorks Group, The 15, 204, 228

Earthworms, Dirt, and Rotten Leaves: An Exploration in Ecology 17
Easy Menu Ethnic Cookbooks (series) 74
Easy-Read Geographic Activities (series) 16
Ebb, Fred 183
Eco-Heroes: Twelve Tales of Environmental Victory 230
Eco-Journey (series) 83, 104, 125, 137, 158
Ecology and Conservation [Gareth Stevens Information Library] 230
Ecology Watch (series) 94, 104, 114, 137, 148, 159, 168, 181
EcoZones (series) 84, 94, 114, 125, 149, 159, 169
Edge of the Sea, The 85
Egyptian Farmers [Beginning History] 192
Eldredge, Douglas 16
Electric Power Research Institute 51, 234
Electricity from Faraday to Solar Generators 50
Electricity Turns the World On! [Science in Action] 49
Elektra Nonesuch 70, 234
Elkington, John 204, 228
Ellis, Chris 38
Emerald Rim: Earth's Precious Rain Forests, The 116
Emergence of Man, The (series) 194
Enchantment of the World (series) 74, 168
Encyclopedia of the Animal World (series) 193
Encyclopedia of the Animal World: Mammals (series) 149
End Hunger Network 194, 234
Endangered Animals [New True Books] 216
Endangered Animals [Ranger Rick Books] 215
Endangered Animals (series) 62, 74, 94, 126, 149, 216
Endangered Forest Animals [Endangered Animals] 126
Endangered Grassland Animals [Endangered Animals] 149

Endangered Habitats [Our Fragile Planet] 114, 216
Endangered Island Animals [Endangered Animals] 74
Endangered Ocean Animals [Endangered Animals] 62
Endangered Peoples [Impact] 116, 160
Endangered Plants [First Books — Our Environment] 215
Endangered Savannah Animals [Endangered Animals] 149
Endangered Species [Earth Alert] 216
Endangered Species [Overview Series: Our Endangered Planet] 215
Endangered Species Coalition 218, 234
Endangered Wetland Animals [Endangered Animals] 94
Endangered Wildlife [World Issues] 215
Endangered Wildlife of the World 74, 216
Endangered World, The [Using and Understanding Maps] 216
Energy [New True Books] 49
Energy [Science Frontiers] 50
Energy [Science Through Art] 50
Energy (series) 192
Energy: Making It Work [Science in Action] 49
Energy Alternatives [Overview Series: Our Endangered Planet] 49
Energy and Growth [Fun with Science] 50
Energy Crisis, The [Opposing Viewpoints] 50
Energy Crisis, The [World Issues] 49
Energy Demands [Green Issues] 49
Energy from Oil and Gas [Facts About] 49
Energy from Wind and Water [Facts About] 27, 49
Energy Gap [Operation Earth] 49
Energy Resources [World's Resources] 50
Energy Supply A–Z [Environment Reference] 50
Energy Technology [Technology in Action] 50
Engel, Leonard 63, 75

Environment [Our Endangered Planet] 215, 228

Environment, The [American Issues] 230

Environment, The [Let's Investigate Science] 230

Environment, The [World Issues] 230

Environment Alert! (series) 115, 125, 137, 148, 159, 192, 205, 229

Environment Reference (series) 17, 50, 217

Environmental Action Coalition 29, 183, 206, 230, 234

Environmental America: The Northeastern States [American Scene] 28

Environmental Atlas (series) 216

Environmental Awareness: Air Pollution 27

Environmental Awareness: Water Pollution 37

Environmental Career Guide: Job Opportunities with the Earth in Mind, The 229

Environmental Defense Fund 18, 29, 116, 170, 230, 235

Environmental Disasters [The World's Disasters] 228

Environmental Diseases [First Books—Medicine and Diseases] 228

Environmental Experiments About Air [Science Experiments for Young People] 27

Environmental Experiments About Land [Science Experiments for Young People] 17, 206

Environmental Experiments About Water [Science Experiments for Young People] 39

Environmental Issues (series) 28, 50, 114, 230

Environmental Literacy: Everything You Need to Know About Saving the Planet 205

Environmental Literacy: The A-to-Z Guide 230

Environmentalist [Be an Expert] 229

Esbensen, Barbara Juster 106

Eskimo: The Inuit and Yupik People, The [New True Books] 169

Eskimo Boy: Life in an Inupiag Village 169

Eskimos: The Inuit of the Arctic [Original Peoples] 169

Eugene, Toni 125

Ever-Living Tree: The Life and Times of a Coast Redwood, The 126

Everglades 91

Everglades [National Parks] 94

Everglades, The [The American Wilderness] 95

Every Drop Counts: A Book About Water [Target Earth] 38

Every Kid's Guide to Saving the Earth 228

Expanding Deserts [Environment Alert!] 159

Expeditions of Amundsen, The [Exploration Through the Ages] 169

Experimental Cities 183, 235

Experiments That Explore Acid Rain [Investigate!] 28

Experiments That Explore Oil Spills [Investigate!] 39

Experiments That Explore the Greenhouse Effect [Investigate!] 28

Experiments with Air [New True Books] 28

Experiments with Heat [New True Books] 49

Experiments with Water [New True Books] 37

Exploration Through the Ages (series) 38, 169

Explore a Spooky Swamp [Books for Young Explorers] 95

Explore a Tropical Forest [National Geographic Action Book] 115

Explorer (series) 70

Exploring Deserts [Eco-Journey] 158

Exploring Energy Sources [Exploring Science] 50

Exploring Forests [Eco-Journey] 125

Exploring Humans and the Environment [Exploring Science] 230

Exploring Lakeshores [Eco-Journey] 104

Exploring Mountains [Eco-Journey] 137

Exploring Our Living Planet 73

Exploring Our World (series) 15, 105, 125, 137, 159

Exploring Science (series) 15, 50, 230

Exploring Seashores [Eco-Journey] 83
Exploring Soil and Rocks [Exploring
    Science] 15
Exploring the Great Swamp 94
Exploring the Seashore [Books for
    Young Explorers] 84
Exploring the Unknown (series) 217
Exploring Uses of Energy [Exploring
    Science] 50
Exploring Woodlands [Eco-Journey]
    125
Extinct (series) 217
Extinct Alphabet Book, The 217
Extinction [Earth at Risk] 217
Extinction A–Z [Environment Refer-
    ence] 217
Extinction Is Forever 217
Extinction of the Dinosaurs, The [Ex-
    ploring the Unknown] 217
Eye-Openers (series) 28
Eyewitness Books (series) 16, 62, 84,
    94, 105
Eyewitness Explorers (series) 84
Eyewitness Science: Electricity 49
Eyewitness Visual Dictionaries
    (series) 17

*Fabled Cities, Princes & Jinn from
    Arab Myths & Legends* 183
Facing the Future (series) 194
Facklam, Howard 137, 217
Facklam, Margery 137, 194, 215, 217
Facts About (series) 27, 49, 104, 124,
    137, 158, 159, 181, 192
Facts About the 50 States [First
    Books—American History] 125
Facts on (series) 50, 194, 206
*Facts on Domestic Waste and Indus-
    trial Pollutants* [Facts on] 206
Facts on File Children's Atlas, The
    137, 159
Facts on Fossil Fuels [Facts on] 50
Facts on Future Energy Possibilities
    [Facts on] 50
Facts on Nuclear Energy [Facts on]
    50
*Facts on Pesticides and Fertilizers in
    Farming* [Facts on] 194
Famine, Drought and Plagues
    [Natural Disasters] 159, 193

Famine in Africa [Issues] 160, 194
Famous First Facts 125, 169
Fantastic Flying Paper Toys 28
*Fantastic Painted Desert & the Phe-
    nomenal Petrified Forest, The* 160
Far North [Vanishing Cultures] 169
Farb, Peter 116, 126
Farewell to Shady Glade 217
Farm Aid 194, 235
Farm Animal Discovery Library
    (series) 193
Farm Animals 192
Farm Animals [New True Books] 192
Farm Animals Reform Movement
    194, 235
Farm Committee for Sustainable
    Agriculture 194, 235
Farm Machinery [Picture Library] 193
Farmer Boy 194
Farmer Through History, The [Jour-
    ney Through History] 192
Farmers [Facts About] 192
Farming 193
Farming [New True Books] 192
Farming [Ways of Life] 193
Farming and the Environment [Con-
    serving Our World] 192
Farming and the Environment [En-
    vironment Alert!] 192
Farming Technology [Technology in
    Action] 192
*Farming the Land: Modern Farmers
    and Their Machines* [Photo Books]
    192
Farming Today Yesterday's Way
    [Photo Books] 192
Farms [Great Places to Visit] 193
Farris, John 160
Feeding the World [First Starts] 193
Feeding the World [Today's World]
    192
Feris, Jeri 170
Few, Roger 105, 115, 149, 216
Fiarotta, Noel 205
Fiarotta, Phyllis 205
Field Guide to Geology, The 17, 106,
    139
Fielder, Erica 183
*50 Simple Things Kids Can Do to
    Save the Earth* 15, 204, 228
Finding-Out Books (series) 228

Fine, John Christopher 63
Fire in the Valley [Stories of the States] 39
Fire Mountains: The Story of the Cascade Volcanoes, The [Interpreting the Great Outdoors] 138
First Books (series) 170, 181
First Books—American History (series) 125
First Books—Examining the Past (series) 63
First Books—Famous Rivers of the World (series) 104
First Books—Indians of the Americas (series) 94, 150, 160
First Books—Medicine and Diseases (series) 228
First Books—Our Environment (series) 94, 114, 215, 217
First Books—Planets (series) 17
First Books—Space Science and First Flights (series) 28
First Books—War (series) 106
First Facts (series) 27
First Farmers, The [The Emergence of Man] 194
First Flight: The Story of the Wright Brothers, The [First Books—Space Science and First Flights] 28
First Look (series) 16, 27, 48, 104, 125, 138
First Look at Rivers [First Look] 104
First Look at Using Energy [First Look] 48
First Look in the Air [First Look] 27
First Look in the Forest [First Look] 125
First Look Under the Ground [First Look] 16
First Starts (series) 63, 115, 138, 160, 169, 193, 204, 216, 229
Fischetto, Laura 115
Fish [Eyewitness Books] 62
Flaherty, Steven 75
Fleming, Ronald Lee 182
Flight [Science Through Art] 28
Flight and Flying Machines [See & Explore Library] 28
Flint, David 37, 75, 150
Flood [World Disasters!] 37, 105
Florian, Douglas 84

Flying Start Science (series) 37
Focus on—Science (series) 126
Fodors . . . Europe's Great Cities 182
Follow the Water from Brook to Ocean [Trophy Let's-Read-and-Find-Out Stage 2] 38
Food [Discovering Art] 194
Food and Farming [Energy] 192
Food and Farming [Green Issues] 194
Food and Farming [Young Geographer] 192
Food and Fasting [Comparing Religions] 194
Food and Water: Threats, Shortages and Solutions [Our Fragile Planet] 37, 193
Food Cycle, The [Nature Cycles] 193
Food Energy [Science Through Cookery] 50
Food Facts (series) 193
Food for the World [Discovering Science] 194
Food for the World [Facing the Future] 194
Food or Famine? [World Issues] 192
Food Resources [World's Resources] 194
Food We Eat, The [We Can Save the Earth] 193
Foods We Eat (series) 192
Footprints in the Swamp 95
For the Love of Our Earth 229
Forces and Energy [Project Science] 50
Foreman, Michael 84
Forest 126
Forest, The [Life Nature Library] 116, 126
Forest Ecosystem Rescue Network 116, 127, 235
Forest Is Reborn, A 126
Forest Life [Look Closer] 126
Forest Year, A 125
Forests [Facts About] 124
Forests [Franklin Watts Picture Atlas] 125
Forsyth, Adrian 114
Fosse, Bob 183
Fossil Factory, The 16
Fossil Fuels [World About Us] 50

Fossils Tell of Long Ago [Let's Read-and-Find-Out] 15
Foster, Joanna 206
Foster, Sally 75
Foster, Stephen 106
4-H Program and Youth Development 194, 235
Fowler, Allan 38
Foxfire: A Play Based on Materials from the Foxfire Books 138
Fradin, Dennis 49, 192
Fragile Mountains [Environment Alert!] 137
Franklin Watts Picture Atlas (series) 125, 137, 148, 159
Franklin Watts Science World (series) 16
Freedman, Russell 148
Freshet, Berniece 95
Freshwater Foundation, The 39, 106, 235
Friedman, Judi 217
Friends in Danger (series) 216
Friends of the Earth 18, 29, 39, 64, 85, 116, 160, 170, 230, 235
Friends of the Everglades 96, 235
Friends of the River Foundation 106, 235
From Cacao Bean to Chocolate [Start to Finish] 114
From Grain to Bread [Start to Finish] 149, 193
From Grass to Butter [Start to Finish] 193
From Oil to Gasoline [Start to Finish] 50
From Ore to Spoon [Start to Finish] 17
From Rubber Tree to Tire [Start to Finish] 114
From Sand to Glass [Start to Finish] 159
From Sea to Salt [Start to Finish] 63
From Sea to Shining Sea (series) 74
From Swamp to Coal [Start to Finish] 95
From Tree to Table [Start to Finish] 126
From Wood to Paper [Start to Finish] 126
Frontiers of America (series) 64

Frozen Land [Vanishing Cultures] 170
Fuel and Energy [Information Library] 49
Fuel and Energy [Read About Science] 48
Fueling the Future [Saving Planet Earth] 50
Fun with Science (series) 50, 126
Future Energy and Resources [Today's World] 50
Future Farmers of America 194
Future Sources [World About Us] 50
Future World of Agriculture, The [Walt Disney World Epcot Center Book] 192
Fyson, Nance Lui 192

Galápagos [National Parks] 73
Gallant, Roy A. 114, 125, 170, 181
Gallencamp, Charles 116
Ganeri, Anita 64, 94, 95, 104, 126
Ganges Delta and Its People, The [People and Places] 106
Garbage [Overview Series: Our Endangered Planet] 204
Garbage! The Trashiest Book You'll Ever Read 205
Garbage! Where It Comes from, Where It Goes [Nova Books] 206
Gardens from Garbage: How to Grow Plants from Recycled Kitchen Scraps 206
Gardiner, Brian 49, 205
Gareth Stevens Information Library (series) 230
Gas [Resources] 49
Gas Research Institute 51, 235
Gates, Richard 228
Gay, Kathlyn 181
Geiger, John 170
Gelbart, Larry 183
Gelman, Rita Golden 73
Gentle Desert: Exploring an Ecosystem, The 159
Geology: Rocks, Minerals and Fossils [Franklin Watts Science World] 16
George, Jean Craighead 115, 126, 138, 149, 159, 169, 170
George, Lindsey Barrett 95

George, William T. 95
Georges, D. V. 169
Geothermal Education Office 51, 235
Geothermal Energy [Alternative Energy] 49
Geraghty, Paul 216
Giant Sequoia and Kings Canyon National Parks, The 126
Giants in the Land 126
Gibb, Christopher 192
Gibbons, Gail 28, 74, 84, 182, 193, 205
Gibson, Michael 49
Gilliland, Judith Heide 105, 115
Gilman, Phoebe 205
Gittins, Anne 75
Glaciers [New True Books] 169
Glaciers: Ice on the Move [Earth Watch] 169
Glaciers and Ice Caps [Earth Science Library] 170
Glass, Paul 138
Glimmerveen, Ulco 169
Global Cities [Project Eco-City] 182
Global Coral Reef Alliance 75, 235
Global ReLeaf Through Learning 116, 127, 183, 235
Global Villages (series) 116
Global Warming [Our Fragile Planet] 27
Global Warming: Assessing the Greenhouse Threat 27
Glorious Flight: Across the Channel with Louis Bleriot, The 28
Godall, John S. 84
Godman, Arthur 50
Gods & Heroes from Viking Mythology [World Mythologies] 75
Going for Oysters 74
Going Green: A Kid's Handbook to Saving the Planet 204, 228
Golden Guides (series) 16, 83, 84, 94, 125
Gone Forever (series) 217
Gonzalez, Christina 138
Goodall, John S. 182
Goodman, Billy 15, 75, 116, 137, 182, 206, 228
Gore, Sheila 94
Gove, Doris 229

Gowell, Elizabeth Tayntor 85
Grace, Theresa 95
Graff, Nancy Price 194
Graham, Ada 160
Graham, Frank 160
Grandfather's Dream 229
Granfield, Linda 104
Grass Songs: Poems 150
Grasshopper Summer 150
Grassland Animals [Tell Me About It] 148
Grassland Heritage Foundation 150, 235
Grasslands 149
Grasslands [Ecology Watch] 148
Grasslands [Franklin Watts Picture Atlas] 148
Grasslands [Habitats of the World] 148
Grasslands [The Living World] 148
Grasslands [Nature Search] 150
Grasslands [Our World] 148
Grasslands and Deserts [Vanishing Animal Pop-Ups] 149
Grasslands and Tundra [Planet Earth] 150
Gray Wolf, Red Wolf 217
Great Barrier Reef: A Living Laboratory, The [Discovery!] 73
Great Cities (series) 181
Great Disasters (series) 50
Great Dismal: America's Scariest Swamp, The 96
Great Journies (series) 169, 170
Great Kapok Tree, The 115
Great Lakes, The [New True Books] 105
Great Lakes United 106, 235
Great Newspaper Crafts 205
Great Places to Visit (series) 193
Great Plains Agricultural Council 150, 235
Great Red River Raft, The 106
Greek Myths: Tales of the Gods, Heroes and Heroines 17
Green Issues (series) 16, 49, 192, 194, 206, 217, 229
Green Planet Rescue: Saving the Earth's Endangered Plants [Cincinnati Zoo Books] 217
Green World (series) 114, 125, 160

Greenaway, Theresa 94, 125, 160
Greenburg, Judith E. 16, 63, 115
Greene, Carol 28, 38, 216, 229
Greenhouse Crisis Foundation 29, 235
Greenhouse Effect, The [New True Books] 28
Greenhouse Effect: Life on a Warmer Planet, The [Discovery!] 27, 114
Greening the City Streets: The Story of Community Gardens 183
Greenland [Enchantment of the World] 168
Greenpeace U.S.A. 64, 170, 235
Greenway, Shirley 125
Greenwillow Read-Alone (series) 37
Grolier World Encyclopedia of Endangered Species, The 216
Gross, Ruth Belov 193
Groundwater [Our Endangered Planet] 37
Groves, Seli 206
Growing Up Masai 149
Growing Up with Science 27
Guiberson, Brenda Z. 63, 95
Guinness Book of World Records, The 16, 84, 105, 115, 137, 159
Gunby, Lise 192
Gunzi, Christiane 16, 28, 39, 50, 84

Habitats: Making Homes for Animals and Plants 217
Habitats: Saving Wild Places [Better Earth] 217
Habitats: Where the Wild Things Live 217
Habitats and Environments [More Science in Action] 217, 230
Habitats of the World (series) 115, 137, 148, 159
Hacker, Randi 217
Hackwell, W. John 170
Hadingham, Evan 206
Hadingham, Janet 206
Haines, Gail B. 50
Haley, Gail E. 138
Hallinan, P. K. 229
Hallstead, William F. 170
Halpern, Robert R. 217
Hamilton, Jean 114

Hammerstein, Oscar 75, 106, 194
Handelman, Judith F. 206
Hands on Science (series) 28, 37, 39, 116
Hansen, Judith 83
Hare, Tony 27, 28, 37, 62, 114, 204, 206, 215, 230
Hargreaves, Pat 64
Hargrove, Jim 138
Harlow, Rose 50, 126
Harris, Colin 230
Harris, Geraldine 94
Harrison, Ted 169
Hartford, John 105
Harvey, Brett 149
Hauptmann, William 106
Hausherr, Rosemarie 193
Havill, Juanita 216
Hawaii Volcanoes National Park 75, 139, 235
Hawke, Sherryl Davis 181
Hawkes, Nigel 192, 204
Hazardous Waste [Saving Planet Earth] 205
Heart of the Forest 111
Heart of the Wood, The 125
Hecht, Jeff 83, 104
Heinrichs, Susan 63
Henderson, Kathy 105
Herda, D. J. 228, 230
Here Comes the Recycling Truck! 205
Here Is the Arctic Winter 169
Hereniko, Patricia 73
Hereniko, Vilsoni 73
Hester, Nigel 83, 94, 105, 125, 181
Hewitt, Garnet 170
Hey! Get Off Our Train 216
Heyman, LeRoy 28
Hiawatha 105
Hickman, Pamela M. 217
Hidden Life (series) 94, 125, 159
Hidden Life of the Desert, The [Hidden Life] 159
Hidden Life of the Forest, The [Hidden Life] 125
Hidden Life of the Pond, The [Hidden Life] 94
Hidetomo, Oda 83
High Cities of the Andes 139
High Mountain Challenge: A Guide for Young Mountaineers 138

Higham, Charles 182
Hilton, Suzzanne 183
Himalaya [Vanishing Cultures] 138
Hintz, Martin 114
Hirschi, Ron 85, 94, 95, 105, 126, 138, 150
Hiscock, Bruce 168
History of the World (series) 158, 181
Hoban, Russell 50
Hobbs, Will 106
Hoff, Mary 37, 62, 105, 215
Hogan, Paula 115, 137, 159
Holiday Handbook: Activities for Celebrations Every Season of the Year and More, The 125
Holling, Holling Clancy 85, 106, 126
Holmes, Anita 228
Homes in Cold Places [Houses and Homes] 168
Homes in Hot Places [Houses and Homes] 114, 159
Homes in the Future [Houses and Homes] 49, 181
Honor the Earth Powwow: Songs of the Great Lakes Indians 101
Horton, Casey 148
Horwitz, Elinor Lander 138
Hotel Boy 182
Houghton, Graham 49, 204
House for Hermit Crab, A 84
Household Hazardous Waste Project 206, 235
Houses and Homes (series) 49, 114, 159, 168, 181
How and Why Books (series) 229
How and Why Wonder Book of the Environment and You [How and Why Books] 229
How Did We Find Out About . . . ? (series) 27, 50
How Did We Find Out About the Atmosphere? [How Did We Find Out About . . . ?] 27
How Do Big Ships Float? [Ask Isaac Asimov] 38
How Energy Is Made 48
How Nature Works 228
How on Earth Do We Recycle Glass? 206

How Our Bodies Work (series) 27
How Safe Is Our Food Supply? [Impact] 194
How the Earth Works [Science in Our World] 15, 137
How the Sea Began 74
How the World Works (series) 38, 49
How They Lived (series) 138, 148, 149
How They Lived in Cities Long Ago 182
How to Be an Ocean Scientist in Your Own Home 64
How to Dig a Hole to the Other Side of the World 17
How's the Weather? (series) 27
Hoyt, Erich 217
Huff, Barbara 183
Hughs, Jill 159, 168
Hughs, Susan 181
Human Body, The (series) 27
Humane Farming Association, The 194, 235
Humble, Richard 169
Humphrey, Kathryn Long 63
Hunter, The 216
Huntley, Beth 115
Hyden, Tom 138

I Am Leaper 160
I Can Read Book (series) 193
I Can Save the Earth: A Kid's Handbook for Keeping the Earth Healthy and Green 228
I Draw, I Paint (series) 38
I Know America (series) 105, 126
I Live in a City [In My World] 181
Ice Age, The [New True Books] 170
Ice Ages, The [First Books] 170
Ice Caps and Glaciers: Projects with Geography, The 170
Icebergs and Glaciers 38, 169
Igloo, The 169
Illustrated History of the World, The (series) 182
Imagine Living Here (series) 115, 138, 159, 169, 182
Impact (series) 95, 116, 160, 181, 193, 194, 206
In My World (series) 181

In Peril (series) 75, 217
In the Desert [Living Spaces] 160
In the Mountains [Living Spaces] 137
In the Polar Regions [Living Spaces] 170
In the Soil [Use Your Eyes] 17
In the Town [Use Your Eyes] 182
In the Village of the Elephants 149
In the Woods [Use Your Eyes] 126
Inca Civilization [World Heritage] 138
Inca Farmer, An [How They Lived] 138
Incredible Facts About the Ocean: Volumes 1,2,3,4 [Ocean World Library] 64
Indians of the Andes [Original Peoples] 139
Information Library (series) 49
Information Please Almanac, The 169
Information Please Environmental Almanac, The 49, 95, 105, 115, 125, 149, 169, 182, 205
Information Please Kids Almanac, The 205
Ingrams, Doreen 160
INKISHU: Myths and Legends of the Maasai 150
Inner City Mother Goose, The 183
Inside-Outside Book of London, The 182
Institute of Andean Studies 139, 235
Institute of Scrap Recycling Industries 206, 235
International Erosion Control Association 18, 235
International Mountain Society 139, 235
International Water Resources Association 39, 235
Interpreting the Great Outdoors (series) 138
Into the Woods 126
Into the Woods (sound recording) 126
Inuit [Threatened Cultures] 168
Inunguaki: The Little Greenlander 169
Inventor Through History, The [Journey Through History] 49
Investigate! (series) 28, 39, 50
Irvine, Georgeanne 217

Island [The Story of the Earth] 73
Island Boy 74
Island of the Blue Dolphins 75
Islands 73
Islands and Their Mysteries 73
Islands in the Sea Discovery Library (series) 74
Islands of the Pacific Rim and Their People [People and Places] 75
Issues (series) 160, 194
Issues Atlases (series) 95, 115, 159, 193, 216, 229
Issues in Focus (series) 192
Issues Update (series) 204
It Could Still Be Water [Rookie Read-About Science] 38
Izaak Walton League of America, The 39, 235, 236, 237

Jackman, Wayne 49
Jacobs, Linda 49
Jacobs, Una 17
Jacobsen, Karen 192
James, Alan 114, 159, 168
James, Barbara 168, 183, 204
James, Diane 193
James, Elizabeth 125
James, J. Alison 160
James, Simon 126
Jarman, Cathy 149
Jaspersohn, William 63
Jauck, Andrea 74
Jennings, Terry 15, 83, 105, 125, 137, 159
Jenson, Anthony 63
Johnson, Annabel 160
Johnson, Jean 206
Johnson, Jinny 170
Johnson, Rebecca L. 27, 73, 114
Johnson, Sylvia A. 73, 83, 138, 150, 194
Johnston, Ginny 95
Johnston, Tom 27, 49
Johnstone, Hugh 50, 206
Joseph, Lynn 74
Josepha: A Prairie Boy's Story 149
Journey Through a Tropical Jungle 114
Journey Through History (series) 37, 49, 62, 192

*Journey to the Center of the Earth,
A* 17
Journey to the North Pole, The [Great
Journies] 170
Julie 170
Julie of the Wolves 170
Jungle 111
Jungle Book 116
Jungle Book, The (sound recording)
115
*Jungle Gym: A Monkey's Eye View of
the World's Jungles, Yesterday, To-
day, and Tomorrow?* 116
Jungle Is My Home, The 115
*Jungle Rescue: Saving the New World
Tropical Rain Forest* 114
Jungles (Catchpole) 114
Jungles (Dixon) 114
Jungles [A Closer Look at] 114
Jungles [Last Frontiers for Mankind]
114
Jungles [The Living World] 114
*Jungles and Forests: Projects with
Geography* [Hands on Science]
116
Jungles and People [Nature's Land-
scapes] 114
Junior Library of Ecology, The
(series) 27, 62, 104, 125, 181
Just a Dream 230
Just for a Day Books (series) 63

Kahl, Jonathan D. 27
Kalahari Bushmen [Threatened Cul-
tures] 160
Kalbacken, Joan 204
Kalman, Bobbie 39, 168, 181, 204
Kane, Joseph Nathan 125, 169
Kaufman, Curt 182
Kaufman, Gita 182
Kaufman, Jackie 217
Kaufman, Les 39
Keeler, Barbara 49
Keep America Beautiful 230, 235
*Keepers of the Animals: Native Amer-
ican Stories and Wildlife Activities
for Children* 95
Keeping the Air Clean [The Junior
Library of Ecology] 27
Keller, Holly 229

Kelly, Walt 95
Kendall, Russ 169
Kern, Jerome 106
Kerr, Jim 192
Kerrod, Robin 17, 27, 50, 194, 230
Khanduri, Kamini 168
Kidron, Michael 27, 38, 63, 159
Kids' EarthWorks Group, The 18,
230, 235
Kids for Saving the Earth 183, 230,
235
*Kid's Guide to How to Save the
Planet, A* 206, 228
Kimball, Debi 206
King, John 159
Kipling, Rudyard 116
Knapp, Brian 15, 37, 83, 105, 114,
138, 148, 159, 160, 194
Koch, Frances K. 64
Kovacs, Deborah 105
Kramer, S. A. 138
Kramer, Sydelle 206
Kricher, John C. 85
Krull, Kathleen 183
Krupinski, Loretta 74
Kudlinsky, Kathleen V. 96, 126
Kurelek, William 150

Lafferty, Peter 49
Lake [Land Shapes] 105
Lake [The Story of the Earth]
104
Lambert, David 17, 64, 73, 83,
94, 106, 139, 148, 168, 228, 230
Lambert, Mark 27, 28, 39, 49, 50,
181, 192
Lampton, Christopher 64, 75
Land Animals [Our Endangered
Planet] 215
Land Institute, The 150, 235
Land Masses [Easy-Read Geographic
Activities] 16
Land Shapes (series) 83, 105, 159
Land Under the Sea 73
Land Use A–Z [Environment Refer-
ence] 17
Land Use and Abuse [Science, Tech-
nology & Society] 230
Land We Live In, The [We Can Save
the Earth] 17

Landau, Elaine 114, 137, 150, 215
Landforms in the U.S.A. (series) 83
Lands and Peoples 74, 105, 115, 149,
   159, 193
Langley, Andrew 95, 150
Lapine, James 126
Lapps: Reindeer Herders of Lapland
   [Original Peoples] 168
Large Plant-Eaters, The [Encyclopedia
   of the Animal World: Mammals]
   149
Lasky, Kathryn 73, 139
Last Frontiers for Mankind (series)
   62, 114, 137, 159, 169
Latin American and Caribbean Crafts
   [Crafts Around the World] 74
Lauber, Patricia 16, 17, 126, 137
Lavies, Bianca 95, 96, 126, 206
Law, Felicia 75
Lawler, Laurie 150
Laycock, George 17, 73, 94
Lazier, Christine 85
Lazo, Caroline Evensen 216
Lee, Martin 94
Lee, Sally 206
Lefkowitz, R. J. 228
Leggett, Dennis 37, 62, 105, 192, 228
Leggett, Jeremy 27, 37, 49, 62, 105,
   125, 192, 204, 228
Leinwand, Gerald 230
L'Engle, Madeleine 170
Leonard, Jonathan Norton 194
Leone, Bruna 50
Leopold, Luna B. 39, 106
Lepthien, Emilie U. 168, 204, 217
Lerner, Carol 125, 148, 159
Let's Explore the River [Books for
   Young Explorers] 105
Let's Investigate S ience (series) 230
Let's Read-and-Find-Out Science
   (series) 84
Let's Take a Trip (series) 126, 138
Let's Talk About (series) 193
Let's Visit Places and Peoples of the
   World (series) 75
Let's-Read-and-Find-Out (series) 15
Let's-Read-and-Find-Out Science
   (series) 205
*Letting Off Steam: The Story of Geo-
   thermal Energy* [Earth Watch] 49
Letting Swift River Go 106

Lewington, Anna 114, 115
Lewis, Naomi 160
Ley, Willey 170
Library of Congress (series) 150
Life at the Seashore 85
Life in (series) 62, 114, 137, 158, 168
Life in a Tidal Pool 84
Life in the Deserts [Life in] 158
Life in the Mountains [Life in] 137
Life in the Oceans [Life in] 62
Life in the Oceans [Planet Earth] 63
Life in the Polar Lands [Life in] 168
Life in the Polar Regions 169
Life in the Rainforests [Life in] 114
Life Nature Library (series) 17, 63,
   75, 116, 126, 139, 170
Life on a Coral Reef 74
Life on Land [Our Endangered
   Planet] 215
Life Science Library (series) 39, 106
Lighter Look, A (series) 204
Lily Pad Pond 95
Lindblad, Lisa 149
Linsley, Leslie 28
Lion and the Savannah, The [Ani-
   mals and Their Ecosystems] 149
Liptak, Karen 94, 116, 160, 217
Lisle, Janet Taylor 126
Little House on the Prairie 150
Living Desert, The [The Living
   World] 160
Living Forest, The [Living World]
   126
*Living in the Tropics: A Cultural
   Geography* 114
Living Music Records 59, 225, 235
Living Ocean, The [The Living
   World] 62
Living on Islands [Cultural Geog-
   raphy] 75
Living Pond, The [Watching Nature]
   94
Living River, The [Watching Nature]
   105
Living Seashore, The [Watching
   Nature] 83
Living Spaces (series) 137, 160, 170
Living Town, The [Watching Nature]
   181
*Living Treasure: Saving Earth's
   Threatened Biodiversity* 216

Living Tree, The [Watching Nature] 125

Living World, The (series) 62, 114, 126, 138, 148, 158, 160

Livingston, Myra Cohen 229

Llewelyn, Claire 27

Lobstein, Tim 194

Locker, Thomas 105

Logging and Lumbering 124

Logging Machines in the Forest 125

London, Jonathan 217

Long Ago Lake: A Child's Book of Nature Lore and Crafts, The 126

Longfellow, Henry Wadsworth 105

Look Closer (series) 16, 75, 84, 94, 105, 115, 126, 149, 159

Looking at Islands (series) 74

Loon Lake 105

Loons on Mirror Lake 102

Lopez, Barry 229

Lorbiecki, Marybeth 204, 216, 228

Lord, Suzanne 205

Lost Cities [First Books] 181

Lost Lake, The 105

Lost Wild America: The Story of Our Extinct and Vanishing Wildlife 217

Lostman's River 95

Lots of Rot 205

Lourie, Peter 116

Love, Ann 216

Lowery, Linda 204, 216, 228, 229

Lucas, Eileen 27, 37, 49

Lungs and Breathing, The [How Our Bodies Work] 27

Lungs and Breathing, The [The Human Body] 27

Lye, Keith 17, 83, 137, 138, 159, 168

Lynn, Sara 193

McCall, Edith 64

Macaulay, David 183

McCauley, Jane R. 105, 126

McCay, J. J. 194

McCloskey, Robert 74

McClung, Robert M. 96, 217

McConnell, Anita 16, 64, 73, 83

McCormick, Maxine 73

MacDonald, Fiona 181

MacDonald, Robert 75

McFarland, Cynthia 192

McGovern, Ann 74

McGrath, Susan 217

McGugan, Jim 149

McHugh, Christopher 38, 182, 194

Mackie, Dan 62

McKie, Robin 50

MacLachlan, Patricia 150

McLaughlin, Molly 17

McLeish, Ewan 159

McMillan, Bruce 85, 217

McNeese, Tim 106

McNulty, Faith 17

McWilliams, Karen 63

Madden, Margaret L. 230

Magic Purse, The 95

Magic School Bus (series) 16, 38, 63

Magic School Bus at the Water Works, The [Magic School Bus] 38

Magic School Bus Inside the Earth, The [Magic School Bus] 16

Magic School Bus on the Ocean Floor, The [Magic School Bus] 63

Magley, Beverly 138

Mail Preference Services, Direct Marketing Association 206, 235

Malkuri: Traditional Music of the Andes 134

Mallory, Kenneth 116

Malnig, Anita 83

Man-Made Disasters (series) 29

Manatees [New True Books] 217

Manci, William E. 192

Mangrove Wilderness: Nature's Nursery 96

Margery Stoneman Douglas: Guardian of the Everglades 96

Margolies, Barbara A. 149

Mariculture: Farming the Fruits of the Sea [New England Aquarium Books] 64

Mariner, Tom 16, 62, 105, 137, 159

Markham, Adam 230

Markl, Julia 75

Markle, Sandra 16, 50, 137

Marsh, Carole 96, 116, 126, 160

Marshes and Swamps [New True Books] 94

Martin, Ana 17

Martin, James 64

Maruska, Edward J. 96

Masey, Mary Lou 150

Mason, Helen 85
Mason, John 50
Matthews, Rupert 169
Mattson, Mark 27, 95, 105, 169, 205, 229
Mattson, Robert A. 62
Maxwell, Roxie 182
May, Robin 148, 149
Mayle, Peter 216
Maynard, Thane 216
Mbugua, Kioi wa 150
Meadow [Look Closer] 149
Meat [Foods We Eat] 192
Mebane, Robert C. 17, 28, 39, 206
Mediterranean and Its People, The [People and Places] 75
Mellett, Peter 50
Mermaid Tales from Around the World 64
Merriam, Eve 183
Meyer, Carolyn 116
Meyerson, A. Lee 64
Middleton, Nick 49, 95, 115, 159, 193, 216, 229
Migrant Farm Workers [Impact] 193
Miles, Betty 206, 229
Milkins, Colin S. 94
Millbrook Arts Library (series) 229
Millea, Nicholas 183
Miller, Christina G. 28, 84, 114
Miller, Jane 193
Miller, Roger 106
Milne, A. A. 28
Milne, Lorus J. 17, 96, 139
Milne, Margery 17, 96, 139
Milner, Cedric 160
Mineral Resources [World's Resources] 17
Minn of the Mississippi 106
Mitgutsch, Ali 17, 50, 63, 95, 114, 126, 149, 159, 193
Moeri, Louise 50
Mojave 160
Month in the Brazilian Rainforest, A 111
Moon of the Mountain Lions, The [Thirteen Moons] 138
Moonlight on the River 105
Moore, Randy 160
Moran, Tom 106

More Power to You! [How the World Works] 49
More Science in Action (series) 217, 230
Morgan, Gareth 50, 126
Morgan, Gillian 114
Morgan, Patricia G. 138
Morning Girl 75
Morris, Neil 115
Morris, Ting 115
Morrison, Gordon 85
Morrison, Marion 116, 138, 139
Mosques and Minerets 160
Mountain [The Story of the Earth] 137
Mountain Adventure, A [Let's Take a Trip] 138
Mountain Climbing [Superwheels and Thrill Sports] 138
Mountain Jack Tales 138
Mountain Music of Peru 134
Mountain People, Mountain Crafts 138
Mountain Stream 102
Mountaineers 139, 235
Mountains (Brandt) 137
Mountains (Simon) 138
Mountains [Earth in Action] 137
Mountains [Earth Science Library] 137
Mountains [Ecology Watch] 137
Mountains [Exploring Our World] 137
Mountains [Facts About] 137
Mountains [First Look] 138
Mountains [First Starts] 138
Mountains [Franklin Watts Picture Atlas] 137
Mountains [Habitats of the World] 137
Mountains [Last Frontiers for Mankind] 137
Mountains [The Living World] 138
Mountains [New True Books] 137
Mountains [Our World] 137
Mountains [Picture Library] 137
Mountains, The [Life Nature Library] 139
Mountains and Earth Movements [Planet Earth] 137
Mountains and People [Nature's Landscapes] 138

Mountains and Volcanoes [Young Discoverers] 138
Moving Continents: Our Changing Earth [Earth Processes] 15, 137
Müller, Jorg 182
Multicultural Cookbook for Students, The 75
Multicultural Portrait of Life in the Cities, A [Perspectives] 182
Murphy, Wendy 192
Mutel, Cornelia F. 114
My First Green Book 229
My Mama's Little Ranch on the Pampas 149
My Prairie Year 149
My Side of the Mouuntain 138
My Sister Sif 75
Mysteries of the Unknown (series) 137
Mystery of, The... (series) 16, 138
Mystery of the Ancient Maya, The 116
Mystery of the Bog Forest 96

Nadler, Ellis 206, 230
Nardo, Don 217
National Arbor Day Foundation 127, 235
National Audubon Society 85, 96, 127, 218, 235
National Coalition Against the Misuse of Pesticides 231, 235
National Coalition for Marine Conservation 64, 236
National Environmental Development Association/Resource Conservation and Recovery Act Project 206, 236
National FFA Organization 194, 236
National Geographic Action Book (series) 115
National Geographic Society 160, 170, 218, 236
National Grange 194, 236
National Institute for Urban Wildlife, The 183, 236
National Parks (series) 17, 73, 94, 149
National Parks and Conservation Association 127, 139, 218, 236
National Recycling Coalition 206, 236

National Speleological Society 18, 236
National Wildlife Federation 85, 96, 127, 150, 183, 218, 234, 236
National Wildlife Federation Staff 95
Nations, James D. 114
Native Grasslands [Circle of Life] 149
Natural Disasters (series) 159, 193
Natural Disasters [The World's Disasters] 17
Natural Fire: Its Ecology in Forests 125
Natural Resources [Young Geographer] 50
Natural Resources Defense Council 29, 39, 51, 85, 127, 170, 236
Natural Science (series) 73, 83, 150, 194
Natural Wonders and Disasters [Planet Earth] 15, 75, 137
Naturalist [Be an Expert] 229
Nature Close-Ups (series) 83
Nature Company, The 225
Nature Company Catalog, The 236
Nature Conservancy, The 96, 127, 150, 218, 236
Nature Cycles (series) 193
Nature Detective (series) 95
Nature Detective: How to Solve Outdoor Mysteries 229
Nature in Action (series) 62, 84
Nature in Art [Millbrook Arts Library] 229
Nature Library (series) 75, 83
Nature Recordings 12, 59, 69, 91, 102, 111, 121, 155, 225, 236
Nature Search (series) 95, 150
Nature Study Book (series) 95
Nature Watch (series) 62, 83, 216
Nature's Children (series) 149
Nature's Disasters (series) 137
Nature's Hidden World (series) 148
Nature's Landscapes (series) 104, 114, 138, 158
Near the Sea: A Portfolio of Paintings 74, 84
New Book of Knowledge, The 38
New Book of Popular Science, The 49, 95, 169, 193
New England Aquarium Books (series) 39, 64, 73, 74, 85

New England Aquarium—Endangered
  Habitats Books (series) 94, 116
New Mexico People and Energy Col-
  lective 50
*New Providence: A Changing City-
  scape* 182
New State of the World Atlas, The 27,
  38, 63, 159
New True Books (series) 16, 27, 28,
  37, 49, 62, 63, 94, 104, 105, 137,
  149, 160, 169, 170, 192, 204, 216,
  217, 228
Newton, David E. 17
Newton, James R. 126, 159
Night and Day in the Desert, A 158
*Night Bird: A Story of the Seminole
  Indians* [Once Upon America] 96
*Night Reef: Dusk to Dawn on a Coral
  Reef* [New England Aquarium
  Books] 73
Nile, Richard 159
Niles, Gregory 16
*1993 Earth Journal: Environmental
  Almanac and Resource Directory*
  229
*1993 Information Please Environmen-
  tal Almanac, The* 229
Nixon, Hershell H. 73
Nixon, Jean Lowery 73
Nomads [Facts About] 159
Norman, Lilith 17
Northern Alphabet: A Is for Arctic, A
  169
Nottridge, Rhoda 62
Nova Books (series) 206
Nuclear Energy [New True Books] 49
*Nuclear Energy: Troubled Past, Uncer-
  tain Future* [Science for Survival]
  49
Nuclear Energy Information Service
  51, 236
Nuclear Waste [World About Us] 205
Nuclear Waste Disposal [Save Our
  Earth] 206

Ocean, The [Earth Alert] 64
Ocean Dreams 59
Ocean Moods 59
Ocean World [Young Readers' Nature
  Library] 62

Ocean World Library (series) 64
Ocean World of Jacques Cousteau,
  The (series) 64
Oceanic Society, The 39, 64, 75, 236
Oceans 62
Oceans [Earth in Action] 62
Oceans [Earth Science Library] 63
Oceans [First Starts] 63
Oceans [Last Frontiers for Mankind]
  62
Oceans [New True Books] 62
Oceans [Our Endangered Planet] 62
Oceans [Strange and Amazing
  Worlds] 62
Oceans and Arctic [Vanishing Animals
  Pop-Ups] 170
*Oceans Atlas: A Pictorial Atlas of the
  World's Oceans, The* 64
Oceans in Peril 63
O'Connor, Karen 204
O'Dell, Scott 75, 85, 170
Oil [Resources] 49
Oil Spill! [Let's-Read-and-Find-Out
  Science] 84
Oil Spills [New True Books] 63
Oil Spills [Saving Planet Earth] 37,
  48, 62
Okefenokee Swamp, The [The Ameri-
  can Wilderness] 96
Oklahoma! (sound recording) 194
Oklahoma! A Musical Play 194
Olbalbal: A Day in Masailand 149
Old Farmer's Almanac, The 193
Olesky, Walter 49
Oliphant, Margaret 182
On My Own (series) 125, 229
*On the Brink of Extinction: The
  California Condor* 216
On the Farm [Use Your Eyes] 193
On the River ABC 105
On the Seashore [Use Your Eyes]
  84
Once on This Island (sound record-
  ing) 75
Once on This Island: A New Musical
  75
Once Upon America (series) 95
One Day in the Alpine Tundra 138,
  169
One Day in the Desert 159
One Day in the Prairie 149

One Day in the Tropical Rain Forest 115

One Day in the Woods 126

One Earth (series) 85, 94, 95, 126, 150

One Rainy Night 229

One Small Square: Backyard [Scientific American Books for Young Readers] 17

One Small Square: Cave [Scientific American Books for Young Readers] 17

One Small Square: Seashore [Scientific American Books for Young Readers] 84

One World 84

Operation Earth (series) 27, 37, 49, 62, 105, 125, 192, 204, 228

Operation Siberian Crane: The Story Behind the International Effort to Save an Amazing Bird 217

Opposing Viewpoints (series) 50, 206

Organic Foods Production Association of North America 194, 236

Original Peoples (series) 73, 139, 148, 150, 159, 168, 169

Osborne, Mary Pope 64

Osinski, Alice 169

Other Side: How Kids Live in a California Latino Neighborhood, The [A World of My Own] 183

Our Changing World (series) 83, 105

Our Changing World: The Forest 125

Our Endangered Planet (series) 17, 37, 62, 105, 114, 169, 182, 215, 228, 229

Our Fragile Earth (series) 193

Our Fragile Planet (series) 27, 37, 62, 114, 125, 205, 216

Our Great Rivers and Waterways [I Know America] 105

Our National Parks [I Know America] 126

Our Planet (series) 94

Our Poisoned Sky 28

Our Vanishing Farm Animals [Saving America's Rare Breeds] 194

Our Violent Earth [Books for World Explorers] 16

Our Wild Wetlands 94

Our World (series) 83, 105, 126, 137, 148, 159, 168, 230

Outdoor Science Book, An (series) 94

Overview Series: Our Endangered Planet (series) 49, 204, 215

Oxfam America 194, 236

Oxford Scientific Films (series) 125

Ozark Society 139, 236

Ozone Layer, The [Save Our Earth] 27

Pacific Ocean, The [New True Books] 63

Pacific Whale Foundation 64, 236

Pack, Janet 50

Paddle-to-the-Sea 106

Paddock: A Story in Praise of Earth, The 17

Padget, Sheila 84

Pagoo 85

Paladino, Catherine 194

Pallotta, Jerry 217

Palmer, Joy 63, 115, 160, 169, 204

Park, Ruth 75

Parker, Philip 182

Parker, Steve 17, 27, 28, 49, 62, 84, 94, 105

Patent, Dorothy Hinshaw 85, 125, 149, 192, 217

Paulson, Gary 170

Peaceful Pond 91

Peacock, Graham 38

Peckham, Alexander 16, 192, 229

Peet, Bill 217

Pelicans 85

Penan: People of the Borneo Jungle, The [Global Villages] 116

Penny, Malcolm 216, 230

People and Places (series) 75, 106, 116, 138, 150, 160, 170

People Trap [Operaton Earth] 192, 228

People We Live With, The [We Can Save the Earth] 182

Peppin, Anthea 229

Perspectives (series) 182

Pesticides: Necessary Risk [Issues in Focus] 192

Peters, Lisa Westberg 149

Petersen, David 49, 63

Petersen, Palle 169

Peterson First Guide to Seashores 85

Pets and Farm Animals [Encyclopedia of the Animal World] 193
Philip, Neil 169
Phillips, Anne W. 64
Photo Books (series) 115, 192, 205
Physical World, The [Using and Understanding Maps] 169
Picture Book of..., A (series) 95
Picture Book of Swamp and Marsh Animals, A [A Picture Book of...] 95
Picture Library (series) 137, 168, 193
Picture Library—Science (series) 74
Picture Science (series) 17
Pieck, Anton 160
Piero Ventura's Book of Cities 182
Pifer, Joan 50
Pioneers [Library of Congress] 150
Pirates [First Books—Examining the Past] 63
Pirates and Privateers [Frontiers of America] 64
Places and Peoples of the World (series) 74
Plains Indian Warrior, A [How They Lived] 148
Plains Indians of North America [Original Peoples] 148
Planes [Eye-Openers] 28
Planes [What's Inside] 28
Planes and Flight [Technology Craft Topics] 28
Planet Earth (series) 15, 63, 75, 84, 116, 137, 150
Planet Earth [Your World 2000] 228
Plant Life (series) 160
Plants: Extinction or Survival? 217
Plastics Recycling Foundation 206, 236
Play & Discover (series) 193
Playful Slider: The North American River Otter 106
Podendorf, Illa 49
Points, Larry 74
Poisoned Food? [Issues] 194
Polar Lands [Ecology Watch] 168
Polar Lands [First Series] 169
Polar Lands [Last Frontiers for Mankind] 169
Polar Lands [Picture Library] 168
Polar Regions [Our World] 168

Polar Wildlife [Usborne World Wildlife] 168
Poles, The [Life Nature Library] 170
Poles and Tundra Wildlife [Close-Up] 170
Pollard, Michael 27, 37
Pollock, Steve 216
Polluting the Air [Save Our Earth] 28
Polluting the Sea [Save Our Earth] 62
Pollution [First Starts] 229
Pollution and Conservation [Our World] 230
Pond & River [Eyewitness Books] 94, 105
Pond Life [Golden Guides] 94
Pond Life [Look Closer] 94
Pond Life [New True Books] 94
Ponds and Pond Life [Nature Detective] 95
Pope, Joyce 84
Population Growth [Our Endangered Planet] 182, 229
Population of the World [Using and Understanding Maps] 229
Porritt, Jonathan 206, 230
Portraits of the Nations (series) 74
Posell, Elsa 160
Power Station Sun: The Story of Energy [Discovering Science] 50
Power Up: Experiments, Puzzles, and Games Exploring Electricity 50
Powerful Waves [Nature in Action] 62, 84
Poynter, Margaret 16
Prairie Alphabet, A 149
Prairie Animals [Treasury of American Wildlife] 149
Prairie Boy's Summer, A 150
Prairie Boy's Winter, A 150
Prairie Dogs 149
Prairie Songs 150
Prairie Visions: The Life and Times of Solomon Butcher 148
Prairies [EcoZones] 149
Prairies and Grasslands [New True Books] 149
Prairies and Their People, The [People and Places] 150
Pratt, Kristin Joy 115
Prehistoric Stone Monuments [World Heritage] 17

Primary Ecology (series) 39
Prince William 63
Pringle, Laurence 27, 37, 49, 125, 159, 169, 204, 216, 230
Private World of Smith Island, The 75
Project Eco-City (series) 182
Project Ecology (series) 230
Project Science (series) 50
Project Wildlife (series) 217
Projects That Explore Energy [Investigate!] 50
Protecting Endangered Species at the San Diego Zoo 217
Protecting Our Forests [The Junior Library of Ecology] 125
Protecting Our Rivers and Lakes [The Junior Library of Ecology] 104
Protecting Our World [Conservation Guides] 229
Protecting the Oceans [Conserving Our World] 62, 83
Protecting the Planet [Young Geographer] 230
Protecting Trees and Forests [Conservation Guide] 125
Protecting Wildlife [Conserving Our World] 216
Provensen, Alice 28, 182, 193
Provensen, Martin 28, 182, 193
Puddles and Ponds [An Outdoor Science Book] 94
Purcell, John Wallace 149

Question and Answer Book (series) 73, 96

Race to the South Pole, The [Great Journies] 160
Radlauer, Ruth 75
Radlauer Geo (series) 75
Rain Forest 115
Rain Forest [Look Closer] 115
Rain Forest [Planet Earth] 116
Rain Forest [Sticky Fingers] 115
Rain Forest, The [Science Adventures] 115
Rain Forest Amerindians [Threatened Cultures] 114

Rain Forests [EcoZones] 114
Rain Forests [First Starts] 115
Rain Forests [Habitats of the World] 115
Rain Shadow 159
Rain to Dams: Projects with Water [Hands on Science] 39
Rainforest Action Network 116, 236
Rainforest Alliance 116, 236
Rainforest Destruction [Save Our Earth] 114
Rainforest Secrets 114
Rainforests [Ecology Watch] 114
Rand, Gloria 63
Rand McNally Children's World Atlas 16, 182
Randle, Damian 50
Random House Book of 1001 Questions and Answers About Planet Earth, The 17
Random House Library of Knowledge (series) 16, 137
Ranger Rick Books (series) 215
Ranger Rick's Nature Club 218, 236
Ransome, Arthur 116
Ravaged Temperate Forests [Environment Alert!] 125
Raynor, Ralph 39
Razon, Mark J. 38, 114
Read About Science (series) 48
Reader's Guide to Periodical Literature 27, 63, 84
Reading, Susan 160
Recycle! A Handbook for Kids 205
Recycle It! Once Is Not Enough! [We Can Save the Earth] 205
Recycler's Handbook, The 204
Recycling [Earth at Risk] 204
Recycling [New True Books] 204
Recycling [Saving Planet Earth] 204
Recycling [World About Us] 204
Recycling: Meeting the Challenge of the Trash Crisis 206
Recycling in America [Contemporary World Isssues] 206
Recycling Metal [Waste Control] 204
Recycling Paper [Waste Control] 204
Recyclopedia: Games, Science Equipment, and Crafts from Recycled Materials 206
Red Ribbons for Emma 50

Reducing, Reusing, Recycling [The Crabtree Environment Series] 204

Reed-King, Susan 192

Reefs [Radlauer Geo] 75

Reference Guide to Clean Air, A [Science, Technology, and Society] 28

Reid, George K. 94

Reindeer 169

Reiser, Lynn 95

Remember Me to Harold Square 183

Renew America 18, 51, 231, 236

Renewable Natural Resources Foundation 231, 236

Resources (series) 37, 49

Resources Control [Green Issues] 229

Restoring Our Earth 230

Reynolds, Jan 115, 138, 160, 169, 170

Reynolds, Tony 182

Rice, Paul 216

Rice, Tony 62

Rice [Natural Science] 194

Richardson, Jack 39, 183

Richardson, Joy 17

Richardson, Wendy 39, 183

Rickard, Graham 27, 37, 49, 50

Rime of the Ancient Mariner, The 170

Rinard, Judith E. 139, 216

River 105, 115

River [Land Shapes] 105

River [The Story of the Earth] 104

River, The [Our Changing World] 105

River and Canal 104

River Dream 105

River Life [Look Closer] 105

River Ran Wild, A 105

River Thrill Sports [Superwheels and Thrill Sports] 106

Riverkeeper 105

Rivermen [The Wild West in American History] 105

Rivers [Earth in Action] 105

Rivers [Exploring Our World] 105

Rivers [Facts About] 104

Rivers [New True Books] 104

Rivers and Lakes [Earth Science Library] 106

Rivers and Lakes [Our Endangered Planet] 105

Rivers and Lakes [Our World] 105

Rivers and Oceans: Geography Facts and Experiments [Young Discoverers] 63, 105

Rivers and People [Nature's Landscapes] 104

Rivers of the World (series) 106

Rivers, Ponds and Lakes [Ecology Watch] 94, 104

Roald Amundsen and Robert Scott [The World's Great Explorers] 170

Robinson, W. Wright 64

Rock Climbing Is for Me [Sports for Me Books] 138

Rock Pool, The [Our Changing World] 83

Rocks [Earth in Action] 16

Rocks & Minerals [Eyewitness Books] 16

Rocks and Minerals [A Golden Guide] 16

Rocks and Minerals of the World [Using and Understanding Maps] 16, 49, 74, 137

Rocks and Soil [Picture Science] 17

Rocks and Soil [The Young Scientist Investigates] 15

Rockwell, Jane 96

Rodgers, Mary M. 17, 37, 62, 105, 114, 169, 182, 215, 229

Rodgers, Richard 75, 194

Rom, Christine Sotnak 94

Rood, Ronald 95

Rookie Read-About Science (series) 38

Root, Phyllis 73

Rosen, Michael J. 95

Rosen, Mike 170

Rosenblum, Richard 28

Ross, Harriet 17

Ross, Suzane 115

Rossiter, Jane 50

Roth, Charles E. 230

Rott, Joanna R. 206

Rounds, David 106

Rowan, James P. 149

Rowe, Julian 49

Rowland-Entwistle, Theodore 105

Royston, Angela 28

Royston, Robert 182

Russell, Franklin 96

Rybolt, Thomas R. 17, 28, 39, 206

Rydell, Wendy 73
Ryder, Joanne 63
Rykodisc 70, 101, 111, 236
Rylant, Cynthia 138

Saami of Lapland [Threatened Cultures] 170
Sabin, Francene 126
Sabin, Louis 63, 84, 149, 160, 193
Safari Beneath the Sea: The Wonder World of the North Pacific Coast 85
Sahara [Vanishing Cultures] 160
Sahara and Its People, The [People and Places] 160
Sailor Through History, The [Journey Through History] 37, 62
Salisbury, Mike 170
Salmon Story 63
Salt Marsh Summer 95
Sam Ellis's Island 75
Sanchez, Isidro 38
Sand and Egg: Adventures in Southern Africa 159
Sand Dunes [Earth Watch] 83
Sandak, Cass 28
Sandler, Martin W. 150
Sanitation Workers A to Z [Community Helpers] 205
Santrey, Laurence 229
Sarah, Plain and Tall 150
Sargent, William 73
Sato and the Elephants 216
Savage, Candice 204
Save It! Keep It! Use It Again!: A Book About Conservation and Recycling [Finding-Out Books] 228
Save My Rainforest 115
Save Our Earth (series) 27, 28, 37, 62, 114, 206, 230
Save Our Forests [One Earth] 126
Save Our Oceans and Coasts [One Earth] 85
Save Our Prairies and Grasslands [One Earth] 150
Save Our Species (series) 217
Save Our Streams 106, 236
Save Our Wetlands [One Earth] 94
Save the Earth 206, 229
Save-the-Redwoods League 127, 236

Saving America's Rare Breeds (series) 194
Saving Endangered Mammals: A Field Guide to Some of Earth's Rarest Animals [Cincinnati Zoo Books] 216
Saving Our Ancient Forests 126
Saving Our Animal Friends [Books for Young Explorers] 217
Saving Our Wetlands and Their Wildlife [First Books — Our Environment] 94, 217
Saving Planet Earth (series) 27, 37, 48, 49, 50, 62, 95, 125, 183, 204, 205
Saving the Peregrine Falcon [Nature Watch] 216
Sawyer, Kem Knapp 96
Say, Allen 105
Schachtel, Roger 138
Schaub, Janine 39, 204
Schmid, Eleonore 38
Schmidt, Jeremy 149
Scholastic Environmental Atlas of the United States 27, 95, 105, 169, 205, 229
Schoonmaker, Peter K. 126
Schwartz, David M. 94, 125
Schwartz, Linda 206, 229
Science Activities (series) 38
Science Adventures (series) 16, 63, 115
Science Book of Air, The 26
Science Book of Energy 49
Science Experiments for Young People (series) 17, 28, 39, 206
Science Fair (series) 17
Science for Survival (series) 37, 49
Science Frontiers (series) 50
Science in Action (series) 27, 49
Science in Our World (series) 15, 38, 125, 137
Science Project Book (series) 17
Science Starters (series) 39
Science, Technology, and Society (series) 28, 230
Science Through Art (series) 28, 38, 50
Science Through Cookery (series) 50
Scientific American Books for Young Readers (series) 17, 84

Scoones, Simon 160
Scooter 183
Scoots the Bog Turtle 95
Sea, The 59
Sea, The (series) 63
Sea, The [Life Nature Library] 63, 75
Sea and Seashore [The Young Scientist Investigates] 83
Sea Disasters [The World's Disasters] 62
Sea Elf [Just for a Day Books] 63
Sea Jellies: Rainbows in the Sea [New England Aquarium Books] 85
Sea of Grass: The Tallgrass Prairie, A 149
Sea Otter Rescue: The Aftermath of an Oil Spill 64
Sea, Salt, & Air 84
Seal Oil Lamp, The 169
Search for Delicious, The 38
Seas and Oceans (series) 64
Seas and Oceans [The World of Science] 64, 73, 83
Seashells in My Pocket: A Child's Guide to Exploring the Atlantic Coast from Maine to North Carolina 83
Seashells of the World: A Guide to the Better-Known Species [Golden Guides] 83
Seashore [Eyewitness Books] 84
Seashore, The [Action Science] 84
Seashore Book, The 84
Seashore Life [Nature Library] 75, 83
Seashore Life [Young Discovery Library] 85
Seashore Life on Rocky Coasts 85
Seashores [EcoZones] 84
Seashores [Golden Guides] 84
Seasons of the Tallgrass Prairie 148
Seasons on the Farm 193
Seawater: A Delicate Balance [Earth Processes] 63
Secret of the Seal, The 170
Secrets of Animal Survival [Books for World Explorers] 217
Secrets of Science (series) 27
See & Explore Library (series) 28, 62
Seed, Deborah 39
Seeing Earth from Space 17
Segal, Ronald 27, 38, 63, 159

Seidenberg, Steven 49, 230
Seixas, Judith S. 37
Selley, Lyndsey 149, 170
Seltzer, Meyer 205
Seminoles, The [First Books — Indians of the Americas] 94
Serengeti [National Parks] 149
Serengeti Migration: Africa's Animals on the Move, The 149
Settlements [Young Geographer] 183
Shabanu, Daughter of the World 160
Shachtman, Tom 149
Shaffer, Carolyn 183
Shaffer, Paul R. 16
Shaker Lane 182
Shapiro, Irwin 75
Sharks and Other Creatures of the Deep [See and Explore Library] 62
Shells [Eyewitness Explorers] 84
Shells [What's Inside?] 84
Shepard, John 106
Shifting Shores: Rising Seas, Retreating Coastlines 83, 104
Ship Technology [Technology in Action] 39
Shipwrecks: Terror and Treasure [First Books — Examining the Past] 63
Shoreline [Look Closer] 84
Shoshoni, The [First Books — Indians of the Americas] 160
Shovelful of Earth, A 17
Show Boat 106
Showers, Paul 205
Shrinking Forests [Our Fragile Planet] 114, 125
Siebert, Diane 138, 160
Siegal, Alice 205
Siegel, Beatrice 75
Sierra 138
Sierra Club 29, 85, 96, 127, 139, 150, 160, 218, 236
Sierra Club Book of Our National Parks, The 230
Sign of the Seahorse, The 63
Silent Spring 194
Silver, Donald M. 16, 17, 84, 115, 137, 217
Silver Burdett Color Library, The (series) 215
Silverstein, Alvin 84, 206
Silverstein, Virginia 84

Simon, Noel 216
Simon, Seymour 16, 17, 38, 62, 64, 138, 159, 169
Simons, Robin 206
Sing for a Gentle Rain 160
Singer, Louis C. 138
Sink or Swim: The Science of Water [Step into Science] 38
Sioux, The [First Books—Indians of the Americas] 150
Sipiera, Paul P. 170
Sirimarco, Elizabeth 229
Sis, Peter 170
Siy, Alexandra 116, 125, 149, 169
Skidmore, Steve 204
Skylark 150
Small Tale from the Far North, A 170
Smith, David 193
Smith, J. H. Greg 169
Smith, Judy 50
Smith, Roland 64
Smithsonian Book of Flight for Young People, The 27
Smithsonian/Folkways Recordings 70, 134, 155, 236
Smokejumpers and Forest Firefighters [At Risk] 126
Smoky Night 182
Snodgrass, Mary Ellen 27, 37
Society for the Preservation of Birds of Prey 218, 236
Soil [Our Endangered Planet] 17
Soil and Water Conservation Society 18, 39, 236
Soil Erosion and Pollution [New True Books] 16
Solar Energy [Alternative Energy] 49
Solar Energy at Work [New True Books] 49
Solar Power [World About Us] 50
Something from Nothing 205
Sondheim, Stephen 126
Songs Are Thoughts: Poems of the Inuit 169
Songs of Hill and Mountain Folk 138
Songs of the Humpback Whale 59
Sotnak, Lewann 17
Soundings of the Planet 59, 91, 121, 134, 155, 225, 236
South Pacific (sound recording) 75
South Pacific: A Musical Play 75

South Pacific Islanders [Original Peoples] 73
Souza, D. M. 62, 84
Space Junk: Pollution Beyond the Earth 206
Spence, Margaret 50, 205
Spenser, Guy 126
Spit Is a Piece of Land, A [Landforms in the U.S.A.] 83
Spoonbill Swamp 95
Sports for Me Books (series) 138
Spotlight on American History (series) 160
Spread of Deserts, The [Conserving Our World] 159
Spring Pool: A Guide to the Ecology of Temporary Ponds [New England Aquarium—Endangered Habitats Books] 94
Sproule, Anna 194
Stanley, Jerry 160
Staples, Suzanne Fisher 160
Starburst (series) 85
Start to Finish (series) 17, 50, 63, 95, 114, 126, 149, 159, 193
Starting Points (series) 38
Staub, Frank 126
Steamboat in a Cornfield 105
Steele, Philip 28, 62, 63, 182, 217
Stefoff, Rebecca 204, 217
Stein, R. Conrad 106, 149
Steiner, Barbara 170
Stenstrup, Allen 205
Step into Reading (series) 138
Step into Science (series) 28, 38
Stephen, R. J. 193
Stephens, William M. 73
Steven Foster Songbook 106
Stevenson, Robert Louis 75
Stewart, Gail 105, 126, 137, 160, 170
Steyn, H. F. 159
Sticky Fingers (series) 115
Stidworthy, John 149, 229
Stille, Darlene R. 16, 27, 28, 37, 63, 170
Stone, Lynn M. 84, 94, 114, 125, 126, 137, 149, 150, 159, 169, 193, 216
Stonehenge [The Mystery of...] 16
Stories from the Arabian Nights 160
Stories of the States (series) 39

Stories of the Steppes: Kazahk Folk-lore 150

Storm [The Violent Earth] 16

Storms: Causes and Effects [Weather Watch] 28

Story of a Main Street, The 182

Story of the Earth, The (series) 15, 73, 104, 137, 158

Story of the Erie Canal, The [Cornerstones of Freedom] 106

Story of the Homestead Act, The [Cornerstones of Freedom] 149

Story of the Seashore, The 84

Strange and Amazing Worlds (series) 62

Stream Team on Patrol, The [Target Earth] 106

Street Music: City Poems 183

Streib, Sally 85

Strength in the Hills: A Portrait of a Family Farm, The 194

Stuart, Gene S. 183

Student Environmental Action Coalition 231, 236

Stutson, Caroline 105

Stwerka, Eve 39

Submarines [New True Books] 63

Sukay 134, 236

Summer of Fire: Yellowstone, 1988 126

Super Kids Recycling Program 206, 237

Superwheels and Thrill Sports (series) 106, 138

Surrounded by Sea: Life on a New England Fishing Island 74, 84

Surtsey: The Newest Place on Earth 73, 139

Survival (series) 215, 216

Swallow, Su 38, 194

Swallows and Amazons 116

Swamp Life [Look Closer] 94

Swamp Spring 95

Swamps [Our Planet] 94

Swan, Robert 170

Swanson, Diane 85

Switch on, Switch Off 50

Symes, R. F. 16

Szumski, Bonnie 206

Take a Trip (series) 75, 168

Take a Trip to Antarctica [Take a Trip] 168

Take Action: An Environmental Book for Kids [World Wildlife Fund] 216

Tale of Antarctica, A 169

Tales from the South Pacific Islands 75

Target Earth (series) 38, 106, 230

Taylor, Barbara 28, 38, 39, 63, 75, 84, 94, 105, 115, 126, 138, 149, 159

Taylor, Dave 62, 74, 94, 126, 149, 216

Taylor, Kim 37

Taylor, Richard L. 28

Taylor, Ron 194

Tayntor, Elizabeth 74

Technology Craft Topics (series) 28

Technology in Action (series) 28, 39, 50, 192

Tell Me About It (series) 148

Temperate Forests [EcoZones] 125

Temperate Forests [Exploring Our World] 125

Temperate Forests [Our World] 126

Tentacles: The Amazing World of Octopus, Squid, and Their Relatives 64

Terrible Wave, The 38

Tesar, Jenny 27, 37, 62, 114, 125, 193, 205, 216

Thames Doesn't Rhyme with James 183

Thirteen Moons (series) 138

This Place Is Cold [Imagine Living Here] 169

This Place Is Crowded: Japan [Imagine Living Here] 182

This Place Is Dry [Imagine Living Here] 159

This Place Is High [Imagine Living Here] 138

This Place Is Wet [Imagine Living Here] 115

Thomas, Margaret 137

Thomas, Robert B. 193

Thornhill, Jan 126

Threatened Cultures (series) 114, 159, 160, 168, 170

Threatened Oceans [Our Fragile Planet] 62

Three Days on the River in a Red Canoe 106

Throwaway Generation [We Can Save the Earth] 205
Throwaway Society, The [Impact] 206
Throwing Things Away: From Middens to Resource Recovery 204
Tidal Wave [Disaster!] 64
Tide Pool [Look Closer] 84
Tiger 216
Tilling, Robert I. 139
Timber Country [Back Roads] 126
Timberlake, Lloyd 160, 194
Time of Wonder 74
Time Quest (series) 170
Timelines (series) 181
To the Top! [Step into Reading] 138
Today's World (series) 50, 192
Tomorrow on Rocky Pond 95
Tompkins, Terry 125
Town and Country [Discovering Art] 182
Town Life [Project Eco-City] 182
Towns and Cities [Ecology Watch] 181
Toxic Waste [Save Our Earth] 206
Toxic Waste [World About Us] 205
Toxic Waste and Recycling [Issues Update] 204
Toxic Waste Time Bomb, The [Environment Alert!] 205
Toxic Wastes: Examining Cause and Effect Relationships [Opposing Viewpoints] 206
Trailblazers (series) 170
Trapped in Tar: Fossils from the Ice Age 16
Trash! [Photo Books] 205
Trash Attack [Earth Care] 204
Trash Busters (series) 205
Treasure Island 75
Treasures by the Sea [Starburst] 85
Treasury of American Wildlife (series) 149
Tree Amigos Project 116, 126, 237
Tree City U.S.A. Community Improvement Program 183, 237
Tree in the Forest, A 126
Tree in the Trail 126
Tree of Life: The World of the African Baobab [Tree Tales] 148
Tree Tales (series) 148, 158
Tree Trunk Traffic 126
Trees [Focus on — Science] 126

Trees [Golden Guides] 125
Trees and Leaves [Fun with Science] 126
Trees of the Tropics [Green World] 114
Trip of a Drip, The [How the World Works] 38
Trophy Let's Read-and-Find-Out Stage 2 (series) 38
Tropical Rain Forests [Our Endangered Planet] 114
Tropical Rain Forests Around the World [First Books — Our Environment] 114
Tropical Rain Forests of Central America [World Heritage] 115
Tropical Rainforest [World About Us] 115
Tropical Rainforests 114
Tropical Rainforests: Endangered Environment [Environmental Issues] 114
Troubled Waters [Operation Earth] 37, 62, 105
Troubling a Star 170
Trust for Public Land 183, 237
Tundra 170
Tundra: The Arctic Land 168
Turner, Ann 150, 193
Turtle Watch 216
Twain, Mark 106
24 Hours (series) 84, 150
24 Hours in a Game Reserve [24 Hours] 150
24 Hours on a Seashore [24 Hours] 84
Twist, Clint 39, 50, 116, 159, 170

Uchida, Yoshiko 95
Under the Sea [Science Adventures] 63
Underground 183
Undersea [CHP Technology Series] 62
Undersea Mission [Young Explorers] 63
Undersea Technology [Technology in Action] 39
United Citizens Coastal Protection League 85, 237
Unstead, R. J. 182
Up Goes the Skyscraper! 182

Up, Up and Away! The Science of Flight [Step into Science] 28

Upper Mississippi River Conservation Commission 106, 237

Urban Roosts: Where Birds Nest in the City 181

Urban Wildlife [The American Wilderness] 183

Usborne World Wildlife (series) 168

Use of Land [Young Geographer] 183

Use Your Eyes (series) 17, 84, 106, 126, 182, 193

Using and Understanding Maps (series) 16, 49, 74, 137, 169, 193, 216, 229

Van Allsburg, Chris 230

Vangelis 165

Vanishing Animal Pop-Ups (series) 149, 170

Vanishing Cultures (series) 115, 138, 160, 169, 170

Vanishing Forests [Saving Planet Earth] 125

Vanishing Habitats [Survival] 216

Vanishing Habitats [World About Us] 215

Vanishing Rain Forests [Environment Alert!] 115

Vanishing Species [Green Issues] 217

Vanishing Wetlands, The [Impact] 95

Ventura, Piero 182

Verne, Jules 17

Versfield, Ruth 193

Viera, Linda 126

Violent Earth, The (series) 16

Visual Dictionary of the Earth, The [Eyewitness Visual Dictionaries] 17

Visual Geography (series) 74

Vitebsky, Piers 170

Vodopich, Darrell S. 160

Voices of the Rainforest 111

Voices of the River: Adventures on the Delaware 106

Voices of the Wild 217

Volcano! [Nature's Disasters] 137

Volcano [World Disasters] 138

Volcano: The Eruption and Healing of Mount St. Helens 16, 137

Volcanoes: Fire from Below [Wonderworks of Nature] 16, 137

Von Tscharner, Renata 182

Wading into Wetlands 95

Wakefield, Celia 139

Walden Forever Wild 96, 237

Walk in the Rainforest, A 115

Walk on the Great Barrier Reef, A [Nature Watch] 62

Walker, Jane 29, 159, 193

Walker, Sally M. 37, 169

Wallace, Aubrey 230

Walpole, Brenda 38

Walt Disney World Epcot Center Book (series) 192

Walter, F. Virginia 205

War and the Environment [Environment Alert!] 229

War of 1812: Second Fight for Independence, The [First Books—War] 106

Ward, Alan 50

Waste and Recycling [Conserving Our World] 204

Waste and Recycling [First Starts] 204

Waste Control (series) 204

Waste Crisis, The [Our Fragile Planet] 205

Waste Disposal and Recycling [Green Issues] 206

Waste War [Operation Earth] 204

Watching Nature (series) 83, 94, 105, 125, 181

Water 38

Water [Discovering Art] 38

Water [Flying Start Science] 37

Water [Life Science Library] 39, 106

Water [Resources] 37

Water [Science Activities] 38

Water [Science in Our World] 38

Water [Science Through Art] 38

Water [Starting Points] 38

Water: A Resource in Crisis [Saving Planet Earth] 37

Water: The Next Great Resource Battle [Science for Survival] 37

Water: Through the Eyes of Artists [Artists of the World] 39

Water: What It Is, What It Does
[Greenwillow Read-Alone] 37
Water and Life [Science Starters] 39
Water at Work [Science Starters] 39
Water Energy [Alternative Energy]
37, 49
*Water Hole: Life in a Rescued Tropical
Forest* [New England Aquarium—
Endangered Habitats] 116
Water Pollution [New True Books] 37
Water Science 39
Water Travel [The World on the
Move] 37, 62
*Water Up, Water Down: The Hydro-
logic Cycle* [Earth Watch] 37
*Water Wars: The Fight to Control and
Conserve Nature's Most Precious
Resource* [Earth Care] 38
Water, Water Everywhere 38
Water We Drink, The [We Can Save
the Earth] 38
Watercolor [I Draw, I Paint] 38
*Waterfalls: Nature's Thundering
Splendor* [Wonderworks of
Nature] 38, 105
Waters, John F. 64
Water's Journey, The 38
Watts, Barrie 84, 150
Wave in Her Pocket, A 74
Ways of Life (series) 193
We Can Save the Earth (series) 17,
28, 38, 50, 182, 193, 205, 230
We Live In... (series) 74
Weather [Earth Science Library] 28
*Weather and Climate: Geography
Facts and Experiments* [Young
Discoverers] 28
*Weather and Climate: Projects with
Geography* [Hands on Science] 37
Weather Watch (series) 28
Weatherwatch 27
Weatherwise [How's the Weather?] 27
Webb, Lois Sinaiko 75
Weber, Michael 126
*Webster's New World Pocket Geo-
graphical Dictionary* 137
Welch, Catherine A. 150
Welcome to the Green House 115
West, Tracey 39
Wetland Walk, A 95
Wetlands [EcoZones] 94

Wetlands [Nature Search] 95
Wetlands [Nature Study Book] 95
Wetlands Watch 96, 237
Whale Brothers 170
What a Load of Trash! [A Lighter
Look] 204
*What Do We Know About Grass-
lands?* [Caring for Environments]
148
*What Do We Know About Rainfor-
ests?* [Caring for Environments]
114
What Food Is This? 193
*What Makes It Rain? The Story of a
Raindrop* 38
What We Can Do About (series) 38,
49, 205, 229
*What We Can Do About Conserving
Energy* [What We Can Do About]
49
What We Can Do About Litter [What
We Can Do About] 205
*What We Can Do About Protecting
Nature* [What We Can Do About]
229
*What We Can Do About Recycling
Garbage* [What We Can Do About]
205
*What We Can Do About Wasting
Water* [What We Can Do About]
38
What We Eat [Play & Discover] 193
*What's in the Rainforest? One Hun-
dred Six Answers From A to Z* 115
What's Inside? (series) 28, 84
What's on My Plate? 193
Wheat [Natural Science] 150, 194
Wheeler, Jill 17, 28, 38, 50, 182, 193,
205
When I Was Young in the Mountains
138
When the Stars Begin to Fall 106
When the Tide Is Low 84
Where Animals Live (series) 217
*Where Are My Swans, Whooping
Cranes, and Singing Loons?* [One
Earth] 95
Where Does the Garbage Go? [Ask
Isaac Asimov] 205
Where Does the Garbage Go? [Let's-
Read-and-Find-Out Science] 205

Where Food Comes From 192
Where the Forest Meets the Sea 115
Where the River Begins 105
Where the Waves Break: Life at the Edge of the Sea [Nature Watch] 83
White, E. B. 193
Whitfield, Philip 17, 62, 74, 216
Whitlock, Ralph 17, 84, 106, 126, 182, 193
Who Lives in . . . (series) 138
Who Lives in the Mountains? [Who Lives in . . .] 138
Why Are People Hungry? [Let's Talk About] 193
Why Are Some Beaches Oily? [Ask Isaac Asimov] 83
Why Are the Animals Endangered? [Ask Isaac Asimov] 216
Why Are the Rain Forests Vanishing? [Ask Isaac Asimov] 115
Why Do Volcanoes Erupt? 17, 74
Why Does Litter Cause Problems? [Ask Isaac Asimov] 204
Why Doesn't the Sun Burn Out? 50
Why Is the Air Dirty? [Ask Isaac Asimov] 28
Why Save the Rainforest? 115
Why Throw It Away? (series) 205
Wiewandt, Thomas 159
Wiggers, Raymond 17
Wilcox, Charlotte 205
Wild West in American History, The (series) 105
Wild Woods, The 126
Wilder, Laura Ingalls 150, 194
Wildlife: Making a Comeback [Books for World Explorers] 216
Wildlife at Risk (series) 217
Wildlife in Danger (series) 217
Wildlife in Danger [The Silver Burdett Color Library] 215
Wildlife Preservation Trust International 218, 237
Wildlife Rescue: The Work of Dr. Kathleen Ramsay 216
Wilkes, Angela 114, 229
Wilkins, Marne 126
Will We Miss Them? Endangered Species 217
Williams, Brenda 17

Williams, Brian 17, 193
Williams, Lawrence 62, 114, 137, 159, 169
Williams, Terry Tempest 95
Williams, Vera B. 106, 183
Wilson, Barbara Ker 183
Winckler, Suzanne 17, 169, 182, 229
Wind and Water Power [World About Us] 50
Wind Energy [Alternative Energy] 27, 49
Wings: The Early Years of Aviation 28
Wings Along the Waterway 95
Winnie the Pooh and the Blustery Day 28
Winston, James 74
Wolf, Bernard 75
Wonderful Water [Primary Ecology] 39
Wonders of Swamps and Marshes 94
Wonders of the Desert 160
Wonders of the Forest 126
Wonders of the Sea 63, 84
Wonderworks of Nature (series) 16, 38, 63, 74, 84, 105, 137
Wood, Jenny 16, 38, 63, 74, 84, 105, 115, 137, 159
Wood, Tim 17, 27
Woodburn, Judith 205
Woodland Life [Science in Our World] 125
Woodland Trees [Green World] 125
World About Us (series) 50, 115, 204, 205, 215
World Almanac and Book of Facts, The 16, 27, 38, 49, 63, 74, 105, 125, 169, 182
World Aquaculture Society 64, 237
World Beneath Us, The [The World of Science] 16
World Book Encyclopedia 137, 182
World Book's Young Scientist, Vol. 4—Planet Earth 16
World Cities (series) 181
World Contemporary Issues (series) 49
World Disasters! (series) 15, 37, 105, 138, 160, 194
World Explorers, The (series) 105
World Heritage (series) 17, 115, 138

World in View (series) 74
World Issues (series) 49, 182, 192, 215, 230
World Mythologies (series) 75
World Nature Association 160, 237
World of Art, The (series) 183
World of My Own, A (series) 183
World of Science, The (series) 16, 64, 73, 83
World on the Move, The (series) 27, 37, 62
World Resources Institute 49, 95, 105, 115, 125, 149, 169, 182, 205, 229
World Wildlife Fund 116, 139, 150, 216, 218, 237
World's Disasters, The (series) 17, 27, 62, 228
World's Great Explorers, The (series) 170
World's Population, The [Young Geographer] 230
World's Resources (series) 17, 50, 194
World's Wild Shores, The 85
Worldwatch Institute 64, 75, 106, 160, 231, 237
Wright, Alexandra 217
Wright, David 137, 159, 182
Wright, Jill 137, 159
Wu, Norbert 63, 64
Wyatt, Valerie 27
Wyler, Rose 94

Year at Maple Hill Farm, The 193
Year on Muskrat Marsh 95
Yellowstone Fires: Flames and Re-birth 125
Yellowstone's Cycle of Fire [Earth Watch] 126

Yep, Laurence 29
Yepsen, Roger 183
Yeti: Abominable Snowman of the Himalayas [Mysteries of the Unknown] 137
Yolen, Jane 106, 115
You Breathe In, You Breathe Out: All About Your Lungs [Discovering Science] 27
Young, Donald 230
Young Discoverers (series) 28, 63, 105, 138
Young Discovery Library (series) 85
Young Explorers (series) 63, 115, 160, 170
Young Geographer (series) 17, 50, 85, 183, 192, 230
Young Readers' Nature Library (series) 17, 62
Young Scientist 149
Young Scientist Investigates, The (series) 15, 83
Young Scientist, Volume 8: Energy, Conservation 229
Your Earth 2000 (series) 228
Your Living Home [Project Eco-City] 182
Your Wild Neighborhood [Project Eco-City] 182
Your World 2000 (series) 182
Ytek and the Arctic Orchid: An Inuit Legend 170
Yue, Charlotte 169
Yue, David 169

Zak, Monica 115
Zero Population Growth 231, 237
Zim, Herbert S. 16, 84, 125
Zolotow, Charlotte 84
Zuckerman, Seth 126